CREDO SERIES

Living and Loving as Disciples of Christ

Based on the Curriculum Framework
Course VI: Life in Jesus Christ

WRITERS
Amalee Meehan, PhD
Daniel O'Connell, PhD
Ailís Travers, MA

GENERAL EDITOR
Thomas H. Groome, EdD

Professor Theology and Religious Education
Boston College

VERITAS

USA Office: Frisco, Texas

www.veritasreligion.com

The Subcommittee on the Catechism, United States Conference of Catholic Bishops, has found that this catechetical high school text, copyright 2015, is in conformity with the *Catechism of the Catholic Church* and that it fulfills the requirements of Core Course VI of the *Doctrinal Elements of a Curriculum Framework for the Development of Catechetical Materials for Young People of High School Age.*

CREDO SERIES CONSULTANT: Maura Hyland
PUBLISHER, USA AND THEOLOGICAL EDITOR:
Ed DeStefano
CATECHETICAL CONSULTANTS: Patrick Manning;
Brendan O'Reilly
COPY EDITOR: Elaine Campion
DESIGN: Lir Mac Cárthaigh
TYPESETTING: Heather Costello
COPYRIGHT RESEARCH: Emma O'Donoghue

INTERNET RESOURCES
There are internet resources available to support this text. Log on to *www.credoseries.com*

NIHIL OBSTAT
Rev. Msgr. Robert M. Coerver, S.T.L.
Censor Librorum

IMPRIMATUR
† Most Reverend Kevin J. Farrell, D.D.
Bishop of Dallas
August 9, 2013

The *Nihil Obstat* and *Imprimatur* are official declarations that the work contains nothing contrary to Faith and Morals. It is not implied thereby that those granting the *Nihil Obstat* or *Imprimatur* agree with the contents, statements or opinions expressed.

SEND ALL INQUIRIES TO:
Veritas, Customer Service
P.O. Box 789
Westerville, OH 43086
Tel. 866-844-0582
info@veritasreligion.com
www.veritasreligion.com

ISBN 978 1 84730 604 3 (Student Edition)
ISBN 978 1 84730 418 6 (Teacher Resource Edition)
ISBN 978 1 84730 606 7 (E-book: Student Edition)

Printed in the United States of America
2 3 4 5 6 7 / 14 15 16 17

CONTENTS

CHAPTER 1

God Desires What Is Best for Us

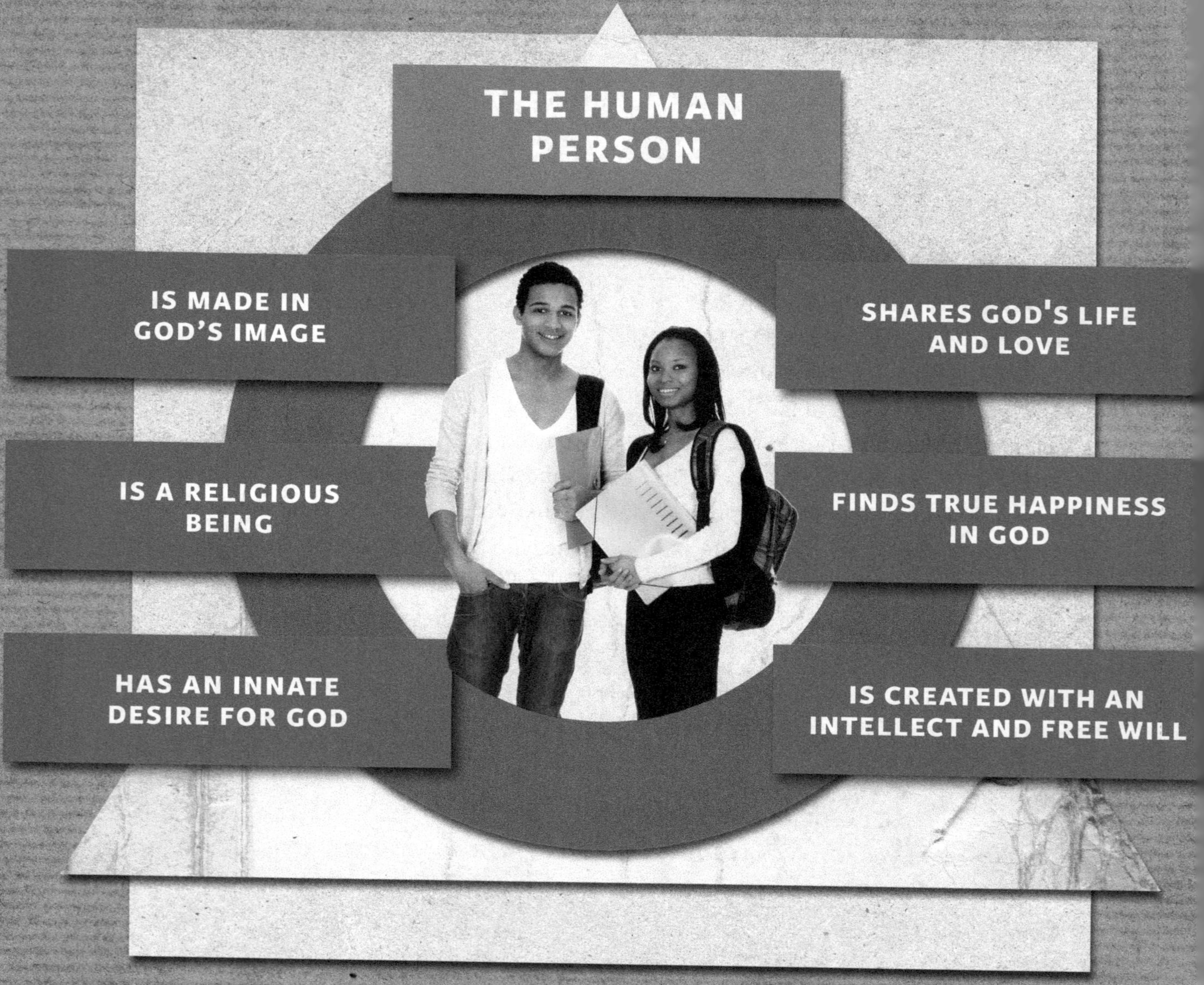
THE HUMAN PERSON
IS MADE IN GOD'S IMAGE
SHARES GOD'S LIFE AND LOVE
IS A RELIGIOUS BEING
FINDS TRUE HAPPINESS IN GOD
HAS AN INNATE DESIRE FOR GOD
IS CREATED WITH AN INTELLECT AND FREE WILL

GOD HAS CREATED US TO KNOW AND EXPERIENCE THE happiness that living in friendship with him brings during our life on earth and forever in heaven. In other *Credo* texts you have explored how the universality of the human search for happiness gives evidence of the truth of this Revelation. In this opening chapter we review that learning. The moral choices we make as individuals and as a society are choices for happiness. In making those choices Christians follow the lead of Christ who "always did what was pleasing to the Father (see John 8:29), and always lived in perfect communion with him" (CCC, no. 1693).

WE ARE PART OF GOD'S DIVINE PLAN OF GOODNESS

OUR HAPPINESS IS ROOTED IN OUR RELATIONSHIP WITH GOD

LIFE IN CHRIST IS THE PATH TO HAPPINESS

Faith Focus: These teachings of the Catholic Church are the primary focus of the doctrinal content present this chapter:

- Every person has a built-in desire for happ
- Our happiness is rooted in our relationshi
- God creates us out of love to share in the love of God.
- God creates the human person in his imag likeness.
- God creates the human person with the ab know and the freedom to choose what is avoid what is evil.
- Sin is choosing freely what we know is evi
- God always gives us the grace to live as his and as disciples of Jesus Christ.
- Life in Christ is the path to happiness.

Discipleship Formation: As a result of studying chapter and discovering the meaning of the fa Catholic Church for your life, you should be be

- identify and evaluate how you are seeking h
- come to understand and make God's will fo happiness your life-plan;
- understand and live out the role you have in plan of goodness for all humanity;
- recognize the presence of the Holy Spirit in
- cooperate with the Holy Spirit in making yo decisions to live as a child of God and discip Christ.

Scripture References: These Scripture referenc quoted or referred to in this chapter:
OLD TESTAMENT: Genesis 1:27, 28–30 and 31, 2: and 15, 4:1–25, 6:1—10:32, 11:1–9; **Psalm** 139:13–
NEW TESTAMENT: Matthew 4:1–11, 5:15 and 33, and 13; **Luke** 6:20–21, 24–25, 12:13–21; **John** 1:16– 47, 10:10, 14:1, 2, 6–7 and 15–21; **Romans** 5:12–21 11, 7:19; **2 Corinthians** 4:4; **Hebrews** 9:15, **Coloss** 2:12; **Revelation** 21:1

Faith Glossary: Familiarize yourself with the me these key terms. Definitions are found in the Gl **consumerism, creation, Creator, freedom, free grace, human person, intellect, Kingdom (Reign morality, Original Sin, Paschal Mystery, redemp secularism, sin, temptation**

Faith Word: human person
Learn by Heart: John 1:16–17
Learn by Example: St. Augustine of Hippo

How do you seek happiness?

OPENING REFLECTION

⊙ What does "happiness" mean for you? How do you go about seeking happiness?

⊙ Slowly and quietly read these words of Jesus: "I came that they may have life, and have it abundantly" (John 10:10).

⊙ Read Jesus' words again and allow Jesus to speak to you. What is he saying to you about your own search for happiness? About what is best for you?

JOURNAL EXERCISE

Complete these sentences.

⊙ Happiness is. . . .

⊙ I will be happy if. . . .

⊙ I would be happier if. . . .

THE PURSUIT OF HAPPINESS

On July 4, 1776, the fifty-six representatives of the original thirteen States signed the Declaration of Independence. In the opening of the Declaration we read: "We hold these truths to be self-evident, that all men are created equal, that they are endowed by their Creator with certain unalienable Rights, that among these are Life, Liberty and the pursuit of Happiness."

In recent years Black Friday has become a symbol of how many Americans use their liberty to pursue happiness, to live a "good" life. Retailers have created that frantic day of bargain-hunting to lure consumers to spend and spend in that pursuit. It is one sign that **consumerism** drives the American "pursuit of Happiness." Consumerism encourages the purchase of goods and services in ever-greater amounts as a partial solution to our desire for happiness. This attitude is deeply rooted in secularism. **Secularism** is a vision and philosophy of life that separates religion and life. It denies that God is the source

DECLARATION OF INDEPENDENCE | 19TH-CENTURY ENGRAVING

and center of all life and of our desire for true happiness.

In his annual message at the beginning of Lent 2011 Pope Benedict XVI denounced consumerism. He warned of the violence it does to the dignity of the **human person**. Benedict XVI, who was elected Pope on April 19, 2005 and resigned the papacy, or the Petrine ministry, on February 28, 2013, taught: "The idolatry of goods . . . not only separates us from others but empties the human person and leaves him [or her] unhappy." Pope Francis has also directly and firmly addressed the evil of consumerism and the idolatry of goods. In his Apostolic Exhortation, *The Joy of the Gospel*, Pope Francis taught that we are to say "No to the new idolatry of money":

The worship of the ancient golden calf (see Exodus 32:1–35) has returned in a new and ruthless guise in the idolatry of money and the dictatorship of an impersonal economy lacking a truly human purpose. The worldwide crisis affecting finance and the economy lays bare their imbalances and, above all, their lack of real concern for human beings; man is reduced to one of his needs alone: consumption.

—*The Joy of the Gospel (Evangelii Gaudium)*, no. 55

TALK IT OVER

⊙ What do you think of the pope's evaluation of the pursuit of happiness?

⊙ How common or uncommon is it to travel the path of consumerism in the pursuit of happiness? How willing are young people to travel that road?

⊙ Does such a choice really lead to "happiness"?

WHAT ABOUT YOU PERSONALLY?

⊙ How do you determine what is "best" for you? Is it working? Give it some real thought!

Can money buy happiness?

A few years ago Lexus marketed its new range of cars with the tag line, "Whoever said money can't buy happiness isn't spending it right." In July 2006 CNNMONEY did an intriguing evaluation of the thesis behind Lexus' marketing strategy, namely, money can buy happiness. Its analysis opened, "What made the ads so intriguing, but also so infuriating, was that they seemed to offer a simple—if rather expensive—solution to a common question: How can you transform the money you work so hard to earn into something approaching the good life? Later in the article we read, "We always think if we just had a little bit more money, we'd be happier, but when we get there, we're not. . . . Once you get basic human needs met, a lot more money doesn't make a lot more happiness."

THINK, PAIR AND SHARE

The above articulates the wisdom that Scripture and the Church have always taught—a wisdom that many reject as folly.

⊙ Share with a partner what you see to be the factors that contribute to the "money vision" of happiness—of the good life.

⊙ Think about some of the reasons people may pursue happiness in primarily material terms. What might the implications of such a pursuit be for one's personal life? For society? For the Church?

⊙ Share your views with the rest of the class.

LET'S PROBE DEEPER

⊙ Read Luke 6:20–21, 24–25 and Luke 12:13–21.

⊙ In your own words summarize Jesus' teaching on the pursuit of possessions as the path to happiness.

⊙ With a partner, compare Jesus' teaching with the Lexus ad and with other media portrayals of the connection between happiness and the pursuit and accumulation of possessions.

OVER TO YOU

⊙ How can you take the wisdom of Jesus' teaching and apply it to your own life?

A UNIVERSAL PURSUIT

Philosophers and theologians have addressed the human pursuit of happiness, as Scripture does. For example, the great Greek philosopher Aristotle (384–322 BC) taught that happiness is the chief desire of the human heart. In the fifth century, St. Augustine of Hippo wrote, "You have made us for yourself alone and our hearts are restless until they rest in you" (*Confessions*). The Christian French philosopher Blaise Pascal (1623–62) wrote, "There is a God-shaped vacuum in the heart of

every person which cannot be filled by any created thing, but only by God the Creator made known through Jesus Christ." The German Catholic theologian Karl Rahner, S.J. (1904–84) taught the same truth; he wrote, "We all have an innate desire for God—because we are made in the image and likeness thereof; God has implanted a 'God seed' in each of us, it is to grow and blossom throughout life." The contemporary Catholic American spiritual writer and Franciscan Friar Fr. Richard Rohr, O.F.M. describes this desire and search for happiness as a "homesickness" for God.

Every person has a built-in desire to pursue happiness. In some way, this pursuit is the "human story." The Catholic Church teaches that human beings can only find true happiness by pursuing a life lived in relationship with God, who is Father, Son and Holy Spirit. Any other path to "happiness" leads to a pale imitation of that lasting happiness and joy that Jesus revealed. This is good news! Jesus, the Incarnate Son of God, assures us that we can come to true happiness—we can fulfill the deepest desire of our heart by living our life in Christ, by following the way Jesus lived and taught and summed up in the Beatitudes. "The Beatitudes take up and fulfill God's promises from Abraham by ordering them to the Kingdom of heaven. They respond to the desire for happiness that God has placed in the human heart" (CCC, no. 1725).

This course of study explores Christian

morality. **Morality** refers to the goodness or evil of human acts, and is rooted in the moral law. The moral law, urges us "to do what is good and avoid what is evil" (Vatican II, *Pastoral Constitution on the Church in the Modern World*, no. 16; quoted in CCC, no. 1713). This law "makes itself heard in conscience and is fulfilled in love of God and love of neighbor" (CCC, no. 1706).

We will examine the concepts and precepts of the moral law that govern the lives of Jesus' disciples, who "incorporated in *Christ* by Baptism . . . are 'dead to sin and alive to God in Christ Jesus' and so participate in the life of the Risen Lord (Romans 6:11; see also Romans 6:5 and Colossians 2:12)" (CCC, no. 1694). This study will prepare you to live out, more fully, God's plan of goodness and his will for your happiness—and for the happiness of all people.

OVER TO YOU

- ⊙ Revisit the "Opening Reflection." How has studying this section of the chapter challenged you to evaluate any assumptions about happiness and the pursuit of what is best for you? How might you be challenged to change those assumptions?
- ⊙ What might happen to your pursuit of happiness when you make those changes?
- ⊙ How might making those changes impact the lives of other people?

The divine path for the human pursuit of happiness

The Summer Day

Who made the world?
Who made the swan, and the black bear?
Who made the grasshopper?
This grasshopper, I mean—
the one who has flung herself out of the
    grass,
the one who is eating sugar out of my hand,
who is moving her jaws back and forth
    instead of up and down—
who is gazing around with her enormous and
    complicated eyes.
Now she lifts her pale forearms and
    thoroughly washes her face.
Now she snaps her wings open, and floats
    away.
I don't know exactly what a prayer is.
I do know how to pay attention, how to fall
    down

into the grass, how to kneel down in the
    grass,
how to be idle and blessed, how to stroll
    through the fields,
which is what I have been doing all day.
Tell me, what else should I have done?
Doesn't everything die at last, and too soon?
Tell me, what is it you plan to do
with your one wild and precious life?

—Mary Oliver (b. 1935)

OPENING REFLECTION AND CONVERSATION
"Who made us?" "Who is God?" "Why did God make us?" "What must we do to gain happiness?" These are fundamental human questions about the origins and purpose of human existence. "The Summer Day" by the American Pulitzer Prize-winning poet Mary Oliver invites us to reflect on these questions.

⊙ Read "The Summer Day" quietly, pausing and reflecting as you read. What stands out and speaks to your heart?

⊙ Choose three of the questions the poet poses and answer them from a faith perspective.

⊙ Share your thoughts with a partner.

JOURNAL EXERCISE
⊙ Write your personal response to the final question in the poem.

FROM THE CATECHISM
God created the world to show forth and communicate his glory. That his creatures should share in his truth, goodness, and beauty—this is the glory for which God created them.

—CCC, no. 319

GOD THE CREATOR—OUR BEGINNING AND OUR END
The Catholic Church, from her beginning, has taught—as our ancestors in faith, the Jews have taught—that God created the world out of love. The Church continues to pass on this Revelation: "By love God has revealed himself and given himself to man" (CCC, no. 68). The two creation stories that open the Book of Genesis reveal the divine plan of goodness for humankind and the world. They reveal God's best desire for us. They

reveal that the will of God at the heart of the divine plan of **creation** is that our happiness is rooted in our relationship with God our **Creator** who is Father, Son and Holy Spirit.

God wills to share his divine life—his love, truth, goodness and beauty—with us. This is God's plan for humanity. In reflecting on Scripture and, in particular, on the life, Death, Resurrection and Ascension of Jesus, St. Irenaeus (c. 125–c. 202), Bishop of Lyons, Father of the Church and early Church theologian and apologist, summed up the divine will for us when he taught, "The glory of God is the human person fully live; moreover, human life is the vision of God" (*Against Heresies* 4, 20, 7).

THINK, PAIR AND SHARE

- Think about St. Irenaeus' statement. With a partner, discuss how a person can be "fully alive" today.
- Describe someone you know whom you believe is fully alive.
- How do you imagine that faith in God can encourage and help people to become fully alive?

LET'S PROBE DEEPER

- Brainstorm with a partner what you remember about the first story of creation in Genesis 1:1—2:3. These questions may help you recall the details.
  - What does this account say about the origin of the world?
  - What does it say about the creation of human beings?
  - What did God do on the seventh day?
  - What did God say when he looked at everything he had created?
- Now think about and share what you can recall about the second story of creation in Genesis 2:4–24. These questions may help you recall the details.
  - According to this account, how did God make human beings?
  - What instructions did God give to Adam?
  - Why did God create Adam and Eve?
  - How should humans relate to each other?
- Now read the two creation accounts and see how accurately you remembered them.

WHY DID GOD CREATE US?

Recall this teaching of St. Irenaeus: "The glory of God is the human person fully alive; moreover, human life is the vision of God." We have received the precious gift of life to unwrap and to live for the glory of God. The Creator has given us responsibility for our own lives, for the rest of God's creatures and for the earth. This includes a responsibility to respect the dignity of every person, including ourselves.

God the Creator invites each of us to be part of the unfolding of the divine plan of goodness for all creation. He invites us to bring life and love and goodness and truth and beauty to the earth; he invites us to respect all life, to care for all his creation (see Genesis 1:28–30).

God is the sovereign master of his plan. But to carry it out he also makes use of his creatures' co-operation. This use is not a sign of weakness, but rather a token of almighty God's greatness and goodness. For God grants his creatures not only their existence, but also the dignity of acting on their own, of being causes and principles for each other, and thus of co-operating in the accomplishment of his plan.

—CCC, no. 306

God invites you to join with him in bringing about the changes for good that he desires in the world. God the Creator awaits your response. You are capable, with God's **grace**, of shaping your own life—of crafting who you become. Grace is the "free and undeserved gift that God gives us to respond to our vocation to become his adopted children" (CCC, Glossary, "Grace"). You can make a positive difference for good in the lives of those around you and in the world. You can bring the leaven of the Gospel into the world. You can work to rebuild the world according to God's original plan of goodness. You can work to bring about the **Kingdom (Reign) of God** that Jesus inaugurated.

Jesus, the Incarnate Son of God, came to live among us to show us how to fulfill that responsibility. Jesus promised that he would always be with us and would send the Holy Spirit to be our teacher and helper as we undertake that task. (Check out John 14:15–21.) Remember, life in Christ always demands the works of justice. We are to be salt and light to the world. We are to live our Christian faith in a visible way.

"Even I could make a better world than this!"

A university student who was having a hard time getting his act together decided to take his frustrations out on God. He went into the university chapel, sat in a pew, looked heavenward and said, "All we have on this earth are problems and a bunch of dummies who will never figure out how to solve them. Even I could make a better world than this one." And somewhere deep inside him the student heard God's answer: "That's what you are supposed to do."

GROUP ACTIVITY
- Work in groups and share your ideas for making the world a better place. Pick one area to focus on: school, neighborhood, state, country or the wider world.
- Design a group poster to illustrate the change you would most like to see happen.
- Discuss how *you* can contribute to making this change a reality.
- Share ideas on ways people can work together to contribute to making this change a reality.

WHAT ABOUT YOU PERSONALLY?
- What does it mean to you to know that you have a role to fulfill in God's will for creation and human history?

We are images of God

In the beginning. . . .

For it as you who formed my inward
parts;
you knit me together in my mother's
womb.
I praise you, for I am fearfully and
wonderfully made.
Wonderful are your works;
that I know very well.
My frame was not hidden from you,
when I was being made in secret,
intricately woven in the depths of the
earth.
You eyes beheld my unformed substance.
—Psalm 139:13–16a

OPENING REFLECTION AND CONVERSATION

⊙ Read and reflect quietly and prayerfully on these psalm verses.

⊙ What message do they convey about creation? About your life?

⊙ Share your reflections

THE GIFTS OF INTELLECT AND FREE WILL

The first creation story tells us that God looked at his creation after the first five days and declared what he had created to be "good." Then on the sixth and final day of creation, after he had created human beings, male and female, "God saw everything that he had made, and indeed, it was very good" (Genesis 1:31).

The human person is the summit of God's plan. God created the human person "in his image, / in the image of God he created them; / male and female he created them" (Genesis 1:27). In this statement Scripture reveals the fundamental dignity of the human person, which the New Testament further reveals: "It is in Christ, 'the image of the invisible God' (Colossians 1:15; see also 2 Corinthians 4:4), that man has been created 'in the image and likeness' of the Creator" (CCC, no. 1701).

The second creation account opens up the meaning of Genesis 1:31. We read: "[T]he LORD God formed man from the dust of the ground, and breathed into his nostrils the breath of life; and the man became a living being" (Genesis 2:7). God created Adam by sharing the very breath of the life of God with him. Thus, each one of us is alive with the very breath of God. The Church has come to understand this Revelation to mean:

Endowed with "a spiritual and immortal soul" (*Pastoral Constitution on the Church in the Modern World*, no. 14), the human person is "the only creature on earth that God has willed for its own sake" (*Pastoral Constitution on the Church in the Modern World*, no. 24). From his conception, he is destined for eternal beatitude.

—CCC, no. 1703

This second story of creation also reveals that Adam and Eve had the ability to know and choose between good and evil. In other words, God creates the human person with an **intellect** and **free will**.

By virtue of his soul and his spiritual powers of intellect and will, man is endowed with freedom, an "outstanding manifestation of the divine image" (*Pastoral Constitution on the Church in the Modern World*, no. 17).

—CCC, nos. 1705

Our intellect and free will are God-given powers that are signs of God's unconditional love for us. By the use of our intellect we have the ability to recognize the will of God and to choose freely what is good and avoid what is evil and to know the difference between the two. (Read Genesis 3:1–7.)

Genesis clearly teaches that God does not program us. God gives us the **freedom** to say "yes" or "no" to him. "Freedom is the power given by God to act or not to act, to do this or to do that, and so to perform deliberate actions on one's own responsibility. Freedom characterizes properly human acts. The more one does what is good, the freer one becomes. . . . The choice of evil is an abuse of freedom and leads to the slavery of sin" (*Compendium of the Catechism of the Catholic Church*, no. 363). The *Catechism* teaches:

God's free initiative demands man's free response, for God has created man in his image by conferring on him, along with freedom,

By the use of our intellect we can recognize the will of God and choose freely what is good

the power to know and love him. . . . He has placed in man a longing for truth and goodness that only he can satisfy. The promises of "eternal life" respond, beyond all hope, to this desire.

—CCC, no. 2002

In other words, God has implanted in the human heart a desire for happiness that we can know and freely choose to pursue. Our eternal destiny, the ultimate purpose and goal of human life, is to respond to God's grace and live in the loving presence of the one God, who is Father, Son and Holy Spirit, in the divine communion of love for all eternity. The great St. Augustine of Hippo (354–430) put it this way:

"If at the end of your very good works . . ., you rested on the seventh day, it was to foretell by the voice of your book that at the end of our works, which are indeed 'very good' since you have given them to us, we shall also rest in you on the sabbath of eternal life" (*Confessions*, 13, 36, 51).

—CCC, no. 2002

TALK IT OVER

⊙ Share your understanding of our responsibilities in relation to the gifts of intellect and free will.

JOURNAL EXERCISE

⊙ In view of what you have learned so far, describe in your own words what you understand by the dignity of the human person.
⊙ Explain its practical implications for a person's life. For your life now.

Human person

The human individual, made in the image of God; not some thing but some one, a unity of spirit and matter, soul and body, capable of knowledge, self-possession, and freedom who can enter into communion with other persons—and with God. The human person needs to live in society, which is a group of persons bound together organically by a principle of unity that goes beyond each one of them.

—CCC, Glossary, "Person, Human"

Overcoming obstacles to happiness

OPENING REFLECTION

- Create a life map. Illustrate the path your life has taken so far—perhaps on a piece of paper or on your iPad or Notebook.
- Recall any crossroads you encountered along the way. Crossroads are situations where you had to make a choice of what you would do or say or not do or not say. Mark these on your life map. How were your choices influenced by your search for happiness?
- As you look over your life journey so far, can you recall times when you felt God guided your direction or when you asked God for help?

TURNING OUR BACKS ON GOD AND THE DIVINE PLAN FOR OUR HAPPINESS

Some of the crossroads on your life journey may have led to choices that kept you on the road to happiness; others tried to deceive and convince you they were the better directions to travel.

We sometimes do not live up to our identity and dignity, nor do we fulfill our responsibilities of being images of God. We do not acknowledge evil and often label it "good"; we choose evil over good. That is the power of temptation. Temptation presents evil as good. Temptation is "an attraction, either from outside oneself or from within, to act contrary to right reason and the commandments of God" (CCC, Glossary, "Temptation").

Recall the story of the original, or the first, temptation, and how the serpent—a biblical symbol for the Devil, or Satan, and evil—tempted Eve to believe the lie that God did not really have her and Adam's good at heart. Eve, in turn, convinced Adam. They knowingly and freely gave in to temptation. They sinned. The Church names that choice Original Sin. (Now read Jesus' words in John 8:42–47.) As a consequence of this sin, the human person can make errors of judgment about good and evil and is inclined to choose evil in the exercise of freedom.

Everyone faces temptation. Temptation comes in many forms and from many sources. Sometimes we can see through the deceit of a temptation, and resist and reject it. Other times we are not so insightful and strong. We may freely and knowingly choose what is evil and follow a road that leads to our unhappiness and that of others. When we do, we misuse or abuse our God-given gift of free will and freedom. The true exercise of freedom is following the natural law which God has implanted in every human heart to choose and do good and not to choose evil. When we knowingly and freely give in to temptation and exercise our freedom to choose and do what is evil, we sin.

Sin "is an abuse of the freedom that God gives to created persons so that they are capable of loving him and loving one another" (CCC, no. 387). It is an "offense against God as well as a fault against reason, truth, and right conscience. Sin is a deliberate thought, word, deed, or omission contrary to the eternal law of God" (CCC, Glossary, "Sin"). Sin is a reality that we need to name and acknowledge. We have the responsibility to encourage and support one another to use our freedom to seek what is good and live a life free of sin.

Christ himself was tempted, or put to the test, by the father of lies. (Read Matthew 4:1–11.) This gospel passage reveals the opposition between Jesus and the Devil and the triumph of God's saving work over Satan (see CCC. no. 538). Jesus shows us how to use our gift of free will as God intends to resist temptation—to choose what is good and true over what is evil and a lie.

(We will explore the teachings of Sacred Scripture and the Catholic Church on sin in more detail in chapter 4.)

THINK, PAIR AND SHARE
St. Paul struggled with the inner conflict of temptation. He wrote: "For I do not do the good I want, but the evil I do not want is what I do" (Romans 7:19).

⊙ Identify with a partner some of the common temptations that young people face today in their search for happiness. How do those challenges tempt us to abuse our freedom?

⊙ Why can't we use our freedom any way we desire?

⊙ Discuss what Catholic young people can do to support one another to use their gift of freedom to choose what is good and to resist temptations to sin.

OVER TO YOU
⊙ Reflect on your own pursuit of happiness. What temptations do you face in your life at this time? How are they obstacles to your finding true happiness?

⊙ What role does your participation in the life of the Church play in your efforts to seek happiness?

FROM THE CATECHISM
With infinite power God could always create something better. But with infinite wisdom and goodness God freely willed to create a world "in a state of journeying" toward its ultimate perfection.

—CCC, no. 310

THE PURSUIT CONTINUES
The Book of Genesis tells us that from the beginning human beings continued to vacillate between turning their backs on God's love and accepting the divine plan of goodness. Through it

CAIN | JOSEPH CAILLÉ

all, time and time again, God did not respond by turning his back on humanity. For example, recall the stories of Cain and Abel in Genesis 4:1–25, of Noah in Genesis 6:1—10:32, and of the Tower of Babel in Genesis 11:1–9.

This dimension of the human story continues today. We partner with God in doing the work of God in the world when we strive to know and choose freely to do God's will. But we can also knowingly and freely make choices that are contrary to God's will and run counter to the divine plan of goodness. As St. Paul did, we know that we can seek happiness in ways that lead to a deep inner conflict and unhappiness. So we pray daily as Jesus taught us to pray. We pray the Lord's Prayer with the Church and ask for God's grace to know, resist and reject temptation and to open our hearts and minds to God's will and desire for us.

"Our Father in heaven, . . .
Your kingdom come.
Your will be done on earth as it is in heaven. . . .
And do not bring us to the time of trial,
but rescue us from the evil one."
—Matthew 6:9–10, 13

Christ, the Incarnate Son of God, who himself rejected temptation, gives us God's pledge and assurance that the will of God, who is truth and love, remains unchanged. God never gives up on us; the divine plan of goodness will come about.

THE MOUNT OF TEMPTATION, ISRAEL

In Christ we share in the saving work of making God's kingdom a reality. St. Thomas Aquinas captured the essence of Jesus' mission when he taught: "The only-begotten Son of God, wanting to make us sharers in his divinity, assumed our nature, so that he, made man, might make men gods" (*Opusculum* 57:1–4; quoted in CCC, no. 460). Jesus' redeeming work was to offer humanity the grace of holiness of life (sanctifying grace), which is "a habitual gift of God's own divine life, a stable and supernatural disposition that enables us to live with God and to act by his love" (USCCA, Glossary, "Grace," 514). God also offers us actual graces. These graces support us in cooperating with the Holy Spirit in bringing about our own conversion and the ongoing transformation of all creation into the Kingdom of God, which was announced and inaugurated by Jesus Christ.

"The form of this world, distorted by sin, is passing away, and we are taught that God is preparing a new dwelling and a new earth in which righteousness dwells, in which happiness will fill and surpass all the desires of peace arising in the hearts of men" (*Pastoral Constitution on the Church in the Modern World*, no. 39).
—CCC, no. 1048

This transformation of creation into a "new heaven and a new earth" (Revelation 21:1) remains a mystery and will only and finally come about at the end of time when Christ comes again in glory. "It will be the definitive realization of God's plan to bring under a single head 'all things in [Christ], things in heaven and things on earth' (see Ephesians 1:10)" (CCC, no. 1043). St. Paul taught this truth of faith:

If, because of the one man's trespass, death exercised dominion through that one, much more surely will those who receive the abundance of grace and the free gift of righteousness exercise dominion in life through the one man, Jesus Christ. . . . so that, just as sin exercised dominion in death, so grace might also exercise dominion through justification leading to eternal life through Jesus Christ our Lord.
—Romans 5:17, 21

> ## "Do not let your hearts be troubled. Believe in God, believe also in me."
>
> **JOHN 14:1**

THE LAST SUPPER (DETAIL) | ORATORIO DI SAN LORENZO ALL'ALPE SECCIO, VERCELLI, ITALY

Through the **Pascal Mystery** of Jesus' Death, Resurrection and Ascension, God fulfilled the divine promise of **redemption** first announced in Genesis 3:15. Jesus has fulfilled that promise and has freed us from the power of evil and the "evil one." "By his Passion, Christ delivered us from Satan and from sin. He merited for us the new life in the Holy Spirit. His grace restores what sin had damaged in us" (CCC, no. 1708). (Read Romans 5:12–21.)

At the Last Supper Jesus assured the Apostles (and all humanity):

"Do not let your hearts be troubled. Believe in God, believe also in me. In my Father's house there are many dwelling places. If it were not so, would I have told you that I go to prepare a place for you". . . "I am the way, and the truth, and the life. No one comes to the Father except through me. If you know me, you will know my Father also. From now on you do know him and have seen him."

—John 14:1, 2, 6–7

All Scripture points to and is fulfilled in Jesus. "Jesus did not abolish the Law of Sinai, but rather fulfilled it (see Matthew 5:15) with such perfection (see John 8:46) that he revealed its ultimate meaning (see Matthew 5:33) and redeemed the transgressions against it (see Hebrews 9:15)" (CCC, no. 592). Joined to Christ in Baptism and by God's abundant grace, we can now pursue happiness successfully. Life in Christ is the path to happiness.

JOURNAL EXERCISE

- Recall St. Paul's words: "For I do not do the good I want, but the evil I do not want is what I do" (Romans 7:19).
- Describe the wisdom you have gained from this chapter for your own struggle to live as a disciple of Christ.

We will continue to examine throughout this course of study how and why following Jesus, who is "the Way," is our surest path to happiness in this life and in life after death.

JUDGE AND ACT

REVIEW AND SHARE WHAT YOU HAVE LEARNED IN THIS CHAPTER

Look back over this chapter and reflect on the teachings of Scripture and Tradition on the human search for happiness. Share the teachings of the Catholic Church on these statements:

- ⊙ The human pursuit of happiness can only be fulfilled in God.
- ⊙ The human person is an image of God, whom God created to share in the life and love of God.
- ⊙ Human beings have an intellect and free will.
- ⊙ Adam and Eve sinned; they turned away from God and his love.

- ⊙ Sin is an abuse of the freedom that God gives to us.
- ⊙ Sin is the road to unhappiness.
- ⊙ God does not abandon human beings when they sin.
- ⊙ Jesus has saved humanity from the power of sin.

REFLECT AND DISCERN

- ⊙ What wisdom for your life have you learned from reflecting on the teachings of the Catholic Church presented in this chapter?
- ⊙ How can you integrate that wisdom into your pursuit of happiness?

LEARN BY EXAMPLE

St. Augustine of Hippo, the story of finding happiness in living one's life in Christ

Augustine was a born questioner; he was an original thinker, continually wondering, searching and seeking for truth and happiness. Augustine, in his teenage and young adult years, might be described today as a "seeker."

Augustine was born in modern-day Algeria in AD 354. His father, Patricius, was a pagan, and his mother, St. Monica, a devout Christian. By the age of twenty Augustine, in his search for happiness, read the works of the Latin philosopher-poet Cicero, the Greek philosopher-poet Plato, and many others who were recognized, in his day, as great thinkers. Augustine's search eventually took him to a crossroad in his life journey where he "detoured" from the way of Christianity, the faith his mother so diligently tried to pass on to her son.

Alongside all of his intellectual and spiritual searching, Augustine wrestled with the way he was living—with his moral life. He struggled intensely with the truth that he was not living his life in accordance with the values his mother instilled in him and continually urged him to live by. In his

deep inner conflict he prayed, "Make me pure, O Lord, but not yet!" Why "not yet"? The young Augustine was reluctant to face the choices he knew he would need to make—particularly the thought of ending his long-term relationship with the mother of his illegitimate son.

During all the years of Augustine's long and painful struggle, his mother, Monica, never stopped praying and believing that her son would eventually respond to God. This is one of the reasons the Catholic Church has named Monica a saint and the patron saint of mothers.

In spite of, or perhaps because of, his yearning for happiness and his inner conflicts, and through his cooperating with God's grace, Augustine has become a model of the human search for happiness. By the time he came to write the story of his life, Augustine knew and could say from both the pains and joys of his experiences, "Our hearts, O God, were made for you, and they are restless until they rest in you." This prayer in his *Confessions,* Book X, sums up his pursuit of happiness:

Belatedly I loved you, O Beauty so ancient
    and so new, belatedly I loved you.
For see, you were within and I was without,
and I sought you out there.
Unlovely, I rushed heedlessly among the
    lovely things you had made.
You were with me, but I was not with you.
These things kept me far from you;
    even though they were not at all unless they
        were in you.
You did call and cry aloud, and did force
    open my deafness.
You did gleam and shine, and did chase away
    my blindness.
You did breathe fragrant odors and I drew in
    my breath; and now I pant for you.
I tasted, and now I hunger and thirst.
You did touch me, and I burned for your
    peace.

TALK IT OVER
◉ What is the best lesson we can learn from Augustine's pursuit of happiness?
◉ How valuable is it for young people today to know the story of Augustine? Give specific reasons.

WHAT ABOUT YOU PERSONALLY?
◉ What aspects of Augustine's story reflect your own life story?
◉ How does Augustine's faith journey encourage you to follow the way of Jesus?

SHARE FAITH WITH FAMILY AND FRIENDS
◉ Discuss with family and friends how you can help one another to pursue happiness in ways that will lead to communion with God.
◉ Share how you can help one another to avoid searching in places that will not lead to God.

WHAT WILL YOU DO NOW?
◉ Think of something you can do personally this week to embrace the challenge of living "an abundant life"—of giving glory to God by becoming "fully alive."
◉ Whatever you do, take time to thank God the Creator—Father, Son and Holy Spirit—for giving you the opportunity to live your life abundantly—no matter what those circumstances may be.

JOURNAL EXERCISE
Our Christian faith teaches us that God has created us to be happy in this life and in our life after death.
◉ Write out any quotes that you came across in this chapter from Scripture or from people of faith that you think will assist you in your personal search for fulfillment and happiness. In this way you can start your personal 'Words of Wisdom' anthology for this course.

LEARN BY HEART

From his fullness we have all received, grace upon grace. The law indeed was given through Moses; grace and truth came through Jesus Christ.

JOHN 1:16—17

LEADER

Our prayer today will use the *lectio divina* prayer technique. *Lectio divina* is a method used to read and mediate on Sacred Scripture and other texts so that it becomes a prayer. This method of prayer traditionally includes vocal prayer, meditation and contemplation. We read, reflect, try to understand and listen to hear how God may be speaking to us, right here and right now. We then act upon what the Lord is asking of us. We will apply that prayer format to a prayer of Blessed John Henry Cardinal Newman.

Read

Quiet your mind and heart. Place yourself in the presence of God as you pray this prayer:

God has made me for a special reason.
Something has been given to me
which God has given to no one else.
I have my mission.
I may not know everything about it now;
but one day I will look back on life and see what it was.
God has not created me for nothing.
No matter who or what I am, I can never be put away.
Even if I am sick or unwell, I can do God's work.
God's plans always work out.
God knows the right thing.
My friends may be gone.
The only people around me may be strangers.
I may feel depressed.
I may worry about the future.
Still God knows what is right.
So, I will trust in God.

Now, silently and slowly pray the prayer once again, being alert for what stands out for you or seems significant for your life right now.

Meditate

Pray the prayer again, pausing and talking silently in your heart to God the Father, Son and Holy Spirit about what you are hearing.

Contemplate

Pray the prayer once again, as you listen to hear what God may be saying to you.

Pray

Acknowledge God's presence and pray for whatever may be the deep desire of your heart.

Act

LEADER

Let us respond to these questions to help us decide what we can and will do to put our prayer into action. If you wish, share your reflections on these questions with a partner:

- What does this study and prayer time call you to do?
- How will you take it to heart in your life now?

Let us share a sign of peace and go forth and glorify God by our lives.

God has made me for a special reason. Something has been given to me which God has given to no one else

CHAPTER 2

Jesus' Response Our Response

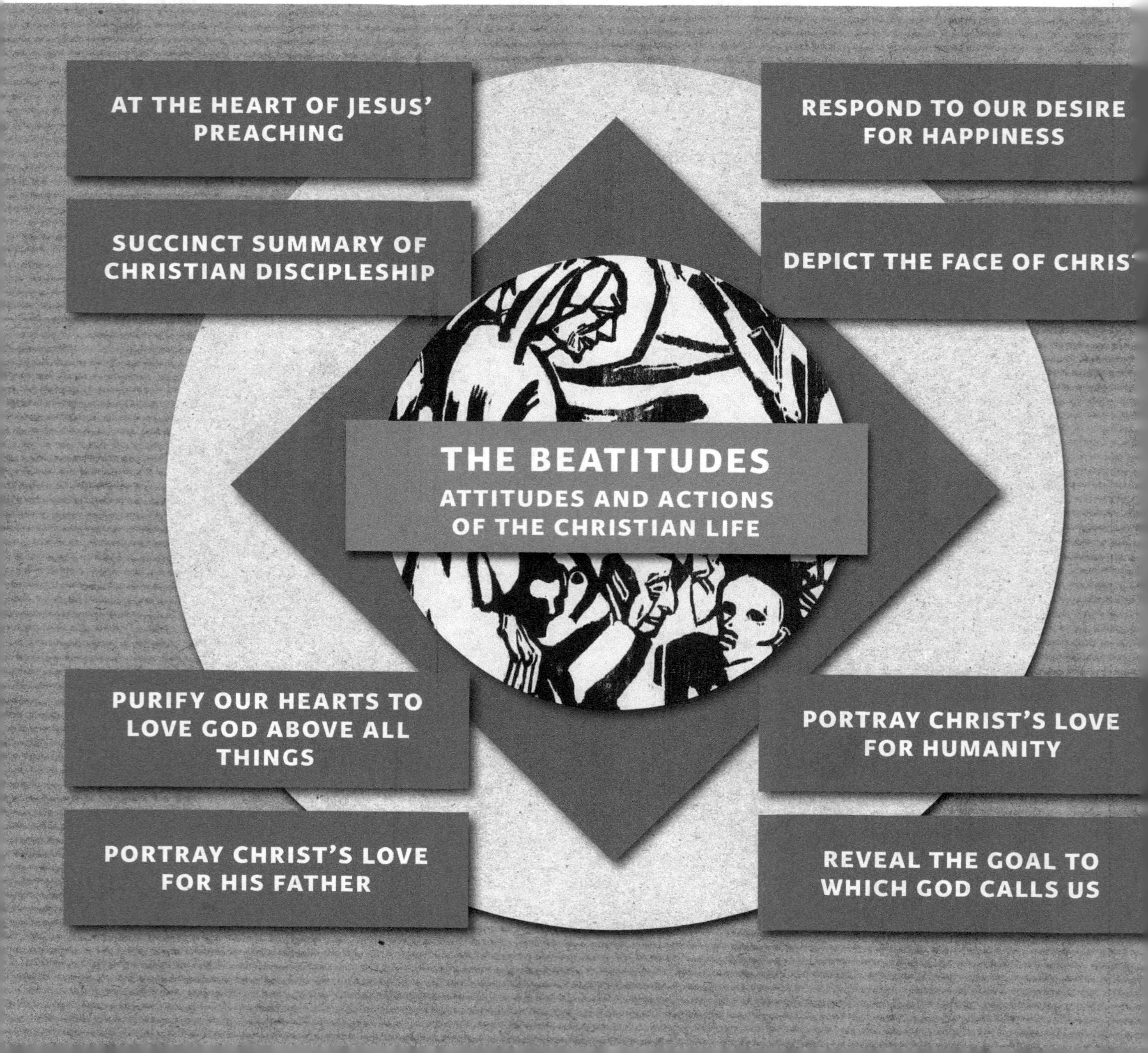
AT THE HEART OF JESUS' PREACHING
SUCCINCT SUMMARY OF CHRISTIAN DISCIPLESHIP
RESPOND TO OUR DESIRE FOR HAPPINESS
DEPICT THE FACE OF CHRIST
THE BEATITUDES
ATTITUDES AND ACTIONS OF THE CHRISTIAN LIFE
PURIFY OUR HEARTS TO LOVE GOD ABOVE ALL THINGS
PORTRAY CHRIST'S LOVE FOR HIS FATHER
PORTRAY CHRIST'S LOVE FOR HUMANITY
REVEAL THE GOAL TO WHICH GOD CALLS US

THE BEATITUDES ARE AT THE HEART OF JESUS' teaching; they portray the face of Christ and his love for his Father and for humanity. In this chapter we deepen our understanding of the Beatitudes, which are the attitudes and actions characteristic of the Christian life. We explore what it means for us to discern and freely choose to live the Beatitudes by responding to God the Father's will as Christ did.

BLESSED ARE:

- THE POOR IN SPIRIT
- THOSE WHO MOURN
- THE MEEK
- THOSE WHO HUNGER AND THIRST FOR RIGHTEOUSNESS
- THE MERCIFUL
- THE PURE IN HEART
- THE PEACEMAKERS
- THOSE WHO ARE PERSECUTED FOR RIGHTEOUSNESS' SAKE
- THOSE WHO ARE REVILED AND PERSECUTED ON JESUS' ACCOUNT

Faith Focus: These teachings of the Catholic Church a the primary focus of the doctrinal content presented in this chapter:

- ⊙ Divine love is a mystery beyond our full comprehensio
- ⊙ We are called to love as Jesus, the Incarnate Son of Go loved and as God loves.
- ⊙ The Beatitudes teach that we are to love God above all things.
- ⊙ The Beatitudes are the sure way to fulfill the human desire for happiness.
- ⊙ The Beatitudes reveal the central message of Jesus' life and preaching.
- ⊙ The Beatitudes reveal the good and being in the world.
- ⊙ The Beatitudes are guide Heaven.
- ⊙ The Beatitudes provide clear cr Christian life.

Discipleship Formation: As a result of stud chapter you should be better able to:

- ⊙ grow in your conviction of God's love for you "good" times and "bad" times;
- ⊙ discern the real difference between true happiness pretenders to happiness;
- ⊙ discover the Sermon on the Mount as the blueprint for living your life in Christ;
- ⊙ understand humility as strength of character commit yourself to living a life of humilit
- ⊙ commit yourself to working for ju
- ⊙ find the joy that comes from sacrificing love.

Scripture References: These Scrip quoted or referred to in this chapter:
OLD TESTAMENT: Exodus 3:7, 19:20; **Deuteronomy** 10:17–18; **Psalms** 1:1, 24:4–5, 34:8, 37:1–11, 65:4, 99:4, 103:8, 128:1; **Isaiah** 1:10–20, 55:8, 58:6–7, 61:1–11; **Jeremiah** 3:10; **Amos** 2:6–7, 5:24; **Micah** 6:8
NEW TESTAMENT: Matthew 4:17, 5:1—7:29,10:38, 15:7–9, 16:24, 23:37–39, 25:34–40; **Mark** 8:34, 10:21; **Luke** 2:14, 4: 19, 6:20–26 and 17–49, 9:23, 14:27, 16:13; **John** 11:3 and 17 13:1–17 and 33–38, 14:6, 20:19; **Romans** 12:1–21; 1 Corint 16:13 14; **Galatians** 6:12; **Ephesians** 2:4; **Philippians** 2:1 **Colossians** 1:20; **1 Timothy** 1:14; **1 John** 4:8, 19

Faith Glossary: Familiarize yourself with the mean of these key terms in the Glossary: *agape*, beatitu **Beatitudes, Beatific Vision, compassion, divine** **providence, hope, humility,** *kenosis*, materialis **Law, Sermon on the Mount, Sermon on the Pla** (the)

Faith Word: humility
Learn by Heart: The Beatitudes
Learn by Example: St. Maria Faustina, Apos

How should we respond to God, who is love?

OPENING REFLECTION

⊙ Think about people whom you know love you.
  - How do you know that they love you?
  - How do you generally respond to the love that you experience?
⊙ Think about the people whom you love.
  - What do you do that is a sign for them that you love them?
  - How do you find others whom you love responding to you?

GOD'S LOVE FOR US

In the Credo text *Son of God and Son of Mary* you spent some time learning about the love that is the inner life of the Blessed Trinity. You learned that the Triune God—God the Father, Son and Holy Spirit—is one God in Three Divine Persons who is a divine community of self-giving love.

Divine love is a mystery beyond our comprehension. In the First Letter of John we read: "God is love" (1 John 4:8). The Greek word for love

used in this passage is *agape*. **Agape** is a love that is *totally self-giving*; it is the selfless, self-emptying love (which the New Testament describes as **kenosis**) revealed and lived by Jesus, the Incarnate Son of God. It is love that does not expect anything in return. (Read Philippians 2:1–11.)

Jesus' awareness of and confidence in his Father's love was such that he freely took upon himself his suffering and dying on the Cross. Jesus' love redeemed and restored us to a life lived in the love of God—the holiness of life that Adam and Eve rejected.

We are called to love as Jesus, the Incarnate Son of God, loved and as God loves. We are called to love with a totally self-giving love. When we open our hearts to the grace of the Holy Spirit of love and live the way of love revealed in the Person and life of Jesus (see John 13:1–17, 33–38), we live in "the spiritual freedom of the children of God" (*Catechism of the Catholic Church* [CCC], no. 1828). When we do, we can come to know and experience the joy and **beatitude** (blessedness) that God wills and desires for us now and in the **Beatific Vision** when we will enjoy the presence of God, face-to-face, after death.

THINK, PAIR AND SHARE

⊙ What passages can you recall and name in the four accounts of the Gospel that reveal, in concrete ways, what God's love looks like?
⊙ Which of these is your favorite passage, and why?
⊙ Share your reflections with a partner.

WHAT ABOUT YOU PERSONALLY?

⊙ What experiences of God's love mean most to you in your life right now?
⊙ How do you respond to the conviction that God shows his love for you in these and many other ways?

Recognizing God's love in "unexpected places"

Patrick Henry Hughes was born without eyes and with scoliosis and a tightening of his joints, which left him physically challenged for life. As a child, Patrick was fitted with artificial eyes and had two steel rods surgically attached to his spine to correct the scoliosis. Despite such challenges, Patrick managed to excel as a musician and student. Before his first birthday he had discovered the piano. His mom recalls, "I could hit any note on the piano, and within one or two tries, he'd get it." By his second birthday Patrick was playing such tunes as "You Are My Sunshine" and "Twinkle, Twinkle Little Star." His father was ecstatic, commenting, "We might not ever play baseball, but we can play music together."

Patrick eventually became a student in the University of Louisville. There he excelled in Spanish language studies and as a virtuoso pianist, vocalist and trumpet player. Even more than his unbelievable achievements, it was Patrick's "attitude of gratitude" that inspired others. He talked to people about his life and about how blessed he was. Not ignoring or overlooking his challenges, Patrick said, "God gave me the ability . . . the musical gifts I have and the great opportunity to meet new people."

JOURNAL EXERCISE

⊙ What wisdom for your own life have you gleaned from Patrick Henry Hughes's story?

⊙ What signs of God's love for you can you find in the challenges you face in your own life?

FROM THE CATECHISM

The Beatitudes are at the heart of Jesus' preaching and they take up and fulfill the promises that God made starting with Abraham. They depict the very countenance of Jesus and they characterize authentic Christian life. They reveal the ultimate goal of human activity, which is eternal happiness.

—*Compendium of the Catechism of the Catholic Church* (*Compendium*), no. 360

THE BEATITUDES: THE ATTITUDES AND ACTIONS CHARACTERISTIC OF THE CHRISTIAN LIFE

The **Beatitudes** proclaim Jesus' attitude to life in the world. Our whole life, including our moral life, is focused on and in Jesus. "The Beatitudes are at the heart of Jesus' preaching" (CCC, no. 1716). They teach us the final end to which God calls us: the kingdom, the vision of God, participation in the very life and love of God, our identity as the beloved, adopted daughters and sons of God, and eternal life and rest in God.

The Beatitudes appear in the synoptic Gospels of Matthew and of Luke. In Matthew they are part of the **Sermon on the Mount** (Matthew 5:1—7:29) and in Luke they are part of the **Sermon on the Plain** (Luke 6:17–49). Here is Matthew's listing of the Beatitudes:

Blessed are the poor in spirit, for theirs is the kingdom of heaven.
Blessed are those who mourn, for they will be comforted.
Blessed are the meek, for they will inherit the earth.
Blessed are those who hunger and thirst for righteousness, for they will be filled.
Blessed are the merciful, for they will receive mercy.

Blessed are the pure in heart, for they will see God.
Blessed are the peacemakers, for they will be called children of God.
Blessed are those who are persecuted for righteousness' sake, for theirs is the kingdom of heaven.
Blessed are you when people revile you and persecute you and utter all kinds of evil against you falsely on my account. Rejoice and be glad, for your reward is great in heaven, for in the same way they persecuted the prophets who were before you.

—Matthew 5:3–12

In his teachings in the Sermon on the Mount Jesus makes it very clear that God's way of thinking is not our way of thinking; our ways of acting are not always God's way of acting. (Read Isaiah 55:8.) God's ways can be radically different from the values and standards that the world recommends as the source of our happiness. (We will explore the Sermon on the Mount in more detail in the next section of this chapter.)

TALK IT OVER
Read and reflect on each of the Beatitudes.

- What is your immediate response to each Beatitude?
- Who are the people described in the Beatitudes whom you would consider blessed by God? Why do you think these people might be considered "blessed" or "not blessed"?

OVER TO YOU
- In what ways have you come to know Pope Francis to be a "Beatitude" person?
- How does he model for you living an authentic Christian life?

LET'S PROBE DEEPER
The Hebrew and Greek words for "beatitude" have been translated into English as both "happy" and "blessed." The word "happy" is open to many interpretations, and often these are subjective, depending on an individual's experience and expectations. What makes one person happy may not do so for another. The word "blessed" names the gifts of joy and happiness that come from faith in God and the conviction of being loved by God. Through his teaching on the Beatitudes Jesus reveals *the good and true way*—his way—of our being in the world. These eight fundamental *attitudes* and *actions* provide the focus for our attitude toward the world and how God creates us to act in the world. When we are true to our origin and purpose we are among those people whom Scripture identifies as "blessed"; those who know the joy that brings true happiness.

REFLECT AND SHARE
- Read and compare the Beatitudes in the Sermon on the Mount in Matthew 5:3–12 with the Beatitudes in the Sermon on the Plain in Luke 6:20–26.
- What do you recognize as major similarities and major differences?
- Why do you think Luke adds the section from verse 24 to 26, which contains a list of woes?

JOURNAL EXERCISE
- Name the Beatitude that speaks most clearly to your life right now.
- How does living according to this Beatitude make a difference to your life? To the life of other people?

We are called to be "blessed"

OPENING ACTIVITY

⊙ Conduct a class vox pop asking: "What do you think is the best way to become the person God wants you to be?" and "What do you imagine you still need to learn in order to be able to do this?"

THE SERMON ON THE MOUNT

Matthew situates the Sermon on the Mount on the side of a mountain. In the Old Testament, a "mountain" is a symbol for the presence of God; it is where God often speaks to his people; for example, we read, "When the LORD descended upon Mount Sinai, to the top of the mountain, the LORD summoned Moses to the top of the mountain" (Exodus 19:20). In locating the Sermon on the Mount on a mountain, Matthew is teaching that Jesus has come to fulfill and not to abolish the Law and the Prophets. (Pause and read Matthew 5:17–20.)

The Sermon on the Mount has been described as "the blueprint" for Christian living. It summarizes the New Law, which Jesus taught and lived. The **New Law** is the law of love because it calls us to act out of love for God and for one another. It is the law of grace because it gives us the grace of the sacraments to help us to live out of love. It is the law of freedom because it frees us from the status of servant, as in the Old Testament Law, to the status of children of God. The teachings of Jesus in the Sermon on the Mount are a succinct summary of Christian discipleship. The whole Sermon portrays the vision of Jesus for his disciples. Being a disciple of Jesus involves formation in fundamental attitudes and actions, that is, conforming to a certain way of being in the world. Imagine how empowering it must have been for the people listening to Jesus, many of whom were the "poor" of his times, as they heard his words, "You are the salt of the earth; . . . You are the light of the world" (Matthew 5:13 and 14). Imagine how uplifted they must have been that they could be such salt and light by obeying and teaching God's commandments, avoiding sin, being reconciled as needed, living faithful lives, turning the other cheek instead of seeking revenge, going the extra mile, loving even enemies, caring for the needy, praying and fasting regularly, depending on **divine providence** instead of on possessions, and judging all with kindness.

As the Sermon draws to a close, Jesus gives them "the golden rule" for finding happiness and joy in life. He teaches, "In everything do to others as you would have them do to you; for this is the law and the prophets" (Matthew 7:12).

instead it uses what might be called rhyming ideas, which serve to facilitate memorizing the verses. A biblical beatitude is a "technical term found for a literary form found in both the OT and NT. A beatitude is a declaration of blessedness on the ground of some virtue or good fortune. . . . The beatitude is common in the NT, most frequently for faith or sharing in the kingdom of God" (John L. McKenzie, S.J., *Dictionary of the Bible*, "Beatitude," 84).

Matthew, one of the **Twelve**, under the inspiration of the Holy Spirit, wove together a summary of Jesus' most important teachings and placed them at the beginning of his Gospel account as a prelude for what was to come. These teachings, which were first passed on by word of mouth (oral tradition), were eventually written during the third stage of the formation of the Gospel, and were recognized by the Church as authentic and included in the canon of Scripture.

THE BEATITUDES FOR US TODAY: THE HEART OF JESUS' TEACHING

In the Sermon on the Mount, and in particular in the Beatitudes, Jesus invites us to see life as a blessing. God "first loved us" (1 John 4:19). We are truly "blessed." Such a worldview sees the world as God sees it. It provides us with the truth that our life is good and rooted in God's love for us. St. Basil the Great (c. AD 330–379), one of the Eastern Fathers and a Doctor of the Church, put it this way:

"If we turn away from evil out of fear of punishment, we are in the position of slaves. If we pursue the enticement of wages, . . . we resemble mercenaries. Finally if we obey for the sake of the good itself and out of love for him who commands . . . we are in the position of children" (St. Basil, *The Rule of St. Basil*, prologue, 3).

—CCC, no. 1828

JOURNAL EXERCISE
⊙ Summarize the best thing you have learned so far from the Sermon on the Mount.

LET'S PROBE DEEPER: SCRIPTURE ACTIVITY
⊙ Read the Sermon on the Mount in Matthew 5:1—7:29 with a partner.
⊙ Choose three moral teachings that stand out for you and share your thoughts about them.

OVER TO YOU
⊙ What might these teachings mean for the lives of young people today

LITERARY FORM AND HISTORICAL CONTEXT OF THE SERMON ON THE MOUNT

A beatitude is a form of Hebrew poetry found in several books of the Old Testament. (Check out Psalms 1:1, 34:8, 65:4, 128:1.) This form of Hebrew poetry does not use rhyming words, as you might be used to reading in some forms of poetry;

The Beatitudes and God's free gift of joy

The Beatitudes turn much of conventional human thinking upside down. How can the "poor in spirit," "those who mourn," "the meek," those who are "persecuted for righteousness' sake" and reviled on Jesus' account be blessed, be happy, be filled with joy?

OPENING REFLECTION

- ☉ Reread the Beatitudes in the first section of this chapter. What do you honestly think of such claims and promises?
- ☉ How willing and ready are you personally to accept those claims?

FROM THE CATECHISM

The Beatitudes depict the countenance of Jesus Christ and portray his charity. They express the vocation of the faithful associated with the glory of his Passion and Resurrection; they shed light on the actions and attitudes characteristic of the Christian life; they are paradoxical promises that sustain hope in the midst of tribulations; they proclaim the blessings and rewards already secured, however dimly, for Christ's disciples; they have begun in the lives of the Virgin Mary and all the saints.

—CCC, no. 1717

JESUS REVEALS THE NATURE OF TRUE HAPPINESS

The Beatitudes respond to the natural desire for happiness that God has placed in every human heart. They reveal the goal of human existence to which God calls us. Let's take a closer look at the actions and attitudes revealed in each of the Beatitudes. They "confront us with decisive choices concerning earthly goods; they purify our hearts in order to teach us to love God above all things" (CCC, no. 1728).

"Blessed are the poor in spirit, for theirs is the kingdom of heaven" (Matthew 5:3):

The "poor in spirit" are not necessarily the economically poor. Jesus does not bless economic poverty, but commands us to work to alleviate it and the suffering associated with it. In the Scriptures the "poor in spirit" are all those who keep God at the center of their life and have absolute trust in him. The virtue of **humility** is the foundation of their life.

The actions and attitudes of the poor in spirit reveal the emptiness of the deceit of **materialism**, which drives one to pursue and turn created goods into idols, into "gods." In Luke's Sermon

on the Plain Jesus teaches, "No slave can serve two masters; for a slave will either hate the one and love the other, or be devoted to the one and despise the other. You cannot serve God and wealth" (Luke 16:13). Jesus admonishes those who choose to focus their lives on the pursuit of wealth or on anything or anyone other than God—no matter what its form.

OVER TO YOU

◉ What people do you recognize to be "poor in spirit"?

◉ Do you see the qualities of the "poor in spirit" in your own attitudes and actions? Why is that?

MOURNER | 15TH-CENTURY TOMB SCULPTURE

Humility

The virtue by which a Christian acknowledges that God is the author of all good. Humility avoids inordinate ambition or pride, and provides the foundation for turning to God in prayer. Voluntary humility can be described as "poverty of spirit."

—CCC, Glossary

"Blessed are those who mourn, for they will be comforted" (Matthew 5:4):

In the Psalms, mourning is often connected to sorrow for sin and its consequences on one's personal life and on society. People who mourn experience a sense of sadness not only over their own personal suffering and sin but also over the suffering and sin of others, especially the sinful and oppressive structures of society. For example, Jesus mourned (wept) over the city of Jerusalem for turning its back on God and the covenant: "Jerusalem, Jerusalem, the city that kills prophets and stones those who are sent to it! How often have I desired to gather your children together as a hen gathers her brood under her wings, and you were not willing! See, your house is left to you, desolate. For I tell you, you will not see me again until you say, 'Blessed is the one who comes in the name of the Lord'" (Matthew 23:37–39).

LET'S PROBE DEEPER

Jesus joined Martha and Mary and mourned over the loss of their brother, Lazarus (see John 11:33–35). Through his words and actions Jesus, the Son of God made flesh, reveals that God is our companion during our times of mourning. Jesus' action transformed Martha's and Mary's sorrow into joy. In our times of sorrow, disappointment or bereavement, we too can know and experience the comfort of the compassionate God with us.

◉ Read and reflect on John 11:17–44.

◉ Share with a partner your insights on how mourning can be transformed into joy.

ECCE HOMO

"Blessed are the meek, for they will inherit the earth" (Matthew 5:5):

The word "meek" is often used to describe a person as "weak." This usage in English is contrary to its use in the Scriptures. In the Scriptures "meek" is often translated as "slow to anger and abounding in steadfast love" (Psalm 103:8). Meekness is an attribute of God that Jesus calls his disciples to "image" in their lives. The meek are gentle and generous; they are forgiving, even of their enemies (check out Matthew 5:43–44). They treat others with kindness, **compassion** and tenderness (check out Matthew 5:21–26). The words and actions of the meek manifest non-violence; not only do they "not kill," but they avoid acting out of anger, hatred and vengeance. The meek will "inherit the earth"—the goodness God wills for all people.

PAUSE AND REFLECT

⊙ Read Psalm 37:1–11. Recall a time when you refrained from anger and treated people with gentleness and kindness.

In the Scripture often translated as "slow to anger and abounding in steadfast love"

⊙ How was that an expression of your strength of character?
⊙ What response did you receive? How did you feel about the reaction?

"Blessed are those who hunger and thirst for righteousness, for they will be filled" (Matthew 5:6):

The Hebrew word *sedeqah* and the Greek *dikaiosyne* can be translated as "righteousness" or "justice." So this Beatitude can be read as "Blessed are those who hunger and thirst for *justice*"—those who hunger to live according to God's original plan of holiness and justice for his creation; those who seek to live in right relationship with God and others and all creation. Authentic disciples of Jesus hunger for justice, fairness and equality in the world, as Jesus did. (Reread Luke 4:16–19; then check out Isaiah 61:1–11.) To work for justice is to embrace what God wills and desires for everyone. Those who "hunger and thirst for righteousness" work with the Holy Spirit to bring about the kingdom that Jesus inaugurated.

LET'S PROBE DEEPER: SCRIPTURE ACTIVITY

- ⊙ Look up and quietly read Exodus 3:7, Deuteronomy 10:17–18, Psalm 99:4, Isaiah 58:6–7, Amos 2:6, 7 and 5:24, and Micah 6:8.
- ⊙ What do these passages say about justice, or righteousness?
- ⊙ In light of these Old Testament passages, what does this Beatitude teach us as we strive for justice in our world today?

"Blessed are the merciful, for they will receive mercy" (Matthew 5:7):

Human misery is a universal sign of the consequence of Original Sin and the need for salvation and healing of our human condition. Throughout his ministry the Lord, who freely took upon himself our human condition, constantly identified himself with people who were suffering from sin and other evils and addressed their misery. The Church since her beginning, at the command of Christ, has done the same.

St. Thomas Aquinas taught that the virtue of mercy is second only to love in the Christian life. God is a God of mercy who is "rich in mercy" (Ephesians 2:4). Mercy is the generous, practical expression of undeserved love. Those who are merciful do not judge others harshly. (Check out Matthew 7:1–5.) They love the sinner and hate the sin. They forgive those who trespass against them (Lord's Prayer).

Mercy for others, expressed in compassion and concern, is always a responsibility of a disciple of Christ. (Check out Matthew 6:1–4.) As disciples of Jesus we are called to love our neighbor, especially those most in need, because of our love for God.

"Hence, those who are oppressed by poverty are the object of a *preferential love* on the part of the Church which, since her origin and in spite of the failings of many of her members, has not ceased to work for their relief, defense, and liberation, through numerous works of charity which remain indispensable always and everywhere" (Congregation for the Doctrine of the Faith, *Instruction on Christian Freedom and Liberation*, 68.)

—CCC, no. 2448

JOURNAL EXERCISE

◉ Write about a time when you showed mercy or had mercy shown to you. Try to articulate what wisdom you learned from that experience.

Those who are merciful do not judge others harshly; they love the sinner and hate the sin

THE WOMAN TAKEN IN ADULTERY | GUERCINO

"Blessed are the pure in heart, for they will see God" (Matthew 5:8):

Take a moment and read Psalm 24:4–5, Isaiah 1:10–20 and Jeremiah 3:10. The "pure in heart" keep their eyes on God. They desire to please God and to do the will of God above everything else. They strive for a perfect correspondence between their inner thoughts and desires and their external actions, and between their worship of God and their moral life. They avoid being hypocrites. The Church passes on this truth of our faith when she teaches: "The moral life is a spiritual worship" (CCC, 2047). Jesus admonished the Pharisees about separating our "heart" from our actions:

"You hypocrites! Isaiah prophesied rightly about you when he said:
'This people honors me with their lips,
    but their hearts are far from me;

in vain do they worship me,
    teaching human precepts as doctrines.'"
—Matthew 15:7–9

The divine promise to the pure in heart is that they will glimpse the face of God now and will enter into the joy of seeing God face to face eternally after death. St. Irenaeus captured the heart of the promise when he wrote: "[B]ecause of God's love and goodness toward us, and because he can do all things, he goes so far as to grant those who love him the privilege of seeing him" (*Against Heresies*, 4, 20; quoted in CCC, no. 1722).

TALK IT OVER
- With a partner, read Matthew 25:34–40.
- How you might "catch a glimpse" of God now?

"Blessed are the peacemakers, for they will be called children of God" (Matthew 5:9):

The Hebrew word for peace, *shalom*, points to all the goodness, all the best, that God wills and desires for us. This Beatitude teaches that disciples of Jesus, who have become adopted children of God through Baptism, are called to bring about this reality. When the angels first announced the birth of Jesus, they said he brought "on earth peace" (Luke 2:14). The first words the risen Christ said when he appeared to his disciples were, "Peace be with you" (John 20:19). Peacemakers work to restore harmony in every situation of violence, tension or division—as Jesus, the Prince of Peace, did and as the Spirit of Jesus continues to do. They work to reconcile people with God and with one another. (See Colossians 1:20.)

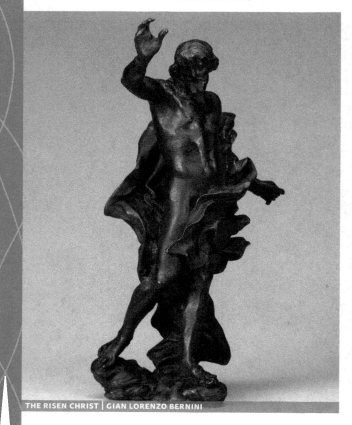

THE RISEN CHRIST | GIAN LORENZO BERNINI

The first words the risen Christ said when he appeared to his disciples were, "Peace be with you."

Have you ever been put down for your religious beliefs or for acting on those beliefs?

READ, REFLECT AND SHARE

- Reflect on these words of St. John Paul II, who was the pope from October 16, 1978 to his death on April 2, 2005: "Wherever the strong exploit the weak; wherever the rich take advantage of the poor . . . there the work of making peace is undone."
- Let the Pope's words speak to your heart.
- Share your reflections with the class.

"Blessed are those who are persecuted for righteousness' sake, for theirs is the kingdom of heaven" (Matthew 5:10):

Jesus clearly taught that there is a cost to being his disciple. The authentic disciple of Jesus will accept carrying the Cross (see Matthew 10:38, 16:24; Mark 8:34, 10:21; Luke 9:23, 14:27; Galatians 6:12); this will include being persecuted, as Jesus was persecuted.

Pope Francis in his first homily on March 14, 2013 echoed the words of Christ. The Pope said, "When we walk without the Cross, when we build without the Cross, and when we profess Christ without the Cross, we are not disciples of the Lord." Jesus began his public ministry by announcing: "Repent, for the kingdom of heaven has come near" (Matthew 4:17). When we suffer in the cause of justice, we work to bring about the Kingdom of Heaven.

JOURNAL EXERCISE

- Have you ever been put down for your religious beliefs or for acting on those beliefs? Have you ever not acted on those beliefs for fear of being put down? Write about these experiences.
- Describe how the insights you have gained from studying the Beatitudes might help you "stand firm in your faith" (1 Corinthians 16:13) in Christ in the future.

What it means to live the Beatitudes

are aware of another voice within you and all around you, a contradictory voice. It is a voice which says, "Blessed are the proud and violent, those who prosper at any cost, who are unscrupulous, pitiless, devious, who make war not peace, and persecute those who stand in their way." And this voice seems to make sense in a world where the violent often triumph and the devious seem to succeed. "Yes," says the voice of evil, "they are the ones who win. Happy are they!"

OPENING REFLECTION

◉ What sense does St. John Paul II's message make to you? How willing are you to be called a "loser" in order to be a "winner" for Christ?

◉ Write your thoughts in your journal.

BE GLAD AND REJOICE IN THE LORD
Matthew's listing of the Beatitudes concludes with this final Beatitude:

"Blessed are you when people revile you and persecute you and utter all kinds of evil against you falsely on my account. Rejoice and be glad, for your reward is great in heaven, for in the same way they persecuted the prophets who were before you."

—Matthew 5:11

CAN LOSERS REALLY BE WINNERS?
This is an extract from a homily St. John Paul II addressed to young people on the Mount of Beatitudes in March 2000.

It is strange that Jesus exalts those whom the world generally regards as weak. He says to them, "Blessed are you who seem to be losers, because you are the true winners: the kingdom of heaven is yours!" These words present a challenge which demands a deep and abiding *metanoia* of the spirit, a great change of heart. You young people will understand why this change of heart is necessary! Because you

Christians are people whose faith and love are strengthened by **hope**. Hope is a gift of God; along with faith and love it is one of the three theological virtues. Hope is "the theological virtue by which we desire and expect from God both eternal life and the grace we need to attain it" (CCC, Glossary, "Hope"). Hope gives us the strength to cooperate with the grace of the Holy Spirit to transform our life, our attitudes and actions, and truly become "Beatitude" people.

Hope deepens our faith and commitment to love as Jesus loved and commanded us to love—even when that may not be the popular thing to do.

JESUS CALLS US TO LIVE THE BEATITUDES

Jesus' teaching in the Beatitudes is crystal clear, and the Church passes on this teaching: "True happiness is not found in riches or well-being, in human fame or power, or in any human achievement—however beneficial it may be—such as science, technology and art, or indeed in any creature, but in God alone, the source of every good and of all love" (CCC, no 1723).

There is a cost in choosing to live by the wisdom of Jesus. Putting your faith and hope in Jesus means choosing to believe in him and in what he teaches—no matter how costly it may be. It means recognizing the deceit of evil and rejecting the claims of evil, no matter how sensible or attractive or wise and good they may seem.

We learned earlier in this chapter: "The Beatitudes depict the countenance of Jesus Christ" (CCC, no. 1717). Jesus does not merely speak the Beatitudes, he lives the Beatitudes.

Jesus is the Beatitudes "made flesh." Looking at Christ and the mystery of his whole life, Death, Resurrection and Ascension, we see what it means to be "poor in spirit," to "mourn," to be "meek," to "hunger and thirst for righteousness," to be "merciful," to be "pure in heart," to be "peacemakers," to be "persecuted for righteousness' sake" and "reviled" on his account.

THINK, PAIR AND SHARE
- Look through the Gospels. Find examples of Jesus living each of the Beatitudes.
- Share your findings with a partner.

NEW LIFE IN CHRIST
We too have received God's grace to enable us to live as adopted children. We have the grace to meet the challenge of living a life of holiness and justice. As St. Paul, who knew he had received the grace of God abundantly through Christ, said to Timothy, "I received mercy, . . . and the grace of our Lord overflowed for me with the faith and love that are in Christ Jesus" (1 Timothy 1:14). So it is for us. The Beatitudes reveal the fundamental attitudes and actions that undergird the moral choices we make to live the life in Christ that we

were incorporated into, professed and promised to live at Baptism. The Spirit of Christ is always offering us the grace to follow Jesus, who is the only way to the Father.

LET'S PROBE DEEPER: SCRIPTURE ACTIVITY

A coach will often summarize what she or he expects of the members of the team. Throughout the year the coach and players will use this statement to measure their efforts. In a way, the Beatitudes serve a similar purpose for Christians. St. Paul wrote to the Church in Rome to help them understand and measure how we are to live as members of the Body of Christ.

⊙ Carefully read Romans 12 and take note of its main points.
⊙ Divide into groups; ask each member to share their most compelling insights.
⊙ Conclude with what you think this passage means for the lives of Christian youth today.

A team can measure their efforts against what the coach expects from them; Christians can measure their efforts against the Beatitudes

OVER TO YOU

⊙ How do you think what you have read in this chapter can influence your attitudes and actions?
⊙ What might change in the way of your "being" in the world?
⊙ What will help you to bring about that change?

REVIEW AND SHARE WHAT YOU HAVE LEARNED IN THIS CHAPTER

Look back over this chapter and reflect on the teachings of Scripture and Tradition on the Beatitudes. Share your understanding of the teaching of the Catholic Church on these statements:

⊙ The moral life and the human search for happiness are inseparable.

⊙ Living the Beatitudes is the way to happiness.

⊙ Jesus' life and ministry modeled the Beatitudes.

⊙ The Beatitudes teach that we are to love God above all things.

⊙ The Beatitudes teach us how we are to treat our neighbors.

⊙ The Beatitudes provide a blueprint for living the Christian life.

⊙ The Beatitudes are eight fundamental *attitudes* and *actions* that provide the focus for how God creates us to act in the world.

OVER TO YOU

⊙ What wisdom have you learned for your life from this chapter?

LEARN BY EXAMPLE

St. Maria Faustina, Apostle of Mercy

Helen Kowalska, St. Maria Faustina, was born in a small village west of Lodz, Poland on August 25, 1905. She was the third of ten children. She came from a very poor family that had struggled hard on a small farm during the terrible years of World War I. After only three years of very basic education, at the age of fifteen she started work as a housekeeper to support her family.

When she was almost twenty Helen entered the Congregation of the Sisters of Our Lady of Mercy. The following year she received her religious habit and was given the name Sister Maria, to which she added "of the Most Blessed Sacrament." Sr. Maria performed the humblest of tasks in the convent, usually in the kitchen or the vegetable garden or as a porter.

During her time in the convent Sr. Maria experienced a series of private revelations and visions of Jesus. She recalled Jesus saying to her in one of these apparitions, "My mercy is so great that no mind, be it of man or of angel, will be able to fathom it throughout all eternity" (*Divine Mercy in My Soul* [*Diary of Saint Maria Faustina*], 699). Jesus asked Sr. Maria to model in her own life the mercy of God. This would remind people that if they wanted divine mercy for themselves, they had to be merciful to others. Sr. Maria took to heart the gospel command to "be merciful even as your heavenly Father is merciful" and lived as an apostle of mercy. Sr. Maria Faustina died of tuberculosis in Krakow, Poland, on October 5, 1938.

St. John Paul II beatified Sr. Maria in 1993 and canonized her in 2000. On the day of Sr.

Maria's canonization, the Pope also officially instituted the Feast of the Divine Mercy, which the Catholic Church celebrates on the Second Sunday of Easter. The Catholic Church also celebrates the memory and the life of St. Maria Faustina on October 5. The message of mercy that St. Maria Faustina lived and taught is now being spread throughout the world. Her diary has become the handbook for devotion to Divine Mercy.

TALK IT OVER

⊙ What is the best spiritual wisdom that you have learned for your life from the story of St. Maria Faustina?

SHARE FAITH WITH FAMILY AND FRIENDS

⊙ Pope Francis, in his first *Angelus* address to over 100,000 pilgrims in St. Peter's Square, said: "A little mercy makes the world less cold and more just."

⊙ Talk with family and friends about what that mercy might look like. How might it make a difference in people's lives?

⊙ How might you be an apostle of mercy?

JUDGE AND DECIDE

⊙ How have your ideas about true happiness changed as you worked through this chapter?

⊙ What changes would you suggest in our society to bring about the fullness of the values of the Beatitudes?

⊙ What can you do right now to begin living a life of beatitude?

LEARN BY HEART

Working in pairs, help each other to memorize the Beatitudes in Matthew 5:3–12.

Pray the Sign of the Cross together.

LEADER

What Jesus says is not always what we say. Nor is it always what we want. Sometimes there's a gap between what God wants and what we want. Jesus says, "Blessed are the poor in spirit, for theirs is the kingdom of heaven" (Matthew 5:3).

READER

Yet sometimes people think, "Money, success and power: these are what matter in life." (*Pause*) God, you invite us to be our true selves and not to depend on anything to give us false confidence.

ALL

God, help us to trust and place our hope in you.

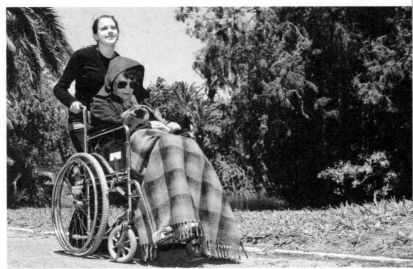

God, keep us true to what is just and right

LEADER

Jesus says, "Blessed are those who mourn, for they will be comforted" (Matthew 5:4).

READER

Yet sometimes people say, "Be tough! Hide your tears." (*Pause*) God, you invite us to enter into life, even when it is painful.

ALL

God, send us the Comforter, the Holy Spirit.

LEADER

Jesus says, "Blessed are the meek, for they will inherit the earth" (Matthew 5:5).

READER

Yet sometimes people say, "Take advantage of every situation, even if others lose out." (*Pause*) God, you invite us to be gentle with others and to respect the earth.

ALL

God, help us to be caring and kind.

LEADER

Jesus says, "Blessed are those who hunger and thirst for righteousness, for they will be filled" (Matthew 5:6).

READER

Yet sometimes people say, "Why should I care about anyone else but me?" (*Pause*) God, you invite us to be concerned about justice and fair play.

ALL

God, keep us true to what is just and right.

LEADER

Jesus says, "Blessed are the merciful, for they will receive mercy" (Matthew 5:7).

READER

Yet sometimes people say, "Be tough with others, especially when they go wrong or make a mistake." (*Pause*) God, you invite us to make allowances and to give others a chance.

ALL

God, make us more compassionate and understanding.

LEADER

Jesus says, "Blessed are the pure in heart, for they will see God" (Matthew 5:8).

READER

Yet sometimes people say, "Be casual. It's okay to use others to get what we want." (*Pause*)

God, you invite us to be noble and to appreciate the people in our lives.

ALL

God, help us to do what is decent and right.

LEADER

Jesus says, "Blessed are the peacemakers, for they will be called children of God" (Matthew 5:9).

READER

Yet sometimes people say, "Revenge is sweet. I'll get my own back." (*Pause*)

God, you invite us to let go of our resentment, our grudges and our fear.

ALL

God, help us to reconcile with all who trespass against us and to make peace.

LEADER

Jesus says, "Blessed are those who are persecuted for righteousness' sake, for theirs is the kingdom of heaven" (Matthew 5:10).

READER

Yet sometimes people say, "Don't stand up for others. It's only trouble." (*Pause*)

God, you invite us to be true to what we know to be right, even if it makes us unpopular or makes us suffer.

ALL

God, keep us loyal to what is true and right.

LEADER

Jesus says, "Blessed are you when people revile you and persecute you and utter all kinds of evil against you falsely on my account. Rejoice and be glad, for your reward is great in heaven, for in the same way they persecuted the prophets who were before you" (Matthew 5:11–12).

READER

Yet sometimes people say, "I'll keep my religion and beliefs to myself. I'll avoid any hassle." (*Pause*)

God, you invite us to follow Jesus even when others ignore him and what he says.

ALL

God, help us to believe in Jesus, your Son, and to honor him and revere his Holy Name.

LEADER

Loving God of mercy and love,
send the Holy Spirit to help us each day to practice the Beatitudes
so that we can preach the Gospel with our lives.
May all people know we are followers of your Son by our mercy, trust, purity of heart, works of justice, peacemaking, and perseverance under persecution.
We ask this in the name of Jesus Christ, our Lord. Amen.

All pray the Sign of the Cross together.

CHAPTER 3

God's Law for a Good Life

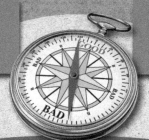

NATURAL
REVEALED
GOOD
BAD
BAD
BAD
THE DIVINE AND ETERNAL LAW OF GOD
PART OF GOD'S DIVINE PLAN
EXPRESSES THE DIGNITY OF THE HUMAN PERSON
THE FOUNDATION OF MORAL RULES AND CIVIL LAW
NATURAL LAW IS INSCRIBED IN THE HUMAN HEART AND KNOWN BY HUMAN REASON
REVEALED LAW IS FOUND IN THE OLD AND NEW TESTAMENTS

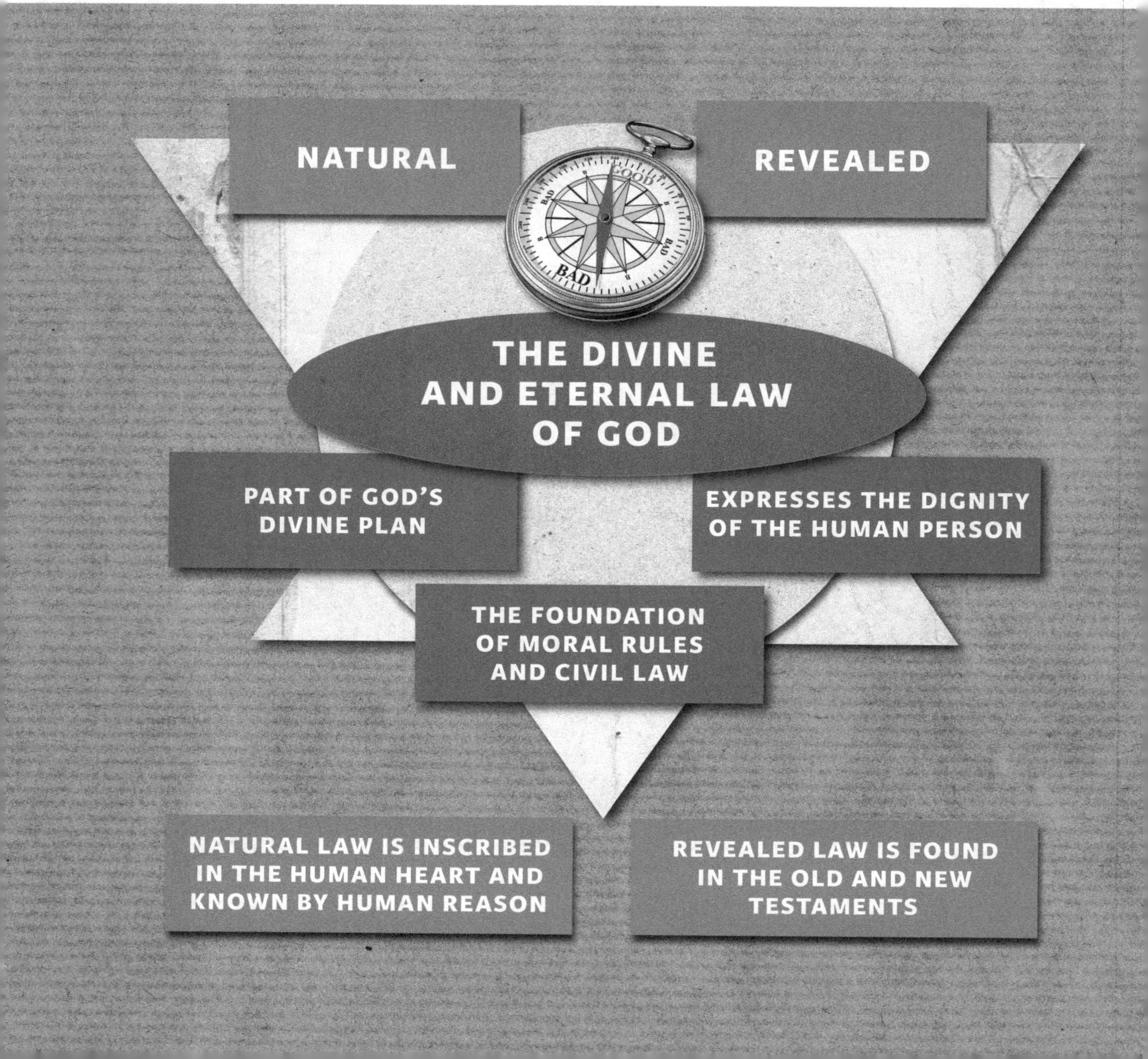

GOD HAS IMPLANTED IN EVERY PERSON HIS DIVINE and eternal natural moral law. This law enables us to know right from wrong, good from evil. In this chapter we explore the role of the natural law and of our conscience in our making decisions and choices to live a moral life. We also look briefly at the relationship between this natural law and the law of God revealed in Sacred Scripture and Sacred Tradition and taught by the Church.

LIVING A MORAL LIFE INVOLVES

THE GIFTS OF THE HOLY SPIRIT

REFLECTION AND INTROSPECTION

INFORMED CONSCIENCE

MORAL VIRTUES

SACRED SCRIPTURE

SACRED TRADITION

Faith Focus: These teachings of the Catholic Church are the primary focus of the doctrinal content prese[...] this chapter:

⊙ God is the source of all true and just law.
⊙ The divine or eternal moral law can be eith[...] or revealed.
⊙ Natural moral law can be known by reason.
⊙ God assists us with his grace to live a moral [...]
⊙ The natural moral law is the foundation for a [...] society.
⊙ Conscience helps us judge whether an act is g[...] evil, in accordance with God's law or not.
⊙ Each person has the responsibility to form thei[...] conscience in accordance with the moral law.
⊙ Human beings have the right and duty to follow [...] conscience in making their moral decisions.

Discipleship Formation: As a result of studying this [...] chapter you should be better able to:

⊙ discern with more clarity the fundamental natural [...] moral laws that guide all human life;
⊙ understand the relationship between natural moral [...] law and the revealed law of God;
⊙ evaluate whether civil laws are in ke[...] natural and revealed law and express th[...] the human person;
⊙ commit yourself to developing a well-inform[...] well-formed conscience;
⊙ recognize the forces in your life that lead you away [...] from following your conscience;
⊙ grow in your experience of the joy of livi[...] freedom of a disciple of Jesus.

Scripture References: These Script[...] quoted or referred to in this chapter:
OLD TESTAMENT: **Deuteronomy** 15:11; **2 Sa**[...]
1 Kings 3:9; **Psalms** 119:105, 160; **Jeremiah** 22[...]
NEW TESTAMENT: **Matthew** 5:21–30, 7:12, 13:1–[...]
22:34–40, 25:31–46; **Luke** 16:19–31, 22:54–62; **John** [...]
and 66–67, 10:10; **Romans** 1:20, 2:14–16, 10:4, 14:21;
2 Corinthians 9:8; **Galatians** 5:1

Faith Glossary: Familiarize yourself with the meaning of these key terms in the Glossary: **conscience, Examen,** [...] **freedom, law, Magisterium, moral law, moral virtu**[...] **natural law, passions, temptation, virtue**[...]

Faith Word: natural law
Learn by Heart: Psalm 119:105
Learn by Example: St. Thomas More, [...]

What is the source of moral law?

ADDRESS TO CLERGY AND LAITY CONCERNED

In his 1967 address to the anti-war group Clergy and Laity Concerned, Martin Luther King Jr. said:

> When I speak of love I am not speaking of some sentimental and weak response. I am speaking of that force which all of the great religions have seen as the supreme unifying principle of life. Love is somehow the key that unlocks the door which leads to ultimate reality. This Hindu–Moslem–Christian–Jewish–Buddhist belief about ultimate reality is beautifully summed up in the first epistle of Saint John: "Let us love one another; for love is of God; and everyone that loveth is born of God and knoweth God. . . . " Along the way of life, someone must have the sense enough and morality enough to cut off the chain of hate. This can only be done by projecting the ethic of love to the center of our lives.

OPENING CONVERSATION

- ⊙ Share whether you agree or disagree with Dr. King's vision, and give your reasons.
- ⊙ Draw up a list of "just laws" that are built on love. What makes them just? What do they have in common?

THE HEART OF ALL "JUST" LAWS

There are many times when we need both skills and knowledge to deal well with the various demands of our daily lives. For example, the responsibilities connected with driving a car include driving according to a set of laws. It is not enough for you to have driving skills, such as knowing how to brake, how to accelerate, how to turn and so on. You must also know the "laws of the road"; you must know the speed limits, the correct passing lanes, parking regulations and so on.

The same is true of living a moral life. Living a moral life includes having a set of **moral virtues**. The moral human virtues are "stable dispositions of the intellect and will that govern our acts, order our passions, and guide our conduct in accordance with reason and faith" (*United States Catholic Catechism for Adults* [USCCA], Glossary, "Virtue," 531). They are good habits learned by practicing certain actions, and using those habits in accordance with **moral law**.

As we begin this chapter, it is important that we understand how the Catholic Church defines moral law. Here is the definition of moral law as it appears in the *Catechism of the Catholic Church* (CCC):

CREATION | PAOLO UCCELLO

God created all that exists out of love and he created humanity to share in the very life and love of God

A rule of conduct established by competent authority for the common good. In biblical terms, the *moral* law is the fatherly instruction of God, setting forth the ways which lead to happiness and proscribing those which lead to evil. The *divine* or eternal law can be either *natural* or revealed (*positive*). Natural moral law is inscribed in the heart, and known by human reason. Revealed law is found in the *ancient* law (Old Testament), notably the ten commandments, and in the *new* law (Law of the Gospel), the teaching of Christ, notably the Sermon on the Mount, which perfects the ancient law.

—CCC, Glossary, "Law, Moral"

In his "Address to Clergy and Laity Concerned" Dr. King refers to love as "the supreme unifying principle of life" that people of all great religions have come to know. This reflects the teaching of the Catholic Church on the moral law. God created all that exists out of love and he created humanity to share in the very life and love of God. All moral law is part of the divine plan of original justice and original holiness that God willed for his creation. This divine plan and law finds its

fulfillment and unity in Jesus Christ. who "is the end of the law (see Romans 10:4); only he teaches and bestows the justice of God" (CCC, no. 1977).

FROM THE CATECHISM
Law is declared and established by reason as a participation in the providence of the living God, Creator and Redeemer of all.

—CCC, no. 1951

THE DIVINE AND ETERNAL NATURAL LAW

The divine or eternal law can be either natural or revealed. The **natural law** is called "natural" because it is part of our human nature. "The natural law, present in the heart of each man and established by reason, is universal in its precepts and its authority extends to all men. It expresses the dignity of the person and determines the basis for his fundamental rights and duties" (CCC, no. 1956). The natural law is unchangeable and permanent throughout human history. It is the foundation on which moral rules and civil law are built.

The natural law reflects our belief that God created the universe according to an overarching design and with certain purposes in mind. "It expresses the dignity of the human person and forms the basis of his fundamental rights and duties" (CCC, no. 1978). Catholic Tradition teaches that God, who is Father, Son and Holy Spirit, continues to rule the universe with wisdom and directs it toward divine fulfillment.

So God is the source of all just and true law. The natural moral law is not the same as physical, biological or chemical laws of nature. These latter work inevitably. For example, if an apple becomes loose from its branch it will fall to the ground. On the other hand, the natural moral law is fulfilled only in so far as we make good moral choices. The natural law is a participation in God's wisdom and goodness. God created men and women in the image of God the Creator. He created us with an intellect and free will. God has given us a moral capacity which is part of our human nature—and so it is "natural." It is a law in the sense that its moral force comes from its reasonableness. To act contrary to the natural law is foolish, for us and for others.

We have the intellectual ability to look at the natural world and to use our reason in order to recognize God's design. We can come to an understanding of what God's providential plan of goodness for the world might be. We can come to know what the truth of God's will or law is for ourselves and comprehend how we are to work in partnership with God's plan of goodness for the world. We have the God-given abilities to think about our life, to weigh evidence and consequences, and so to decide how we can best live according to the will of God.

TALK IT OVER

⊙ Explain the difference between the natural law and a scientific law.

⊙ Since the beginning of time, all peoples have recognized that murder, stealing, lying and so on are wrong. Why do you think this is so?

⊙ Name some shared human values that apply to everyone. How do we know them? Why can we agree upon them?

NATURAL MORAL NORMS AND LIVING THE GOOD LIFE

The natural law tradition teaches that when people use *human reason* to reflect on human

All people possess the natural law within their being; through reason, they can come to know what is right and just

When Gentiles, who do not possess the law, do instinctively what the law requires, these, though not having the law, are a law to themselves. They show that what the law requires is written on their hearts, to which their own conscience also bears witness; . . .

—Romans 2:14–15

Building on Paul's point, the Second Vatican Council taught: "For [men and women] have in their hearts a law inscribed by God. Their dignity rests in observing this law, and by it they will be judged" (*Pastoral Constitution on the Church in the Modern World*, no. 16).

OVER TO YOU
- Do you recognize this "law inscribed by God" in your own heart? If so, give examples.
- Why does obeying this law enhance your own dignity?

nature and experience, they can arrive at the moral law and know what it means to live according to God's plan of goodness for his creation. This is not only true for Christians; it is true for all people. All people possess this natural law within their very being; through reason, they can come to know what is right and just.

St. Paul often made this point in his writings. For example, he wrote:

An understanding mind

In 2011, when he was the Pope, Benedict XVI addressed the German Parliament. In his address he referred to the prayer of King Solomon in which the king asked God for "an understanding mind" (1 Kings 3:9). Solomon did not ask for success, wealth or a long life. He prayed that he might govern God's people with justice and be able to discern well between good and evil. Pope Benedict XVI commented further on what should ultimately matter for all public servants who have authority over people. He said, "The fundamental criterion and motivation for their work as politicians must not be success, and certainly not material gain. They must strive for justice. . . . "

OPENING CONVERSATION

Though he referenced the story of Solomon in Scripture, Pope Benedict XVI was also appealing to good reason to make his case to the members of the German Parliament.

- ◉ Why might this approach be effective?
- ◉ Work with a partner. In your own words share what Benedict XVI was saying to the German Parliament.

OVER TO YOU

- ◉ What might following the example of King Solomon and putting into practice the teaching of Pope Benedict XVI cost a politician, or anyone, who works for justice?
- ◉ How willing are you to pay that price?

THE TEACHINGS OF PHILOSOPHERS ON THE MORAL LIFE

In appealing to reason, Pope Benedict XVI was using the natural law. He was appealing to our shared human nature as a source of moral enlightenment to guide our personal lives and our common life in society. Such an approach has been used throughout history by pagan as well as Christian philosophers. We will take a brief look now at the Greek and Roman philosophical traditions. We will then explore the teachings of St. Thomas Aquinas.

The Greek tradition: Stoicism was among the earliest philosophies of life based on following the natural law. It was founded by Zeno of Citium around 300 BC. The Stoics taught that the "good life" must be a moral life and can be lived only by conforming to the laws that we can discern within nature. The ancient Greek Stoic philosopher Epitectus (AD 55–135) taught, "I am formed by nature for my own good" (*Discourses*, iii. 24.83). The Stoics believed that people must discern the patterns and movements within nature and live a disciplined life in accordance with them. Such discipline, they taught, simply depends on our own efforts. (We often use the word "stoic" to describe a person who is very determined and disciplined.) For Stoics, it is disastrous for both individuals and society just to "do your own thing."

The Roman tradition: The Roman Empire was based entirely on the "rule of law." The Romans believed the natural law to be innate in everyone, a power that comes from using reason to direct our behavior. The laws of the land must be in keeping with the laws of nature. Cicero (106–43 BC), one of the great Roman philosophers, taught that people must live in harmony with the law given in nature, a law everyone can discover through the use of right reason. He wrote:

"For there is a true law: right reason. It is in conformity with nature, is diffused among all men, and is immutable and eternal; its orders summon to duty; its prohibitions turn away from offence. . . . To replace it with a contrary law is a sacrilege; failure to apply even one of its provisions is forbidden; no one can abrogate it entirely" (Cicero, *Republic* III, 22, 33).
—CCC, no. 1956; see also CCC, no. 1979

St. Paul, the Apostle to the Gentiles, preached the Gospel to both Greeks and Romans. Speaking of people who refused to live a moral life in keeping with God's law, St. Paul wrote to the Church in Rome: "Ever since the creation of the world [God's] eternal power and divine nature, invisible though they are, have been understood and seen through the things he has made. So they are without excuse. . . " (Romans 1:20).

REFLECT AND DISCUSS
- What is the connection between Pope Benedict XVI's teaching in his address to the German Parliament and the teachings of the ancient Greeks and the Romans?
- How might you use that connection to dialogue with others about what it means to live a moral life?

ST. THOMAS AQUINAS ON THE NATURAL LAW
We have briefly explored the concept of the natural law in Greek and Roman philosophical traditions. We now take a look at the teachings of St. Thomas Aquinas (1225–74). Aquinas is one of

MARCUS TULLIUS CICERO

> There is a true law: right reason. It is in conformity with nature, is diffused among all men, and is immutable and eternal.

CICERO

the Church's philosopher theologians who wrote extensively on the natural law. Aquinas taught that through honoring the natural law the human person participates in the eternal law of God, who is the ultimate source of all moral law and obligations.

Aquinas reasoned that the most fundamental principle of the natural law is to do what is good and avoid evil. He taught that human beings, unlike non-rational animals, can come to know and understand something of God's own divine providential plan for the world. They do this through the use of their reason and through reflection on human experience. (See *Summa Theologiae*, I–II, q. 91, a.2.)

For Aquinas, reason in this context is not just an intellectual pursuit; it also includes such things as intuition, affection, common sense and one's aesthetic sense of what is fitting—whatever it takes to come to understand human reality. Natural reason is like a "divine light," he argued, which is reflected onto the person by the face of God. Such a "light" helps the person follow

their moral sense in order to live in a way that is true to their own best nature. However, such a norm might not clearly enlighten us in a given situation, in a particular place, where we grapple with competing choices. This is why God in his goodness has revealed his law. Revelation, both Sacred Scripture and Sacred Tradition, assists our moral discernment and decision-making.

TALK IT OVER
- What is the core idea of the natural law according to Aquinas?
- Do you think that broad, overarching principles such as "Do good and avoid evil" are sufficient to guide us in dealing with the everyday difficulties of life? Why?

NATURAL LAW AND DIVINE REVEALED LAW
Sacred Scripture clearly reveals and teaches that all people share in and are guided by God's natural law. Much of the explicit law of God that we learn from the Scriptures enhances and clarifies this natural law. For example,

Aquinas reasoned that the most fundamental principle of the natural law is to do what is good and avoid evil

the Wisdom literature in the Old Testament encourages God's people to reflect on their own experiences to discover moral rules by which they are to live.

Many of the parables of Jesus invite his listeners to reflect on the laws of nature in order to gain an understanding of the mysteries of faith that he was revealing. These parables appeal to and open up the meaning of the natural law—what people can know by listening with good reason to their own hearts. For example, read the kingdom parables in Matthew 13:1–53.

Recall Romans 2:14–16, in which St. Paul insisted that people who did not have access to God's explicit Revelation in Scripture were still held responsible for their good or bad deeds. Why? Because they can discern God's natural moral law from their own conscience and by looking at life in the world. Conscience, in other words, helps us to judge whether an act is good or evil, whether or not it is in accordance with God's law. (We will explore the nature and role of conscience in more detail in the next section of this chapter.)

What is the relationship of the natural law to the explicit law of God revealed in Scripture? First, Scripture constantly echoes the great moral principles and precepts that we can know from natural law. For example, Scripture, as the natural law does, condemns murder and adultery. Murder and adultery are contrary to what is good for humanity. Jesus not only reaffirmed these truths but he clarified and expanded his listeners' understanding of these natural law precepts. (Check out Matthew 5:21–30.)

Second, Scripture and Tradition not only deepen and clarify the natural law, they also motivate us to obey its dictates. For example, Scripture makes very clear that all people must do the works of justice, oppose injustice of every kind, and help to see to it that all can have what they need in order to live with dignity. The Scriptures add to our motivation to obey this law of God, which Jesus explicitly taught in his teaching on the Great Commandment in Matthew 22:34–40. We must love our neighbors as ourselves because of God's unconditional love for all people.

Third, there are revealed laws of God that we might not immediately detect in nature. For example, we can know from reason the law of justice for all; as Aristotle put it, we must "give everyone their due." Scripture, however, in both the Old Testament and the New Testament, clarifies that what God intends is not just that we give everyone their due but that we should have a special favor for those most in need; we should have what our Church calls "a preferential option for the poor." (Check out Deuteronomy 15:11 and Jeremiah 22:15–16. Also look up and read Jesus' conversation with the wealthy man in Luke 16:19–31 and his teaching to his disciples in the parable of the judgment of nations in Matthew 25:31–46.)

MEETING THE DEMANDS OF THE NATURAL LAW

Christians believe that more than human effort alone (as the Stoics taught) is necessary to live the natural law or the revealed law. Scripture and Tradition reveal that we cannot depend simply on our own disciplined efforts. We need and are empowered by the grace of God through Jesus Christ. St. Paul often writes about God's abundant grace that is now available to us through Jesus so that we "may share abundantly in every good work" (2 Corinthians 9:8). Add to this that by Baptism every Christian receives the gifts of the Holy Spirit. These seven gifts, namely, wisdom, understanding, counsel, fortitude, knowledge, piety, and fear of the Lord, dispose and strengthen us to respond knowingly and freely to God's holy will in the very circumstances of daily life.

Jesus Christ, the Incarnate Word and Son of God, is the best model we have of how to live by the natural law and the revealed law. Catholics rely on the teachings of Jesus, now taught with authority by the Church. The moral teachings of the Church help us come to know with confidence the dictates of the divine law, both natural and revealed. This is how we are to live a moral life. "The Word of God is a light for our path. We must assimilate it in faith and prayer and put it into practice. This is how moral conscience is formed" (CCC, no. 1802).

THINK, PAIR AND SHARE

⊙ Read Psalm 119:105. Discuss with a partner your understanding of the relationship between natural and revealed law.

⊙ Take one of the gifts of the Holy Spirit and share how you think it might help you to fulfill the law of God.

Developing an "understanding heart"

Lawmakers have an awesome responsibility. In our society there are many laws that people agree with and many with which they disagree. The Golden Rule is an example of a natural law that many religions and societies agree is foundational to how people should treat one another. In the Sermon on the Mount Jesus taught, "In everything do to others as you would have them do to you; for this is the law and the prophets" (Matthew 7:12). The Golden Rule gives us insight into the nature of what a true and just law should be.

OPENING CONVERSATION

- ⊙ Review this definition of law: "Law is a rule of conduct enacted by competent authority for the sake of the common good" (CCC, no. 1951).
- ⊙ Name several civil laws that reflect this definition of law. Give reasons for your choices.
- ⊙ Name several civil laws that do not reflect or are contrary to this definition of law. Give reasons for your choices.

FROM THE CATECHISM

"The natural law is a participation in God's wisdom and goodness by man formed in the image of his Creator. It expresses the dignity of the human person and forms the basis of his fundamental rights and duties" (CCC, no. 1978). "The natural law is immutable, permanent throughout history. . . . It is a necessary foundation for the erection of moral rules and civil law" (CCC, no. 1979).

NATURAL AND CIVIL LAW

All the human laws that are enacted in society should be formed according to good reasoning.

In other words, reason can help establish the moral obligations and responsibilities that bind us as a society.

Over time the members of a society can agree on the civil moral rules that foster their human well-being. They create human laws that provide the rules for people to live with dignity and with one another in a way that leads to wholeness and fullness of life for all. When the legislators of a society discover these rules and formulate laws accordingly, they are on the way to guiding their citizens to live by the divine and eternal law of God.

There can be great debates and disputes about the natural law, especially by people from one culture to another. On this point the Catholic Church teaches:

The precepts of natural law are not perceived by everyone clearly and immediately. In the present situation sinful man needs grace and revelation

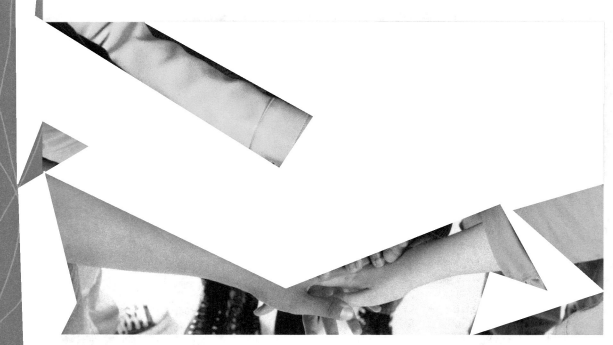

so moral and religious truths may be known. . . . The natural law provides revealed law and grace with a foundation prepared by God and in accordance with the work of the Spirit.

—CCC, no. 1960

Through looking closely at the structures of nature, including our own bodies and our healthy instincts, desires and inclinations, it is possible for all people to reach basic agreement on the laws that should govern our societies. Many rules of social order—for example, not to steal, lie, harm, cheat—are based on the natural inclination for people to live justly and peacefully with one another. The *Catechism* summarizes this important aspect of the approach of the natural law to civil law:

The natural law, the Creator's very good work, provides the solid foundation on which man can build the structure of moral rules to guide his choices. It also provides the indispensable moral foundation for building the human community. Finally, it provides the necessary basis for the civil law with which it is connected, whether by a reflection that draws conclusions from its principles, or by additions of a positive and juridical nature.

—CCC, no. 1959

We live in a pluralistic society. This means that the citizens of the United States of America are diverse ethnically and politically, religiously and philosophically. Americans do not agree universally on how the dictates of the natural law are to be interpreted. This diversity can lead to civil laws that the Catholic Church judges to be contrary to both the natural law and the revealed law. It is a great strength of the Catholic tradition that we engage in moral discernment with people of any or no faith. We work together to reach agreement on civil laws that govern society with "an understanding heart" as King Solomon did. Our Catholic tradition believes that all people can agree upon a limited set of standards for moral behavior in a society. It is a great blessing for Christians that God's divine law, revealed through Scripture and Tradition, deepens and amplifies our sense and understanding of what is required by the moral law, both natural and revealed.

REFLECTIVE EXERCISE

- ⊙ Imagine that you are debating a moral issue, for example, abortion or the death penalty, with a non-Christian person. How might you make your argument entirely from the natural law?
- ⊙ Can you think of an image for the natural law? Draw that image.

Natural law and justice: The Church teaches that "humanity. . . is and it ought to be the beginning, the subject and the object of every social organization" (*Pastoral Constitution on the Church in the Modern World*, no. 25). The natural law, in particular, lends a common basis for the requirement of justice at every level of our lives: personal, interpersonal, social, economic, political and ecological. The natural law provides universal principles that are immutable and eternal. "Even when [the natural law] is rejected in its very principles, it cannot be destroyed or removed from the heart of man. It always rises again in the life of individuals and societies" (CCC, no. 1958).

THINK, PAIR AND SHARE

⊙ Work with a partner, each choosing a principle, or moral rule, of the natural law.
⊙ Discuss how each natural law principle guides legislators to write laws that foster the good of citizens.
⊙ Share reasons why ignoring the principles of the natural law contributes to injustice within a society.

Natural law and conscience: Our God-given gift of freedom separates natural law from physical and other laws of nature. For example, the law of gravity will always prevail. However, a person has the freedom to choose. A person can choose whether or not to live by the natural moral law that God has planted in our hearts. For example, a person, for a variety of reasons, may choose to steal. They may erroneously conclude that the end justifies the means.

This is where conscience comes into play. Conscience is a judgment of reason that allows us to know whether some concrete act—past, present or future—is in harmony with or contrary to natural and revealed law. That is why we have the responsibility to develop and form our moral conscience correctly.

TALK IT OVER

⊙ What does it mean to "follow your conscience"?
⊙ How do we ensure that our conscience is correctly informed?

Conscience is a judgment of reason that allows us to know whether an act is in harmony with or contrary to natural and revealed law

CONSCIENCE

Conscience is present at the heart of every person. It informs our choices. It not only helps us to do what is good and to avoid evil, but it also approves good decisions and denounces bad ones. In this way our conscience links us with God who "is Truth itself, whose words cannot deceive. That is why one can abandon oneself in full trust to the truth and faithfulness of his word in all things" (CCC, no. 215). (Check out Psalms 119:160, 2 Samuel 7:28.)

Blessed John Henry Cardinal Newman described conscience this way:

"[Conscience] is a messenger of him, who, both in nature and in grace, speaks to us behind a veil, and teaches and rules us by his representatives. Conscience is the aboriginal Vicar of Christ" ("Letter to the Duke of Norfolk," V).

—CCC, no. 1778

FROM THE CATECHISM

A well-formed conscience is upright and truthful. It formulates its judgments according to reason, in conformity with the true good willed by the wisdom of the Creator. Everyone must avail himself of the means to form his conscience.

—CCC, no. 1798

FORMING OUR CONSCIENCE

Each one of us has the responsibility to listen to and to follow the voice of our conscience. This responsibility is vital to the exercise of our God-given gift of freedom. This requires honest and diligent reflection and introspection. We have the responsibility to form our conscience according to the law that God has implanted in our heart and revealed in Sacred Scripture and Tradition.

When we follow our own personal instincts and feelings or blindly and uncritically follow the opinion of the crowd, we are not using our gift of freedom responsibly. We form our conscience

BUST OF CARDINAL NEWMAN, TRINITY COLLEGE, OXFORD, ENGLAND

[Conscience] is a messenger of him, who, both in nature and in grace, speaks to us behind a veil, and teaches and rules us by his representatives.

CARDINAL NEWMAN

correctly by using our reason and the teachings of divine law that we find in Sacred Scripture and that are taught to us with authority by the Church. When we form our conscience in this manner, we can not only rely on it but we must follow its dictates.

TALK IT OVER
⊙ What is the relationship between natural law and an informed Christian conscience?
⊙ Why do you have a responsibility to educate and then to follow your conscience?

A well-formed, or certain, conscience is "upright and truthful." For Catholics, this means our conscience makes practical judgments according to reason that are in conformity with the will of God as revealed in Scripture and Tradition and taught by the Magisterium of the Church. The Church is our Teacher and has the authority and responsibility to teach on moral issues. Because life is so full of negative influences that tempt us to turn away from God, it is important that we constantly educate our consciences. This is a lifelong task that begins in childhood in the family, which is "a community of grace and prayer, a school of human virtues and of Christian charity" (CCC, no. 1666).

Inform and form your conscience

The wisdom of the Church has identified certain key disciplines you can follow to inform and form your conscience well. These include:

⊙ Read frequently and study Scripture diligently. "We must assimilate it in faith and prayer and put it into practice. This is how moral conscience is formed" (CCC, no. 1802).
⊙ Study the teachings of the Catholic Church. The Church is the temple of the Spirit of Christ. The Holy Spirit guides the Church to understand and teach authentically all that Jesus, the Incarnate Word of God, has revealed and taught.
⊙ Take part in the sacramental and prayer life of the Church. The sacraments and prayer offer us the grace and strength to live a moral life. Celebrate the Sacrament of Eucharist and the Sacrament of Penance and Reconciliation frequently and regularly.
⊙ Seek the counsel of others, both living and deceased; for example, seek the advice of a spiritual counselor, parent and teacher, your parish priest or youth minister whom you trust; read about the saints, whom the Church offers us as models to live our life in Christ.
⊙ Examine your conscience daily. For example, in the evening talk with the Lord about how your day went. Share the efforts you made to live as his disciple and those times your efforts were not so good. No matter what our bad deed, our conscience always holds out a pledge of conversion and hope. God always offers us his forgiving and supportive grace.

A PRIEST HEARING CONFESSION DURING WORLD YOUTH DAY, SPAIN, 2011

If we do a deed that is contrary to the law of God, our conscience will attest to that reality

Our well-formed conscience will rest easy with the truth and good that we choose to do or say. If, on the other hand, we do a deed that is contrary to the law of God, our conscience will make us aware of our bad judgment and wrongdoing. God will respond, as Jesus responded to St. Peter, by offering us the grace to see and accept responsibility for what we have done wrong and to correct our choice. We can accept that grace and return to and practice the good. Take a few moments and look up and read Luke 22:54–62. We must practice choosing and doing what is good and true. From good practices, we develop good habits and grow in living a life of virtue. We build up our ability to make good choices.

We can never reach the point where we can say, "Yes! Now my conscience is fully formed and fully educated according to God's word." To draw that conclusion is to risk complacency and making erroneous judgments. But we can form our conscience correctly. We can act with certainty and out of freedom and live with peaceful hearts. We must also always remember that we are finite human beings. In humility we need to accept and trust that God knows, sees and understands more than any one of us can.

TALK IT OVER
- How is it possible to "choose one's attitude"?
- What helps and what prevents us from doing so?
- What is the relationship between a person's attitude and their actions?

JOURNAL EXERCISE
- Create a practical plan that will guide you in forming your conscience.
- Pray to the Holy Spirit for guidance.
- Write your plan in your journal.

The freedom to choose to follow Jesus

In his book *Man's Search for Meaning*, Victor Frankl (1905–97), a survivor of the Holocaust, reflected: "We who lived in concentration camps can remember the men who walked through the huts comforting others, giving away their last piece of bread. They may have been few in number, but they offer sufficient proof that everything can be taken away from a man but one thing: the last of the human freedoms— to choose one's attitude in any given set of circumstances, to choose one's own way."

OPENING CONVERSATION

⊙ How do you understand Frankl's words in light of what you have learned so far in this chapter?

⊙ What things challenge people today to abandon the "last of the human freedoms"?

⊙ When have you been pressured *not* to "choose your own way?" How did you respond?

AUSCHWITZ, WHERE VICTOR FRANKL WAS PROCESSED IN 1944

FROM THE CATECHISM

Man has the right to act in conscience and in freedom so as personally to make moral decisions. "He must not be forced to act contrary to his conscience. Nor must he be prevented from acting according to his conscience, especially in religious matters" (Vatican II, *Declaration on Human Freedom [Dignitatis Humanae]*, no. 3).

—CCC, no. 1782

THE FREEDOM OF FOLLOWING ONE'S CONSCIENCE

We have learned that the Catholic Church teaches that a "human being must always obey the certain judgment of his conscience" (CCC, no. 1800). God created us; and he has given each one of us the freedom to make moral decisions and to act according to our conscience.

As Christians, we direct that freedom toward living as the People of God. We freely choose to cooperate with the Holy Spirit and follow Jesus, the Incarnate Son of God, who revealed the way to live as children of God.

Jesus revealed to his disciples, "I came that they may have life, and have it abundantly" (John 10:10). You will recall that St. Irenaeus rephrased Jesus' words and taught that "the glory of God is the human person fully alive." By following a well-formed conscience, we can become fully alive human beings who give glory to God.

Following our conscience is not always easy in practice. There are many forces that tempt us to abuse our freedom. These forces try to deceive us into believing that not following our conscience will set us free to be our true selves. In a commencement address at Stanford

University in 2005, Steve Jobs (1955–2011), the well-known CEO of Apple, warned of the danger of such a **temptation**. He said: "Don't let the noise of others' opinions drown out your own inner voice."

Peer pressure is one example of "the noise of others." Such pressure may tempt you to follow the conscience of the group, which can be contrary to your own conscience. It is never right to choose evil so that good may result from it—for example, the good of being accepted by your friends. Likewise, you have the obligation not to pressure a friend or anyone else to make judgments and to act contrary to their conscience. St. Paul spoke on this issue to the Church in Rome. He wrote:

> It is good not to . . . do anything that makes your brother or sister stumble.
>
> —Romans 14:21

You may wonder, "Why bother forming a good conscience at all?" We are faced with many situations each day in which we feel or are told that we do not really have freedom to choose.

We may be tempted by the lie that our decisions are determined by genetics, social trends and the circumstances of our daily life. This argument presents the human person as no more than a programmed robot.

Some people accept this argument and decide simply to go along with the crowd; others use this argument and claim that they do not have to take responsibility for their choices, actions and the consequences of their actions. Human nature knows better; Scripture and Tradition teach the opposite. Whatever our limits—and we need to be aware of those limits—we can live freely within those limits.

We act responsibly when we freely cooperate with God's grace and form our choices in accordance with the teachings of the Church. We are also to respect and respond to the authority of others who exercise their authority over us legitimately and morally, for example, legitimate civil authority. Children exercise true freedom when they listen to and obey their parents and other competent persons who share in their parents' responsibility for their spiritual and bodily welfare.

"Don't let the noise of others' opinions drown out your own inner voice."

STEVE JOBS

- What is the relationship between Christian faith and a well-formed conscience?
- Give an example of someone whom you know or have learned about who took a stand because their conscience would not allow them to do otherwise.
- What difference did taking that stand make?

WHAT ABOUT YOU PERSONALLY?

- Name some of the challenges to following your conscience in your own life right now. How do you want to respond?
- What will help you to know and to do what is right?

ERRONEOUS JUDGMENTS

Faced with a moral choice, a person can make a right judgment in accordance with reason and the divine law. However, sometimes we get it wrong. A good judgment does not always flow from a well-formed conscience. A judgment of a person's conscience can, at times, be erroneous. This happens when a conscience makes a judgment that is contrary to natural or revealed law while intending to make a good one. An erroneous judgment can happen through lack of effort that results in ignorance—not knowing clearly what is bad or good in a particular situation. "Conscience can remain in ignorance or make erroneous judgments. Such ignorance and errors are not always free of guilt" (CCC, no. 1801). The *Catechism* names these possible sources of erroneous judgment:

- ignorance of Christ and the Gospel;
- following bad example given by others;
- allowing our **passions** and desires to take over and enslave us;
- rejection of the Church's authority and teaching;
- lack of compassion for others.

When you make a sincere and honest effort to form your conscience and follow its judgment, even when an error is made, the dignity of your conscience is not compromised. No one can be blamed for acting irresponsibly if he or she has sincerely, diligently and honestly worked at forming their conscience. On the other hand, you are not free of guilt if you take little trouble to find out what is true and good, and if your judgments, actions and the consequences of those actions are based on ignorance or erroneous information.

REFLECT AND DISCUSS

- What do you understand by "erroneous judgment"?
- Taking the possible sources above, discuss how each can contribute to an erroneous judgment of conscience.

EXAMINATION OF CONSCIENCE

Regularly examining one's conscience is an ancient practice and discipline of the Church. The **Examen** is one such discipline that you can use to form your conscience well. Christians have used the Examen down through the centuries as a method of discernment to guide them in living according to God's will by responding to the promptings of the Holy Spirit. The Examen is a powerful and proven spiritual discipline for tuning in to ourselves and becoming aware of our good and bad judgments. Ultimately, the Examen

Live in the freedom of the children of God. The alternative is to live under a "yoke of slavery"

is a tool that helps us open our minds and hearts to allow the Spirit to work in our lives.

At the end of your day, before going to sleep, is a good time to examine your conscience. It is an opportune time to reflect on how well you used your gifts and also on your gaffes during that day. In the Examen you name the situations in which you were wise or stupid, compassionate or self-indulgent, courageous or cowardly, just or unfair. You give praise and thanks to God and ask for his forgiveness. You pray for God's grace to use the gift of freedom well and for his glory. This discipline helps you identify how well you responded to the Spirit of Christ and will challenge you to respond appropriately in the future.

OVER TO YOU
⊙ How often do you examine your conscience?
⊙ How willing are you to examine your conscience daily if you are not already doing so? You might use or adapt the examination of conscience in the Prayer Reflection for this chapter.

FREEDOM TO FOLLOW JESUS
The Gospel according to John tells of a time when some of Jesus' disciples found his message difficult to accept. We read: "When many of his disciples heard it, they said, 'This teaching is difficult; who can accept it?'. . . Because of this many of his disciples turned back and no longer went about with him. So Jesus asked the twelve, 'Do you also wish to go away?'" (John 6:60, 66–67).

The call to live a moral life in Christ, the law embedded in our hearts and revealed by Christ, is an invitation. It is an invitation to live in the freedom of the children of God. The alternative is to live, as St. Paul described it, under a "yoke of slavery" (Galatians 5:1)—the slavery of sin. (We will explore the teaching of Scripture and Tradition on sin in the next chapter.)

JOURNAL EXERCISE
⊙ Think of times when your choices and actions brought you a sense of true freedom. Describe what that was like.
⊙ Now think of times when your choices and actions brought you a sense of having a "yoke" around your neck. Again, describe that experience.

REVIEW AND SHARE WHAT YOU HAVE LEARNED IN THIS CHAPTER

Look back over this chapter and reflect on the teachings of Scripture and Tradition on the revealed moral law and on the natural law, which also comes from God, and on the role of conscience in one's moral life. Share the teachings of the Catholic Church on these statements:

⊙ God is the source of all true and just law.
⊙ The law of God can be either natural or revealed.
⊙ The human person can come to know the natural moral law through the use of our reason.
⊙ Revealed law opens up the meaning of and explains natural law.

⊙ Living a moral life includes developing virtues, or habits, to do good.
⊙ Conscience is present at the heart of every person. Conscience helps us to judge whether an act is good or evil, in accordance with God's law or not.
⊙ Every person has the responsibility both to form their conscience correctly and to follow their conscience.

REFLECT AND DISCERN

⊙ What is the best insight or wisdom that you have learned from this chapter?
⊙ What difference can a correctly formed conscience make in your life and in the lives of other young people today?

LEARN BY EXAMPLE

St. Thomas More (1478–1535), the king's good servant but God's first

SIR THOMAS MORE | HANS HOLBEIN THE YOUNGER

Thomas More was an English barrister, or attorney, who was a trusted advisor to King Henry VIII of England from October 1529 to May 1532. After studying law, More became a barrister in 1501 and a member of Parliament in 1505. In 1505 he married Jane Colt, with whom he had four children: Margaret, Elizabeth, Cicely and John. After Jane died in 1511 More married Alice Middleton.

King Henry VIII knighted More in 1521 and appointed him Lord Chancellor of England in 1529. The Lord Chancellor was the keeper of the royal seal, the secretary to the king and the bridge between the king and the Parliament. The office of Lord Chancellor was customarily held by a priest; Thomas More was the first layperson appointed to serve as the Lord Chancellor.

More came into irreconcilable conflict with the king over Henry's decision to divorce

Catherine of Aragón and marry Anne Boleyn. When Pope Clement VII refused to annul Henry's marriage to Catherine, the king responded by rejecting the authority of the Pope and he set himself up to be the head of the Church in England.

Thomas More resigned his office in 1532, partly due to ill health but also to his opposition to the king over his marriage to Anne. In April 1534 More refused outright to take an oath of allegiance to the Act of Succession and the Oath of Supremacy. The Act of Succession declared that the children of Henry and Anne were the legitimate heirs to the throne. The Oath of Supremacy required all people taking public office to acknowledge Henry to be the head of the Church in England. On April 17 Henry VIII had More arrested and imprisoned in the Tower of London.

More's wife, daughter and many others visited him in prison; they urged More to take the oaths, but he remained steadfast in his refusal. On July 6, 1535 Henry VIII "resolved" his conflict with More by having him beheaded alongside Bishop Fisher. Bishop Fisher had staunchly stood by the side of Queen Catherine and defended her marriage to Henry VIII.

Standing on the scaffold, More spoke his final words: "I die the King's good servant, but God's first." On May 19, 1935 Pope Pius XI declared Thomas More to be a saint of the Church. The Catholic Church celebrates the life and memory of the martyrs St. John Fisher and St. Thomas More on June 22.

Sir William Stanley, K.G. — 1495
James Tuchet, 7th Baron Audley — 1497
Edward Plantagenet, Earl of Warwick — 1499
Edward Stafford, 3rd Duke of Buckingham — 1521
John Fisher, Bishop of Rochester — 1535
Sir Thomas More — 1535
Thomas Darcy, Lord Darcy of Templehurst, K.G. — 1537

REFLECT AND DISCERN
⊙ What does the way More handled the conflict between his conscience and the king's demands say to you about the role of conscience?

SHARE FAITH WITH FAMILY AND FRIENDS
⊙ Share ideas on how the natural law expresses the dignity of the human person and how it is the foundation of all moral rules and civil law.

JUDGE AND DECIDE
⊙ Work with a partner and create a list of all the "justice" principles that flow from the natural law or are revealed in Scripture.
⊙ Prioritize the principles; make the most important principle number 1.
⊙ Choose one of those principles and give specific examples of how living it can contribute to bringing about the justice and peace of the Kingdom of God.

JOURNAL EXERCISE
⊙ Write down all the principles you identified in the "Judge and Decide" activity.
⊙ Begin with the first principle and create a plan to integrate that principle into your life.
⊙ Do the same for the remaining principles throughout your course of study this year.

LEARN BY HEART

Your word is a lamp to my feet and a light to my path.

PSALM 119:105

PRAYER REFLECTION

Pray the Sign of the Cross together.

Pause for a few moments so that all of you may become quiet and still. Become aware of your breath as it passes in and out of your body . . . slowly.

LEADER
Lord God, Father, Son and Holy Spirit,
we gather in your presence.
We thank you for the gift of this day and every day.
Come, Spirit of Christ, our Advocate and Teacher,
enlighten our minds and open our hearts.
Give us the grace to see this day with the eyes of faith, hope and love
and to discern both our response and lack of response to your presence.
We ask this in the name of our risen Lord.

ALL
Amen.

LEADER
Let us begin by asking ourselves: Where are my choices and actions leading me? (*Pause and reflect*)

The Lord says: "You shall love the Lord your God with all your heart, and with all your soul, and with all your mind" (Matthew 22:37).

Now review your day slowly, using the Great Commandment as your guide. Recognize the God moments, how you responded to the promptings of the Holy Spirit, and what was or was not of God's reign. Close your eyes as you think about these questions in the silence of your heart:

- ◉ Was your heart set on God? Did your words and actions show clearly that you love God above all things? (*Pause and reflect*)
- ◉ Were you faithful to living the Commandments, the Beatitudes, the New Commandment of Jesus, and the precepts of the Church? (*Pause and reflect*)
- ◉ Were you wholehearted in accepting and following the Church's moral teachings?

When the occasion arose, were you strong and fearless in professing your faith in God and the Church? (*Pause and reflect*)
- ◉ Are you growing as a person of prayer? Do you set time aside regularly to talk things over with God? Do you read the Scriptures and take the time to celebrate the Eucharist and Penance when the opportunity presents itself? (*Pause and reflect*)
- ◉ How well did you show your love and reverence for God by the way you talked about God, the Blessed Virgin Mary and the saints, and the Church? (*Pause and reflect*)

LEADER
The Lord says: "You shall love your neighbor as yourself" (Matthew 22:39).

Now continue to review your day:
- ◉ Have you shared your faith in Christ with others? Have you chosen not to do so out of laziness or to avoid criticism? (*Pause and reflect*)

- Have you used the gifts of time, your health and knowledge, and other talents that God has given you, wisely and generously and compassionately? (*Pause and reflect*)
- In what ways have you worked for peace and justice to the best of your ability? Have you shared your possessions with people in need, especially with the poor, with victims of violence and with people suffering from other forms of injustice? (*Pause and reflect*)
- What are some of the ways you have supported and shown respect for the dignity of others? Have you bullied others, or treated them with violence, or treated them unjustly and disrespectfully in any other way? (*Pause and reflect*)
- Did you show respect toward or choose not to obey those who are exercising their responsibility to help you grow as a person and as a disciple of Christ? Have you listened to or rejected their wisdom? (*Pause and reflect*)
- Have you been truthful and fair, forgiving and a peacemaker? Have you gossiped or spread lies about others or sought revenge just to set things straight? (*Pause and reflect*)
- Have you honored your body as a temple of the Holy Spirit? What have you done to keep your body and mind healthy and chaste? Have you dieted well and responsibly? Have you indulged in reading or watching videos or looking at images, or texted messages and images that offend against Christian and human decency? (*Pause and reflect*)
- Have you acted against your conscience out of fear or hypocrisy? Have you always acted in the true freedom of the children of God by following the law of the Spirit? (*Pause and reflect*)

—Based on *Rite of Penance*, Appendix III, "Form of Examination of Conscience"

LEADER
Jesus came to preach the good news of God's presence with us. Let us open our hearts to God with trust and humility as we pray:

ALL
Our Father. . . .

All exchange a sign of peace.

CHAPTER 4

The Reality of Sin

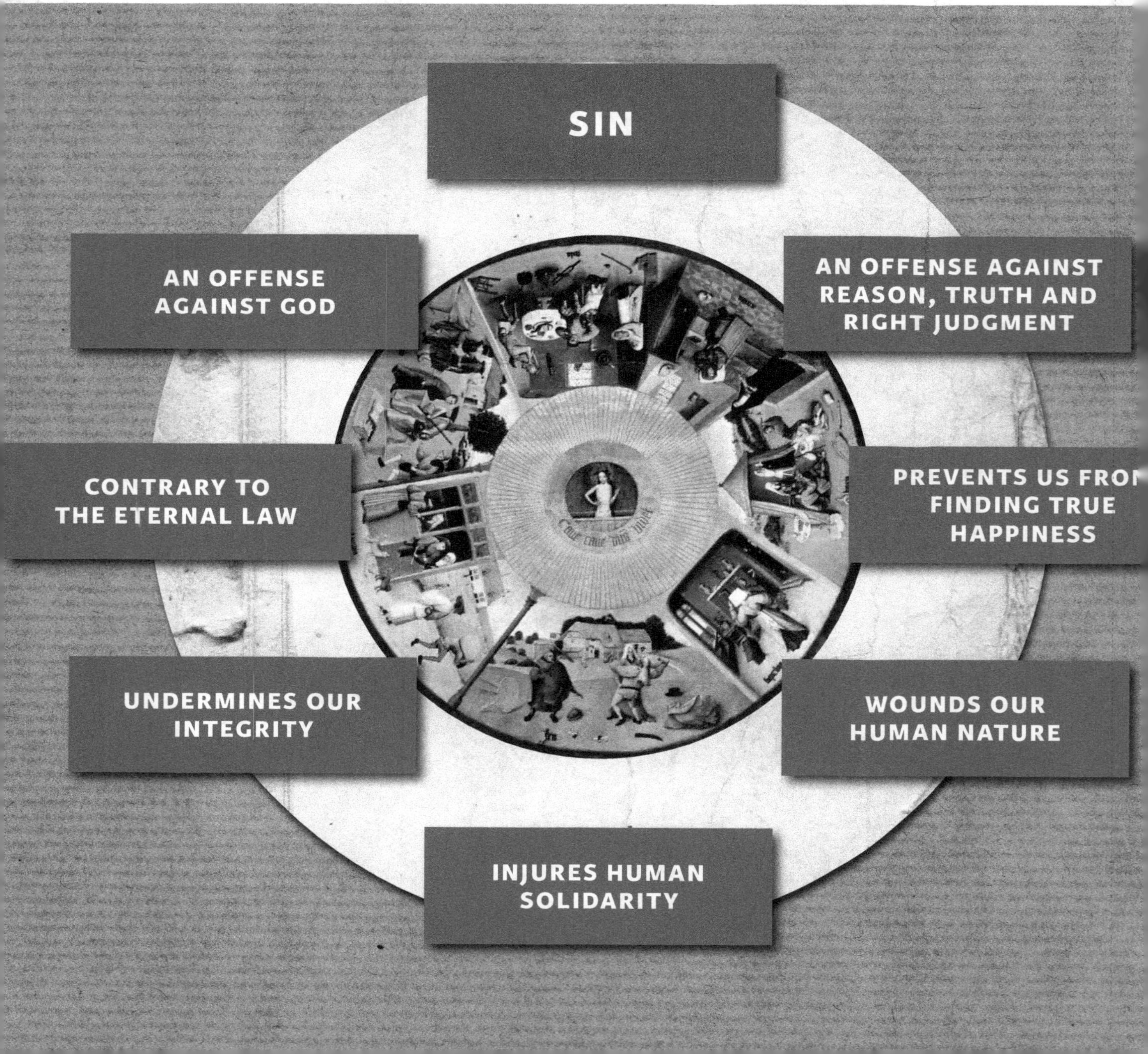

SIN

AN OFFENSE AGAINST GOD

AN OFFENSE AGAINST REASON, TRUTH AND RIGHT JUDGMENT

CONTRARY TO THE ETERNAL LAW

PREVENTS US FROM FINDING TRUE HAPPINESS

UNDERMINES OUR INTEGRITY

WOUNDS OUR HUMAN NATURE

INJURES HUMAN SOLIDARITY

SIN IS THE DELIBERATE CHOICE TO TURN ONE'S back on God's love and the divine plan of goodness. In this chapter we explore the reality and the consequences of sin. Jesus Christ, the Incarnate Son of God, is the Savior of the world. By his Death and Resurrection he has freed humanity from the power of sin and death. He is the source of hope for humankind.

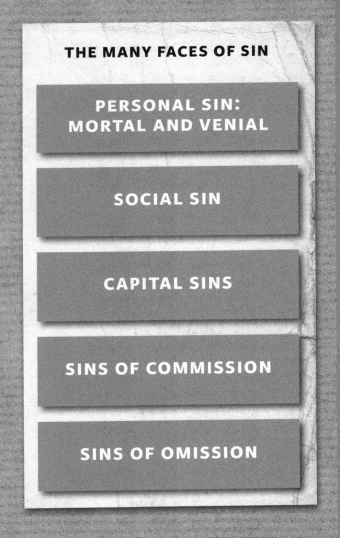

THE MANY FACES OF SIN

PERSONAL SIN: MORTAL AND VENIAL

SOCIAL SIN

CAPITAL SINS

SINS OF COMMISSION

SINS OF OMISSION

Faith Focus: These teachings of the Catholic Church the primary focus of the doctrinal content presente this chapter:

- ☉ Sin is present in the world as a consequence of Original Sin.
- ☉ God always loves us and is faithful to us even whe we sin.
- ☉ The object, the intention and the circumstances a the sources of the morality of human acts.
- ☉ By the Paschal Mystery of his Death and Resurrect Jesus Christ freed humanity from the power of sin.

Discipleship Formation: As a result of studying this chapter you should be better able to:

- ☉ acknowledge and take responsibility for your sins;
- ☉ identify and work against racism and other social sins;
- ☉ learn to hate sin but be compassionate toward and forgiving of the sinner;
- ☉ understand that your sin is given gift of freedom;
- ☉ be more aware of your inner struggl choosing good and choosing evil;
- ☉ join with the Church to work against the stru social sin within our society and against the injus and violence that such structures bring upon people.

Scripture References: These Scripture references are quoted or referred to in this chapter:
OLD TESTAMENT: **Genesis** 3:8 and 15, 4:10, 18:20, 19:13; **Exodus** 3:7–10, 20:20–22; **Leviticus** 26:12; **Deuteronon** 24:14–15; **1 Samuel** 20:1; **2 Kings** 8:20; **Psalms** 25:1, 6–7 and 10, 51:1–2; **Proverbs** 19:2
NEW TESTAMENT: **Matthew** 5:3, 6:19–21, 7:1–5, 9:2–8 and 9–13, 11:19, 12:22–32, 15:10–11 and 17–20, 18:21–3 25:31–46, 26:26–29; **Mark** 2:1–12, 7:14–23; **Luke** 7:36 15:1–7 and 11–32, 16:19–31; **John** 8:1–11 and 21–24, 9 15:18–25; **Romans** 1:28–32, 6:5 and 9–11, 7:21–23; **1 Corinthians** 6:9–11; **Galatians** 5:19–21; **Ephesian** **Colossians** 3:5–9; **1 Timothy** 3:2–6; **1 John** 2:1–2

Faith Glossary: Familiarize yourself with the me these key terms in the Glossary: **Capital Sins, c good, genocide, mortal sin, original innocenc Sin, proverb, relativism (moral) , sanctifying sin of commission, sin of omission, social si venial sin, vice**

Faith Word: sin
Learn by Heart: Romans 6:10–11
Learn by Example: St. Claudine Thévenet, faith, courage and commitment

Where is the evidence for sin in the world?

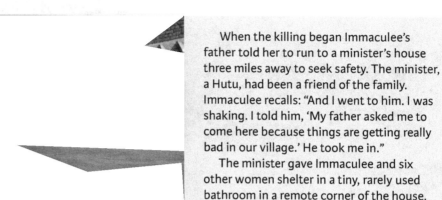

When the killing began Immaculee's father told her to run to a minister's house three miles away to seek safety. The minister, a Hutu, had been a friend of the family. Immaculee recalls: "And I went to him. I was shaking. I told him, 'My father asked me to come here because things are getting really bad in our village.' He took me in."

The minister gave Immaculee and six other women shelter in a tiny, rarely used bathroom in a remote corner of the house. When a horde of Hutus stormed the house, Immaculee heard one of them shout her name, saying, "I have killed 399 cockroaches." Immaculee says, "He wanted me to be the 400th. I was so scared that he knows where I am. He's so sure. It was like dying alive. When I remember the pain of that place it was like every day you are dying, slowly dying thousands of times, yeah."

After French troops arrived in Rwanda to protect the Tutsis, Immaculee persuaded the minister to bring them to a French encampment in the middle of the night. Soon after Immaculee learned that her two brothers and her mother and father had all been murdered. Her father had been shot trying to get food for his neighbors' children.

More than 800,000 Tutsi men, women and children (three out of four), along with thousands of Hutu who opposed the killing, perished at the hands of the Hutu.

The Horror of Genocide

Rwanda, in East Africa, is a country slightly smaller than Maryland. Three major tribes make up its population of about ten million people. The history of this small country is scarred by the horrific effects of genocide. Genocide is "the deliberate and systematic destruction of a racial, political, or cultural group" (Merriam Webster Online Dictionary). This story of Immaculee and her family reveals the horror of the sin of genocide.

Immaculee realized life would never be the same. People were screaming all over the country. No gas chambers here—but the killing was real and bloody. The Hutus, the majority tribe, wielding machetes, spears and knives, were approaching her village with the intention of eliminating the Tutsis.

OPENING CONVERSATION
- ⊙ What does the genocide in Rwanda reveal about the reality of sin?
- ⊙ What examples of violence and injustice exist in today's world? How are they impacting people?

OVER TO YOU
- ⊙ How might your actions have harmed other people? What did you do to heal the harm you caused?
- ⊙ Did you recognize your actions to be sins? Why or why not?

TURNING A BLIND EYE

Much of the world remained in silence and turned a blind eye to the genocide in Rwanda. Standing up against violence and injustice is a command of the Gospel. Christians have the mandate to work toward bringing about the Kingdom of God that Jesus inaugurated. In light of this mandate, we might wonder, "How could others stand by idly and watch?" Unfortunately, history is full of examples of people turning a blind eye and pretending not to notice what is happening around them. Recall Jesus' admonishment of the wealthy man in Luke 16:19–31.

People do not always respond to their conscience. They do not always *do the good* the moral law names; rather, they *do the evil* the moral law prohibits. They abuse their freedom and sin. Some psychologists use the terms "motivational blindness" and "bystander effect" to describe why people do not reach out to others in need. Many philosophers and theologians, schools of ethics and religions, teach moral systems that address this weakness of the human person by responding to the inner struggle of human beings to live a good life. They emphasize the importance of forming good habits and other practices to help people deal with their inclinations toward evil. The political commentator and Op-Ed columnist David Brooks (born 1961) commented in the *New York Times*:

These systems . . . helped people make moral judgments and hold people responsible amidst our frailties. . . . We live in a society oriented around our inner wonderfulness. So when something atrocious happens, people look for some artificial, outside force that must have caused it—like the culture of college football, or some other favorite bogey. People look for laws that can be changed so it never happens again.

We sometimes blame our parents, teachers, neighborhood, classmates and upbringing for the evil we do. It is very difficult to take responsibility for our actions and simply say, 'It was my fault.'

THINK, PAIR AND SHARE

- ⊙ What are the consequences of a society turned in on itself and oriented around its "inner wonderfulness"?
- ⊙ Share your thoughts on this with a partner.

THE ORIGIN OF SIN AND ITS CONSEQUENCES

Scripture reveals, beginning with the account of Adam and Eve in Genesis 3, that human beings can misuse and abuse their God-given gift of freedom. Tempted by the serpent (which the Church has come to understand to be a symbol for Satan or

Some psychologists use the terms 'motivational blindness' and 'bystander effect' to describe why people do not reach out to others in need

the Devil), Adam and Eve opted out of God's plan of holiness and justice for them and for the whole of humanity and creation. In their freedom, they chose to disobey God and to reject their original relationship with God the Creator. They sinned.

Adam and Eve desired to be "like God" but on their own terms and in their own way. They chose to make themselves equal to God and free from God's power. In choosing this path they became afraid of God and scorned him. Separation and isolation became features of human life and sin became a reality in the world. As the *Catechism* reminds us: "Sin sets itself against God's love for us and turns our hearts away from it" (*Catechism of the Catholic Church* (CCC), no. 1850).

This biblical narrative reveals a great truth about our present human condition. After Adam and Eve's sin—which Tradition names **Original Sin**—their harmonious relationship with God, within themselves and between each other, and with the rest of creation, started to come asunder. They lost the peace and harmony of living in the state of **original innocence**. "Original innocence" is the term used for this teaching of the Church: "The first man was not only created good, but was also established in friendship with his Creator and in harmony with himself and with the creation around him, in a state that would be surpassed only by the glory of the new creation in Christ" (CCC, no. 374).

Some Christians interpret these events to mean that as a consequence of Original Sin the human person has become and remains intrinsically corrupt, that is, corrupt by nature. The Catholic Church rejects this view and teaches that the human person, while wounded by Original Sin, remains intrinsically good by nature. As a consequence, we are inclined to error in making moral judgment and acts. In other words, as a consequence of Original Sin there is an *inclination* in human nature that engages every person in a spiritual battle between good and evil. "Man is divided in himself. As a result, the whole life of men, both individual and social, shows itself to be a struggle, and a dramatic one, between good and evil, between light and darkness" (*Pastoral Constitution on the Church in the Modern World*, no. 13; quoted in CCC, no. 1707).

TALK IT OVER
- ◉ Recall the biblical account of Eve's response to the serpent. Describe her attitude and her actions.
- ◉ What was Adam's response to Eve?
- ◉ Compare Adam and Eve's attitudes and actions with those named in the Beatitude, "Blessed are the poor in spirit, for theirs is the kingdom of heaven" (Matthew 5:3).

Adam and Eve desired to be "like God" but on their own terms and in their own way

GOD THE FATHER WITH ADAM AND EVE | ST. ZENO MONASTERY, BAD REICHENHALL, GERMANY

God did not turn his back on Adam and Eve; he did not abandon them and humanity after the Fall

GOD IS ALWAYS FAITHFUL

God did not turn his back on Adam and Eve; he did not abandon them and humanity after the fall. God entered into conversation with Adam and Eve and slowly revealed that he is not only God the Creator but also God the Savior and Liberator. We read that, after Adam and Eve became aware of their choice and its consequences:

They heard the sound of the LORD God walking in the garden at the time of the evening breeze, and the man and his wife hid themselves from the presence of the LORD God among the trees of the garden.

—Genesis 3:8

God also admonished Adam and Eve and the serpent. This admonishment, found in Genesis 3:15, "in a mysterious way heralds the coming victory over evil and his restoration from his fall" (CCC, no. 410). The Church has named this passage in Genesis "The First Gospel," or the *Protoevangelium*. Genesis 3:15 is "the first announcement of the Messiah and Redeemer, of a battle between the serpent and the Woman, and of the final victory of a descendant of hers" (CCC, no. 410). It is God's assurance that sin and evil would not prevail. At the time appointed by God, God would fulfill his promise. Jesus Christ, the Incarnate Son of God, would come to save and redeem humanity.

Through the Sacrament of Baptism we first share in the saving work of Jesus. We receive the gift of **sanctifying grace**. "Sanctifying grace is the gratuitous gift of his life that God makes to us; it is infused by the Holy Spirit into the soul to heal it of sin and to sanctify it" (CCC, no. 2023). God restores us to a state of holiness. He offers us the graces we need to resist the effects of Original Sin and to live holy and just lives. No religion or philosophy has a more life-giving moral code than our Christian faith.

JOURNAL EXERCISE

⊙ Describe how you deal with the struggle of choosing the good over evil, and how celebrating the sacraments and praying help you in your efforts to win that struggle.

The divine plan of goodness versus sin

The Deceit of Sin

In J.R.R. Tolkien's *The Hobbit,* Gollum, originally called Sméagol, is a character around whom the struggle between good and evil centers. One birthday, Sméagol goes fishing with his cousin Déagol. After being pulled into the water by a large fish, Déagol finds a gold ring. Sméagol demands the ring as a birthday present and he strangles Déagol when Déagol insists on keeping it.

Sméagol is quickly corrupted by the Ring, is banished by his people and forced to find a home in a cave. The Ring's malignant influence twists his Hobbit body and mind and prolongs his life far beyond its natural limits.

During his centuries under the Ring's influence, Sméagol develops a sort of identity disorder: his *good* personality (Sméagol) still vaguely remembers such moral qualities as friendship and love, while his *bad* personality (Gollum) becomes so enslaved to the Ring that he would kill anyone who tries to take it from him.

The two sides of his personality often quarrel. This is highlighted when he talks to himself, as Tolkien writes, "through not having anyone else to speak to." This inner conflict between a love–hate relationship mirrors Gollum's love and hatred for the Ring and for himself.

OPENING CONVERSATION

⊙ What is Gollum's inner conflict? How is it a source for sin?

JOURNAL EXERCISE

⊙ Might you be so attached to something that your attachment is a temptation to sin?
⊙ How are you dealing with that attachment?
⊙ Write your thoughts on this in your journal.

FROM THE CATECHISM

Sin is present in human history. This reality of sin can be understood clearly only in the light of divine revelation and above all in the light of Christ the Savior of all. Where sin abounded, he made grace to abound all the more.

—*Compendium of the Catechism of the Catholic Church (Compendium)*, no. 73

THE NATURE OF SIN

To understand the nature of sin we need to place the reality of sin within the context of God's ultimate plan of goodness and salvation in Christ. Sin corrodes our character and undermines our integrity. It prevents us from finding true happiness, both here on earth and in the hereafter. The *Catechism* describes sin:

Sin is an offense against reason, truth, and right conscience; it is failure in genuine love for God and neighbor caused by a perverse attachment to certain goods. It wounds the nature of man and injures human solidarity. It has been defined as "an utterance, a deed or a desire contrary to the eternal law" (St. Augustine, *Reply to Faustus the Manichaean* 22; St. Thomas Aquinas, *Summa Theologiae* I–II, 71, 6).

—CCC, no. 1849

The morality of human acts depends on three sources:

- **Object chosen**: The act itself, either a true or apparent good.
- **Intention of the person acting, or end of the act**: The purpose, or intention, for which a person acts; an evil purpose corrupts the action, even when the object is good in itself; a good purpose does not make an evil act good.
- **Circumstances of the act**: Circumstances, such as fear, ignorance, duress and other social or psychological factors, can increase or diminish the responsibility of the person acting, but they do not change the moral quality of the act; they can never make good an act that is in itself evil.

—Based on *Compendium*, nos. 367 and 368

At its fundamental level "the root of sin is in the heart of man, in his free will" (CCC, no. 1853). For example, Gollum's pursuit of the Ring twisted and corrupted him; it prevented him from being his best and truest self. The effect of our sinning is similar; it corrodes and spoils our best selves.

LET'S PROBE DEEPER

- Read Jesus' teaching in Matthew 6:19–21. The passage concludes: "For where your treasure is, there your heart will be also."
- What insights does this teaching of Jesus give us into sin?

THE RESPONSE (OR NON-RESPONSE) TO SIN

Jesus, who is true God and true man, revealed God's response to sin and the appropriate human response to sin and to the sinner. We will now take a brief look at two gospel passages. The first is from the Sermon on the Mount; the second is from Jesus' encounter with the woman caught in adultery.

The Sermon on the Mount

"Do not judge, so that you may not be judged. For with the judgment you make you will be judged,

> ## "Do not judge, so that you may not be judged."
>
> **MATTHEW 7:1**

THE SERMON ON THE MOUNT | BRUSSELS CATHEDRAL, BELGIUM

and the measure you give will be the measure you get. Why do you see the speck in your neighbor's eye, but do not notice the log in your own eye? Or how can you say to your neighbor, 'Let me take the speck out of your eye,' while the log is in your own eye? You hypocrite, first take the log out of your own eye, and then you will see clearly to take the speck out of your neighbor's eye."

—Matthew 7:1–5

The Woman Caught in Adultery

Early in the morning he came again to the temple. All the people came to him and he sat down and began to teach them. The scribes and the Pharisees brought a woman who had been caught in adultery; and making her stand before all of them, they said to him, "Teacher, this woman was caught in the very act of committing adultery. Now in the law Moses commanded us to stone such women. Now what do you say?" They said this to test him, so that they might have some charge to bring against him. Jesus bent down and wrote with his finger on the ground. When they kept on questioning him, he straightened up and said to them, "Let anyone among you who is without sin be the first to throw a stone at her." And once again he bent down and wrote on the ground. When they heard it, they went away, one by one, beginning with the elders; and Jesus was left alone with the woman standing before him. Jesus straightened up and said to her, "Woman, where are they? Has no one condemned you?" She said, "No one, sir." And Jesus said, "Neither do I condemn you. Go your way, and from now on do not sin again."

—John 8:2–11

Jesus' response to sin and to the sinner is to be our response. Jesus' actions and words teach that while we are to hate and reject the sin, we are to love and welcome the sinner. We are not to condone the sin or to show that we accept the sin. Jesus is also clear about the need not to sin again. The spiritual works of mercy guide us to follow the example of Jesus: we are to admonish and help those who sin; we are to teach those who are ignorant of God's law; and we are to forgive those who trespass against us. (Check out Jesus' teaching in Matthew 18:21–35).

CHRIST AND THE WOMAN TAKEN IN ADULTERY | VALENTIN DE BOULOGNE

JOURNAL EXERCISE

- ◉ How similar to Jesus' response to sin is your response? Write about what you might you need to work on.
- ◉ What does Jesus' response to sin and sinners say to you about God's response to your sin?

THOU SHALL NOT JUDGE

Following the way and teachings of Jesus is difficult. There is a lot of pressure in our culture today to practice *tolerance* toward all and not to criticize or condemn those who do not live by our standards. *Tolerance* can be a distortion of Jesus' teaching, "Do not judge, so that you may not be judged."

Tolerance does not include ignoring the true moral nature of the actions of others. When those actions are contrary to moral law, to the teachings of the Gospel and of the Church, we are to name those actions as such. Moral actions must always be measured by **truth**. There are some actions that are just plain evil and contrary to the moral law by nature. The nature of such immoral acts is not changed by the circumstances surrounding the act or by the intention or purpose of the person committing the act. In other words, the end never justifies the means. We must not show by our words or actions that we agree with the evil act of another person in order to avoid confronting or hurting their feelings. In all this we are to remember, as Pope Francis has so often reminded us, that even when we see an act committed that is by its very nature gravely evil and a grave offense against God and the moral law, it is not ours to judge the person who commits such acts. "We must entrust judgment of persons to the justice and mercy of God" (CCC, no. 1861).

The inclination to keep our views to ourselves may also be due to the prevalence of **moral relativism**. Moral relativism is a common philosophy of life today. It denies that there is objective truth and teaches that moral rules and standards are irrelevant. It teaches that no act is good or evil in and of itself. In other words, it erroneously claims that the morality of any act is "relative" to what a person thinks, the circumstances of a person's life, the time and culture in which a person lives. It is easy to see how moral relativism leads to anarchy and chaos. If everyone were to live by a relative moral code, this would lead to anarchy and chaos and a loss of happiness.

In such an atmosphere it can be extraordinarily stressful to express a view that is contrary to someone else's or public opinion or to a

Clever use of language can soften the reality of an evil that has taken place

public policy. Disagreement is often labeled as "disrespectful" or as forcing one's "personal views" on others. On the contrary, when we speak the truth as Jesus did, we are showing deep respect for those with whom we disagree. When the Church teaches about the moral law, for example, in the development of public policy, she is not imposing her views or her own ecclesiastical disciplines on other people. She is fulfilling her responsibility to teach about how God has revealed people are to live, act and treat one another. She is promoting the universal moral law and the common good.

There are many ways in which we can refuse to face up to the reality of sin and deny our responsibilities in relation to its evil and harmful consequences. A favorite is to use language to soften the reality of an evil that has taken place. For example, we can describe direct abortion as "termination of a pregnancy," or the "violation of freedom of choice"; the killing of innocent people during war as "collateral damage"; and embezzlement as "creative accounting." You can probably add many other examples.

As Christians, we must not remain silent when we come face to face with evil and its consequences. To point out evil and sin as such

is an act of Christian faith and love, just as it is a sign of love and respect to point out and advise a teammate on how to correct a faulty habit. It is also a sign of love and respect to show our care and concern for a person who is acting contrary to the moral law of God. We are to love the sinner and hate the sin.

THINK, PAIR AND SHARE

- With a partner, choose a social policy in the United States of America. Discuss the morality of that policy using the three sources of the morality of human acts.
- Talk about the responsibilities that should guide a Catholic's response to the policy you have discussed.

JOURNAL EXERCISE

- Describe a situation where someone has trespassed against you. How did it make you feel? How did you deal with it? If you were to deal with it again, what might you do differently?
- Write about what you can learn from Jesus' example of loving the sinner while hating the sin.

"Do you reject Satan, and all his works, and all his empty promises?"

After a "give-and-take" with the Pharisees and scribes about observing Jewish laws, Jesus teaches:

"Listen and understand: it is not what goes into the mouth that defiles a person, but it is what comes out of the mouth that defiles. . . . But what comes out of the mouth proceeds from the heart, and this is what defiles. For out of the heart come evil intentions, murder, adultery, fornication, theft, false witness, slander. These are what defile a person, but to eat with unwashed hands does not defile."

—Matthew 15:10–11, 18–20

JESUS DISPUTES WITH THE PHARISEES | JAN LUYKEN

OVER TO YOU

⊙ How does this teaching of Jesus speak to the inner struggle to live as a disciple of Jesus?

FROM THE CATECHISM
Sin sets itself against God's love for us and turns our hearts away from it.

—CCC, no. 1850

OLD TESTAMENT TEACHING ON SIN
The heart of the Old Testament is the story of the covenant between God and his people. It is the Revelation of God's fidelity to his people even when they turn their backs on him and on the covenant. God reveals himself to the Israelites, saying: "I will walk among you, and will be your God, and you shall be my people" (Leviticus 26:12). *Chesed* is the Hebrew word that the inspired sacred authors of the Scriptures of Ancient Israel used to describe the loving and faithful covenantal commitment of the Lord God to his people. *Chesed* has a depth of meaning that no one English word or phrase can capture.

Chesed includes steadfast loyalty and faithfulness, love and devotion, kindness and mercy, justice and righteousness. God's *chesed* toward his people never diminishes. It remains even when they turn away from God, when they sin. The psalmist, speaking for God's people, acknowledges the sin of God's people and appeals to God's chesed:

To you, O Lord, I lift up my soul.
O my God, in you I trust; . . . .

Be mindful of your mercy, O Lord, and of your
steadfast love,
for they have been from of old.
Do not remember the sins of my youth or my
transgressions;

according to your steadfast love remember
me,
for your goodness' sake, O LORD! . . . .

All the paths of the LORD are steadfast love and
faithfulness,
for those who keep his covenant and his
decrees.

—Psalm 25:1–2, 6–7, 10

The biblical account of salvation testifies to the fact that God's people were unfaithful to the covenant. They rejected in part or as a whole their covenantal relationship with God and with one another. They worshiped and placed their trust in the idols (gods) of their neighbors and conquerors. They violated and oppressed their own people by injustice and lack of compassion toward the poor.

In our day, these false gods—these idols—remain. They are more likely to be things such as money or power, fame or pleasure. We continue to neglect or turn our backs on those living in poverty; we do this through our personal decisions and through our approval of unjust social policies. If, as Christians, we do not center our lives on God and do not show love, either through the evil we do or the good we do not do, we fail to live our covenant with God which we entered into at our Baptism.

PAUSE, REFLECT AND PRAY

⊙ Take a moment to reflect on times when you did not honor your covenant with God. Pray Psalm 25.

THE HARM BROUGHT ABOUT BY SIN

The Old Testament offers over fifty words to describe the "harm" that is the consequence of sin. We will look now at three of these words, namely, *hattah*, *pescha* and *awon*.

Hattah. *Hattah* is a quality of people who are so distracted that they make erroneous judgments.

THE ADORATION OF THE GOLDEN CALF | NICOLAS POUSSIN

Sin distorts the sinner. It limits severely the exercise of our freedom. It disables us from being our best selves

As a result, they do not achieve the goal they set out to accomplish. In Proverbs 19:2 we read: "Desire without knowledge is not good, and one who moves too hurriedly misses the way." This proverb describes God's people when they act on the erroneous judgments they make. As a result, their lives are off course. They sin and "miss living the way of the covenant."

Pescha. *Pescha* refers to a rebellious spirit. In 2 Kings 8:20 we read, "In his days Edom revolted against the rule of Judah, and set up a king of their own." *Pescha* describes the attitude that leads people not to fulfill their responsibilities to those in lawful authority. When used in a religious context, *pescha* names the deliberate refusal of a person to adhere to their obligations and commitments to God. The sacred human authors of the Bible also use other words that are very similar to *pescha*. These include *marah*, *pesa* and *marad*. *Marah* is the defiance of a child toward their parent; *pesa* is rebellion toward one who has political authority; *marad* points to obstinacy and being argumentative.

Awon. *Awon* often has the sense of a "heavy burden" associated with the guilt a person experiences over sinning. In 1 Samuel 20:1 we read,

"David fled from Naioth in Ramah. He came before Jonathan and said, 'What have I done? What is my guilt? And what is my sin against your father that he is trying to take my life?'" *Awon* also portrays the image of a person who has become physically crooked or twisted and is unable to stand upright and move freely. (Think of Gollum in *The Lord of the Rings*.) Sin distorts the sinner. It limits severely the exercise of our freedom. It disables us from being our best selves.

WHAT ABOUT YOU PERSONALLY?
- ⊙ Which of these words, namely, *hattah*, *pescha* or *awon*, best describes your understanding of sin? Explain your choice.
- ⊙ Think of times when you may have found yourself in the disposition described by any one of these biblical words for sin. How do you think being in this disposition limited you as a person?

LET'S PROBE DEEPER: SCRIPTURE ACTIVITY
The Scriptures of Ancient Israel also speak of the sins that cry to heaven.
- ⊙ Look up and read these passages from the Torah: Genesis 4:10, Genesis 18:20 and Genesis 19:13; Exodus 3:7–10 and Exodus 20:20–23;

THE RESURRECTION | CHURCH OF SANTIAGO, CUILAPAN, OAXACA, MEXICO

NEW TESTAMENT TEACHING ON SIN

Jesus Christ is the Savior and Redeemer of the world. By his Death, Resurrection and Ascension he freed humanity from the power of sin and from its consequence, death. St. Paul affirmed and taught this truth of our faith. He wrote:

> For if we have been united with him in a death like his, we will certainly be united with him in a resurrection like his. . . . We know that Christ, being raised from the dead, will never die again; death no longer has dominion over him. The death he died, he died to sin, once for all; but the life he lives, he lives in God. So you also must consider yourselves dead to sin and alive to God in Christ Jesus.
>
> —Romans 6:5, 9–11

The First Letter of John, in its teaching on obeying God's commandments, states:

> My little children, I am writing these things to you so that you may not sin. But if anyone does sin, we have an advocate with the Father, Jesus Christ the righteous; and he is the atoning sacrifice for our sins, and not for ours only but also for the sins of the whole world.
>
> —1 John 2:1–2

SCRIPTURE ACTIVITY

⊙ Working with a partner, page through the four gospel accounts for passages that reveal Jesus' teachings on sin. Here are some examples: Matthew 9:2–8 and 9–13, 11:19, 12:22–32, 26:26–29; Mark 2:1–12, 7:14–23; Luke 7:36–50, 15:1–7; John 8:1–11 and 21–24, 9:1–9, 15:18–25.

⊙ Write a summary of Jesus' teachings on sin and share it with the class.

We see many of these elements in the parable of the prodigal and his brother (Luke 15:11–32). In that parable the younger son *chooses* to ask for his inheritance and leaves home; he *abuses his freedom* and squanders his inheritance; he comes to his senses and accepts responsibility for his decisions after he hits rock bottom; he *decides* to return home and seek his father's forgiveness.

The Father, who did not hinder the son's decision to take his share of the family

Deuteronomy 24:14–15. As you do so, identify and write down the sins referred to in each passage.

⊙ Share the results of your reading with a partner.

⊙ Discuss how these passages speak to moral issues that the People of God face today.

FROM THE CATECHISM

[A]t the very hour of darkness, the hour of the prince of this world (see John 14:30), the sacrifice of Christ secretly becomes the source from which the forgiveness of our sins will pour forth inexhaustibly.

—CCC, no. 1851

inheritance, watches as his son leaves him; he awaits his son's return; and he embraces the son upon his return, even before his son can apologize and ask for forgiveness.

The son comes to realize that his sin is not so much the squandering of his share of the inheritance or his dissolute living. While these are serious, his gravest sin is the rupturing of the relationship of love with his loving parent and his family. The words of the younger son's apology reveal that this is what he wants to repair. The son says, "Father, I have sinned against heaven and before you; I am no longer worthy to be called your son" (Luke 15:21). He wants to reclaim his status as a "son."

In the New Testament as in the Old Testament: "There is never any question . . . whether sin is a deliberate and willful act for which man must bear full responsibility. . . . Sin is indeed a breakdown of society, and the prophets often speak of this; but society breaks down because of the failure of its members" (John L. McKenzie, S.J., *Dictionary of the Bible*).

THINK, PAIR AND SHARE
- Choose one of Jesus' teachings about sin and complete the sentence: "This truth has meaning for my life right now because. . . ."
- Share your reflection with a partner.

SIN IN THE NEW TESTAMENT LETTERS
The Apostle Paul (Saul) was a Pharisee who was steeped in Jewish law and the teachings of the Scriptures of Ancient Israel. We need to read Paul in light of this background. Paul's teaching on sin is summarized in chapter 6 of his Letter to the Romans.

THE PRODIGAL SON | ST. GEORGE'S CHURCH, HATTINGEN, GERMANY

> "Father, I have sinned against heaven and before you; I am no longer worthy to be called your son."
>
> LUKE 15:21

Paul often portrays sin within the context of the old self and the new self. Reflecting on his personal life, Paul vividly describes human life as a battle with sin. He often finds himself behaving in ways contrary to how he would like to behave: his body is at war with his mind! When sin has a power over him, Paul finds himself doing the very things he does not want to do. You will recall that he wrote to the Church in Rome:

I find it to be a law that when I want to do what is good, evil lies close at hand. For I delight in the law of God in my inmost self, but I see in my members another law at war with the law of my mind, making me captive to the law of sin that dwells in my members.

—Romans 7:21–23

St. Paul often portrays sin within the context of the old self and the new self

OVER TO YOU

- How close is Paul's description of his life to the life of young people today?
- Do you feel the battle Paul described going on inside you? What are some of the protagonists in the struggle?

LET'S PROBE DEEPER: SCRIPTURE ACTIVITY

- Search these passages to discover what they say about the different kinds of sin that sunder relationships. Create a list and share it with a partner.
  - Romans 1:28–32
  - 1 Corinthians 6:9–11
  - Galatians 5:19–21
  - Ephesians 5:3–5
  - Colossians 3:5–9
  - 1 Timothy 3:2–6

Sin, at its root, is a deliberate and progressive sundering of one's relationship with God, with one's neighbors, with creation. Sin is also a hardening of our heart, of our own best self. The human heart has not been created nor is it born this way. This hardening takes place over time. It is the consequence of Original Sin and is the result of our deliberate evil and sinful choices.

REFLECT AND DISCERN

- Review what you learned in this chapter about what is involved in a moral act, namely, the object, the intention and the circumstances.
- In view of these three sources of a moral act, review some choices you have made recently.
- What wisdom did you learn from this exercise?

The many faces of sin and our response

Sin or No Sin?

In William Golding's Lord of the Flies *a group of school children kill one of their schoolmates, a boy called Simon. Two of the children, Ralph and Piggy, are talking about it afterward. Ralph is very upset by what has just happened and Piggy is in denial and tries to make excuses.*

At last Ralph stopped. He was shivering.
"Piggy."
"Uh?"
"That was Simon."
"You said that before."
"Piggy."
"Uh?"
"That was murder."
"You stop it!" said Piggy, shrilly. "What good're you doing talking like that?"
He jumped to his feet and stood over Ralph.
"It was dark. There was that—that bloody dance. There was lightning and thunder and rain. We was scared!" . . .
"Didn't you see, Piggy?"
"Not all that well. I only got one eye now. You ought to know that, Ralph."

Ralph continued to rock to and fro.
"It was an accident," said Piggy suddenly, "that's what it was. An accident." His voice shrilled again. "Coming in the dark—he had no business crawling like that out of the dark. He was batty. He asked for it. It was an accident."
"You didn't see what they did—"
"Look, Ralph. We got to forget this. We can't do no good thinking about it, see?"
"I'm frightened. Of us. I want to go home. O God I want to go home."

OPENING CONVERSATION

- What forces or trends in life today blind us to the many faces of sin that we encounter?
- Why might some people want to explain sin away?

FROM THE CATECHISM

Sin creates a proclivity to sin; it engenders vice by repetition of the same acts. . . . Thus sin tends to reproduce itself and reinforce itself, but it cannot destroy the moral sense at its root.
—CCC, no. 1865

THE MANY FACES OF SIN

We can encounter sin in many forms. Being aware of the many faces of sin can help us recognize sin in our personal lives as well as in the social structures and policies of the communities to which we belong.

Capital Sins: The Church names seven sins Capital Sins, which are also called "deadly sins." They are avarice (greed), anger, envy, gluttony, lust, pride and sloth. Capital Sins lead us into other more serious sins and vices. A vice is "the habitual practice of repeated sin" (*United States Catholic Catechism for Adults* [USCCA], 531).

The Capital Sins

Anger: Anger is that passion which leads one to either harm a person or want to harm a person because of a desire for vengeance.

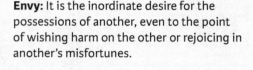

THE SEVEN DEADLY SINS (DETAIL) | HIERONYMUS BOSCH

Envy: It is the inordinate desire for the possessions of another, even to the point of wishing harm on the other or rejoicing in another's misfortunes.

Gluttony: Actions of eating and drinking more than what is necessary.

Greed (Avarice): An inordinate attachment to the goods of creation, frequently expressed in the pursuit of money or other symbols of wealth, which leads to sins of injustice and other evils.

Lust: It is an inordinate desire for earthly pleasures, particularly sexual pleasures.

Pride: It involves excessive self-esteem and a strong desire to be noticed and honored by others; excessive pride sets one in opposition to God.

Sloth: It involves a lack of effort in meeting duties and responsibilities to God, to others, and to oneself.

—USCCA, Glossary

Sins of commission and sins of omission: You may think that a person sins only by doing or saying something that is contrary to the will and law of God. That is only half the story. A person who knowingly and freely chooses to do or say something that is contrary to God's law and will commits a sin of commission. Sins of commission may be of thought, of word, or of deed. A person can also sin by failing to do or say something good. A person who knowingly and freely chooses not to do something good that he or she has the responsibility to do and can do commits a sin of omission.

Personal sin and social sin: Personal sin refers to sins of commission or omission committed by an individual person. We can also contribute to a group or a society developing a sinful attitude that infects its very structure. We can do so by supporting one another in sinful actions or by taking part in the sin of a group or by not speaking out against sin. The *Catechism* teaches, "we have a responsibility for the sins committed by others when *we cooperate in them*" (CCC, no. 1868). The *Catechism* reminds us:

> "Structures of sin" are the expression and effect of personal sins. They lead their victims to do evil in their turn. In an analogous sense, they constitute a "social sin" (St. John Paul II, *On Reconciliation and Penance*, no. 16).
> —CCC, no. 1869

From your study of history and current events you will be aware of sinful situations such as the Holocaust, slavery and other faces of social sin. Racism is at the heart of the Holocaust and slavery. Racism is the "unjust discrimination on the basis of a person's race; a violation of human dignity, and a sin against justice" (CCC, Glossary, "Racism"). The social doctrine of the Catholic Church teaches:

> The equality of men rests essentially on their dignity as persons and the rights that flow from it: "Every form of social or cultural discrimination in fundamental personal rights on the grounds of sex, race, color, social conditions, language, or religion must be curbed and eradicated as incompatible with God's design" (*Pastoral Constitution on the Church in the Modern World*, no. 29).
> —CCC, no. 1935

Every society has the fundamental responsibility to promote and defend the dignity and fundamental personal rights of its members, to reduce excessive social and economic inequalities, and to create the conditions that allow associations and individuals to pursue their God-given rights and responsibly exercise their freedom. When a society strives to meet this fundamental responsibility it promotes the common good of all its members. The common good is "the sum total of social conditions which allow people, either as groups or individuals, to reach their fulfillment more fully and more easily" (*Pastoral Constitution on the Church in the Modern World*, no. 26).

TALK IT OVER
- What other "isms" can you name that identify social sin?
- How do personal sins contribute to these social sins?
- What is the response of the Catholic Church to these social sins? (If necessary, research the Church's response and report back at the appropriate time in your study of the Ten Commandments.)

OVER TO YOU
- What connection do you see between your personal sinful choices and social sin?
- How are you working against social sin?

Discrimination on the grounds of sex, race, color, social conditions, language or religion must be curbed and eradicated as incompatible with God's design

SEGREGATED DRINKING FOUNTAIN, OKLAHOMA, 1939

Mortal, or grave, sin: The Church makes a distinction between mortal sin and venial sin. The word "mortal" means "deadly" or "death-bearing." A mortal sin is a radical "No" to God; it is a total turning of one's back on God, on his offer of life and love, and on the divine plan of goodness for creation. We also call mortal sin "grave sin." Mortal sin seriously or gravely ruptures one's life-giving relationship with God, with people and with creation. Mortal sin also brings serious spiritual and, possibly, physical harm to oneself. Mortal sin "destroys charity in us, deprives us of sanctifying grace, and, if unrepented, leads us to the eternal death of hell" (*Compendium*, no. 395).

This radical "No" to God takes place when three conditions are met. These conditions are:
- The nature of the act is gravely contrary to the law of God.
- The person acting has full knowledge of the gravity of the act.
- The person acts with deliberate and complete consent; external pressures can lessen or take away this consent.

Mortal sin is a *radical possibility* of human freedom. Where such a radical rupture occurs, God respects our freedom and awaits our free choice to respond to his grace and return to the embrace of his love. Jesus clearly revealed this in the parable of the prodigal son. God is always faithful to us; he always offers his grace to us to enable us to repent—but he will not force us to accept his forgiving love. We celebrate this encounter with God in the Sacrament of Penance and Reconciliation. The Church requires that we confess all mortal sins to a priest in this sacrament. The priest is bound by the law of the Church never to reveal the sins we confess to him. This is called the seal of confession.

THINK, PAIR AND SHARE
- With a partner, review the three conditions for a sin to be mortal. Identify some examples of all three being met.
- Discuss: If someone commits a mortal sin, what should they do as soon as possible?

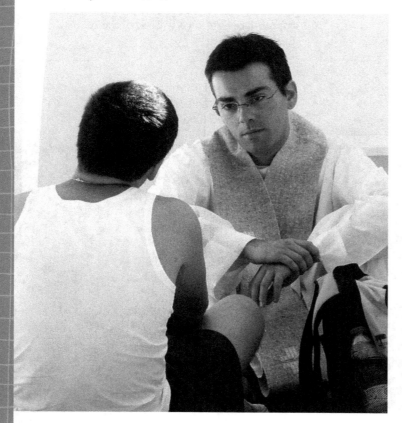

God always offers his grace to us to enable us to repent—but he will not force us to accept his forgiving love

Just as many small acts of indifference and laziness can weaken a friendship, many small sins can weaken our relationship with God

Venial sins: Venial sins are of lesser gravity than mortal sins. Venial sins do not sever our friendship with God and do not deny a person the gift of sanctifying grace. The object of the act is not "grave," and the person acts without full knowledge or does not give complete consent. Even though some venial sins might not be seen to be so terribly serious in the greater scheme of things, a pattern of committing venial sins can weaken a person's ability to do what is right, true and good and "engenders vices, among which are the capital sins" (CCC, no. 1876).

The effects of venial sins can be repaired by acts of love, compassion and justice. While the Church recommends we confess venial sins in the Sacrament of Penance and Reconciliation, this is not necessary, as it is for mortal sins.

Think of venial sin in terms of a friendship. A stable and mature relationship can withstand a little laziness and indifference. However, through many small decisions and actions, for example, not returning phone calls or texts or emails, not saying thank you, taking the other for granted, spending less time with them and more time with others, a friendship can be undermined. The same is true regarding venial sin. Many small sins can weaken our relationship with God.

OVER TO YOU

- ⊙ Pause for a moment of reflection and prayer.
- ⊙ What have you discovered about yourself from exploring the teachings of Scripture and Tradition in this section of the chapter?
- ⊙ How might you integrate that wisdom into your daily life?

FAITH WORD

Sin

Sin is an offense against God as well as against reason, truth, and right conscience; it is a failure in genuine love for God and neighbor caused by a perverse attachment to certain goods. It wounds the nature of man and injures human solidarity.

—*United States Catholic Catechism for Adults (USCCA)*, Glossary, 528

CHRIST'S VICTORY OVER SIN

The presence of sin in our lives is powerful and can be devastating. Our sinfulness can only be overcome by Christ's salvation. Christians face sin with hope and courage. We remember that the power of Christ, the Incarnate Son of God, is far greater than the power of sin. During his

THE RESURRECTION | ALBRECHT DÜRER

TAKE THIS, ALL OF YOU, AND DRINK FROM IT,
FOR THIS IS THE CHALICE OF MY BLOOD,
THE BLOOD OF THE NEW AND ETERNAL
    COVENANT,
WHICH WILL BE POURED OUT FOR YOU AND
    FOR MANY
FOR THE FORGIVENESS OF SINS.
         —Eucharistic Prayer I, *The Roman Missal*

These reassuring words remind us that the very purpose of Jesus' life, Death, Resurrection and Ascension was the forgiveness of sin and the reconciliation of humanity with God. God offers us this same forgiving love in the Sacrament of Reconciliation. The priest assures us of God's loving mercy with these words of absolution:

God, the Father of mercies,
through the death and resurrection of his Son
has reconciled the world to himself
and sent the Holy Spirit among us
for the forgiveness of sins;
through the ministry of the Church
may God give you pardon and peace,
and I absolve you from your sins
in the name of the Father, and of the Son, ✠
and of the Holy Spirit.
—*Rite for Reconciliation of Individual Penitents*

WHAT ABOUT YOU PERSONALLY?

⊙ How have you experienced God's forgiveness in the Sacrament of Penance?
⊙ How might you best overcome sin in your personal life? In structures of society?

PREPARATION FOR THE PRAYER REFLECTION

⊙ Form into two groups. Create a two-part drama. Part one portrays an act of injustice against a person or group. Part two portrays the characters acting in ways that are loving and just.
⊙ Group 1 composes a scene depicting a sin of commission.
⊙ Group 2 portrays a sin of omission.
⊙ Present your drama during the Prayer Reflection at the end of this chapter.

Passion Jesus experienced sin in many forms, namely, hatred, unbelief, mockery, betrayal, cruelty and cowardice. He did not respond in kind. By his Passion, Death, Resurrection and Ascension, Christ overcame the power of sin and death and gave birth to new life.

When we sin, we may sometimes hesitate to reach out to God for forgiveness. If you experience such hesitation, recall Jesus' compassionate actions and words toward people who sinned. Each time you participate in the Eucharist, listen carefully and take heart from the words the priest speaks in the name of Christ during the Consecration. Holding up the chalice he says:

REVIEW AND SHARE WHAT YOU HAVE LEARNED IN THIS CHAPTER

Look back over this chapter and reflect on the teachings of Scripture and Tradition on the reality of sin and the consequences of sin. Share the teachings of the Catholic Church on these statements:

- ⊙ Sin is a reality.
- ⊙ Sin is a failure in genuine love for God and neighbor.
- ⊙ Mortal sin seriously ruptures our relationship with God.
- ⊙ For a sin to be mortal, three conditions are necessary: full knowledge, full consent and grave matter.

- ⊙ Mortal sin must be confessed in the Sacrament of Penance and Reconciliation.
- ⊙ Venial sins weaken our relationships with God and others and can lead to more serious sin.
- ⊙ Structures of sin can come about in society as a consequence of personal sins.
- ⊙ God is always ready to forgive our sins.

REFLECT AND DECIDE

- ⊙ What are the most important insights about the reality of sin that you can take from this chapter?
- ⊙ Is there a particular grace you need to ask of God in your struggle against sin at this time in your life?

LEARN BY EXAMPLE

St. Claudine Thévenet (1774–1837), a woman of faith, courage and commitment

Claudine Thévenet was born in Lyons, France, in 1774, the second child in a family of seven. Claudine had a strong influence on her brothers and sisters, to whom she was affectionately known as Glady. In 1789 the French Revolution brought devastation and chaos into Claudine's life and into the community where she lived when Lyons came under siege, and she witnessed many people, including her two brothers, being executed. Her brothers' last words to her, "Forgive, Glady, as we forgive," spoken on the way to their place of execution, had a huge impact on her life. Inspired by them, she decided to devote herself to the relief of suffering caused by the Revolution. She dedicated her money, time and energy to providing food, clothing, shelter and education to the destitute, particularly the orphaned and abandoned children, whom she saw as being among the weakest and most vulnerable members of society.

Claudine believed that the greatest misfortune is to live and die without knowing God. She wanted to bring God's love to the poor and suffering and to make Jesus and Mary known to as many people as possible.

A priest named Father André Coindre helped her to discover more clearly how she could do this. He encouraged her to form a religious community. On October 6, 1818 Claudine and her companions founded the Congregation of the Religious of Jesus and Mary at Pierres Plantees in Lyons. The main aim of the Congregation was the Christian education of all social classes, with a preference for children, young girls and the poor.

In spite of the many difficulties she encountered, especially the upheaval resulting from the Revolution, Claudine continued her work and bravely undertook all her tasks. Her trust in God's goodness gave her courage and strength. The members of the Congregation were influenced by her strong personality and they praised her courage and commitment. She was a great organizer and always had a strong desire to make others happy. She wanted her Sisters to be like mothers to the children in their care. The only preference she tolerated was for the poor, and working against the sinful structures of the country.

Claudine died in 1837. Her last words, "How good God is!", remain a legacy to her Sisters, who continue to work all over the world, sharing the courage, goodness and forgiving love that Claudine inspired in them. There are now more than 1,800 Religious of Jesus and Mary in 180 communities across the five continents.

Claudine was canonized by St. John Paul II on March 21, 1993.

TALK IT OVER

⊙ In your own words, describe the social sins that Claudine Thévenet worked to alleviate.

⊙ What effect did her response to those social sins have a) on others, and b) on her own spirituality?

⊙ What is the best thing you can learn for your own life from the example of Claudine Thévenet?

SHARE FAITH WITH FAMILY AND FRIENDS

In this chapter we learned about Jesus' teaching that sin has power over people. God the Father calls everyone to turn away from sin and toward 'conversion' to Jesus and his Gospel. Forgiveness is a real possibility for one's sin, and compassion is required toward sinners.

⊙ With your family and friends, call to mind a) Scripture stories and b) some stories from your everyday lives that demonstrate the truth of Jesus' teaching.

⊙ Share what these teachings of Jesus mean for your own life, for your life as a family or as a group of friends.

⊙ What is the best decision you can make in response to what you have learned about sin, about God the Father's grace in Jesus and his loving mercy?

LEARN BY HEART

The death [Christ] died, he died to sin, once for all; but the life he lives, he lives to God. So you also must consider yourselves dead to sin and alive to God in Christ Jesus.

ROMANS 6:10–11

All gather and form a circle around a crucifix.
Pray the Sign of the Cross together.

LEADER

Our Lord promised that he is with us when we gather in his name.
Let us open our hearts and minds to his presence.
(*Pause*)
Together we pray:

ALL

Gracious God, God of mercy,
you call us into relationships of love, loyalty and mercy.
When we bring harm upon others, by our words and actions,
especially upon those people made poor in our society,

we undermine the covenant we entered into with you at Baptism,
we weaken or rupture the mutual covenant that binds us with you and with them.
Send your Holy Spirit to guide and support us to live the covenant we entered with you at Baptism, and to keep our baptismal promises.
We ask this in the name of Jesus Christ, your Son, who is the new and everlasting covenant.
Amen.

Renewal of Baptismal Promises

LEADER

We now take time to remember and renew our baptismal promises.

BAPTISMAL FONT | CATHEDRAL OF CHRIST THE LIGHT, OAKLAND, CALIFORNIA

Dear brothers and sisters, through the Paschal
    Mystery
we have been buried with Christ in Baptism,
so that we may walk with him in newness of
    life. . . .
let us renew the promises of Holy Baptism,
by which we once renounced Satan and his
    works
and promised to serve God in the holy Catholic
    Church.
And so I ask you:
Do you renounce sin,
so as to live in the freedom of the children of
    God?

ALL
I do.

LEADER
Do you renounce the lure of evil,
so that sin may have no mastery over you?

ALL
I do.

LEADER
Do you renounce Satan,
the author and prince of sin?

ALL
I do.

LEADER
Do you believe in God,
the Father almighty,
Creator of heaven and earth?

ALL
I do.

LEADER
Do you believe in Jesus Christ, his only Son, our
    Lord,
who was born of the Virgin Mary,
suffered death and was buried,
rose again from the dead
and is seated at the right hand of the Father?

ALL
I do.

LEADER
Do you believe in the Holy Spirit,
the holy Catholic Church,
the communion of saints,
the forgiveness of sins,
the resurrection of the body,
and life everlasting?

ALL
I do.

—Sunday of the Resurrection,
The Roman Missal

Sharing Faith

LEADER
It is vital that we not only profess but that we
also practice our faith.

*The two groups act out the dramas they have
prepared.*

CONCLUDING PRAYER

LEADER
Let us conclude by acknowledging our sins of
omission and commission and raising up our
voices in prayer.

ALL
Have mercy on me, O God,
    according to your steadfast love;
according to your abundant mercy
    blot out my transgressions.
Wash me thoroughly from my iniquity,
    and cleanse me from my sin.

—Psalm 51:1–2

CHAPTER 5

The Liberating Power of the Ten Commandments

THE TEN COMMANDMENTS (THE DECALOGUE)

OUR GUIDE TO FULLNESS OF LIFE

SUM UP HOW TO LIVE THE COVENANT

BEDROCK OF BOTH JEWISH AND CHRISTIAN FAITH

CENTRAL TO BRINGING ABOUT THE KINGDOM OF GOD

REFLECT THE NATURAL LAW

ADDRESS THE COMMUNITY OF GOD'S PEOPLE

SIGNPOSTS ON THE "PATH OF LIFE"

ARE AFFIRMED BY THE TEACHING OF JESUS

JESUS, THE INCARNATE SON OF GOD AND SAVIOR OF the world, is the fulfillment of the Law and the Prophets. He revealed the power of the Spirit at work in the law of God. In this chapter we explore why the Ten Commandments are at the bedrock of both Jewish and Christian faith, are central to bringing about the Kingdom of God that Jesus inaugurated, and are signposts mapping the path to eternal life. Throughout life we look to the Ten Commandments for directions to living fullness of life in the freedom of the children of God.

Faith Focus: These teachings are the primary focus of the doctrinal content presented in this chapter:
- ⦿ The Old Law prepares for the New Law revealed by Jesus.
- ⦿ The Ten Commandments reveal the natural law that God implanted in the heart of every human being.
- ⦿ Human freedom finds its perfection in choosing to love God above all else.
- ⦿ The theological virtues are the foundation for living the moral life.
- ⦿ The virtue of religion is the habit of centering our life on God.
- ⦿ Acts contrary to the theological virtues and the First Commandment diminish our freedom and lead
- ⦿ Jesus is the fulfillment of the Old Law live the Ten Commandment

Discipleship Formation: As a result should be better able to:
- ⦿ make the connection between the natural Commandments;
- ⦿ live the Ten Commandments in light of the Great Commandment taught and lived by Jesus;
- ⦿ discover the Ten Commandments to be guideposts mapping the path to freedom and abundance of life;
- ⦿ understand and value the Ten Commandments as a expression of God's love;
- ⦿ discover the wisdom of Pope Francis' words Christian is not just about following the it is about letting Christ take possess transform them";
- ⦿ learn from Mary the ways to center you respond to his love for you.

Scripture References: These Scripture references are quoted referred to in this chapter:
OLD TESTAMENT: Genesis 42:1—47:31; **Exodus** 2:1–10 and 16–22, 3:6 and 9–12, 9:1, 12:40–51, 16:1–3, 20:2 **Leviticus** 19:18; **Deuteronomy** 5:1–22 and 32– 29:10–11, 30:16, 34:10–12; **Joshua** 3:10; **Psal** 119:35; **Isaiah** 40:25–26
NEW TESTAMENT: Matthew 4:1–11 and 19, 5:17–22, 33–34, 38–39 and 43–44, 6:19–21 and 24, 12:33–35, 19:16–22, 22:34–40; **Mark** 10:17–22; **Luke** 4:1–13, 11:28, 18:18–30; **John** 1:16–17, 8:31–33, 10:10, 15:9, 12 and 19, 17:11, 20:19–29, 2 **Acts of the Apostles** 8:9–25; **Romans** 8:28, 10:17; 3:17; **Galatians** 5:1; **Colossians** 2:6–10; **1 Timo** 20–21; **1 John** 4:7–21; **James** 2:10–11

Faith Glossary: Familiarize yourself with the key terms in the Glossary: **adoration, apostasy, ark covenant, covenant (the), Decalogue, doubt (voluntary involuntary), Exodus, heresy, idolatry, incredulity, obedience Passover, presumption, religion, sacrilege, schism, simony, sloth, theological virtues, Torah, worship**

Faith Words: Decalogue; worship
Learn by Heart: The Ten Commandments
Learn by Example: Moses, prophet of freedom and liberat

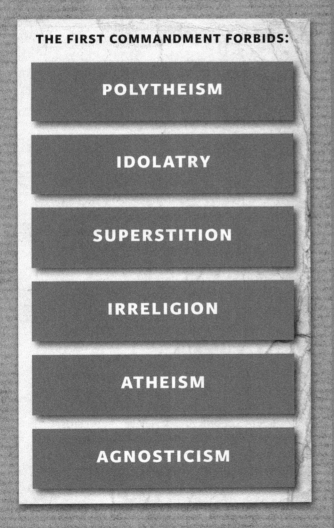

THE FIRST COMMANDMENT FORBIDS:

- POLYTHEISM
- IDOLATRY
- SUPERSTITION
- IRRELIGION
- ATHEISM
- AGNOSTICISM

What good deeds must you do?

task is to structure the legislation that will foster and enable the members to live to their best potential in love, justice and peace.

- ⊙ List the five best laws that will both protect and promote the members' right to live in true freedom and for the society to flourish.
- ⊙ Share your laws with the class.
- ⊙ Identify the laws that most students had in common. List these on a large poster and hang it in a central place in the classroom.

You are by now very familiar with Jesus' conversation with the young man who approached him and asked, "Teacher, what good deed must I do to have eternal life?" (Matthew 19:16). All three authors of the synoptic Gospels include this encounter between Jesus and the young man in their account of the Gospel. This is a sign that this episode is a key to our understanding of Jesus' teachings. (Read the whole passage in Matthew 19:16–22, in Mark 10:17–22 or in Luke 18:18–30.)

OPENING CONVERSATION

- ⊙ How does Jesus' teaching in this passage sum up the heart of the law that God has implanted within every human being? Base your response on what you have learned both in the past and during this course of study.

THINK, PAIR AND SHARE

- ⊙ Work with a partner. Imagine that you are setting up a society for the very first time. There are no laws, rules or regulations. Your

FROM THE CATECHISM

"The Old Law is the first stage of revealed law. Its moral prescriptions are summed up in the Ten Commandments" (*Catechism of the Catholic Church* [CCC], no. 1980). "The Law of Moses contains many truths naturally accessible to reason. God has revealed them because men did not read them in their hearts" (CCC, no. 1981). "The Old Law is a preparation for the Gospel" (CCC. no, 1982).

THE DECALOGUE: "TEN WORDS" OF GOD

The Ten Commandments are often referred to as the **Decalogue**, a word meaning "ten words." The Ten Commandments appear in Exodus 20:2–17 and Deuteronomy 5:6–21. These "Ten Words" sum up and proclaim the law of the covenant that God and the Israelites entered. Coming down from Mount Sinai (also called Mount Horeb), "Moses convened all Israel, and said to them:

"Hear, O Israel, the statutes and ordinances that I am addressing to you today; you shall learn them

The Ten Commandments

1. I am the LORD your God: you shall not have strange gods before me.
2. You shall not take the name of the LORD your God in vain.
3. Remember to keep holy the LORD's Day.
4. Honor your father and your mother.
5. You shall not kill.
6. You shall not commit adultery.
7. You shall not steal.
8. You shall not bear false witness against your neighbor.
9. You shall not covet your neighbor's wife.
10. You shall not covet your neighbor's goods.

and observe them diligently. The LORD our God made a covenant with us at Horeb. Not with our ancestors did the LORD make this covenant, but with us, who are all of us here alive today. The LORD spoke with you face to face at the mountain, out of the fire. (At that time I was standing between the LORD and you to declare to you the words of the LORD; for you were afraid because of the fire and did not go up the mountain.)"

—Deuteronomy 5:1–5

Moses then proclaimed the Decalogue to the Israelites. When he had finished, Moses said:

"These words the LORD spoke with a loud voice to your whole assembly at the mountain, out of the fire, the cloud, and the thick darkness, and he added no more. He wrote them on two stone tablets, and gave them to me."

—Deuteronomy 5:22

The two tablets are called the "tablets of the covenant." They were to be deposited in the **ark of the covenant.** This was the revered chest made to contain the "tablets of stone, written with the finger of God" (Exodus 31:18). The ark was a symbol of God's presence with his people.

Like the ancient Israelites, the Jewish people today and Christians believe the Ten Commandments to be God's word mapping the "path of life." (Check out Psalm 119, especially verse 35.)

The Ten Commandments are the fundamental, practical laws that guide God's people in living the covenant. The essence of the Ten Commandments is summarized in Deuteronomy 6:5 and Leviticus 19:18, the two parts of the Great Commandment. The wording and the numbering of the Ten Commandments has varied in the course of history. The Catholic Church follows the division established by St. Augustine some 1600 years ago. This listing is also shared by Lutheran denominations. The listing and wording used by Orthodox Churches and the Reformed ecclesial communities is based on the Greek Fathers of the Church.

TEN COMMANDMENTS | CHURCH OF SAINT VEIT, BREZJE, SLOVENIA

LET'S PROBE DEEPER

⊙ With a partner, compare the Catholic Church's wording and numbering of the Ten Commandments with Exodus 20:2–17 and Deuteronomy 5:6–21.

THINK, PAIR AND SHARE

⊙ With your partner, look at the list of laws that you assembled for your "society" in the opening exercise of this chapter.

⊙ Identify which of these laws reflect the Ten Commandments and which ones are not connected with the Ten Commandments in any way.

⊙ Discuss whether you still believe that these laws are essential for your society.

THE TEN COMMANDMENTS AND THE NATURAL LAW

As we learned in chapter 3, God has engraved a natural law in the heart of every person, an innate ability to tell good from evil, right from wrong, truth from falsehood. "The Decalogue contains a privileged expression of the natural law. It is made known to us by divine revelation and by human reason" (CCC, no. 2080). This is why it is a blessing from God to have the Ten Commandments as well as the natural law.

When you explore the meaning of any one of the Ten Commandments, you will recognize from the natural law within you that they make eminent good sense. For example, the Seventh Commandment, "You shall not steal," is a pointer toward actions that are harmful to individuals and friends, families and society. It points us toward those attitudes and actions that bring about real freedom and fullness of life. St. Irenaeus put it this way:

"From the beginning, God had implanted in the heart of man the precepts of the natural law. Then he was content to remind him of them. This was the Decalogue" (*Against Heresies*, 4, 15).
—CCC, no. 2070

- Work with a partner. Think through some of the other Ten Commandments. Imagine what life would be like if any one of them were erased.
- With your partner, articulate the wisdom that the specific Commandments you have examined bring to life.

FROM THE CATECHISM

The Decalogue forms an organic unity in which each "word" or "commandment" refers to all the others taken together. To transgress one commandment is to infringe the whole Law (see Letter of James 2:10–11).

—CCC, no. 2079

"BUT I SAY TO YOU": KEEPING THE COMMANDMENTS

"By his life and by his preaching Jesus attested to the permanent validity of the Decalogue" (CCC, no. 2076). This is confirmed in the Gospels, where Jesus also indicates that the Christian life involves more than obeying the letter of the law of the Ten Commandments.

Throughout the Sermon on the Mount Jesus interprets the Old Law six times using the formula, "You have heard that it was said, . . . But I say to you." (Check out Matthew 5:21–22, 27–28, 31–32, 33–34, 38–39 and 43–44.) This formula was commonly used by rabbis. When they used it, they were saying, "You really don't get it so I'll explain it to you." In other words, Jesus was telling the disciples and his other Jewish listeners, "You do not understand the real meaning of the Decalogue and the law of Moses." For example, Jesus unfolds the spirit and true meaning of the Fifth Commandment in this way:

"You have heard that it was said to those of ancient times, 'You shall not murder'; and 'whoever murders shall be liable to judgment.' But I say to you that if you are angry with a brother or sister, you will be liable to judgment; and if you insult a brother or sister, you will be liable to the council; and if you say, 'You fool,' you will be liable to the hell of fire."

—Matthew 5:21–22

THE SERMON ON THE MOUNT | JAN BRUEGHEL THE ELDER

THE TEN COMMANDMENTS AND THE GREATEST COMMANDMENT

Many years ago, St. Augustine noticed that the first three of the Ten Commandments pertain to our love of God and the other seven to our love of neighbor and of one's self. St. Augustine's insight shows us that we are to interpret the Ten Commandments and live them in light of the "twofold yet single commandment of love" of God and neighbor (CCC, no. 2055). We are to love God above all else, and love our neighbor as one's self. (Check out Matthew 22:34–40.) This is our pathway to the fullness of life God created us to have as human beings, both here and now and after our death in the life everlasting.

OVER TO YOU

⊙ Read the Ten Commandments and check out Augustine's insight for yourself.

It was within this context of the centrality of love in our life that Jesus, on the night before he died, told his disciples: "As the Father has loved me, so I have loved you; abide in my love" (John 15:9). What a consolation! Jesus desires that we share in the very love that he and his Father share. Then he continued, "This is my commandment, that you love one another as I have loved you" (John 15:12). Ultimately, we are to share that love with other people—with all people.

What a challenge and an amazing vocation to live up to! Thank God that we have the Ten Commandments to guide us, and God's abundant grace in his Son, Jesus, to sustain our best efforts. The more we obey Jesus' commandment, the more we will flourish, become fully alive and truly free.

THINK, PAIR AND SHARE

⊙ Think about what it means to interpret and live the Ten Commandments in light of the threefold law of love.
⊙ With a partner, take any one of the Ten Commandments and try to see for yourself how it can lead to freedom and fullness of life.
⊙ Identify and share examples of how acting in ways that are contrary to the Ten Commandments leads to slavery of some kind.

JOURNAL EXERCISE

⊙ How are the Ten Commandments your path of life?
⊙ Write your reflections as you explore each of the Ten Commandments.

FAITH WORD

Decalogue

The Ten Commandments (literally, "ten words") given by God to Moses on Sinai. In order to be faithful to the teaching of Jesus, the Decalogue must be interpreted in the light of the great commandment of love of God and neighbor.

—CCC, Glossary

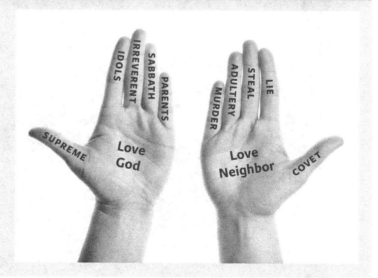

"I am the LORD your God"

Many of our ancestors left their homelands to come to the United States of America, "the Land of Opportunity." Many continue to flee oppression and seek asylum here; others seek the freedom to pursue opportunities to provide the basic necessities of life for themselves and their loved ones and to live with dignity. Sadly, as happened to some of our ancestors, people are still being brought here in slavery by those who abuse their freedom in their pursuit of wealth and power. Human trafficking is a heinous crime and a sin that attacks the very dignity of the human person. Some of our citizens continue to be enslaved by both social structures and other circumstances that are part of their lives.

ELLIS ISLAND WITH THE STATUE OF LIBERTY IN THE BACKGROUND

TALK IT OVER

⊙ In what ways are people in the United States of America enslaved today? What are the forces that contribute to this "slavery"?

⊙ How are the Ten Commandments a force working against such slavery?

⊙ How is the Catholic Church working against slavery in all its forms?

THE ISRAELITES' JOURNEY TO FREEDOM

The **Exodus** and the **covenant** that God and the Israelites entered at Sinai reveal the very heart of God's relationship with his people. The Exodus is God's great liberating action on behalf of his people. It is "God's saving intervention in history by which he liberated the Hebrew people from slavery in Egypt, made a covenant with them, and brought them into the Promised Land" (CCC, Glossary, "Exodus"). Just as Jews do today, the ancient Israelites remembered, recalled and celebrated the Exodus and God's liberating

presence among them during **Passover**, as the law of the covenant commanded. (Check out Exodus 12:40–51.) For Christians, these Passover–Exodus events foreshadow the saving events of Christ's Death and Resurrection.

The Exodus reveals the very identity of the God with whom the Israelites were to live in covenant. At Sinai God declared: "I am the LORD your God, who brought you out of the land of Egypt, out of the house of slavery; you shall have no other gods before me" (Exodus 20:2). God revealed himself to be the one true God whom they were to worship, a God of freedom and justice who has a special love for the oppressed.

This passage from the **Torah** summarizes the Israelites' confession of faith in God. It tells of how the Israelites were to **worship** God when they entered the Promised Land and offer him the gifts from their first harvest:

When the priest takes the basket from your hand and sets it down before the altar of the LORD your God, you shall make this response

When the Egyptians treated us harshly and afflicted us, by imposing hard labor on us, we cried to the LORD. . . .

DEUTERONOMY 26:6—7

before the LORD your God: "A wandering Aramean was my ancestor; he went down into Egypt and lived there as an alien, few in number, and there he became a great nation, mighty and populous. When the Egyptians treated us harshly and afflicted us, by imposing hard labor on us, we cried to the LORD, the God of our ancestors; the LORD heard our voice and saw our affliction, our toil, and our oppression. The LORD brought us out of Egypt with a mighty hand and an outstretched arm, with a terrifying display of power, and with signs and wonders; and he brought us into this place and gave us this land, a land flowing with milk and honey."

—Deuteronomy 26:4–9

LET'S PROBE DEEPER: SCRIPTURE ACTIVITY

⊙ You will remember that the Israelites went to Egypt during a time of great famine. (Check out Genesis 42:1—47:12.) As time wore on, they found themselves oppressed, degraded and enslaved. God heard, saw and responded to their suffering.

⊙ Reread and examine Deuteronomy 26:4–9 to discover this format:
  - People are in distress.
  - They cry out to God.
  - God hears their cry and sees their affliction.
  - God intervenes and delivers them from slavery

⊙ How does this format relate to Christian prayers of petition and of intercession?

WHAT ABOUT YOU PERSONALLY?

⊙ This great story of faith belongs not only to the Jewish people but to Christians as well. What does it tell you about the identity of God and his relationship with you?

MOSES: SHEPHERD, PROPHET OF FREEDOM AND LIBERATOR OF GOD'S PEOPLE

The story of Moses, the prophet of freedom and great liberator, is well known. It has often been portrayed in literature, music, art and film. (There is a profile of Moses in the "Learn by Example" feature in the "Judge and Act" section of this chapter which explores God's command to Moses.)

FAITH WORD

Worship

Adoration and honor given to God, which is the first act of the virtue of religion.

—CCC, Glossary

After he killed an Egyptian when he came to the defense of a Hebrew slave, Moses fled into the desert, where he found refuge among the Midianites, a nomadic tribe. While his flock was grazing near Mount Horeb (also known as Mount Sinai), Moses noticed a bush burning but not being destroyed by the fire. On approaching the bush, Moses heard a voice saying to him, "I am the God of your father, the God of Abraham, the God of Isaac, and the God of Jacob" (Exodus 3:6). Moses hid his face, as the voice called to him and instructed him to lead the Israelites out of their slavery in Egypt into freedom in a new land.

Then the LORD said, "The cry of the Israelites has now come to me; I have also seen how the Egyptians oppress them. So come, I will send you to Pharaoh to bring my people, the Israelites, out of Egypt." But Moses said to God, "Who am I that I should go to Pharaoh, and bring the Israelites out of Egypt?" He said, "I will be with you; and this shall be the sign for you that it is I who sent you: when you have brought the people out of Egypt, you shall worship God on this mountain."

—Exodus 3:9–12

God was asking Moses to be his voice, to be his prophet. God assured Moses that he would be with him and his people. Pharaoh would free the people, and Moses would lead them out of Egypt to Mount Sinai.

On Mount Sinai God and the Israelites entered a covenant and God gave them the Ten Commandments. God then told Moses to give the Israelites this final instruction: "You must therefore be careful to do as the LORD your God commanded you; you shall not turn to the right or to the left. You must follow exactly the path that the LORD your God has commanded you, so that you may live, and that it may go well with you, and that you may live long in the land that you are to possess" (Deuteronomy 5:32–33).

OVER TO YOU

- ⦿ What was Moses' reaction when he heard God's command to him to speak for God to Pharaoh and to be the liberator of his people? Why might he have reacted that way?
- ⦿ When have you felt God calling you to stand up for a person or a group of people who were being treated unjustly? How did you respond?

FROM COERCION TO COVENANT

With God's grace and Moses' leadership, the Israelites began their journey to freedom. But they soon found that the journey was difficult, and it tested their trust in God and in Moses. The Israelites' memories of their oppression became dull and they longed for the comforts of Egypt. When the Israelites were only a month and a half out of Egypt, they began to complain against Moses and Aaron: "If only we had died by the hand of the LORD in the land of Egypt, when we sat by the fleshpots and ate our fill of bread; for you have brought us out into this wilderness to kill this whole assembly with hunger" (Exodus 16:3).

TALK IT OVER

- ⊙ Does it look as if the Israelites were ready to leave coercion and oppression behind and choose to enter a covenant and freely and responsibly commit themselves to living as God's own people?
- ⊙ Why do people sometimes grow so accustomed to things and relationships that enslave them?

THE NEW-FOUND FREEDOM OF LIVING IN COVENANT

At Mount Sinai God invited the ancient Israelites to enter a life-giving and liberating covenant, and they freely agreed. Then God revealed the details of the law of the covenant, which Tradition has summarized in the Ten Commandments. The Ten Commandments begin: "I am the LORD your God, who brought you out of the land of Egypt, out of the house of slavery; you shall have no other gods before me" (Exodus 20:2). In other words, God had freed the Israelites to live in the freedom he wills for all people. Ironically, they could do so only by keeping God's laws. The Ten Commandments point out the conditions of a life freed from the slavery of sin and lived in accordance with God's will.

If you obey the commandments of the LORD your God that I am commanding you today, by loving the LORD your God, walking in his ways, and observing his commandments, decrees, and ordinances, then you shall live and become numerous.

—Deuteronomy 30:16

Why do people sometimes grow so accustomed to the things and the relationships that enslave them?

The Ten Commandments must be understood within the context of the covenant and God's liberating love. The first of the Ten Commandments affirms that God loved his people first. This is an essential point. God reveals the Ten Commandments purely out of love and for our own good. God commands us to so live because God wills nothing but the very best for us—out of love.

The negative commands of the Fifth through the Tenth Commandments not only point to the evil behavior that enslaves people; they also point to those fundamental deeds that undermine the original plan of goodness—of justice and holiness—that God always wills for humanity. Living the Commandments is our response to God's love for humanity. "What God commands he makes possible by his grace" (CCC, no. 2082).

The Ten Commandments do not just address individual persons; they also address the community of God's people. They are the Law God addressed to "the leaders of your tribes, your elders, and your officials, all the men of Israel, your children, your women, and the aliens who are in your camp" (Deuteronomy 29:10–11). The covenant is radically inclusive and radically communal.

The covenant is not simply between God and "me"; it is essentially between God and "us"

The covenant is not simply between God and "me"; it is essentially between God and "us." Every member and the whole community is responsible for living the covenant by obeying the Commandments. The People of God are both a covenant people and a commandment people. Only in a faith community can we live as the People of God.

JOURNAL EXERCISE

⊙ Write about how the Ten Commandments are an expression of God's love for you and about why you need to live by these Commandments.

⊙ Be sure to return to your journal as you explore your faith throughout this course of study.

"*You shall have no other gods before me*"

You will no doubt have heard the adage "Money is the root of all evil." This adage succinctly states the teachings of the Prophets and of the Wisdom literature of the Old Testament, and the teachings of Jesus. St. Paul put it this way: "For the love of money is a root of all kinds of evil, and in their eagerness to be rich some have wandered away from the faith and pierced themselves with many pains" (1 Timothy 6:10).

OPENING CONVERSATION

Take a look at the word *evil*; spell it backward and you get live. Evil leads us in the opposite direction of true living. Evil always tries to deceive us by presenting itself as "good for us."

Choosing and pursuing evil always leads us away from goodness and happiness.

⊙ Take another look at the adage "Money is the root of all evil." Why is money is an appropriate symbol for everyone and everything we turn into a "god"? What other words or terms might you use for money?

⊙ Describe how these people or things might become "gods"? How they might lead us away from "live-ing"?

OVER TO YOU

⊙ When have you pursued evil, convinced that it was good for you? What was the outcome?

Ebenezer Scrooge: A Life Going in the Wrong Direction Until. . . .

Ebenezer Scrooge is the principal character in Charles Dickens' 1843 classic novel, *A Christmas Carol*. Scrooge's life is focused on his love for and pursuit of money. Scrooge has become a cold-hearted businessman who thinks only of making and hoarding money, and who despises Christmas. Dickens tells us: "The cold within him froze his old features, nipped his pointed nose, made his eyes red, his thin lips blue, and he spoke out shrewdly in his grating voice. . . ."

Scrooge's love for and pursuit of money have pierced both himself and others "with many pains"—in particular, his overworked and underpaid humble clerk, Bob Cratchit, and his family. Well, you know the rest of Scrooge's story; his discovery of the meaning of Christmas turns his "e-v-i-l" around and he discovers what it truly means to "l-i-v-e."

THE REFORMED SCROOGE WITH BOB CRATCHIT | JOHN LEECH

- What other "Scrooges" have you learned about? Share your stories.
- What is the common thread running through the lives of these people?

FROM THE CATECHISM

God created the world to show forth and communicate his glory. That his creatures should share in his truth, goodness and beauty—this is the glory for which God created them.

—CCC, no. 319

THE DECEIT OF IDOLS

Choosing any thing or person to replace God is **idolatry**. Idolatry is the "divinization of a creature in place of God; the substitution of some one (or thing) for God; worshiping a creature (even money, pleasure, or power) instead of the Creator" (CCC, Glossary, "Idolatry"). Scrooge's idolatry turned him into a cold-hearted, miserable slave. Every idol, every false "god"—every force of evil—will do that.

In an earlier section of this chapter we explored the inseparable connection between the Ten Commandments and the Great Commandment, the law of love, which Jesus preached, taught and lived. Three ghosts

appeared to Scrooge during the story and moved him to change his heart, "to repent." Each dream, in its own way, motivated Scrooge to change his priorities and turn away from himself and toward the good of others. They helped him see that "money" was his idol and idolatry his way of life.

Jesus said, "Blessed . . . are those who hear the word of God and obey it!" (Luke 11:28). **Obedience** to God's words in the first three Commandments is the pathway that will keep us from following Scrooge's course. The obedience of faith is hearing the word of God and resolving to obey what God is asking. Only when we truly love God with our whole being, can we truly love our neighbor and ourselves (the Fourth through the Tenth Commandments). When we truly and freely and fully respond to God's invitation to know and love and serve him above all else, we will discover what it means to be free and truly "alive."

READ, REFLECT AND SHARE

- Read Matthew 4:1–11 and Matthew 6:24 with a partner.
- Discuss the connection you see between these two gospel passages and *A Christmas Carol*.
- Share other examples from literature, art and music that express these gospel teachings.

Choosing any thing or person to replace God is idolatry

IDOLS IN *OUR* MIDST

There are many idols in our midst that strive for our allegiance. These idols come in many forms. For example, we can make an idol of the latest fashion or high-end car, or college scholarship or money-making career, or excellence in sport, drama or music, or a diet or exercise routine. When a person, a group or a nation travels that path and pursues any idol, they travel deeper and deeper into a self-imposed slavery and run the risk of inflicting the pain of this slavery on themselves and others. Idolatry sucks every ounce of life-giving blood from our hearts.

OVER TO YOU

- ⊙ Look up and prayerfully reflect on Jesus' words (1) in the Sermon on the Mount in Matthew 6:19–21 and 24 and (2) to his disciples and the Pharisees in Matthew 12:33–35.

"WORSHIP THE LORD YOUR GOD AND SERVE ONLY HIM"

During his temptation in the wilderness Jesus admonished his tempter: "Away with you Satan! for it is written, 'Worship the Lord your God, and serve only him'" (Matthew 4:10). Jesus assures us that when we worship God alone, everything in our life will fall into place. St. Paul taught this same truth. He wrote: "We know that all things work together for good for those who love God" (Romans 8:28).

Making Jesus' words and Paul's teaching the motivation behind our moral choices will make us free. This motivation will help us form the attitudes and actions that will put and keep us on the path of life—a life lived in the freedom of the children of God. The Church reminds us of this truth. She teaches: "Human freedom is a force for growth and maturity in truth and goodness; it attains its perfection when directed toward God, our beatitude" (CCC, no. 1731).

READ, REFLECT AND SHARE

- ⊙ With a partner, check out John 8:31–33 and Colossians 2:6–10.
- ⊙ Share what these passages reveal about the life-giving and freeing power of the life, Death, Resurrection and Ascension of Jesus.

WHAT ABOUT YOU PERSONALLY?

- ⊙ Is there some "god" tempting you to place it as the central and primary focus of your life? Think carefully; "gods," or idols, are very skilled deceivers!

- What are some of the signs that this idol may be tempting you?
- What can you do to resist that *E-V-I-L* so you can *L-I-V-E* freely and fully?

JESUS CHRIST, SAVIOR, REDEEMER AND LIBERATOR

God's word to us in Scripture is, from one perspective, the story of God continuously offering his people the grace that will set them free from their own self-imposed slavery to idols. Jesus, the Incarnate Son of God, clearly revealed this to be the heart of his saving work. He taught: "I came that [you] may have life, and have it abundantly" (John 10:10). Earlier in his account of the Gospel the Evangelist teaches: "From his fullness we have all received, grace upon grace. The law indeed was given through Moses; grace and truth came through Jesus Christ" (John 1:16–17).

The People of God—then and now—obey the Commandments not out of grudging submission to dictatorial rules laid down by a God who is bent on keeping us in line; in faith they obey God who has revealed himself to be a God of love. (Check out 1 John 4:7–21.) This is the God whom we have come to know, love and serve in the Incarnate Son of God, Jesus Christ, and who is the fulfillment of the Law and the Prophets. (Check out Matthew 5:17–20.)

All four accounts of the Gospel clearly reveal that God the Father was the center and focus of Jesus' life. His whole life was one of obedience to his Father—an obedience rooted in love. The challenge to us is to freely choose to make God the center of our life, too. Pope Francis shared this wisdom of what it means to follow Jesus: "Being a Christian is not just about following commandments: it is about letting Christ take possession of our lives and transform them" (Twitter/Pope Francis @Pontifex).

MEET THE CHALLENGE

- Work with a partner. Take turns at reading and responding to this statement: Rules get in the way of my being creative. They restrict my freedom so much that I cannot become the person I really want to be.

Living the First Commandment

The Hebrew people did not always strive to worship and serve God who "brought [them] out of the land of Egypt, out of the house of slavery" (Exodus 20:2). Oftentimes they served idols, "which became a snare to them" (Psalm 106:36). A snare is a trapping device, often consisting of a noose, used for capturing birds and small animals. Every idol, every false god that we place at the center of our lives, will enslave us rather than bring us life and freedom, as they deceitfully promise to do. Read "The Snare" by the poet James Stephens (1882–1950) and reflect on what it means to be "ensnared."

The Snare

I hear a sudden cry of pain!
There is a rabbit in a snare:
Now I hear the cry again,
But I cannot tell from where.

But I cannot tell from where
He is calling out for aid!
Crying on the frightened air,
Making everything afraid!

OPENING CONVERSATION
- What kinds of things ensnare young people today?
- How might keeping God first in their lives help young people to avoid being "snared"? How might it set them free?

OVER TO YOU
- How does Jesus' life and teachings help us recognize and avoid the snares in the world?

FROM THE CATECHISM
"The first commandment summons man to believe in God, to hope in him, and to love him above all else" (CCC, no. 2134). "Adoring God, praying to him, offering him the worship that belongs to him, fulfilling the promises and vows made to him, are acts of the virtue of religion which fall under the obedience to the first commandment" (CCC, no. 2135).

GOD'S CONSTANT AND NEVER-ENDING INVITATION
Isn't it amazing that God does not wait for us to love him before he loves us? He freely reaches out to us and invites us into a friendship that is beyond any human friendship we could ever imagine. Jesus, the Word of God made flesh, prayed: "Holy Father, protect them in your name that you have given me, so that they may be one, as we are one" (John 17:11).

God's invitation to come to know, love and serve him is a totally free gift, or grace. First among these graces are the three **theological virtues** of faith, hope and charity (love). Our whole moral life is rooted in and flows from these virtues. The theological virtues are "gifts infused by God into the souls of the faithful to make them capable of acting as his children and of meriting eternal life" (CCC, Glossary, "Virtues, Theological"). They are called "theological" because God (the Greek word for God is *theos*) is "their origin, their motive and their object—God known by faith, God hoped in and loved for his own sake" (CCC, no. 1840).

The *Compendium of the Catechism of the Catholic Church* summarizes the centrality of the theological virtues for living our life in Christ. The *Compendium* teaches that the words "I am the LORD your God . . . you shall have no other gods before me" (Exodus 20:2-3) mean:

. . . that the faithful must guard and activate the three theological virtues and must avoid sins which are opposed to them. *Faith* believes in God and rejects everything that is opposed to it, such as, deliberate doubt, unbelief, **heresy, apostasy and schism**. *Hope* trustingly awaits the blessed vision of God and his help, while avoiding despair and **presumption**. *Charity* loves God above all things and therefore repudiates indifference, ingratitude, lukewarmness, **sloth** or spiritual indolence, and that hatred of God which is born of pride.

—*Compendium*, no. 442

LET'S PROBE DEEPER

- ⊙ Work with a partner.
- ⊙ Read and silently reflect on John 20:19–29, the account of St. Thomas the Apostle's response to hearing the news that his crucified Lord was alive. Then:
  - look up the definitions of "**voluntary doubt**," "**involuntary doubt**," and "**incredulity**" in the "Faith Glossary" of your text;
  - apply the definitions to Thomas' responses in the passage;
  - share your reflections with the whole class.
- ⊙ The whole class then discusses: What positive role can asking questions about the faith of the Church have in our growing in faith?

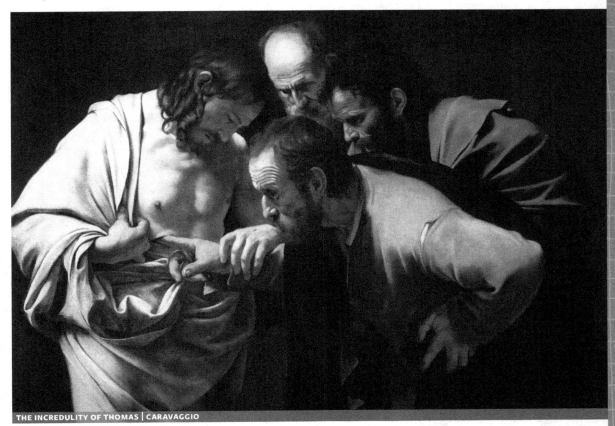

THE INCREDULITY OF THOMAS | CARAVAGGIO

A PEOPLE OF FAITH AND A FAITHFUL PEOPLE

The First Commandment calls us to be a people of faith and a faithful people. It "summons man to believe in God, to hope in him and to love him above all else" (CCC, no. 2134). Faith is both a gift of God and our response to God's invitation to know and believe in him and all that he has revealed. We have the responsibility to nourish and protect our faith and to reject everything that might harm or weaken it. We place our total faith in God with confident hope and we love him above all else.

Mary, the Mother of Jesus, is our model for such faith. She heard God's invitation, responded freely and surrendered her whole self to God. Mary models for us the abundance of life that pours into our own life and into the life of the world when we respond to God with faith, hope and love.

Pope Francis reminds us: "To obey God is to listen to him, to have an open heart, to go on the road that God shows us. This is what makes us free" (from Homily at morning Mass at Domus Sanctae Marthae, April 11, 2013). The wisest way to live is in obedience to God's word. Such obedience, as the lives of Jesus and Mary and the other saints reveal, brings us to true freedom and fullness of life, both here and hereafter. All that we are, and everything we have, ultimately comes from God, who has revealed himself to be the "living God" (Joshua 3:10, Psalm 42:2) who alone gives life to all—our natural life and our supernatural life of grace, our natural birth and our rebirth into new life in Christ.

OVER TO YOU

- ⊙ How do you think placing God first in your life brings true freedom?
- ⊙ How can you embrace such freedom even now?

LIVING THE FIRST COMMANDMENT

When the ancient Israelites' conflict with the Babylonians ended, the prophet Isaiah chided the Israelites. He admonished them for failing to

THE ANNUNCIATION | JAN VAN EYCK

Mary, the Mother of Jesus, heard God's invitation, responded freely and surrendered her whole self to God

trust and honor their own God and the Creator of all that is. He then reminded them of the fidelity and power of "the Holy One" (a name Isaiah used for YHWH). Isaiah asked the Israelites to gaze at the stars (which the Babylonians worshiped as "gods") and he encouraged them to remain steadfast in faith by offering them these words of comfort:

To whom then will you compare me,
    or who is my equal? says the Holy One.
Lift up your eyes on high and see:
    Who created these?
He who brings out their host and numbers
        them,
    calling them all by name;
because he is great in strength,
    mighty in power,
    not one is missing.

—Isaiah 40:25–26

In his First Letter to Timothy St. Paul advises his disciple to warn the Church in Ephesus not to be deceived by false teachers and "not to occupy themselves with myths and endless genealogies that promote speculations rather than the divine training that is known by faith. But the aim of such instruction is love that comes from a pure heart, a good conscience, and sincere faith" (1 Timothy 1:4–5). Paul concludes the letter:

Timothy, guard what has been entrusted to you. Avoid the profane chatter and contradictions of what is falsely called knowledge; by professing it some have missed the mark as regards the faith.
—1 Timothy 6:20–21

THE VIRTUE OF RELIGION

God is the source of our life, our freedom and our every blessing. Only God the Creator is to receive the honor of being first in our lives. The People of God profess this faith in prayer and acts of adoration. Adoration is the "acknowledgement of God as God, Creator and Savior, the Lord and Master of everything that exists" (CCC, Glossary, "Adoration"). The adoration of God sets us free from making ourselves or any other creature the center of the world. It also frees us from the slavery of sin, which is always the consequence

of such choices. It leads us toward holiness of life—life lived in communion and friendship with God—as God always wills for all humanity.

The virtue of religion is the "habit of adoring God, praying to him, offering him the worship that belongs to him, and fulfilling the promises and vows made to him . . . that fall under the obedience of the First Commandment" (*United States Catholic Catechism for Adults* (USCCA), Glossary, "Religion, virtue of," 525).

JOURNAL EXERCISE
⊙ Reflect on and write about your faith in God and his will and desire for you to have freedom and fullness of life.

CHOOSING AN ALTERNATE WAY
From the beginning, many have chosen to center their lives on other "gods" or on "no god." The First Commandment forbids this and reveals the emptiness of living a life rooted in these attitudes and actions:
⊙ *Polytheism* and *idolatry*, which divinizes creatures, power, money, or even demons.
⊙ *Superstition* which is a departure from the worship due to the true God and which also expresses itself in various forms of divination, magic, sorcery and spiritism.
⊙ *Irreligion* which is evidenced: in tempting God by word or deed; in sacrilege, which profanes sacred persons or sacred things, above all the

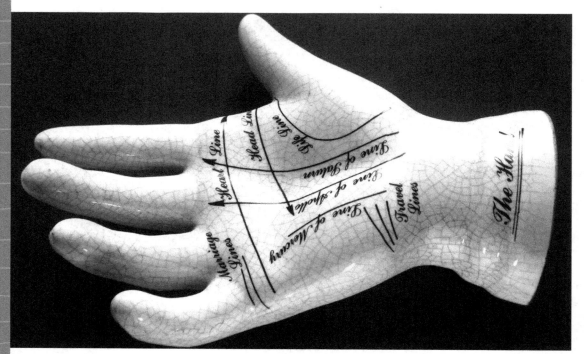

Eucharist; and in simony, which involves the buying or selling of spiritual things.

- ◉ *Atheism* which rejects the existence of God, founded often on a false conception of human autonomy.
- ◉ *Agnosticism* which affirms that nothing can be known about God, and involves indifferentism and practical atheism.

—*Compendium*, no. 445

LET'S PROBE DEEPER

Polytheism, idolatry and superstition: Most obviously, the First Commandment forbids idolatry and superstition. We have explored idolatry in the opening section of this chapter. Superstition involves trying to replace God with magic, or the occult. It can also include fortune-telling or relying on one's horoscope, instead of believing in God's power, providence and blessings. Divinization (trying to foretell future events) and magic are also contrary to the First Commandment.

Irreligion: The First Commandment also warns us not to accept a religion or philosophy that teaches that our life and well-being originate with or depend on anything other than the one true God. It warns us of the evil and enslaving consequences of placing too much trust in earthly goods, such

as money, influence, beauty or success. Ultimately, they will always disappoint and never be enough. Irreligion includes the acts and attitudes of tempting God, sacrilege and simony.

Tempting God consists in putting the divine goodness and power to the test—in other words, it asks God to "prove himself." That is exactly what the Tempter (Satan), the Devil, tried to deceive Jesus into doing. (Check out Luke 4:1–13.) Note that Satan tried to induce Jesus to throw himself down from the Temple and thus force God the Father to act to save him.

Sacrilege and simony are forms of tempting God. Sacrilege consists in profaning, stealing or treating unworthily something sacred. Simony is "the buying or selling of spiritual things which have God alone as their owner and master" (CCC, Glossary, "Simony"). The latter term comes from Simon the magician, who wanted to buy the spiritual power to "obtain God's gift" that he saw at work in the Apostles. (Check out Acts of the Apostles 8:9–25.) Even today people can be tempted to try to buy God's blessings with money; it doesn't work!

TALK IT OVER

- ◉ What are some ways that people can "test" God today?

Atheism: Atheism is "one of the most serious problems of our time, and one that deserves more thorough treatment" (*Pastoral Constitution on the Church in the Modern World*, no. 19). Atheists either do not perceive, or simply reject, that God exists. Others hear and have examined the question of God's existence conscientiously and yet cannot believe. The line between being unable and unwilling to believe is unclear.

Scripture teaches: "Fools say in their hearts, 'There is no God.' They are corrupt, they commit abominable acts; / there is no one who does good" (Psalm 53:1). Atheism easily leads to a world in which everything is relative; one opinion is as true and good as another. Such relativism leads to chaos and a loss of happiness. On the other hand, we must remember that faith is always God's gift that "comes from what is heard, and what is heard comes through the word of Christ" (Romans 10:17).

Agnosticism: Agnostics, unlike atheists, often admit to the existence of a transcendent being, but say that we cannot know anything about this being. Some agnostics make no judgment about God's existence; they simply declare that whether God exists is impossible to prove, or even to affirm or deny. Other agnostics are open to the question of God's existence, but are indifferent to it or are unwilling to grapple with it.

THINK, PAIR AND SHARE

- ☉ Discuss with a partner how each of the acts forbidden by the First Commandment might affect an individual's personal life.
- ☉ How might they affect a society and its citizens?

THE "NONES"

There are nearly 46 million people in America who claim to have no affiliation with religion. In addition to the 13 million atheists and agnostics, some 33 million Americans, most of whom are under thirty, say that they believe in God but they have no need to belong to an organized religion. They identify themselves as spiritual but not "religious." These young people have become known as the "Nones" because when they are asked to identify their religious affiliation, they check off "None."

The number of Nones in the United States of America has risen from about two percent in 1950 to over twenty percent in 2014. This reflects a similar trend among young people under thirty to be "much less involved in many of the main institutions of our society than previous younger generations were" (Robert Putnam, Harvard Professor). Putnam continues: "Even with these recent changes the American religious commitments are incredibly stronger than in most other advanced countries in the world."

Pope Francis has emphasized that faith is both a gift and a free response. Echoing the teaching of St. Paul that "faith comes from what is heard, and what is heard comes through the word of Christ" (Romans 10:17), Pope Francis extended a hand to those who do not belong to any religion. He invited them to join with believers to work for peace and protect the environment.

TALK IT OVER

- ☉ Who do you know who claims to belong to the Nones?
- ☉ What might you say to them about religious belief?

JOURNAL EXERCISE

- ☉ What wisdom have you discovered for your life from your study of the teachings of the Church in this chapter?
- ☉ Describe how that wisdom challenges you.

JUDGE AND ACT

REVIEW AND SHARE WHAT YOU HAVE LEARNED IN THIS CHAPTER

Look back over this chapter and reflect on the teachings of Scripture and Tradition on the nature of the Ten Commandments and the centrality of the First Commandment for one's moral life. Share the teachings of the Catholic Church on these statements:

- The Ten Commandments reveal the natural law.
- The Ten Commandments guide both individuals and the community of God's people in living a moral life.
- Worshiping and serving God alone is the true source of human freedom.
- Faith, hope and charity (love) empower us to live a moral life.

- The virtue of religion focuses our life on our relationship with God.
- Choosing not to obey the First Commandment is an abuse of freedom that leads into the slavery of sin.
- Jesus, the fulfillment of the Law and the Prophets, commands and teaches us to live the Commandments.

REFLECT AND DISCERN

- What wisdom have you learned from this chapter that can enrich your life and the lives of other people?
- How is obeying the First Commandment the best exercise of your freedom?

LEARN BY EXAMPLE

Moses, prophet of freedom and liberator

MOSES | CAST AFTER MICHELANGELO

Moses is one of the most commanding figures of the Hebrew Scriptures. Acting at God's behest, Moses led the Israelites out of

slavery, unleashed the ten plagues against Egypt, guided the freed Israelites for forty years in the wilderness, carried down the Ten Commandments on stone tablets from Mount Sinai and prepared the Israelites to enter the land of Canaan.

Moses was born during a time of political hostility between the Egyptians and the Israelites, whom Scripture also names the Hebrews. Pharaoh decreed that all male Hebrew infants were to be drowned at birth. Moses' mother and sister, whom Scripture does not name, desperate to save him from the Pharaoh's decree, put him in a basket and placed the basket among reeds in the Nile River. Hearing the crying child as she walked by, Pharaoh's daughter was filled with pity, adopted him as her own and raised him in the royal household. (Check out Exodus 2:1–10.)

As a young man Moses became outraged at seeing an Egyptian overseer beating a Hebrew slave, and he defended the Hebrew by killing the Egyptian. Soon after, Moses intervened again when two Hebrews were fighting (Check out Exodus 2:13). And when Pharaoh ordered him to be killed, Moses fled to the desert, where he would find safety with the Midianites, a nomadic tribe. While sitting near a well, Moses went to the defense of the seven daughters of Jethro, a Midianite priest, who had come to draw water from the well. The Midianites welcomed Moses; he married Zipporah, one of the daughters, and settled among the Midianites as a shepherd. (Check out Exodus 2:16–22).

The Pharaoh continued his oppression of the Hebrews. It was during this time that Moses took his flock to graze near Mount Horeb, the "mountain of God." While there, Moses heard the voice of God from the midst of a burning bush, whose fire was not consuming the bush. The voice, which identified itself as "the God of your fathers," commanded Moses to go back to Egypt. Moses resisted strenuously, but eventually he went off carrying the staff God had given him. Joined by his family, Moses began the journey back to Egypt and was met in the wilderness by his brother Aaron, who would speak to Pharaoh in his name.

Facing Pharaoh, Aaron spoke for Moses and made one simple, if revolutionary, demand of Pharaoh. He told him that God had commanded, "Let my people go, so that they may worship me" (Exodus 9:1). Pharaoh resisted over and over again; his heart became harder and harder. After suffering the devastation of ten plagues, Pharaoh freed the Israelites, and then Moses led them on their journey to freedom in the land God had promised them.

Amidst turmoil and dissent among the Israelites, Moses climbed Mount Sinai, where he prayed and encountered the very presence of God. He received the stone tablets on which the Ten Commandments were engraved and gave them to his people. The people received the Commandments as the laws for living the covenant. The closing words of the Book of Deuteronomy, the fifth

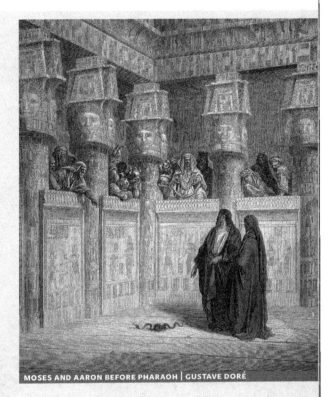

MOSES AND AARON BEFORE PHARAOH | GUSTAVE DORÉ

Aaron spoke for Moses, telling Pharaoh that God had commanded, "Let my people go"

book of the Pentateuch, summarize Moses' commitment to God and his people:

Never since has there arisen a prophet in Israel like Moses, whom the LORD knew face to face. He was unequalled for all the signs and wonders that the LORD sent him to perform in the land of Egypt, against Pharaoh and all his servants and his entire land, and for all the mighty deeds and all the terrifying displays of power that Moses performed in the sight of all Israel.
—Deuteronomy 34:10–12

TALK IT OVER

- Moses had a deep fidelity to God and to the commitment to fighting injustice, wherever he encountered it.
  - Trace the link between a commitment to fighting injustice and the Ten Commandments.
  - How might the Ten Commandments support your attempts to fight injustice today?
- As a prophet, Moses critiqued the oppressive status quo and offered a vision to the people, one that gave them the courage to strike out for freedom. From this chapter:
  - What vision of freedom do you support? How can you work toward that vision?
  - How can you give others energy for change toward true freedom?

SHARE FAITH WITH FAMILY AND FRIENDS

- With your family and/or friends, make a list of your favorite TV shows and the music you most enjoy. Rate the items, making your favorite the first item on the list.
- Evaluate the shows and songs on your list. Which items portray values and lifestyles that are in harmony with the Ten Commandments? Which items portray values and lifestyles that are contrary to the Ten Commandments?

JOURNAL EXERCISE

- Review the list you created for the "Share Faith with Family and Friends" exercise.
- Think about the injustice, sadness and exploitation that result from breaking the Commandments. How does your living the Commandments push back against such injustice, sadness and exploitation? Write your thoughts on this in your journal.

The Ten Commandments

1. I am the LORD your God: you shall not have strange gods before me.
2. You shall not take the name of the LORD your God in vain.
3. Remember to keep holy the LORD's day.
4. Honor your father and your mother.
5. You shall not kill.
6. You shall not commit adultery.
7. You shall not steal.
8. You shall not bear false witness against your neighbor.
9. You shall not covet your neighbor's wife.
10. You shall not covet your neighbor's goods.

Where the Spirit of the Lord is, there is freedom

All gather and form a circle.
Pray the Sign of the Cross together.

LEADER
Gracious God,
when the struggles of life hem us in on every side,
open us to the freedom your presence brings
so that we may see beyond every restriction,
every limit that binds us.
Send your Holy Spirit, for "where the Spirit of the
    Lord is, there is freedom" (2 Corinthians 3:17).
We make our prayer in the name of Jesus Christ,
who "for freedom Christ has set us free"
that we may "stand firm" and "not submit again
    to a yoke of slavery" (Galatians 5:1).

ALL
Amen.

READER
A reading from the holy Gospel according to
Matthew.

ALL
Glory to you, O Lord.

READER
Proclaim Matthew 6:25–33.
The Gospel of the Lord.

ALL
Praise to you, Lord Jesus Christ.

All reflect on how this teaching of Jesus helps us to
understand the meaning of the Ten Commandments.

LEADER
O God, give me the wisdom to see the subtle
    ways people can be enslaved
and the courage to speak for those who have no
    voice.
I ask this for the sake of your love.
O God, when we wake to yet another day of
    wonder and joy in the beauty of your creation,
give us the heart to keep our needs simple, our
    desires soft, our wills pliable,
so that we never participate in the exploitation of
    the earth, or in the oppression of other people.

ALL
Amen.

Pray the Sign of the Cross together.

CHAPTER 6

Love the Lord your God

—The Second and Third Commandments

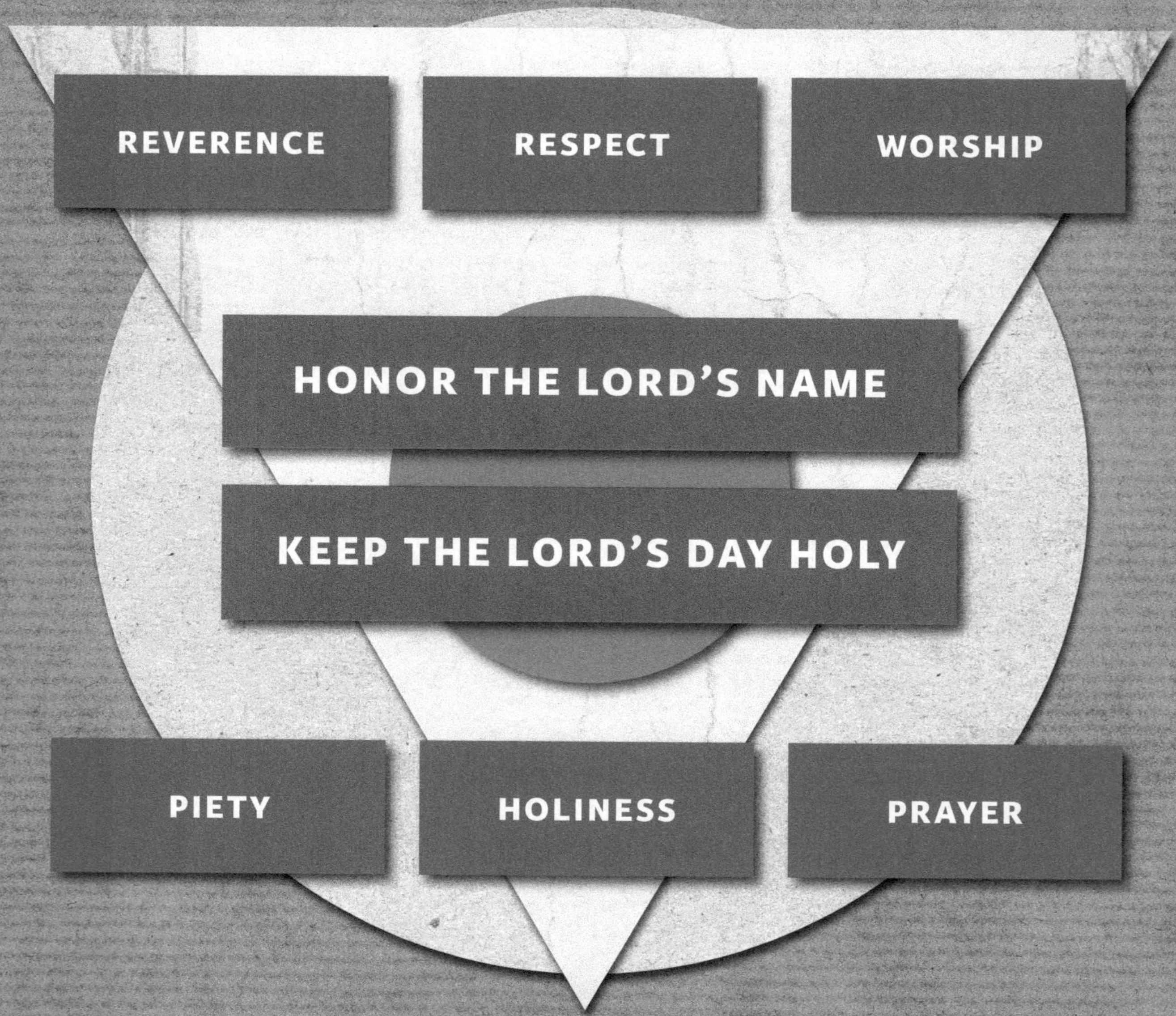

REVERENCE
RESPECT
WORSHIP
HONOR THE LORD'S NAME
KEEP THE LORD'S DAY HOLY
PIETY
HOLINESS
PRAYER

THE FIRST THREE OF THE TEN COMMANDMENTS ARE THE guideposts to living the first part of the Great Commandment: "You shall love the LORD your God with all your heart, and with all your soul, and with all your might" (Deuteronomy 6:5). In this chapter we explore the teachings of the Catholic Church on the Second Commandment, "You shall not take the name of the LORD your God in vain," and the Third Commandment, "Remember to keep holy the LORD's Day." We learn in detail how these two Commandments guide us in keeping God at the center of all that we say and do.

GOD REVEALED HIMSELF GRADUALLY OVER TIME AND UNDER DIFFERENT NAMES

JEWS CELEBRATE THE COMPLETION OF CREATION ON SATURDAY, THE JEWISH SABBATH

CHRISTIANS CELEBRATE THE RESURRECTION OF JESUS ON SUNDAY, THE LORD'S DAY

Faith Focus: These teachings are the primary focus of the doctrinal content presented in this chapter:
- ⊙ Scripture contains divine names God has revealed.
- ⊙ The name of God stands for God himself.
- ⊙ We are to show respect and reverence for the name of God, of Jesus, of Mary and of the saints.
- ⊙ Blasphemy, false promises and false oaths are acts contrary to the Second Commandment.
- ⊙ We are to keep the Lord's Day holy.
- ⊙ Christians fulfill the Third Commandment on Sunday, the day of the Lord's Resurrection.
- ⊙ The precepts of the Church contain the minimal obligation of Catholics to fulfill the Third Commandment.

Discipleship Formation: As a result of studying this chapter you should be better able to:
- ⊙ identify and choose a divine name by which you address God and come to know him more deeply;
- ⊙ reflect on your use of the holy names of God, Jesus, Mary and the saints and commit to using them with reverence and respect;
- ⊙ appreciate the importance of participating in the celebration of Mass on Sundays and holy days of obligation;
- ⊙ grow as a person of prayer.

Scripture References:
OLD TESTAMENT: **Genesis** 2:2–3, 17:1–8, 32:24–30; **Exodus** 3:6 and 13–15, 20:8, 11, 33:18–20, 34:5–6 and 9; **Deuteronomy** 5:12–15, 6:4–5; **Ruth** 1:16; **Psalms** 8:1, 29:2 102:26–27, 115:1, 118:24, 26–27, 119:160, 135:1–3, 138:1–2; **Proverbs** 22:1; **Ecclesiastes** 7:1; **Wisdom** 13:1–9; **Isaiah** 1:1–3, 2:1–4, 30:18, 44:6, 61:8; **Jeremiah** 7:5–7
NEW TESTAMENT: **Matthew** 1:18–24, 21 and 23, 3:16–17, 5:33–34, 15:22, 18:19–20, 28:19, 20; **Mark** 2:23–28; **Luke** 1:26–34 and 42, 2:11, 21 and 49, 3:21, 4:16–21, 5:16, 6:12, 9:18–20 and 28, 10:21–23, 11:1–2, 13:10–17, 22:32 and 41 23:34 and 43; **John** 6:35, 8:12, 10:9 and 11, 11:2–3 and 25–26, 14:6 and 15–17, 15:5, 16:6–7, 17:21–23, 18:37; **Acts** the Apostles 2:42–46, 7:59; **Romans** 1:4, **1 Corinthian** 11:17; **2 Corinthians** 1:23; **1 Thessalonians** 2:19, 5:16–18 **Ephesians** 1:9, 2:4; **Philippians** 2:5–11; **1 John** 1:5, 10, 4 5:20; **Hebrews** 10:24–25; **James** 1:17

Faith Glossary: Familiarize yourself with the meaning of these key terms in the Glossary: **blasphemy, holin holy days of obligation, Jesus (name), Lord's Day, perjury, piety, prayer, precepts of the Church, rever Sabbath, theophany, YHWH**

Faith Word: Sabbath
Learn by Heart: Deuteronomy 6:4–5
Learn by Example: St. Ignatius of Loyola

What does a name tell us?

Imagine you are setting up a business. From the start you want people to know that your business is trustworthy and reliable. In marketing language, you want to "brand" your business. You want to set it apart! You want the name to attract customers so that they will remember it and come back to it.

OPENING CONVERSATION

⊙ What company or product brand names attract you? Why is that?

⊙ What brand names do you deliberately avoid buying or using? Why is that?

OVER TO YOU

Many people have nicknames. A nickname can be similar to a brand name.

⊙ If you could give yourself a nickname, what would it be?

⊙ What would you want your nickname to tell others about you; in other words, how might it brand you?

THE SIGNIFICANCE OF NAMES

Your name identifies you in many ways. When someone hears your name, it brings to their mind the memories and impressions, both good and bad, that they have of the person that is "you." They have come to know you by how you have revealed yourself to them through your words and actions. These memories, in turn, evoke a wide variety of feelings—some good and perhaps some not so good.

For the people of Ancient Israel the name of a person had a particular significance. Oftentimes, personal names expressed some personal characteristic, some incident connected with the person's birth, some hope, desire or wish of the parents. In Sacred Scripture a person's name also often identified the vocation God was calling the person to in order that they might play their part in bringing about God's will for his people. Let's take a look at several key figures from Scripture and how their names point to the role God willed them to have in the divine plan for all humanity:

⊙ **Abraham:** The Hebrew name *Abram* means "exalted father." God had chosen Abram to be the exalted father whose descendants would become the People of God. God changed Abram's name to *Abraham*, which means "father of many." (Check out Genesis 17:1–8.)

⊙ **Israel:** The Hebrew name *Israel* means "let God (El) rule." Israel is the name given to Jacob, the son of Isaac and Rebekah, as a result of his wrestling with God at Penuel. (Check out Genesis 32:24–30.) The twelve sons of Israel (or the sons of Jacob) would be the leaders of the twelve tribes of the People of God. Hence, the name Israelites. Through the twelve tribes of Israel, God would bring about his will for "many" nations.

- **Ruth:** The Hebrew name *Ruth* means "friend," in particular, "lady friend." Naomi, an Israelite, had emigrated to Moab with her husband and two sons during a famine. Ruth, a Moabite, married one of Naomi's sons, and after he died Naomi wished to return to Bethlehem. Ruth refused to abandon Naomi, saying, "Do not press me to leave you / or to turn back from following you! // Where you go, I will go; / where you lodge, I will lodge; // your people shall be my people, / and your God my God" (Ruth 1:16). Ruth left Moab, went to Bethlehem with Naomi, and eventually married Boaz. Their son, Obed, was the grandfather of King David. Ruth's compassion, generosity and fidelity to Naomi are seen as signs pointing to the compassion, generosity and fidelity of God among his people.

- **Isaiah:** The Hebrew name *Isaiah* means "God is salvation." Isaiah lived in Jerusalem in the late eighth century before the birth of Christ. It was a time when the Israelites were recovering from the Assyrians' deportation of many Israelites to live in captivity. God called Isaiah to preach a message of liberation and hope to his people despite their infidelity to and rebellion against him. (Check out Isaiah 1:1–3 and 2:1–4.)

- **Mary:** The name *Mary*, which means "beloved" in Egyptian, is derived from the Hebrew name *Miriam*, whose meaning is disputed. Mary, the mother of Jesus, is beloved of God. All the women of faith named in the Old Testament prefigure Mary. The Catholic Church continues to honor Mary and acknowledge her singular graces and role in God's plan. Catholics have a special devotion to Mary. We honor Mary daily as we pray the Hail Mary and repeat the greeting of her relative Elizabeth, "Blessed are you among women . . . " (Luke 1:42).

THINK, PAIR AND SHARE

- Work with a partner. Think about the names described above.
- Share how these names help you come to know God and his saving and liberating work.

ISAIAH | PIAZZA DI SPAGNA, ROME, ITALY

God called Isaiah to preach a message of liberation and hope to his people

- At their Baptism, many Catholics are given the name of a saint. In light of the above discussion, what is the meaning of this tradition?

FROM THE CATECHISM

Among all the words of Revelation, there is one which is unique: the revealed name of God. God confides his name to those who believe in him; he reveals himself to them in his personal mystery. The gift of a name belongs to the order of trust and intimacy. "The Lord's name is holy." For this reason man must not abuse it.

—*Catechism of the Catholic Church* (CCC), no. 2143

THE YAHWEH TETRAGRAMMATON | ST. CHARLES'S CHURCH, VIENNA, AUSTRIA

GOD REVEALS HIS NAME(S)

How do you greet someone whom you wish to know better? Most often, we say something like, "My name is _____. What is yours?" Hearing someone's name is the first step in coming to know a person; it is the first step of entering a relationship with a person. It is true that we can come to know God—that he exists—from the use of our reason or from reflecting on creation. But God wanted us to know him more intimately, in ways that we could never come to on our own. God wanted us to know him "personally" and address him by name.

Gradually and over time God revealed himself by making his name known. "A name expresses a person's essence and identity and the meaning of this person's life. God has a name; he is not an anonymous force. To disclose one's name is to make oneself known to others; in a way it is to hand oneself over by becoming accessible, capable of being known more intimately and addressed personally" (CCC, no. 203).

God has used different names to help us come to know him and his relationship with us. No one name can ever fully capture the complete identity of God. God is the Mystery who is beyond the full comprehension of our finite minds and hearts. Let us take a look at two of the names that God has revealed. The first is Yнwн, the name God revealed to Moses and to the people of Ancient Israel; the second is Jesus, the name God gave to his only Son who took on flesh and lived among us.

YHWH: The name that God revealed to Moses in the theophany of the burning bush is fundamental to our understanding of who God is. The word "theophany" comes from the Greek words *theos* (God) and *phaneia* (appearance). A theophany is "a revelation or visible appearance of God" (CCC, Glossary, "Theophany"). God appeared to Moses and identified himself, saying, "I am the God of your father, the God of Abraham, the God of Isaac, and the God of Jacob" (Exodus 3:6). God identified himself to be the God who has been with his people from the beginning. He is the God who always remembers and keeps his promises to free his people. "He is the God who, from beyond space and time, can do this and wills to do it, the God who will put his almighty power to work for this plan" (CCC, no. 205). In the Book of Exodus we read:

Moses said to God, "If I come to the Israelites and say to them, 'The God of your ancestors has sent me to you,' and they ask me, 'What is his name?' what shall I say to them?" God said to Moses, "I am who I am." He said further, "Thus you shall say to the Israelites, 'I am has sent me to you.'" God also said to Moses, "Thus you shall say to the Israelites, 'The Lord, the God of your ancestors, the God of Abraham, the God of Isaac, and the God of Jacob, has sent me to you':

This is my name forever,
and this is my title for all
generations."

—Exodus 3:13–15

The Hebrew letters YHWH can be translated "I AM WHO I AM" or "I AM HE WHO IS" or "I AM WHOM I AM." The divine name YHWH "implies that a divine personal being has revealed Himself as the God of Israel through the covenant and the exodus" ("God" in John Mckenzie, S.J., *Dictionary of the Bible*). He is the God who makes himself close to us. (Check out Matthew 1:23, 28:20.)

PAUSE AND REFLECT
⊙ Reflect on those moments when you encounter God "close to you."

Jesus: The English name "Jesus" and the Spanish name *Jesús* are translations of the Hebrew and Aramaic name *Yeshua*, which means "YHWH is salvation." (Check out Matthew 1:21 and Luke 2:21.) Jesus, the Incarnate Son of God, most fully reveals the name and identity of God. He is Lord, a name the Israelites reserved for God. (Check out Matthew 15:22, Luke 2:11, John 11:3, Acts of the Apostles 7:59, Romans 1:4 and 1 Thessalonians 2:19.) He is "I AM" living among his people. (Check out the

seven "I am" statements in John's account of the Gospel and what they tell us about Jesus, about God: John 6:35, 8:12, 10:9, 10:11, 11:25–26, 14:6 and 15:5.) Jesus Christ reveals the saving and liberating work of God, who is always at work in the world. (Check out Philippians 2:5–11.)

READ, REFLECT AND SHARE
⊙ Work with a partner. Read and reflect on Matthew 1:18–24 and Luke 1:26–34.
⊙ What insights do the angel's words "you will name him Jesus" reveal about Jesus?

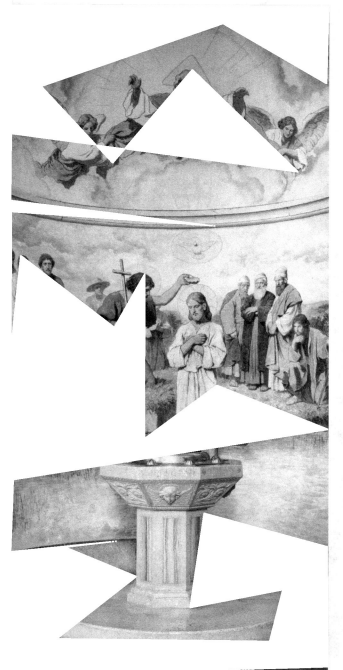

Father/Son/Holy Spirit: Jesus revealed that the name of the one God is Father, Son and Holy Spirit. The four accounts of the Gospel reveal the relationship binding Jesus, the Incarnate Son of God, with God the Father and God the Holy Spirit. Jesus is the beloved *Son* of God the *Father* upon whom the *Spirit of God* descended like a dove. (Check out Matthew 3:16–17 and Luke 4:18.) Jesus and the Father "are one" who will send the Holy Spirit. (Check out John 14:15–17, 16:6–7 and 17:21–23.) When Jesus commissioned the Apostles to baptize all nations, he told them to baptize in the name of God—"in the name of the Father and of the Son and of the Holy Spirit" (Matthew 28:19). The Church has come to understand this Revelation to mean that the Father and the Son and the Holy Spirit are consubstantial, that is, the Three Persons share one divine nature. The divine oneness is expressed in the perfect love of the Three Persons of the Trinity for each other. (Check out 1 John 4:8, 16.). There is one God in Three Divine Persons who are distinct but inseparable from one another. Jesus has fully revealed the God who first revealed himself to Abraham and Moses to be the Holy Trinity.

LET'S PROBE DEEPER: SCRIPTURE ACTIVITY

God revealed himself gradually over time and "under different names" (CCC, no. 204).

- ◉ Work with a partner. Look up all or some of these passages: Exodus 33:18–20, 34:5–6 and 9; Psalms 102:26–27, 119:160, 138:1-2; Wisdom 13:1–9; Isaiah 44:6; John 18:37; Ephesians 2:4; 1 John 1:5, 4:8, 5:20; James 1:17.
- ◉ What names for God are revealed in these passages? What do these names reveal about God?

OVER TO YOU

- ◉ What name or names do you use to address God? Why is that?
- ◉ Spend a few moments in prayerful conversation with God.

"You shall not take the name of the LORD, your God, in vain"

Sadly, name-calling is a common practice. For example, listen to fans at a sports event. Disgruntled fans often yell out all sorts of names at players and referees alike. In short, they take someone's name in vain; they use it in a profane and disrespectful way. However, people also show great respect for and honor others by the way they use their names.

OPENING REFLECTION

- ◉ Reflect on times when someone has used your name to honor you, and also on times when someone has used your name in vain, in a disrespectful way. Why did they do so? What does the way the person used your name say about how they value their relationship with you?
- ◉ Now reflect on situations when you may have used someone's name to honor them or when you might have taken someone's name in vain. Why did you do so? What does that say about how you value your relationship with that person?
- ◉ What wisdom for your life did you learn from those situations?

FROM THE CATECHISM

The second commandment *prescribes respect for the Lord's name.* Like the first commandment, it belongs to the virtue of religion and more particularly it governs our use of speech in sacred matters.

—CCC, no. 2142

"O LORD, OUR SOVEREIGN, HOW MAJESTIC IS YOUR NAME IN ALL THE EARTH!" (PSALM 8:1)

The Second Commandment tells us in a fundamental way how we are to live out the faith we profess in the First Commandment. The Second Commandment speaks to the profound respect and **reverence** we are to have and to show for God himself. The virtue of reverence is an expression of **piety**, which is "one of the seven gifts of the Holy Spirit which leads one to devotion to God" (CCC, Glossary, "Piety"). Reverence "trains us to know and to preserve the difference between the Creator and the creature. Respect for God's name keeps us from reducing him to a mere fact, or even a thing that we can control or manipulate" (*United States Catholic Catechism for Adults* [USCCA], 353). As we would cherish the name of a person whom we love, all the more do we cherish the name of God.

For the ancient Israelites, the name of God was inseparable from God himself. They never spoke or wrote the divine name that God had revealed to Moses. In its place they most often used ADONAI, or LORD. We find a wonderful model of such usage in the Psalms. The psalmist declares:

THE CHURCH OF THE *PATER NOSTER*, JERUSALEM, IS DECORATED WITH THE 'OUR FATHER' IN OVER 100 DIFFERENT LANGUAGES

Ascribe to the LORD the glory of his name;
   worship the LORD in holy splendor.

              —Psalm 29:2

Not to us, O LORD, not to us, but to your name
     give glory,
   for the sake of your steadfast love and your
     faithfulness.

            —Psalm 115:1

Praise the LORD!
   Praise the name of the LORD;
    give praise, O servants of the LORD,
you that stand in the house of the LORD,
   in the courts of the house of our God.
Praise the LORD, for the LORD is good;
   sing to his name, for he is gracious.

           —Psalm 135:1–3

The ancient Israelites had a profound reverence for the name that God had revealed for himself. Jews today continue to show that same reverence for the holy name of God, which they often write G—D.

We see this profound awe and reverence for the holiness of the name of God in Jesus' reply to his disciples. When his disciples asked him to teach them to pray, Jesus said, "When you pray, say: / Father, hallowed be your name. / Your kingdom come" (Luke 11:2). God alone is the Holy, or Hallowed, One. The name of God is hallowed, or holy, as God is holy.

God, the source of all holiness, creates us to live in holiness and to strive for holiness of life—to live a life of friendship in communion with him. "Asking the Father that his name be made holy draws us into his plan of loving kindness for the fullness of time, 'according to his purpose which he set forth in Christ,' that we might 'be holy and blameless before him in love' [Ephesians 1:9, 4]" (CCC, no. 2807).

TALK IT OVER

- All people have the vocation to strive for holiness of life. In light of the above discussion, what does that really mean? What might be some signs that a person is striving to live a life of holiness?
- What insights does the Second Commandment give us?

THE HOLY NAME OF JESUS

Jesus is the Incarnate Son of God. He is the Word of God who took on flesh, lived, died and was buried, and rose from the dead among us. Christians have a profound reverence for the name Jesus. We have the same honor and respect for the name of Jesus that we have for the name of God. One way Catholics show this reverence is by slightly bowing our head when we speak or hear the name Jesus.

Our reverence for the name Jesus is an expression of our belief that Jesus is God. St. Paul passed on this faith of the Apostolic Church. He taught:

> Therefore God also highly exalted him
> and gave him the name
> that is above every name,
> so that at the name of Jesus
> every knee should bend,
> in heaven and on earth and under
> the earth,
> and every tongue should confess
> that Jesus Christ is Lord,
> to the glory of God the Father.
> —Philippians 2:9–11

Jesus Christ is the Son of God, the Second Divine Person of the Holy Trinity. In the Nicene Creed we pray, in part:

> I believe in one Lord Jesus Christ,
> the Only Begotten Son of God,
> born of the Father before all ages. . . .
> For us men and for our salvation
> he came down from heaven,
> and by the Holy Spirit was incarnate
> of the Virgin Mary,
> and became man.
> —*The Roman Missal*

When Christians speak, write and even think of the divine name(s), we are addressing God himself. We enter conversation with God and experience communion with him. Our reverence and awe for God moves us to bless, praise and glorify God and to thank him for all that is associated with him. This moves us to honor and respect the name of Mary and of the other saints, and all people, places and things associated with God and our worship of him. Veneration of Mary and the other saints and praying through them is not contrary to either the First or the Second Commandment. The veneration of the saints and sacred images is based on the mystery of the Incarnation of the Word of God. They remind us of the holiness of God and the holiness of life that God calls us to live.

TALK IT OVER

- Name and describe the ways you and other Christians honor the holy name of God. Of Jesus. Of Mary and the other saints.
- Have you encountered people using the name of God or Jesus profanely? How did you respond? Why did you respond the way you did?

ACTS THAT SHOW LACK OF REVERENCE FOR THE DIVINE NAME

The Lord God's name is holy. The Second Commandment "enjoins respect for the Lord's name" (CCC, no. 2161) and forbids the abuse of the names of God or Jesus Christ, as well as those of Mary and the other saints. We must be ever careful even in casual speech not to use God's name in vain. Let us take a look at three ways we might abuse the name of God:

Blasphemy: Blasphemy is a direct offense to God himself. It is an act of putting oneself before God; it is an act of denying our true relationship with God. **Blasphemy** is "[s]peech, thought, or action involving contempt for God or the Church, or persons or things dedicated to God" (CCC, Glossary, "Blasphemy"). This sin "consists in uttering against God—inwardly or outwardly— words of hatred, reproach, or defiance; in speaking ill of God; in failing in respect toward him in one's speech; in misusing God's name. . . . It is also blasphemous to make use of God's name to cover up criminal practices, to reduce peoples to servitude, to torture persons or put them to death" (CCC, no. 2148). Pope Francis, when he was Cardinal Archbishop of Buenos Aires, said: "To kill in the name of God is blasphemy" (*On Heaven and Earth*). God creates all people in his image and likeness. To kill any person in the name of God shows contempt for God and is blasphemy. This is a truth that we need to heed.

Promises: You have no doubt made a promise or two. When people make a promise, they sometimes "seal the promise" by saying, "I give you my word." Of course, giving one's word is much more than that; it is giving one's entire self as a guarantee of the promise. Promises are sometimes made in God's name. People sometimes use such expressions as, "I promise in the name of God." By so doing they are calling on God to be the guarantor of the promise. They are calling on God to be the witness that they will keep their promise. "To be unfaithful to [promises made in God's name or in the name of Jesus] is to misuse God's name and in some way make God out to be a liar [see 1 John 1:10]" (CCC, no. 2147).

Oaths: An oath "is the invocation of the divine Name as witness to the truth" (*Code of Canon Law* [CIC], canon 1199). As Creator and Lord, God is the norm of all truth. An oath highlights our trust in God when it is truthful and legitimate. A false oath calls on God to be witness to a lie. A person commits perjury when he or she lies under oath. **Perjury** is "[g]iving one's word under oath falsely, or making a promise under oath without

The Divine Praises

An Italian Jesuit priest, Luigi Felici, wrote the Divine Praises at the end of the eighteenth century. He wrote the prayer to make reparation for blasphemy and the profane use of the name of God. Today, the Church prays the Divine Praises at the conclusion of Benediction of the Blessed Sacrament. These four acclamations are included in the Divine Praises the Church prays:

> Blessed be God.
> Blessed be his holy name.
> Blessed be the name of Jesus.
> Blessed be the name of Mary, Virgin and Mother.

You can find the full text of the Divine Praises in the "Catholic Prayers, Devotions and Practices" section of this text.

intending to keep it" (CCC, Glossary, "Perjury"). Perjury violates both the Second Commandment and the Eighth Commandment, "You shall not bear false witness against your neighbor."

When an oath is required by an unjust or illegitimate authority, it may be refused. (Recall the story of St. Thomas More from chapter 3 of this text.) In fact, an oath that is contrary to or harms the dignity of another person or persons must be refused.

REFLECT AND DISCUSS
- ⊙ Why is it a serious matter to swear an oath?
- ⊙ Describe a situation when it would be right and proper to take an oath.
- ⊙ Describe a situation when it would be wrong to take an oath.
- ⊙ In what sorts of ways do you think people take the name of God the Father or Jesus in vain? What is wrong with doing this? Is there anything you need to change about the way in which you use God's name?

LET'S PROBE DEEPER
In the Sermon on the Mount Jesus taught: "Again you have heard that it was said to those of ancient times, 'You shall not swear falsely, but carry out the vows you have made to the Lord.' But I say to you, Do not swear at all" (Matthew 5:33–34). This teaching of Jesus emphasizes the centrality of the Second Commandment and the Eighth Commandment to our relationship with God, with individuals and with the communities of which we are members.

The Tradition of the Church has understood Jesus' words as allowing oaths made in truth and for grave and right reasons. For example, St. Paul calls on God as witness in his dealings with the Church in Corinth. Paul writes: "I call on God as witness against me" (2 Corinthians 1:23).

TALK IT OVER
- ⊙ What wisdom does the Second Commandment offer for growing in our relationship with God and for building strong and healthy relationships with people?
- ⊙ How does living the Second Commandment contribute to building a just society?

WHAT ABOUT YOU PERSONALLY?
- ⊙ How clearly does your use of the name "God" show your reverence for God? What does it say about how you value your relationship with God?
- ⊙ How clearly does your use of the name "Jesus" show your reverence for Jesus? What does it say about how you value your relationship with Jesus?

"Remember to keep holy the LORD's Day"

describe God creating the earth, then filling it with plants and animals and forming it into a dazzlingly beautiful home for the crown of his creation, human beings, in six days. Genesis then tells us: "And on the seventh day God finished the work that he had done, and he rested on the seventh day from all the work that he had done. So God blessed the seventh day and hallowed it" (Genesis 2:2–3). The word "hallowed" means "made holy." God set the seventh day apart from the first six days of creation as holy time.

The biblical account of God resting on the seventh day of creation is the origin of Israel's keeping the seventh day of the week as the **Sabbath**. The Book of Exodus' account of Moses receiving the Ten Commandments refers to Genesis: "For in six days the LORD made heaven and earth, the sea, and all that is in them, but rested the seventh day; therefore the LORD blessed the sabbath day and consecrated it" (Exodus 20:11).

The Hebrew word *shabbath* can mean "end," "cease" or "rest"; and the word *consecrate* means "to set aside for a holy purpose." As God the Creator did, so God's people were to do. The Israelites were to cease from their work. They were to rest and set aside the seventh day of each week for a holy purpose.

Taking time out is a valuable strategy that gives us an opportunity to focus on our priorities. For example, a team takes time out to assess where they are at in a game or to make adjustments so they can better implement their game plan. Students take time out to clear their heads and refocus as they prepare for exams. Christians take time out at the end of the day to "examen" the day—they give thanks to God and ask for his grace to do better in the future. Some people take time out by going on retreat, so that they can give some focused time to rest with God and talk about their relationship with him.

OPENING REFLECTION

- ⊙ There are many other ways people take time out. When have you taken time out?
- ⊙ Why did you take time out? Describe how your taking time out helped you.
- ⊙ Why is it necessary to take time out and reflect on our faith journey?

THE SABBATH DAY

The opening chapters of the Book of Genesis

Observe the sabbath day and keep it holy, as the LORD your God commanded you. Six days you shall labor and do all your work. But the seventh day is a sabbath to the LORD your God; you shall not do any work—you, or your son or your daughter, or your male or female slave, or your ox or your donkey, or any of your livestock, or the resident alien in your towns, so that your male and female slave may rest as well as you. Remember that you were a slave in the land of Egypt, and the LORD your God brought you out from there with a mighty hand and an outstretched arm; therefore the LORD your God commanded you to keep the sabbath day.

—Deuteronomy 5:12–15

FAITH WORD

Sabbath

In Scripture, the Sabbath was the seventh day of the week that the people of Ancient Israel were to keep holy by praising God for the creation and the covenant and by resting from their ordinary work. For Christians, the observance of the Sabbath has been transferred to Sunday, the day of the Lord's Resurrection.

—USCCA, 526

LET'S PROBE DEEPER

Recall the extraordinary and liberating events in the history of the Israelites leading up to and surrounding Moses receiving the Ten Commandments: God freeing them from slavery in Egypt under the leadership of Moses; the miraculous parting of the Red Sea; manna from heaven feeding them in the wilderness; entering a covenant with them at Sinai.

There is an intimate connection between the people of Israel keeping the Sabbath day holy and these events. God had delivered them into freedom and established them as his people. He revealed the Commandments to help his people remember what he had already written in their hearts to guide them in living in freedom. Keeping the Sabbath day holy kept them centered on their covenant relationship with him and with one another. The Sabbath day was and continues to be a concrete sign of the nature of the irrevocable covenant binding God and his people.

TALK IT OVER

⊙ What might have been the value of the Israelites taking time out on the seventh day of each week and keeping it as the Sabbath?

⊙ What is the value of a sabbath, or time out, each week for Christians?

"REMEMBER THE SABBATH DAY, AND KEEP IT HOLY" (EXODUS 20:8)

God the Creator blessed and set the Sabbath aside for a holy purpose. That holy purpose is to *end* our week of work, to *cease* from our daily work, and to *rest* in God, the Holy One, so as to deepen our relationship with him. The holy purpose of the Sabbath is to order not only our work but our whole life to responding to his personal invitation and grace to live a life of holiness. We strengthen our efforts to reject all that tempts us away from striving for holiness of life, which is the "state of goodness in which a person . . . is freed from sin and evil" (USCCA, Glossary, "Holiness," 514).

The Sabbath is a day of total rest for everyone to acknowledge and honor God as the center of their life. All members of a household, as Deuteronomy clearly teaches, were to be given the opportunity to rest from their normal, routine

THE CHILDREN OF ISRAEL CROSSING THE RED SEA | 15TH-CENTURY GERMAN BIBLE

work—even servants, guests and animals—and consciously to turn to God, to the things of God, and offer him worship. By keeping the Sabbath holy the Israelites gave witness to their faith that ultimately everything depends on God—and not on human efforts and work.

TALK IT OVER
- ⊙ What difference does keeping the Sabbath holy make to the life of all human beings?
- ⊙ Describe ways in which people can faithfully keep the Sabbath.

THE WISDOM OF JESUS ON THE TRUE MEANING OF SABBATH LAW

In Jesus' time there were numerous laws detailing the celebration of the sabbath commandment. There were so many laws that the wisdom and life-giving and liberating meaning of the Sabbath was blurred—and sometimes even lost. For example, there were thirty-nine types of work prohibited by sabbath laws. These laws also contained such restrictions as limiting a Jew from walking more than 300 feet from their home on the Sabbath. The legalistic observance of the Sabbath became a source of dispute between Jesus and the Pharisees, who taught and demanded the rigorous observance of all the sabbath laws.

The four accounts of the Gospel give several accounts of Jesus celebrating and teaching on the Sabbath. We will now look at three of those accounts, namely, Luke 4:16–21, Mark 2:23–28 and Luke 13:10–17.

Luke 4:16–21: After his baptism, Jesus returned to Nazareth and "went to the synagogue on the sabbath day, as was his custom" (Luke 4:16). The Greek word *synagogue* means "assembly." In Jesus' time Jews gathered in the synagogue for the reading of their Scriptures, for studying the Law and the Prophets and for worship and prayer. Sacrifice, however, was reserved for the Temple in Jerusalem.

Mark 2:23–28: In this passage a group of Pharisees confront Jesus as his disciples are "plucking heads of grain" to eat on the Sabbath, and they accuse his disciples of breaking a sabbath law. Their accusation, of course, implies that Jesus, a teacher of the Law, should know better and should—as any good rabbi

JESUS' DISCIPLES PLUCK CORN ON THE SABBATH | JAN LUYKEN

would do—not have allowed his disciples to engage in this unlawful work.

Jesus rejects their interpretation and teaches: "The sabbath was made for humankind, and not humankind for the sabbath" (Mark 2:27). In other words, while the plucking of grain to feed oneself when one is hungry is a technical violation of one of the many man-made sabbath laws, it is not a violation of the true purpose of the sabbath commandment. Jesus concludes his teaching with the declaration that he is teaching and acting with the authority of God: "The Son of Man is lord even of the sabbath" (Mark 2:28).

Luke 13:10–17: In this passage we read of a confrontation between Jesus and a leader of the synagogue. This time Jesus is healing a crippled woman on the Sabbath; and the leader of the synagogue, in speaking to the woman, accuses Jesus, "There are six days on which work ought to be done; come on those days and be cured, and not on the sabbath day" (Luke 13:14). Jesus responds, "You hypocrites! Does not each of you on the sabbath untie his ox or his donkey from the manger, and lead it away to give it water? And ought not this woman, a daughter of Abraham whom Satan bound for eighteen long years, be set free from this bondage on the sabbath day?" (Luke 13:15–16). Jesus' response teaches that helping people in need, even on the Sabbath, honors God. Such actions reveal the saving work of God among his people. Obeying the sabbath commandment *includes* spending time with the sick, in reflection and helping those in need. (Check out the teaching of the Catholic Church in CCC, no. 2186.)

Obeying the sabbath commandment includes spending time with the sick

⊙ Work with a partner to compare the similarities in all three passages. Discuss:
  – What is Jesus' common teaching in all three passages?
  – What is the meaning of Jesus' teaching for Christians today?

God the Savior, Jesus, taught the true meaning and spirit of the sabbath commandment. Obeying the Third Commandment enables us, as we have seen, to honor God with our whole lives. "The institution of Sunday helps all to be allowed sufficient rest and leisure to cultivate their familial, cultural, social and religious lives" (*Pastoral Constitution on the Church in the Modern World*, no. 67; quoted in CCC, no. 2194).

THINK, PAIR AND SHARE
⊙ Keep in mind the contexts of the three passages, namely:
  – Jesus kept the sabbath commandment;
  – There were many man-made laws hiding the true meaning of the sabbath commandment;
  – Jesus fulfilled and interpreted the true meaning of the sabbath commandment.

JOURNAL EXERCISE
⊙ Look forward to this coming weekend. Describe how the Third Commandment will guide you in shaping your activities.
⊙ Revisit this exercise weekly to help you prepare for your celebration of Sunday.

Love the Lord your God with your whole mind

OPENING CONVERSATION

◉ Create a "Sunday Profile." Describe a typical Sunday in the lives of Christian families that you know.

◉ How does your "Sunday Profile" match up with what you have learned in this chapter?

WHAT ABOUT YOU PERSONALLY?

◉ How do the activities that make up your typical Sunday match up with what you have learned both in this chapter and in your previous study of the Third Commandment?

FROM THE CATECHISM

Just as the seventh day or Sabbath completes the first creation, so the "eighth day," Sunday, the day of the week on which Jesus rose from the dead, is celebrated as the "holy day" by Christians—the day on which the "new creation" began.

—CCC, Glossary, "Sabbath"

THE LORD'S DAY

Christians pause and rest each week. While our Jewish brothers and sisters continue to keep the sabbath day holy on Saturday, Christians fulfill the Third Commandment on Sunday. Sunday is the **Lord's Day**, the day of the Lord's Resurrection. "The sabbath, which represented the completion of the first creation, has been replaced by Sunday, which recalls the new creation inaugurated by the Resurrection of Christ" (CCC, no. 2190). On the Lord's Day Christians remember and celebrate that Jesus, the Incarnate Son of God, liberated us from sin and death by his own dying and rising. Christians keep the Lord's Day holy in the true spirit of joy that we inherited from our Jewish ancestors in faith. We proclaim aloud with the psalmist:

This is the day that the LORD has made;
    let us rejoice and be glad in it. . . .

Blessed is the one who comes in the name of the
       LORD.
    We bless you from the house of the LORD.
The LORD is God,
    and he has given us light.
           —Psalm 118:24, 26–27

Christians rejoice on the Lord's Day and give adoration and blessing to God. We gather to praise and give thanks to God. We pray for ourselves and for others. In our prayer of adoration and blessing we honor God. We acknowledge the Holy Trinity to be our Creator, Savior and Sanctifier. We exalt God's greatness. We acknowledge God's invitation and respond to his grace to live in holiness, that is, in a life of communion and dialogue with him.

THE SUNDAY EUCHARIST

Christian life finds it nourishment in the Eucharist and the other sacraments. Sunday is a day of grace. On Sundays Catholics rest and respond to God's call to gather for the celebration of the Eucharist, which is "the source and summit of the Christian life" (*Dogmatic Constitution on the Church*, no. 11)" (CCC, no. 1324). Participating in the communal worship of God through the celebration of the Eucharist is "at the heart of the Church's life" (CCC, no. 2177). We refresh ourselves and are fed from the Table of the Word of God and the Table of the Eucharist. God nourishes us with his grace to attend to the importance of family, friends, taking good care of ourselves and of our relationship with him. This practice of the Church dates back to apostolic times. (Check out Acts of the Apostles 2:42–46 and 1 Corinthians 11:17.)

The Letter to the Hebrews addresses the worship of the early Church. The author's main point in this New Testament letter is that the sacrifice of Christ replaced the Old Testament worship in the Temple. In this letter we read:

And let us consider how to provoke one another to love and good deeds, not neglecting to meet together, as is the habit of some, but encouraging one another, and all the more as you see the Day approaching.

—Hebrews 10:24–25

Meeting together with your parish or other local Catholic Church community for the celebration of the Eucharist on Sundays is a serious responsibility. For Catholics, fulfilling this responsibility includes joining with other members of the Catholic Church for the celebration of Mass and refraining "from

engaging in work or activities that hinder the worship owed to God" (CCC, no. 2185). Keeping the Lord's Day holy is so vital to the Christian life, we are to avoid making unnecessary demands of others that prevent them from observing the Lord's Day. This responsibility, known as the "Sunday Obligation," is stated in the first and third precepts of the Church. The precepts of the Church are the "laws made by the Church that indicate basic requirements for her members" (USCCA, 524). They address the fundamental relationship uniting the moral life and the Liturgy of the Church.

THE PRECEPTS OF THE CHURCH AND THE THIRD COMMANDMENT

First precept: "The first precept ('You shall attend Mass on Sundays and on holy days of obligation and rest from servile labor') requires the faithful to sanctify the day commemorating the Resurrection of the Lord as well as the principal liturgical feasts honoring the mysteries of the Lord, the Blessed Virgin Mary, and the saints; in the first place, by participating in the Eucharistic celebration, in which the Christian community is gathered, and by resting from those works and activities which could impede such a sanctification of these days" (*Code of Canon Law* [CIC], canons 1246–1248).

Third precept: "The third precept ('You shall receive the sacrament of the Eucharist at least during the Easter season') guarantees as a minimum the reception of the Lord's Body and Blood in connection with the Paschal feasts, the origin and center of the Christian liturgy" (CIC, canon 920).

—CCC, no. 2042

The Catholic Church has made it all the more possible for us to fulfill these obligations. We can fulfill the Sunday Obligation to take part in the Eucharist by participating in the celebration of Mass on Saturday evening or on Sunday itself. Likewise we can fulfill our obligation to keep holy days of obligation holy by taking part in the celebration of Mass on the evening prior to the holy day or on the holy day itself. This pastoral practice is in keeping with the ancient Jewish tradition of beginning a day at sundown and ending a day on the evening of the following day. This obligation is a serious obligation. We can be excused from keeping it only for serious reasons such as illness, urgent family duties, or for fulfilling essential responsibilities in society, such as protecting members of the community, caring for the sick and so on.

Sins against the Third Commandment include: failing to keep the Lord's Day holy, missing Mass

on Sundays and holy days of obligation without sufficient reason, and failing to pray.

TALK IT OVER
- Why is fulfilling the Sunday Obligation vital to the life of a Catholic?
- What difference does it make for the life of a Catholic to fulfill this responsibility faithfully?
- What are the consequences of not fulfilling it faithfully?

FROM THE CATECHISM
Prayer and *Christian life* are *inseparable*, for they concern the same love and the same renunciation, proceeding from love; the same filial and loving conformity with the Father's plan of love; the same transforming union in the Holy Spirit who conforms us more and more to Christ Jesus; the same love for all men, the love with which Jesus has loved us.

—CCC, no. 2745

A PEOPLE OF PRAYER
The Third Commandment reveals that human beings are people of prayer. The Sunday Eucharist is the preeminent and central prayer of the Church. **Prayer** is a gift. God is always calling each person and the whole Church to encounter him in prayer. Just as it is necessary to spend quality time with a person to build a good and lasting relationship, the same is true of our relationship with God.

We come to the church as a people of prayer and leave the church nourished to be a people of prayer. Our praying is not to be limited to our participation in the celebration of Mass. Our life is to be a prayer. St. Paul taught: "Rejoice always, pray without ceasing, give thanks in all circumstances; for this is the will of God in Christ Jesus for you" (1 Thessalonians 5:16–18).

Praying without ceasing is vital to living the Great Commandment. It means uniting our prayers to good works and good works to our prayers. When we pray, we are more likely to fulfill both parts of the Great Commandment. Yes, right relationship with God, nourished through prayer, encourages us to love and care for one another; in the same way, our acts of love and kindness are a form of prayer.

Praying without ceasing means uniting our prayers to good works and good works to our prayers

READ, REFLECT AND SHARE
Jesus is our model for prayer. By both his preaching and the example of his life Jesus taught that prayer is essential to our daily life.
- Look up, read and reflect on these gospel passages: Luke 2:49; 3:21; 5:16; 6:12; 9:18–20, 28; 10:21–23; 11:1; 22:32, 41–44; 23:34, 43; and John 17.
- Discuss with a partner what these passages reveal to you about the prayer life of Jesus.
- Share how you think they can guide you in becoming a person of prayer?

JOURNAL EXERCISE
- Describe how St. Paul's teaching can guide you in structuring your daily activities.

JUDGE AND ACT

REVIEW AND SHARE WHAT YOU HAVE LEARNED IN THIS CHAPTER

Look back over this chapter and reflect on the teachings of Scripture and Tradition on the Second Commandment and the Third Commandment. Share the teachings of the Catholic Church on these statements:

- ⊙ God has revealed his name.
- ⊙ God and his name are one and the same.
- ⊙ We are to honor, reverence and respect the name of God, of Jesus, of Mary and of all the saints.
- ⊙ God the Creator blessed and set the Sabbath day aside for a holy purpose, to be a day of rest and grace.
- ⊙ Christians fulfill the Third Commandment on Sunday. Sunday is the Lord's Day, the day of the Lord's Resurrection.
- ⊙ The precepts of the Church state the minimal obligations of Catholics to fulfill the Third Commandment.
- ⊙ The Christian life is a life of prayer.
- ⊙ The Eucharist is the central prayer of the Church.

MEETING THE CHALLENGE OF CONTEMPORARY SOCIETY

Society in the United States of America and in other industrialized nations has undergone astonishing changes in recent decades. The daily lives of people are becoming busier and busier. Technological advances that once promised more leisure time now seem only to push us further into our work and our careers. Sometimes we end up feeling out of touch with our friends, our families, even with ourselves, with the world around us and, perhaps most of all, with God. If there ever was a need for "time away" from the hustle and bustle of daily work— for a real sabbath day —it is in our fast-paced contemporary culture.

REFLECT AND DISCERN

- ⊙ How do you experience the pace of life today?
- ⊙ What do you do or can you do to slow down, prioritize your time well and keep things in perspective?
- ⊙ Give some advice to yourself!

St. Ignatius of Loyola (1491–1556): Seeing God in everything

Ignatius of Loyola was born in 1491. He was one of thirteen children of a family of minor nobility in northern Spain. At the age of sixteen he was sent to serve as a page to Juan Velazquez, the treasurer of the kingdom of Castile. As a member of the Velazquez household, Ignatius was frequently at court and he developed a taste for all that it presented. He was much addicted to gambling, very contentious and not above engaging in sword fights on occasion. Indeed, we can safely say that, as a young man, Ignatius' life was not centered on God and living out the demands of the Great Commandment taught by Jesus. He was more motivated by ideals of courtly love, knighthood and doing heroic deeds—all to satisfy his own pride.

In 1521 Ignatius was gravely wounded in a battle with the French. While he was recuperating, he experienced a conversion. Reading the lives of Jesus and the saints aroused in him the desire to do great things; this time, not for himself or to satisfy his own ambitions, but for God. Ignatius realized that these feelings were clues to God's direction for his life.

Over the years, Ignatius became an expert in seeing God in all people and things and centering his life in and on God. He collected his insights, prayers and suggestions in the *Spiritual Exercises*, which is recognized by many as one of the most influential books on the spiritual life ever written. Perhaps Ignatius' most memorable insight was that the Triune God can be seen in everything—every day, every activity and every encounter. For example, when we study astronomy, zoology or quantum physics we can come to see the presence of God. With the eyes of faith, we can come to see God the Creator in the created order and in the life that surrounds us.

With a small group of friends, Ignatius Loyola founded the Society of Jesus, also known as the Jesuits. Over the centuries, many Christians have been touched by Ignatian spirituality and many people have benefited from the education Jesuits provide, which is deeply rooted in their spirituality.

Ignatius died in 1556 and was canonized by Pope Gregory XV in 1622. His legacy includes many Jesuit educational institutions worldwide. In the United States alone there are twenty-eight Jesuit colleges and universities and more than fifty high schools.

ST. IGNATIUS OF LOYOLA | PETER PAUL RUBENS

TALK IT OVER

- What wisdom from Ignatius could help you see the presence of God in your study of science, literature, history, music, art and other courses of study other than theology?
- How and why can these courses of study be a form of prayer?

SHARE FAITH WITH FAMILY AND FRIENDS

- Reflect on these words of wisdom from the Old Testament:
  - "A good name is to be chosen rather than great riches" (Proverbs 22:1)
  - "A good name is better than precious ointment" (Ecclesiastes 7:1)
- Share what your name means to you and why you consider it to be a good name. How do you honor your name?
- Talk together about how you try to keep the Lord's name holy, and how that expresses your love for God.

JUDGE AND DECIDE

- Sacred Scripture teaches that the God who revealed his name to us favors justice. For example, in the writings of the prophets we read:
  - "[T]he LORD is a God of justice" (Isaiah 30:18)
  - "For I the LORD love justice" (Isaiah 61:8)
  - "[I]f you truly act justly one with another, if you do not oppress the alien, the orphan, and the widow, . . . then I will dwell with you in this place" (Jeremiah 7:5–7).
- What do these teachings say to you about how you are to honor the name of God and worship him? Create a list.
- How do your words and actions match up with the items on the list? What can you do to be a living image of God the Creator, Savior and Sanctifier who is "a God of justice"?

LEARN BY HEART

"Hear, O Israel: The LORD is our God, the LORD alone. You shall love the LORD your God with all your heart, and with all your soul, and with all your might."

DEUTERONOMY 6:4–5

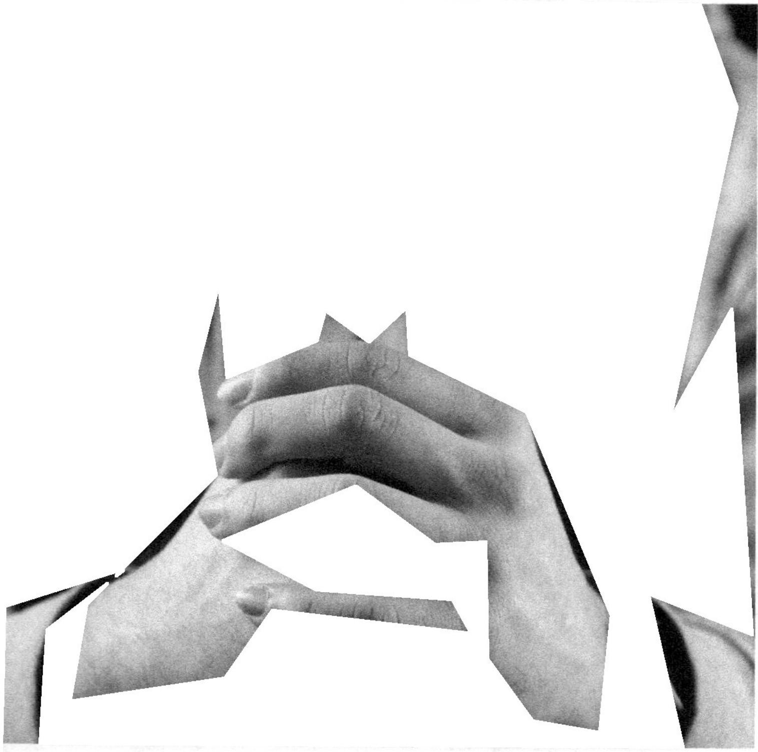

All gather in silence.

Opening Prayer

LEADER
In the name of the Father, and of the Son, and of the Holy Spirit.
ALL
Amen.

LEADER
God the Father has gathered us together in the name of his Son, Jesus.
Empowered with the grace of the Holy Spirit,
we praise the holy name of Jesus, the Incarnate Son of God,
who has promised to be with us when we gather in his name.

The Word of God

READER
A reading from the holy Gospel according to Matthew.
ALL
Glory to you, O Lord.

READER
Proclaim Matthew 18:19–20.
The Gospel of the Lord.
ALL
Praise to you, Lord Jesus Christ.

Response to the Word of God

READER (ALL)
Jesus, Son of the living God (have mercy on us)
Jesus, splendor of the Father (have mercy on us)
Jesus, dawn of justice (have mercy on us)
Jesus, Son of the Virgin Mary (have mercy on us)

THE GOOD SHEPHERD | ALL SAINTS' CHURCH, HAMPSHIRE, ENGLAND

Jesus, mighty God (have mercy on us)
Jesus, God of peace (have mercy on us)
Jesus, father of the poor (have mercy on us)
Jesus, Good Shepherd (have mercy on us)
Jesus, eternal wisdom (have mercy on us)
Jesus, our way and our life (have mercy on us)
By the mystery of your Incarnation (Jesus, save your people)
By your agony and crucifixion (Jesus, save your people)
By your death and burial (Jesus, save your people)
By your rising to new life (Jesus, save your people)
By your return in glory to the Father (Jesus, save your people)
By your gift of the Holy Eucharist (Jesus, save your people)
Lord Jesus, hear our prayer (Lord Jesus, hear our prayer)
—From *Litany of the Holy Name of Jesus*

LEADER
Let us pray.
Lord Jesus, God and Savior of all,
may we honor your holy name,
enjoy your, the Father's and the Holy Spirit's friendship in this life,
and be filled with eternal joy in the kingdom,
where you live and reign for ever and ever.
ALL
Amen.

CHAPTER 7

Honor Your Father and Your Mother

—The Fourth Commandment

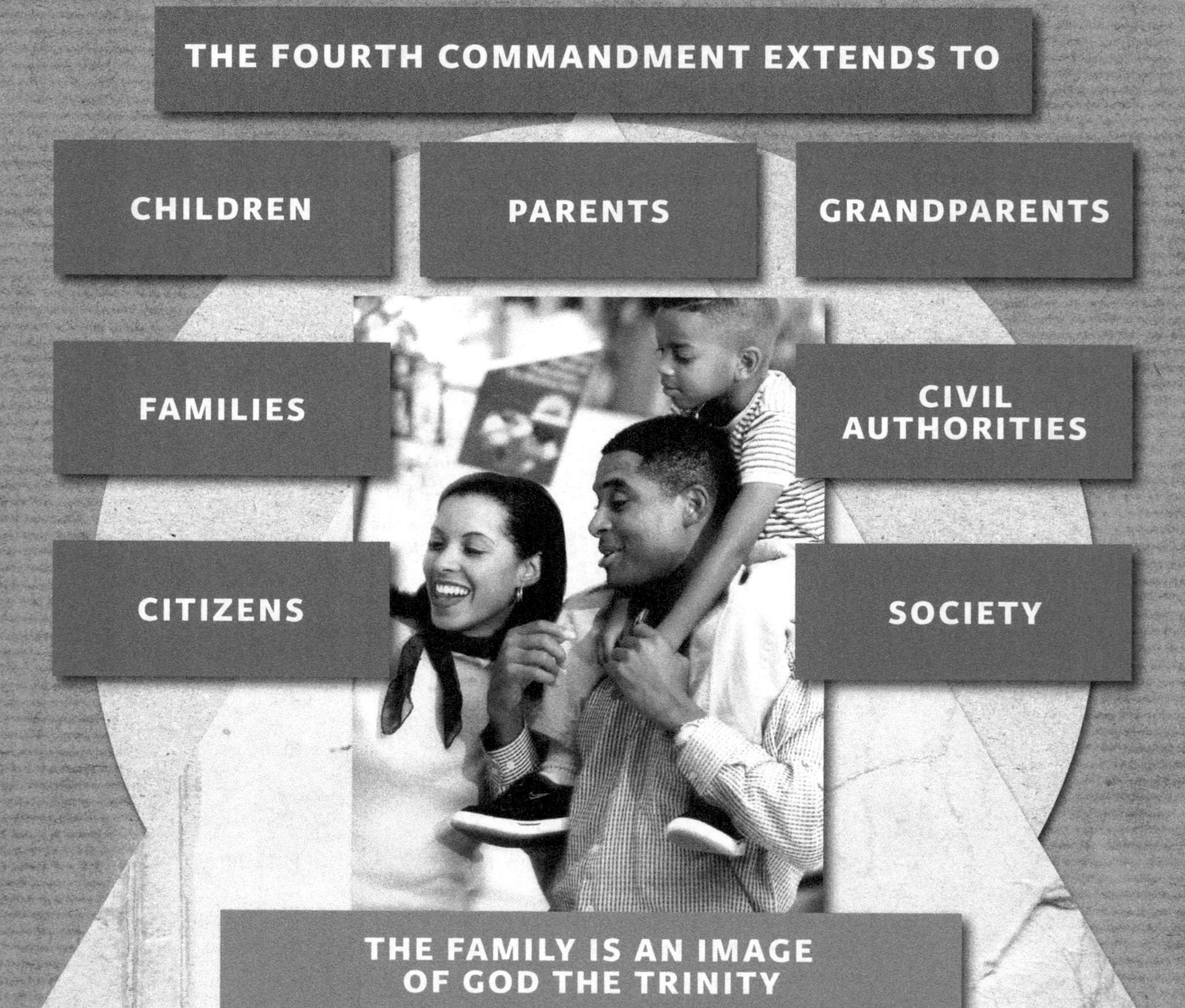
THE FOURTH COMMANDMENT EXTENDS TO
CHILDREN
PARENTS
GRANDPARENTS
FAMILIES
CIVIL AUTHORITIES
CITIZENS
SOCIETY
THE FAMILY IS AN IMAGE OF GOD THE TRINITY

ST. PAUL TAUGHT: "CHILDREN, . . . 'HONOR YOUR father and mother'—this is the first commandment with a promise: 'so that it may be well with you and you may live long on the earth'" (Ephesians 6:2–3). In this chapter we explore the teachings of the Catholic Church on the Fourth Commandment: "Honor your father and your mother." This Commandment addresses not only our relationships with our parents and family but also with all those who exercise legitimate authority over us.

CHILDREN OWE THEIR PARENTS:

RESPECT

GRATITUDE

JUST OBEDIENCE

ASSISTANCE

Faith Focus: These teachings are the primary focus of the doctrinal content presented in this chapter:

⊙ The family is the foundation of society.
⊙ The Christian family is an image of the communion of God, the Holy Trinity.
⊙ Children are to honor their parents; they are to show them respect and gratitude and obey and assist them.
⊙ Parents are to care for the bodily and spiritual needs of their children.
⊙ Civil authorities have the right and responsibility to promote the common good of all the citizens.
⊙ Citizens have the right and the duty to participate in the life of society.

Discipleship Formation: As a result of studying this chapter you should be better able to:

⊙ explore what it means for you and your family to be a living image of the Holy Trinity;
⊙ deepen your ownership of your duty and responsibility to show your parents respect and gratitude;
⊙ contribute to the well-being and harmony of the life of your family;
⊙ resist and speak up against those who exercise authority over you inappropriately and in ways that are contrary to God's law and civil law;
⊙ find the courage to speak up against unjust laws that are contrary to God's law;
⊙ meet your baptismal commitment to live as a "light to the world" in your home and local community.

Scripture References: These Scripture references are quoted or referred to in this chapter:

OLD TESTAMENT: **Genesis** 1:26, 27 and 31, 2:18; **Exodus** 2 **Leviticus** 25:35; **Ruth** 2:2–23; **Tobit** 4:5–11; **Psalm** 131:2–3 **Proverbs** 6:20–21, 31:8–9; **Sirach** 7:27–28; **Isaiah** 1:16–17 49:14–15, 66:13; **Jeremiah** 3:4–19; 22:1–16; **Hosea** 11:1–4 NEW TESTAMENT: **Matthew** 5:14–16, 12:50, 22:16–21, 25 39, 25:31–46; **Luke** 2:41–52, 16:1–13 and 19–31, 22:24–27 **John** 1:6–7, 10:1–18; **Acts of the Apostles** 4:32–35, 5:28 **Romans** 13:1–2; **2 Corinthians** 9:6–15; **Ephesians** 6:2–3 **1 Timothy** 2:1–2; **2 Timothy** 1:5; **James** 2:14–17; **1 Peter** 2:13–17; **1 John** 4:8

Faith Glossary: Familiarize yourself with the meaning of these key terms in the Glossary: **authority, civil disobedience, family, piety, solidarity**

Faith Words: family; solidarity
Learn by Heart: Ephesians 6:2–3
Learn by Example: St. Monica, mother of St. Augustine of Hippo

Why is "family" important?

A Parent's Love

Finding Nemo (Disney Pixar, 2003) is a tale that follows the eventful journeys of two fish, the overly cautious Marlin and his young son, Nemo. The fish are separated from each other in the Great Barrier Reef of Australia. Nemo ventures into the open sea, despite his father's constant warnings about many of the ocean's dangers. Nemo is then netted up and thrust into a fish tank in a dentist's office overlooking Sydney Harbor. Buoyed by the companionship of a friendly but forgetful fish named Dory, Marlin embarks on a dangerous

trek and finds himself the unlikely hero of an epic journey to rescue his son. Meanwhile, the young Nemo hatches a few daring plans of his own to return home safely.

OPENING CONVERSATION

- What is the attraction of the open sea for Nemo?
- What in the relationship between Marlin and Nemo reminds you of the relationships young people often have with their parents today?

Toward the end of *Finding Nemo* Dory gets caught in a fishing net among a school of grouper. Nemo convinces Marlin to let him attempt to save Dory by entering the net and directing the school to swim downward in order to break the net. The fish succeed and escape; and Marlin, Nemo and Dory return to their home at the reef. By now Marlin is no longer overprotective or doubtful of his son's safety. Nemo's brave but responsible actions show that he has learned to honor and respect the wisdom of his father.

WHAT ABOUT YOU PERSONALLY?

- How difficult is it for you to find wisdom in the advice of your parents?
- What is your initial response to your parents when their advice is contrary to what you want for yourself?

THE HUMAN FAMILY—IMAGE OF THE DIVINE FAMILY

We have often explored the meaning and significance of the teachings of Scripture and Tradition on the dignity of the human person. In the Book of Genesis we read that on the sixth day of creation:

God said, "Let us make [man] in our image, according to our likeness; . . ."
So God created [man] in his image,
in the image of God he created them;
male and female he created them. . . .
God saw everything that he had made, and indeed, it was very good.

—Genesis 1:26, 27, 31

The Church passes on this Revelation on the identity and dignity of the human person: "The divine image is present in every man. It shines forth in the communion of persons, in the likeness of the unity of the divine persons among themselves" (*Catechism of the Catholic Church* [CCC], no. 1702).

We often equate God the Creator with God the Father and "attribute" the divine work of creation to God the Father. For example, in the Apostles' Creed we profess, "I believe in God, / the Father almighty, / Creator of heaven and earth." In the Nicene Creed we profess, "I believe in one God, / the Father almighty, / maker of heaven and earth, / of all things visible and invisible."

Christians also profess faith in one God who is the Holy Trinity, Three Divine Persons—Father, Son and Holy Spirit. While we attribute the divine work of creation to the Father, every divine work is the work of the Holy Trinity.

The Catholic Church explains this mystery in her teaching, as we learned in chapter 6 and profess in the Nicene Creed: the Three Persons of the Trinity are *consubstantial*, that is, they share one divine nature. The Father is distinct from the Son and the Holy Spirit, and the Son is distinct from the Father and the Holy Spirit, and the Holy Spirit is distinct from the Father and the Son. God is one, and the Three Divine Persons are inseparable from one another. What the Father does, the Son and the Holy Spirit do. What the Son does, the Father and the Holy Spirit do. What the Holy Spirit does, the Father and the Son do. "Though the work of creation is attributed to the Father in particular, it is equally a truth of faith that the Father, Son, and Holy Spirit together are the one, indivisible principle of creation" (CCC, no. 316).

This teaching has great importance for our understanding of the identity of the **family**. After the creation of Adam, we read: "[The] LORD God said, 'It is not good that the man should be alone; I will make him a helper as his partner' " (Genesis 2:18). God created our first parents to live in "community," in the image and likeness of the Blessed Trinity. The term "Trinity," which means "Three-in-One," teaches that God has revealed himself to be one God in three distinct divine Persons—Father, Son, and Holy Spirit—who share one nature. The divine communion of the Father and Son and Holy Spirit is such that they are inseparable from one another in nature and in their actions. The Christian family is a sign and image of the unity, or communion, of the Three Persons of the Trinity. The Catholic Church teaches: "The Christian family is a communion of persons, a sign and image of the communion of the Father and the Son in the Holy Spirit" (CCC, no. 2205).

- What are the implications of the truth that God the Trinity created the family in the image and likeness of God, Father, Son and Holy Spirit?
- What are some of the ways you see families being true to that identity?

If you could begin to imagine what a "perfect" love of a mother and father would be like, then you can faintly begin to imagine what God is like

FROM THE CATECHISM

In no way is God in man's image. He is neither man nor woman. God is pure spirit in which there is no place for the difference between the sexes. But the respective "perfections" of man and woman reflect something of the infinite perfection of God: those of a mother and those of a father and husband (see Isaiah 49:14–15; 66:13; Psalm 131:2–3; Hosea 11:1–4; Jeremiah 3:4–19).

—CCC, no. 370

GOD AS DIVINE "PARENT," AS "FATHER" AND "MOTHER"

The mystery of the Holy Trinity is a mystery of faith. It is a mystery of faith that we can never fully comprehend; nor could we ever have come to know it unless God revealed it to us. Divine love is at the center of the life of God; for "God is love" (1 John 4:8). If you could begin to imagine what a "perfect" love of a mother and father would be like, then you can faintly begin to imagine what God is like. God is a communion of infinite, self-giving love. God is infinitely and unconditionally loving and faithful, generous and forgiving, caring and life-giving. God is far beyond the limits of any "human" characteristic we use to describe him.

READ, REFLECT AND SHARE

- Sacred Scripture uses the image of mother to help us come to know the depth of God's love for his children.
- Look up, read and reflect on Psalm 131:2–3, Isaiah 49:14–15 and 66:13, Hosea 11:1–4 and Matthew 23:37–39
- Share with a partner what each passage reveals about God's relationship with us, his children.

JOURNAL EXERCISE

God might call you to the vocation of being a parent.

- From what you have learned in this chapter so far, identify up to five key attitudes and actions that are at the heart of being a parent, and of being a family.
- Describe how you might develop those characteristics now.

The heart and foundation of healthy family life

A Parent's Perspective

I am rich in children, but they are driving me stark raving muttering insane.

I think there are three of them, but they sprint through the house and scream piercingly and slam doors. . . . The children call me names and use bad words and hide clothes under their beds and take their mother for granted and get sick all the time and cough darkly on me and put their muddy feet on the couch. . . . They have broken two windows and cracked a door. . . . They lose their homework, their hats, their jackets, their backpacks, their tempers.

Yet when they are sick they drape themselves on me like warm shirts, which I love, and they leave me notes sometimes in my shoes, which I love . . . and when they hug me they hug me desperately and powerfully, and they murmur like small owls when they are sleepy, and they are hilarious twice a day and sometimes, not very often, not as often as I would like, they turn to me and cup my grizzled face in their grubby hands and do the Vulcan mind-lock thing, their sea-green eyes drilling into me, and that is when I am most sure that I am a man wealthy beyond words in the only coin that matters, love, harried though it may be.

OPENING CONVERSATION

- Why does the writer of this piece consider himself "a man wealthy beyond words"?
- What does this piece say to you about a parent's love for their children?
- What does it say to you about God's love?

FROM THE CATECHISM

According to the fourth commandment, God has willed that, after him, we should honor our parents and those whom he has vested with authority for our good.

—CCC, no. 2248

CHILDREN ARE TO HONOR THEIR PARENTS

The Fourth Commandment is the first and foundational expression of how we are to live the second part of the Great Commandment, "You shall love your neighbor as yourself." When he was Pope, Benedict XVI opened up the meaning of the wonderful vocation of the family. In his address at the prayer vigil for the Fifth Meeting of Families in Valencia, Spain, Benedict XVI taught: "Human beings were created in the image and likeness of God for love, and that complete human fulfillment only comes about when we make a sincere gift of ourselves to others. The family is the privileged setting where every person learns to give and receive love."

The Fourth Commandment teaches us how to practice this love: "Honor your father and your mother, so that your days may be long in the land that the Lᴏʀᴅ your God is giving you" (Exodus 20:12). The Catholic Church teaches that children, whether minors or adults, fulfill this Commandment by showing their parents "respect, gratitude, just obedience and assistance" (CCC, no. 2251). The respect children give to their parents, which we name filial respect, and their obedience to their parents' authority is vital to the harmony and well-being of a family.

Filial respect: The Book of Sirach teaches:

> With all your heart honor your father,
> and do not forget the birth pangs of your
> mother.
> Remember that it was of your parents you were
> born;
> how can you repay what they have given to
> you?
>
> —Sirach 7:27–28

The attitudes and actions that flow from the respect we owe our parents derive from the honor and respect we owe God. Reverence and respect for parents and all the members of one's family—siblings, grandparents and others—is at the heart of the Fourth Commandment. Filial respect guides us in those moments when parents and children engage in healthy dialogue about the ups and downs of their relationship.

Gratitude: We also honor our parents when we express our gratitude to them for the gift of life, both our bodily and our spiritual life. We hear the first words of faith and wisdom from our parents and other members of our family. We honor our parents when we acknowledge the many sacrifices they make for us and for the whole family. These sacrifices are the source of the blessings that a family enjoys. Our parents deserve our gratitude for these sacrifices. Perhaps the best way to show this gratitude is by living a life of sacrifice for others as Jesus did and commanded us to do.

Just obedience: Scripture is a treasure of wisdom about the value and role of the virtue of obedience in the life of a family. For example, in the Book of Proverbs we read:

My child, keep your father's commandment,
and do not forsake your mother's teaching.
Bind them upon your heart always;
tie them around your neck.

—Proverbs 6:20–21

Just obedience is the habit of listening and responding to our parents' guidance on how we can live a just and holy life. Children have the obligation to obey their parents when their parents exercise their rightful authority. Parents exercise rightful authority when what they ask of their children is for the good of their children and of the whole family. We call this obedience "just obedience" because it helps to keep us on the path of living in right relationship with our parents, with other family members and other people outside the family, and with God. Developing this virtue in the home prepares children to assume the responsibilities of living outside the home.

There is evidence that the home is sometimes the place where a parent abuses his or her authority. For example, a parent may sexually abuse a child or ask a child to cooperate in committing a crime, such as helping a parent sell drugs illegally. Children, while they sense these acts are terribly wrong, may give in to the demands of the abusing parent because of their love for their parent, because of fear of losing their parent's love or because they do not understand that they have no obligation to obey a parent who asks them to engage in something that is wrong. A child is never obliged to obey a parent, or any person in authority, who asks them to do something that is contrary to God's law, to the Gospel, to the teachings of the Church or to just civil law. Submission to the unjust demands of an abusing parent or other person who exercises authority over us is never an act of "just obedience." A child has the right and the freedom to say "No."

Assistance: The Fourth Commandment reminds children, especially grown children, of their responsibilities toward parents. Parents sometimes need assistance in meeting their basic needs. Most often the need for this assistance comes about as a result of illness or from the reality that adults are living longer today. As parents advance in age, they are often not only without regular income but also without health insurance and other benefits that they were accustomed to receiving while they were employed. Given that the government is looking for ways to reduce the cost of social programs, such as Social Security and Medicare, grown children and their families are stepping up to provide assistance to parents to meet these needs.

Assisting parents is also a responsibility for younger children, who need to acknowledge their parents' generosity. Parents often spend long hours getting their children to and from school and other after-school and weekend

activities. Children who live at home can fulfill the Fourth Commandment by pitching in with chores around the home, not only when they are asked but also by voluntarily doing so.

THINK, PAIR AND SHARE

- ⊙ Discuss with a partner how the attitudes and actions of children toward their parents foster harmony and healthy relationships within a family.
- ⊙ Then discuss how the attitudes and actions of children might also foster disharmony and unhealthy relationships within a family.

GRANDPARENTS

St. Paul shared these thoughts about family with his companion Timothy: "I am reminded of your sincere faith, a faith that lived first in your grandmother Lois and your mother Eunice and now, I am sure, lives in you" (2 Timothy 1:5). Grandparents as well as parents are a blessing. In many cultures, for example in Native American and Chinese families, grandparents are valued as the real heads of the family.

Grandparents are a source of wisdom for family life. They know your family story; they can help you discover your roots. Listen to them and to their stories. They can even share their own experiences of living the demands of the Fourth Commandment with their children (your parents!). You might find out some fun things as well as learn a lot. Your grandparents have much to teach you.

Some grandchildren—more than five million in the United States—live with their grandparents. Others live close to their grandparents, making it easy to visit often. Even when grandchildren live far away, they can express their respect and gratitude by staying in touch regularly by phone, electronically through email or Skype, and through letters. It is a true blessing to include grandparents in the life of one's family.

JOURNAL EXERCISE

- ⊙ Grandparents often tell the best stories, like interesting tales about when they were your age. If possible, ask your grandparents about their own experiences. If your grandparents have died, ask your parents about them.
- ⊙ Write what you learn in your journal. Begin to develop a diary titled "The Wisdom of the (*your family name*) Family."

PARENTS ARE TO HONOR THEIR CHILDREN

The Fourth Commandment also speaks to the duties of parents in relation to their children. "Parents must regard their children as *children of God* and respect them as *human persons*" (CCC, no. 2222). Parents fulfill their vocation and the duties of the Fourth Commandment by providing for their children's education, for their physical and spiritual needs, and by respecting and encouraging their children's vocation.

Education: "The right and duty of parents to give education is essential, since it is connected with the transmission of human life" (St. John Paul II, *The Role of the Christian Family in the Modern World*, no. 36). Parents fulfill this right and duty first and foremost by striving to create a family environment that fosters their children's learning how to live as children of God and disciples of Jesus Christ. In this way the Christian home is a place of apprenticeship and evangelization. It is a school of "apprenticeship in self-denial, sound judgment and self-mastery—the preconditions of all true freedom" (CCC, no. 2223). "[B]y word and example . . . [parents are] the first heralds of the faith with regard to their children" (*Dogmatic Constitution on the Church*, no. 11; quoted in CCC, no. 1656). By their lives parents guide their children to respond to the grace of God to live a life in keeping with the Gospel.

This fundamental right and duty also includes the right of parents "to *choose a school for [their children]* which corresponds to their own convictions. . . . Public authorities have the duty of guaranteeing this parental right and of ensuring the concrete conditions for its exercise" (CCC, no. 2229). The striving to exercise this right is seen in the United States of America in the public policy debate over providing vouchers to families who wish to educate their children in private schools, both religious and non-religious.

Physical and spiritual needs: You will recall that the human person is "a unity of spirit and matter, soul and body, capable of knowledge, self-possession, and freedom, who can enter into communion with other persons—and with God" (CCC, Glossary, "Person, Human"). The Fourth Commandment obliges parents to care for the "whole person" of their children, for their bodily and spiritual needs. This includes providing to the best of their ability for the basic human needs of their children, such as a home and food and clothing and healthcare. Sometimes parents cannot meet this responsibility for a variety of reasons, which are often out of their control. When this happens they have a right and expectation that family, Church and society will support them through their crisis.

Vocation: Every child is a unique person whom God has blessed with a variety of gifts and talents. Parents have the duty to discover the unique gifts and talents of their children and to provide their children, to the best of their ability, with the opportunity to develop those traits. In doing so, parents help children come to discover and discern the vocation to which God is calling them.

In seeking to do what is good for their children, parents sometimes give in to the temptation to re-create their children in their own image and likeness. For example, they force their children to participate and excel in endeavors, such as athletics, even if their children have little interest or limited talents in those areas. Other parents instill such thoughts as "You *will* be a doctor, or a lawyer. If you do, you will *make us* so proud" into the heads of their children from their children's earliest years. The Catholic Church warns parents to be aware of and resist giving into this *not-so-uncommon* temptation. She teaches:

Parents should be careful not to exert pressure on their children either in the choice of a profession or in that of a spouse. This necessary restraint does not prevent them—quite the contrary—from giving their children judicious advice, particularly when they are planning to start a family.

—CCC, no. 2230

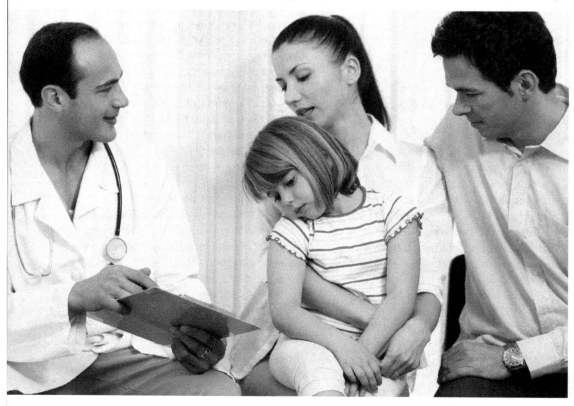

The first vocation of all Christians is "to *follow Jesus*" (CCC, no. 2232). The *Catechism* continues: "Becoming a disciple of Jesus means accepting the invitation to belong to *God's family*, to live in conformity with His way of life: 'For whoever does the will of my Father in heaven is my brother and sister and mother' (Matthew 12:50)" (CCC, no. 2233). Parents are to work with their children to help them discern, develop and use their gifts and talents to fulfill this vocation. If this process leads their child to hear God's call to the priesthood or to the religious life or to the married life or to the single life, parents should be proud and give thanks to God.

OVER TO YOU

- ⊙ What have you discovered at this point in your life to be your gifts and talents?
- ⊙ Answer these questions: What are you good at? What do you enjoy doing? What do you look forward to doing?
- ⊙ Think deeply about your responses. They just might be God's way of helping you to discover the vocation to which he is calling you.

"MOM! THIS IS FOR YOU!"

A mother who had scrimped and saved to put her son through college sat at her son's graduation. She watched as he walked across the platform and received his degree with honors. As he walked down the aisle, instead of turning into the designated row, he kept walking; down to where his mother sat. The young man threw his arms around her neck, kissed her on the cheek, and as he placed his diploma in her hands, he said, "Here, Mom, this is for you. You earned it!"

WHAT ABOUT YOU PERSONALLY?

- ⊙ How does this story reflect the honor parents and their children show each other?
- ⊙ Do you see your relationship with your parents reflected in this story? If so, how?

Parents are to work with their children to help them discern, develop and use their gifts and talents

Responding to the fundamental rights of every person

FAMILY VALUES AND THE HEALTH OF A SOCIETY

There is much concern today about marriage and family life, not only in our nation but also throughout the world. The media and public policies often portray marriage and family life in ways that are contrary to the teachings of the Church. The bishops of the Catholic Church in the United States of America continue to work, as they have always done, to promote public policy rooted in sound "family values." "Strengthening marriage and family life" is one of four strategic priorities of the United States Conference of Catholic Bishops (USCCB). In 2005 our bishops launched the National Pastoral Initiative for Marriage and in 2009 they issued the pastoral letter "Marriage: Love and Life in the Divine Plan." On September 22–27, 2015 our bishops will gather the Church for the World Meeting of Families in Philadelphia. The theme of the meeting is: "Love Is Our Mission: The Family Fully Alive." This gathering will follow the Extraordinary Synod of Bishops held in October 5–19, 2013, whose focus was the pastoral challenges to the family.

OPENING CONVERSATION

- ⊙ What do you think of the media's portrayal of family life? Give specific examples to support your opinion.
- ⊙ Name specific values that strengthen family life. How do these same values contribute to the strength of a society?
- ⊙ Why does the strength of the family strengthen a society? Why does the collapse of the family portend the collapse of a society?

THE FAMILY AND SOCIETY

The Fourth Commandment extends to all who have legitimate authority over us. What we owe in the first place to our parents—respect, gratitude, obedience and assistance—also governs our relationships with people who legitimately guide and supervise us. For the young, this includes teachers, coaches, employers and many others who have legitimate authority over them. Young people are to respect and obey legitimate civil authorities who support their parents and families in caring for the spiritual and bodily welfare of their children.

In the broadest sense, the Fourth Commandment applies to our duties as citizens of society to obey the civil authorities. The home and family are the foundation of society. No nation or community of people is stronger than the family structures within it. As goes the home, so goes the nation and the community. As family members, both parents and children, fulfill their responsibilities and use their rights well within the home; they become good citizens for the common good of society.

Likewise, the family is the foundation of the Church community. As we have already seem, the Second Vatican Council referred to the family as the "domestic church," or the "church of the home." The family, in its own way, must carry on all the ministries of the Church. This includes reaching out to people in need within and outside the family. When the domestic church is strong, the whole Church is stronger.

TALK IT OVER

⊙ Name some of the responsibilities that come from being a member of a Christian family.
⊙ How does fulfilling those responsibilities help you live as a faithful member of society and of the Church?

AUTHORITY

We saw in the Book of Genesis that God created the human person to live in community, or society. "A *society* is a group of persons bound together organically by a principle of unity that goes beyond each one of them. . . . that is at once visible and spiritual" (CCC, no. 1880) The family is the foundational society. All other societies exist to support the family.

All societies need authority to govern them. All authority derives from God and all human authorities are to reflect the authority of God. Authority is "the quality by virtue of which persons or institutions make laws and give orders to men and expect obedience from them" (CCC, no. 1897). The role of legitimate authority is to "preserve [society's] institutions and do all that is necessary to sponsor actively the interests of all its members" (St. John XXIII, *Peace on Earth*, no. 46).

LET'S PROBE DEEPER: SCRIPTURE ACTIVITY

⊙ Work in groups of three or four.
⊙ Check out Luke 16:1–13, 22:24–27; John 10:1–18; Romans 13:1–2; 1 Peter 2:13–17; 1 Timothy 2:1–2.
⊙ Share what these passages say about how people in authority are to exercise their authority.

THE LEGITIMATE AUTHORITY OF CIVIL SOCIETY

Citizens and those who exercise legitimate authority have rights and responsibilities. The primary duty of civil authorities is to lead society in ways that best serve the common good of all the citizens and respect the fundamental rights of

> ## The primary duty of civil authorities is to lead society in ways that best serve the common good

all. You will recall that the common good is "the sum total of social conditions which allow people . . . to reach their fulfillment more fully and more easily" (*Pastoral Constitution on the Church in the Modern World*, no. 26). St. John XXIII spoke of these rights in his encyclical *Peace on Earth*:

But first we must speak of man's rights. Man has the right to live. He has the right to bodily integrity and to the means necessary for the proper development of life, particularly food, clothing, shelter, medical care, rest, and, finally, the necessary social services. In consequence, he has the right to be looked after in the event of ill health; disability stemming from his work; widowhood; old age; enforced unemployment; or whenever through no fault of his own he is deprived of the means of livelihood.

—*Peace on Earth*, no. 11

LET'S PROBE DEEPER: SCRIPTURE ACTIVITY
⊙ Work in small groups. Look up and read these passages from Sacred Scripture: Leviticus 25:35; Ruth 2:2–23; Tobit 4:5–11; Proverbs 31:8–9; Isaiah 1:16–17; Jeremiah 22:1–16; Matthew 25:31–46; Luke 16:19–31; Acts of the Apostles 4:32–35; 2 Corinthians 9:6–15; James 2:14–17.

⊙ How do the teachings in these passages help you understand the wisdom of the teaching in *Peace on Earth*?

THINK, PAIR AND SHARE
⊙ Work with a partner. Review the fundamental human rights named in *Peace on Earth*.
⊙ Discuss how well the social policies of our nation are working to assure those rights.

FROM THE CATECHISM
"The political community and public authority are based on human nature and therefore . . . belong to an order established by God (*Pastoral Constitution on the Church in the Modern World*, no. 74)" (CCC, no. 1920). [This authority] "is exercised legitimately if it is committed to the common good of society" (CCC, no. 1921). "Public authority is obliged to respect the fundamental rights of the human person and the conditions for the exercise of his freedom" (CCC, no. 2254).

THE LEGITIMATE EXERCISE OF CIVIL AUTHORITY
The fundamental rights of every person flow from the dignity of their being images of God. It is for this reason that civil authority exercises its authority legitimately *only* when it is "exercised

The fundamental responsibility of every human community is to protect the life of its members

within the limits of the moral order and must guarantee the conditions for the exercise of freedom" (CCC, no. 1923). The bishops of the Catholic Church in the United States remind us of this foundational teaching of the Catholic Church:

The Catholic tradition teaches that human dignity can be protected and a healthy community can be achieved only if human rights are protected and responsibilities are met. Therefore, every person has a fundamental right to life and a right to those things required for human decency. Corresponding to these rights are duties and responsibilities—to one another, to our families, and to the larger society.
—Website of United States Conference of Catholic Bishops

Right to life: The fundamental responsibility of every human community is to protect the life of its members. The promotion of all other rights is an illusion when the right to life "is not defended with maximum determination" (St. John Paul II, *On the Vocation and Mission of the Lay Faithful* [*Christifideles laici*], no. 38). Societies that legislate and enforce laws that violate this fundamental human right are abusing their authority. They are, in a sense, snubbing their noses at God, who is the source of their authority. "No one can command or establish what is contrary to the dignity of persons and the natural law" (CCC, no. 2235). We will return to the human person's right to life in our study of the Fifth Commandment.

Right to human dignity: Flowing from the fundamental right to life is the right to a "decent" life that honors the dignity of human persons. The right to work is closely associated with this human need. "*Human work* proceeds directly from persons created in the image of God and called to prolong the work of creation by subduing the earth, both with and for one another. Hence work is a duty" (CCC, no. 2427). The exercise of this duty is often restricted by economic and other cultural conditions, which prevent people from adequately meeting those needs that provide them with a decent life.

Societies, including the Church, have in one way or another always recognized this situation, and supported members who are in need. The Church has always enriched herself and the societies of which she is a member by giving witness to this responsibility. The United States of America has a strong commitment to meeting this basic human right. In supporting citizens, however, lawmakers are often conflicted. They try to balance the high financial cost of such programs with other responsibilities that serve the common good. Attempts to resolve this conflict often become contentious and divisive.

The Catholic Church plays a significant role in modeling ways for our nation and for the world community to create a just and compassionate world. Prosperous nations have a duty to share with less fortunate ones. This is a fundamental teaching of Catholic social doctrine. Just as individuals are called to the works of compassion and justice, societies are likewise called to care

Welcoming immigrants is an expression of the principle of solidarity

for those in need and to promote justice for all. This is equally true in the international as well as the national context. Wealthy and powerful nations must promote the peace and prosperity of the poorer and developing peoples.

States work toward achieving this goal by welcoming strangers, or in today's language "immigrants," in search of security and the means of livelihood which they cannot find in their own countries. Welcoming immigrants is an expression of the principle of **solidarity**. In turn, immigrants are obliged to respect and uphold the civic and spiritual heritage of the country that receives them. We see the importance of this responsibility today in the United States in our search for a just and compassionate immigration policy.

Right to religious freedom: We have already learned that the human person is an integrated unity of body and soul. We have fundamental bodily needs and spiritual needs. Every person and every religious community, such as the Church and religious affiliated institutions, such as hospitals and schools, have the fundamental right to the exercise of freedom, especially in religious and moral matters. Society honors the human person when it exercises its authority by protecting and supporting its members to exercise freely their right to fulfill their spiritual

needs. Societies abuse their authority when they make and enforce laws that deny or restrict their citizens' right to religious freedom.

THINK, PAIR AND SHARE

- Take a look at the social policies that you have studied or are currently studying in your American History, Economics or Government courses.
- Discuss with a partner: How well do those polices protect and support the fundamental rights of the human person? Where do we do well? Where can we do better?

FAITH WORD

Solidarity

"The principle of solidarity, also articulated in terms of 'friendship' or 'social charity,' is a direct demand of human and Christian brotherhood" (CCC, no. 1939). This involves a love for all peoples that transcends national, racial, ethnic, economic, and ideological differences. It respects the needs of others and the common good in an interdependent world.
—*United States Catholic Catechism for Adults* (USCCA), 529

⊙ How can your living as a faithful disciple of Jesus support the building of a just and compassionate society?

FROM THE CATECHISM

Every society's judgments and conduct reflect a vision of man and his destiny. Without the light the Gospel sheds on God and man, societies easily become totalitarian.

—CCC, 2257

WHEN LAWS ARE UNJUST

Imagine you are among the elders in Jerusalem making your case to the Sanhedrin for following the way of Jesus. The Sanhedrin was the "Supreme Court" of the ancient Jewish state, in the tradition established in Exodus, chapter 18. According to that tradition, the oral Torah was given to Moses and passed on to Joshua, then to the elders, then to the prophets, then to the Sanhedrin. It decided "difficult cases and cases of capital punishment" (from *Judaism 101*). For example, after much give and take, the Sanhedrin warned Peter and the Apostles, "We gave you strict orders not to teach in this name" (Acts of the Apostles 5:28). This was Peter's response: "We must obey God rather than any human authority" (Acts of the Apostles 5:29).

When a person, in good conscience, judges the directives of civil authorities to be contrary to God's will, to the rights of persons and the moral order, the person is obliged not to obey those directives. The Catholic Church teaches:

Refusing obedience to civil authorities, when their demands are contrary to those of an upright conscience, finds its justification in the distinction between serving God and serving the political community. "Render therefore to Caesar the things that are Caesar's, and to God the things that are God's" (Matthew 22:21). "We must obey God rather than men" (Acts of the Apostles 5:29).

—CCC, no. 2242

This refusal is called **civil disobedience**. The manner in which we fulfill the obligation not to obey directives that we judge to be contrary to the rights of persons and the moral order is also important. We must always respect the rights of others, especially their right to life. Christians are to follow the example and teachings of Christ. Peacemakers are truly children of God. The Christian tradition is filled with models of people using non-violent acts of refusal, such as protests, sit-ins, marches and so on. There is often a cost for citizens who openly resist unjust laws; often they are fined or imprisoned. Sometimes non-violence is met by violence.

REFLECT AND DISCUSS

⊙ What power do Christians have when they work together to change unjust and oppressive laws?

ST. PETER PREACHING | MASOLINO DA PANICALE & FILIPPINO LIPPI

WHAT ABOUT YOU PERSONALLY?

⊙ How willing are you to speak out publicly against laws that oppress people? Have you ever joined others in doing so? Why or why not?

ARMED RESISTANCE

There are situations, such as the conditions that existed at the time of the American Revolution, when the social policies of a country are so oppressive that *armed resistance* is judged to be the last resort. Armed resistance always results in the taking of human life. This includes the life of the innocent—sometimes euphemistically called "collateral damage." The Catholic Church teaches that *armed resistance* to unjust laws and oppressive political authority is legitimate *only when* the following conditions exist:

⊙ There is certain, grave and prolonged violation of fundamental human rights.

⊙ All other means of redress have been exhausted.

⊙ Such resistance will not provoke worse disorders.

⊙ There is well-founded hope of success.

⊙ It is impossible to reasonably foresee any better solution.

TALK IT OVER

⊙ Brainstorm and give specific examples of Christians refusing to obey unjust laws.

⊙ Divide your responses into "Non-violent Resistance" and "Armed Resistance."

⊙ How effective were these acts of "disobedience"? What price did the "resistors" pay?

THINK, PAIR AND SHARE

⊙ Using your knowledge of a recent example of armed resistance to oppression perpetrated by a civil authority, and the criteria listed above, talk with a partner about whether the armed resistance was legitimate or not.

⊙ Share the results of your discussion and research during your study of the Fifth Commandment.

BATTLE OF BENNINGTON, 1777 | 18TH-CENTURY ENGRAVING

Living as faithful citizens

Paying Taxes

In Matthew's Gospel we read: "Then the Pharisees went and plotted to entrap [Jesus] in what he said. So they sent their disciples to him, along with the Herodians, saying, 'Teacher, we know that you are sincere, and teach the way of God in accordance with truth, and show deference to no one; for you do not regard people with partiality. Tell us, then, what you think. Is it lawful to pay taxes to the emperor, or not?' But Jesus, aware of their malice, said, 'Why are you putting me to the test, you hypocrites? Show me the coin used for the tax.' And they brought him a denarius. Then he said to them, 'Whose head is this, and whose title?' They answered, 'The emperor's.' Then he said to them, 'Give therefore to the emperor the things that are the emperor's, and to God the things that are God's.'"

—Matthew 22:16–21

CHRIST AND THE TRIBUTE MONEY | DOMENICO FETTI (AFTER TITIAN)

OPENING CONVERSATION

⊙ What or who might constitute the "emperor" in your world today?

⊙ What sort of things should be rendered to the emperor?

⊙ What sort of things should be rendered to God?

LIGHTS IN THE WORLD

In his encounter with the Herodians (a religious party in opposition to the Pharisees in most matters except in their plot against Jesus), Jesus did not separate faith from the everyday affairs of life in society; in fact, the opposite is true. As we learned in the previous section of this chapter, when the emperor, civil authority, and God are in conflict, it is to God and our conscience that we owe our ultimate allegiance. But it is also true that we are to obey those laws of society that express the natural law and the revealed laws of God. Recall Jesus' description of faithful discipleship:

"You are the light of the world. A city built on a hill cannot be hid. No one after lighting a lamp puts it under the bushel basket, but on the lampstand, and it gives light to all in the house. In the same way, let your light shine before others, so that they may see your good works and give glory to your Father in heaven."

—Matthew 5:14–16

Obeying just civil laws and contributing to the common good is a mandate of our Christian faith. We must live as disciples of Jesus in every arena of our life, personal and social. It is part of letting Christ, the light who came into the world to dispel the darkness, shine in the world. (Check out John 1:6–7.)

TALK IT OVER

Brainstorm responses to these questions:
- What laws of our country support our living the way of life that Jesus revealed?
- What laws of our country are contrary to the way of life that Jesus revealed?
- How do you see the Catholic Church responding to both scenarios?

FROM THE CATECHISM

It is the *duty of citizens* to contribute along with the civil authorities to the good of society in a spirit of truth, justice, solidarity and freedom. The love and service of *one's country* follow from the duty of gratitude and belong to the order of charity.
—CCC, no. 2239

BEING A FAITHFUL CITIZEN

The bishops of the Catholic Church in the United States have offered us guidelines for living our faith as faithful citizens and faithful disciples of Christ. In 2007 the United States Conference of Catholic Bishops (USCCB) issued the document *Forming Consciences for Faithful Citizenship*. In this document our bishops teach: "Responsible citizenship is a virtue, and participation in political life is a moral obligation."

Christians fulfill the responsibility to contribute to the good of society by obeying all just laws. We respect the life of other citizens by obeying safety laws, such as traffic laws, fire laws and gun laws. We exercise the right to vote in a responsible way when we elect representatives whom we judge will build a nation, state or local community that "blesses God." We follow the basic principles of Catholic social doctrine in casting our vote. We pay taxes to contribute to a well-functioning government that protects the life of all its citizens and supports them in their pursuit of a decent life. We serve our country as a member of the armed forces and participate in Church service programs and government service programs that make a difference in people's lives.

We also serve our country, as we learned in more detail in the previous section of this chapter, when we speak out and offer constructive criticism of the State. For example, we can apply what Jesus said of the Sabbath to the State and her laws—the State is there for the person, not the person for the State. In so doing, we are following the example of Jesus.

CATHOLIC YOUTH ARE TO BE FAITHFUL CITIZENS

Catholic youth are called to be "lights in the world." They are obliged to be faithful citizens. The USCCB lists the "Top 10 Ways That You Can Be A Faithful Citizen":

1. Visit *www.faithfulcitizenship.org* and email the link to others.
2. Pick out some issues from *Faithful Citizenship* that you **don't** know much about. Find out more.
3. Pray each day for those who are impacted by injustice, for policymakers, and for the ability to take action.
4. Send letters to your local leaders expressing your opinions and why your faith motivates you to care.
5. Organize a prayer vigil for resolution of an issue you care about.
6. Discuss *Faithful Citizenship* over coffee with your friends.
7. Take part in your diocesan lobby day.
8. Print out the *Faithful Citizenship* cards and ask your pastor if you can pass them out after Mass.
9. Vote if you're old enough, and encourage adults you know to vote.
10. Make a commitment to always defend human life and dignity and promote justice and peace.

THINK, PAIR AND SHARE

⊙ Discuss the "Top 10 Ways" with a partner.
⊙ Which of the ten ways do you see your school, parish or youth ministry group implementing?
⊙ How are these youth being lights to the world by their efforts?

WHAT ABOUT YOU PERSONALLY?

⊙ Which of the "Top Ten Ways" are you already implementing?
⊙ How will you begin to implement the others?

JUDGE AND ACT

REVIEW AND SHARE WHAT YOU HAVE LEARNED IN THIS CHAPTER

Look back over this chapter and reflect on the teachings of Scripture and Tradition on the Fourth Commandment. Share the teachings of the Catholic Church on these statements:

- The Christian family is an image of the Holy Trinity.
- The family is the foundation of society.
- Children are to show respect, gratitude and obedience to their parents.
- Children are to offer assistance to their parents.
- Parents are to provide for the bodily and spiritual needs of their children.
- Civil authorities are to exercise their authority according to the moral law.
- Civil authorities are to promote the common good of all the citizens.
- Citizens are to show respect and obedience to all who exercise legitimate authority over them.
- Citizens have the right and the responsibility to question and not obey unjust laws.
- Citizens are to contribute to the good of society.

TALK IT OVER

- What are the implications of the Fourth Commandment for our life in our family?
- What are the implications of the Fourth Commandment for our relationships with those outside our families who have legitimate authority over us?
- What are the implications of the Fourth Commandment for our living as faithful citizens?

OVER TO YOU

- What is the best wisdom you have learned to guide you to honor your parents?
- Is there a good decision you need to make about obeying and respecting your parents?

St. Monica (333–387), patron of mothers and abused spouses

The love and care of parents for their children has been a constant characteristic of every culture down through the centuries. A parent's love persists even when a beloved child "goes off the rails." Read this story of one mother from the early days of the Church who persevered in love for her wayward child.

Monica and her family lived in North Africa in the fourth century. Monica was a mother who knew all about heartbreak. She was married off at a young age to a bad-tempered and unfaithful pagan husband, Patricius, who was twice her age. But it was her brilliant though lazy and self-centered son, Augustine, who caused her the most tears.

It is a familiar scenario. An academically brilliant son falls in with the wrong crowd. He turns against Christianity, sets up home with a young woman, and fathers a son with her outside of marriage. Later Augustine admitted that he broke all the Commandments except "Thou shalt not kill." Finally, he joined a cult-like religious group called the Manichaeans. Manichaenism was a gnostic religion which had its own mythology to explain its religious understandings. Manichaeans not only rejected, but despised, Christianity.

Monica was so upset that she barred Augustine from her house. Meanwhile she continued to pray fervently for his conversion to a Christian way of life. Then she changed her tactics and decided to stay as close to him as possible, which Augustine found frustrating. At the age of twenty-nine Augustine decided to go to Rome to teach; but in order to keep his mother from following him, Augustine told her he was just going to Hippo to say goodbye to a friend; he set sail for Rome instead. The tenacious mother set off after him, only to find that he had gone to Milan; so she followed him there. It was about

ST. AUGUSTINE & ST. MONICA | OHMENHEIM, GERMANY

this time that Monica went to see a bishop, who consoled her with the now famous words, "The child of those tears shall never perish."

Indeed, Monica's prayers and tears were finally answered some eighteen years later. Her son Augustine had a conversion experience, was baptized, and embraced the Christian faith. He went on to become a priest, then Bishop of Hippo, and one of the most influential scholars in the history of the Church. Augustine was declared a saint of the Church by popular acclaim soon after his death. The Catholic Church celebrates his feast day on August 28, the day of his death.

Monica never gave up. She never lost hope. Her example shows that while instant answers rarely emerge, God's timing is different from ours, and a mother's love and prayers never go to waste. Indeed, as a model to give hope to all parents of wayward children, the Catholic Church remembers and celebrates the life of St. Monica on August 27.

REFLECT AND SHARE

◉ What wisdom for your life can you learn from this story of Monica and Augustine?

SHARE FAITH WITH FAMILY AND FRIENDS

◉ Read and reflect on these scenarios:

Scenario A: Mario wants to express himself. He has run into difficulties with his parents about his hair, his clothes and his friends. Some of the arguments with his father have reached volcanic proportions. He wants to live by his own rules, independent of his parents' authority. He goes to talk to his mom, to get her "on his side."

Scenario B: Elena has always had a wonderful relationship with her parents. However, she is finding it difficult to take on more responsibility and independence for fear of hurting their feelings. Elena feels they still treat her as their "little girl" and want to do everything for her. She decides to talk to her father about her feelings.

◉ Then discuss:

How can Mario work with his parents to resolve their disagreement in a respectful way?

or

How might Elena use her feelings to grow in her relationship with her parents?

◉ Share how the wisdom gained from your discussions can contribute to the life of your family.

JUDGE AND ACT

◉ Choose a social policy or civil law that works against the well-being of family life.

◉ Write a letter to local, state and national leaders expressing your opinions and why your faith motivates you to speak up.

LEARN BY HEART

"Honor your father and mother"—this is the first commandment with a promise: "so that it may be well with you and you may live long on the earth."

EPHESIANS 6:2—3

Pray the Sign of the Cross together.

Opening Prayer

LEADER
Today we join together in Christ's name.
We pray for our families and for all families.
Let us pray: (*Pause*)

O God, in whose eternal design
family life has its firm foundation,
look with compassion on prayers of your
    servants,
and grant that, following the example
of the Holy Family of your Only Begotten Son
in practicing the virtues of family life and in the
    bonds of charity,
we may, in the joy of your house,
delight one day in eternal rewards.
Through our Lord Jesus Christ, your Son,
who lives and reigns with you in the unity of the
    Holy Spirit,
one God, for ever and ever.
ALL
Amen.
—Collect, "Mass for the Family,"
The Roman Missal

The Word of the Lord

READER
A reading from the holy Gospel according to Luke.
Proclaim Luke 2:41–52.
The Gospel of the Lord.
ALL
Praise to you, Lord Jesus Christ.

All pause and reflect on the Word of God.

Prayer of Intercession

LEADER
We now lift up our hearts in prayer. I invite you,
if you wish, to pray your intentions aloud. After
each intention, let us all respond, "Lord Jesus,
hear our prayer."
All who wish to do so offer their petitions.

Concluding Prayer

LEADER
Heavenly Father,
you have given us the model of life
in the Holy Family of Nazareth.
Help us, O Loving Father,
to make our family another Nazareth
where love, peace and joy reign.
May it be deeply contemplative,
intensely eucharistic,
revived with joy.
Help us to stay together in joy
and sorrow in family prayer.
Teach us to see Jesus in the members of our
    families. . . .
May we love one another as God loves us,
more and more each day,
and forgive each other's faults
as you forgive our sins.
Help us, O Loving Father, to take whatever you
    give
and give whatever you take with a big smile.

Immaculate Heart of Mary, cause of our joy,
pray for us.

—Blessed Mother Teresa of Calcutta

ALL
Amen.

Dismissal

LEADER
Go forth and bring the Spirit of God, who is love,
into your families.
ALL
Thanks be to God.

Pray the Sign of the Cross together.

CHAPTER 8

Living the "Way" of Life and Truth

—The Fifth and Eighth Commandments

WE GIVE GLORY TO GOD BY OUR LIVES

OUR HIGHEST CALLING IS TO LIVE AS IMAGES OF GOD, WHO IS TRUTH

WE MUST PROMOTE A CULTURE OF LIFE, NOT A CULTURE OF DEATH

ACTIONS CONTRARY TO THE FIFTH COMMANDMENT INCLUDE:

DIRECT ABORTION

EMBRYONIC STEM CELL RESEARCH

INTENTIONAL EUTHANASIA

SUICIDE

NEGLECT OF ONE'S HEALTH

CHRISTIANS ARE DISCIPLES OF JESUS CHRIST, WHO is "the way, and the truth, and the life" (John 14:6). In this chapter we explore the Fifth Commandment, "You shall not kill," and the Eighth Commandment, "You shall not bear false witness against your neighbor." We discover how these two Commandments guide us in living the way of truth and life, so that we can be living images of God, who is the giver of all life.

ACTIONS CONTRARY TO THE EIGHTH COMMANDMENT INCLUDE:

- LYING AND SELF-SERVING DECEPTION
- GOSSIP
- CALUMNY AND DETRACTION
- RASH JUDGMENT
- IRONY AND SARCASM
- GIVING SCANDAL

Faith Focus: These teachings are the primary focus of the doctrinal content presented in this chapter:

- ⊙ Jesus is "the way, and the truth, and the life" (John 14:6
- ⊙ Individuals and society as a whole have the duty to live life-giving and not death-bearing lives.
- ⊙ Direct abortion, intentional euthanasia, suicide, embryonic stem cell research, and intentional disregard for the bodily and spiritual health of a person or a socie are acts contrary to a person's right to life and to the Fif Commandment.
- ⊙ Individuals and society have the right to defend themselves.
- ⊙ Individuals and society as a whole have the duty to live truthful lives.
- ⊙ Lying, duplicity, dissimulation, hypocrisy, gossip, calumn detraction and rash judgment are acts contrary to truth and to the Eighth Commandment.

Discipleship Formation: As a result of studying this chapter you should be better able to:

- ⊙ resolve that your life will be 'life-giving';
- ⊙ recognize the consequences of taking part in b gossiping and spreading lies;
- ⊙ explore ways you can grow in speaking a truthful life, no matter the cost;
- ⊙ resist judging the moral faults and flaw
- ⊙ appreciate the evil impact of viewing or re pornography and watching films or playing that glorify violence;
- ⊙ contribute to building a culture of life;
- ⊙ deepen your resolve to follow Jesus, "the way, and th truth, and the life."

Scripture References: These Scripture references are quoted or referred to in this chapter:
OLD TESTAMENT: **Genesis** 9:5–6; **Exodus** 20:5–6 and 16, 21:22–25; **Deuteronomy** 30:15 and 19–20; **Psalms** 5:4–6, 100: **Proverbs** 10:11 and 18, 25:11 and 18, 26:20; **Jeremiah** 1:5
NEW TESTAMENT: **Matthew** 5:6, 9, 10, 11, 21–22, 38–39 and 43–45, 6:2, 5 and 16, 7:15–20, 15:7, 18:6–7, 22:18, 23:13–15, 2 and 29; **Luke** 17:1–2; **John** 3:16, 8:1–11 and 44, 10:10, 13:31– 14:6, 17 and 26, 16:25–33, 18:37; **1 Corinthians** 8:1; **Colossi** 3:8–11; **2 Timothy** 1:7; **1 John** 1:5, 4:8 and 11–12; **James** 3:

Faith Glossary: Familiarize yourself with the meaning key terms in the Glossary: **abortion, despair, euthan gossip, hypocrisy, lying, martyrdom, perjury, porn reparation, restorative justice, retributive justice sanctifying grace, scandal, suicide, temperance,**

Faith Word: truth
Learn by Heart: John 14:6
Learn by Example: Sister Helen Prejean, C.S.J.

How are you being true to yourself?

HAMLET AND POLONIUS | ADOLPH VON MENZEL

To Thine Own Self Be True

POLONIUS:
This above all: to thine own self be true,
And it must follow, as the night the day,
Thou canst not then be false to any man.
Farewell, my blessing season this in thee!

LAERTES:
Most humbly do I take my leave, my lord.

OPENING REFLECTION

"[T]o thine own self be true" points to a deep inner urge in every person. These words of Polonius are his last words of advice to his son Laertes, who is about to leave for Paris in search of himself and a better life. All people search for their true selves. We all want to make sense of our lives, to find meaning in what we do and in what happens to us. If we pretend to be someone other than our true self, our whole life is a lie. It will be even more difficult for us to find meaning for our life, and we may bring harm to ourselves and to others.

⊙ Have you ever felt the desire to be someone other than your true self? If so, how did you typically respond?

⊙ What were the consequences of your responses for yourself and for others?

OUR TRUE SELVES

In *Hamlet* the character Polonius is a "man of the world," whose main purpose in life is to protect his own interests. When he gave the advice to his son, Polonius meant, "Be sure to take care of yourself before anyone and anything else." Christians interpret "To thine own self be true" very differently.

Jesus Christ, the Incarnate Son of God, clearly reveals that striving to live as our true selves is not about being selfish and doing what we want, regardless of how that impacts other people. It is about living as people who are created in the image of God, who is love. Our challenge as Christians is to love God, Father, Son and Holy Spirit, to love others and to love our self, as Jesus revealed by his life and teachings. When we do, we act in the best interests of our true self and in the best interests of other people.

- ⊙ Pause for a moment. Look up, read and reflect on: Exodus 20:5–6; Psalms 5:4–6, 100:3; John 3:16; Colossians 3:8–11; 1 John 1:5, 4:8, 11–12; 1 Peter 3:3–4.
- ⊙ What do these passages reveal about God?
- ⊙ What do they reveal about your true self?

LIVING THE TRUTH OF WHO WE ARE

Classically, philosophers and theologians have talked about three key aspects of what it means to be human. First, we are *rational* beings: we have an intellect; we have the ability to reason and think; we can come to know God, ourselves and others. Second, we are *social* beings: we are by nature created to live in relationship with others—human life is a partnership with other people. Third, we are *free* beings: we have a free will; we can make choices to love or hate, tell the truth or lie; we can be life-givers or life-takers. It is in this context that we explore the Fifth Commandment and the Eighth Commandment in this chapter.

Earlier in this text we have seen that God the Creator, the Holy Trinity, creates us in the image of God, who is Father, Son and Holy Spirit. In other words, God creates us to live in the image of the Holy Trinity, a community of Divine Persons rooted in love. The more we live a life of truth and love, the more we show forth our likeness to God and will find meaning for our life.

In the Gospel according to John, Jesus, in his teaching on the Good Shepherd, reveals: "I came that they may have life, and have it abundantly" (John 10:10). Some translations read "have it to the full." The life Jesus shares with us is his own life, the very life of God. You will recall that **sanctifying grace** is the gift of God's own divine life, which he freely shares with us. This grace "enables us to live with God and to act by his love" (*United States Catholic Catechism for Adults* [USCCA], Glossary, "Grace," 514). By living the way of Jesus, our life finds its meaning: we give glory to his Father by our lives and bring the abundance of life that God wills for us (life to the full) to ourselves and to others.

OVER TO YOU

- ⊙ What do you recognize as signs that your own life is life-giving for yourself and for the communities of which you are member?
- ⊙ Can you imagine that you give glory to God the Father, Son and Holy Spirit just by being alive, in the divine image and likeness?
- ⊙ What difference might this make to how you live your life each day?

Living truthful lives

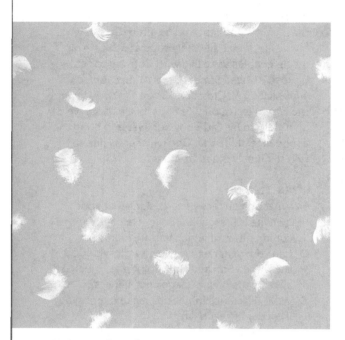

A man confessed to a monk that he had sinned by spreading false rumors about other people. The old monk told him to go, take a pillow to the top of the church belfry, and release its feathers to the wind. The man did as his confessor directed. When he returned, the monk told him to go back out now and pick up all the feathers. The man protested that they had all blown away and it would be impossible for him to retrieve them. "That," the monk said, "is exactly what happened to your careless and malicious words."

OPENING CONVERSATION

⊙ Think of an example where you were aware of the damage done by false rumors. What lesson did you learn from this for your own life?

⊙ How are malicious and false rumors an issue among young people today?

OVER TO YOU

⊙ What wisdom for your life can you learn from the above story?

WORDS

Our words give expression to who we are. Through our words we can be life-givers or life-takers. The Book of Proverbs teaches:

The mouth of the righteous is a fountain of life,
    but the mouth of the wicked conceals
        violence.
Lying lips conceal hatred,
    and whoever utters slander is a fool.
                            —Proverbs 10:11, 18

A word fitly spoken
    is like apples of gold in a setting of silver. . . .
Like a war club, a sword, or a sharp arrow
    is one who bears false witness against a
        neighbor.
                            —Proverbs 25:11, 18

Words can give truthful witness to or can betray our true identity. Living and witnessing to the **truth** involves being true to God, to others and to one's self. In his trial before Pilate, Jesus proclaimed that he came into the world "to testify to the truth" (John 18:37). His disciples, with the grace of the Holy Spirit, are to do the same.

Jesus promised his disciples that the Father, who sent him, would send the Holy Spirit, "the Spirit of truth" (John 14:17), who "will teach you everything, and remind you of all that I have said to you" (John 14:26). Jesus was assuring the disciples and us that God offers us the grace to give testimony about the Lord (see 2 Timothy 1:7).

Christians are to give truthful witness to the Lord. **Martyrdom** is the ultimate form of

DR. MARTIN LUTHER KING JR, ARCHBISHOP ÓSCAR ROMERO AND DIETRICH BONHOEFFER | WESTMINSTER ABBEY, LONDON, ENGLAND

Millions of Christians have given their lives in witness to the truth, who is Jesus Christ

commitment to living a truthful life in the Lord. Throughout history, literally millions of Christians have given their lives in witness to the truth, who is Jesus Christ. This witness continues today. Two modern-day martyrs whom you have encountered in the pages of *Credo* are Blessed Oscar Romero (1917–80) and Maryknoll Sister Maura Clarke (1932–80).

FAITH WORD

Truth

Truth or truthfulness is the virtue which consists in showing oneself true in deeds and truthful in words, and guarding against duplicity, dissimulation, and hypocrisy.
—*Catechism of the Catholic Church*
(CCC), no. 2505

JOURNAL EXERCISE
- Research the life of a Christian martyr.
- Compose a prayer asking for the Holy Spirit's help to give faithful testimony about the Lord.

FROM THE CATECHISM
The eighth commandment forbids misrepresenting the truth in our relations with others. This moral prescription flows from the vocation of the holy people to bear witness to their God who is the truth and wills the truth. Offenses against the truth express by word or deed a refusal to commit oneself to moral uprightness: they are fundamental infidelities to God and, in this sense, they undermine the foundations of the covenant.
—CCC, no. 2464

ATTITUDES AND ACTS CONTRARY TO THE EIGHTH COMMANDMENT
The Eighth Commandment teaches the wisdom and necessity of living a truthful life. It teaches: "You shall not bear false witness against your

neighbor" (Exodus 20:16). The New Testament describes the deadly potential of the tongue to be "a restless evil, full of deadly poison" (James 3:8). Our words and actions, both as individuals and as a society, must give witness to God, who is truth. Let us look briefly at several human acts that are contrary to the truth.

Lying: bearing false witness to the truth: Jesus calls the Devil "a liar and the father of lies" (John 8:44). "Lying is the most direct offense against the truth" (CCC, no. 2483). "Lying consists in saying what is false with the intention of deceiving one's neighbor" (CCC, no. 2508) or misleading others who have the right to know the truth. "The *gravity of a lie* is measured against the nature of the truth it deforms, the circumstances, the intentions of the one who lies, and the harm suffered by its victims" (CCC, no. 2484).

Lying hurts people. It is a form of violence against one's self and one's neighbors. Lying undermines the trust on which every human relationship depends and it tears apart the fabric of the connections between people. When a person lies under oath, it is called **perjury**. Perjury is a serious sin.

Duplicity, dissimulation and **hypocrisy** are other forms of lying. Duplicity is saying one thing or acting in one way and meaning the opposite; for example, a person pretends to be other than who he or she really is. Dissimulation is a form of lying in which one conceals the truth, or speaks in half-truths, in order to deceive someone or a group of people. Hypocrisy is another form of pretending; it is "the practice of claiming to have moral standards or beliefs to which one's own behavior does not conform" (*Oxford Dictionaries* online).

READ, REFLECT AND SHARE
In Matthew's account of the Gospel Jesus uses the word "hypocrites" fourteen times.
⊙ Work with a partner. Look up, read and reflect on Matthew 6:2, 5, 16; 15:7; 22:18; 23:13–15, 25, 27 and 29.
⊙ Discuss the insights the statements of Jesus give about the importance of being truthful.

Other forms of self-serving deception:
Sometimes we try to deceive others for our own good—to serve our own interests, as Polonius did. Boasting or bragging, flattery and adulation are examples of such deception. Boasting or

bragging involves making a false claim to take credit that someone else deserves or to take more credit than we deserve. We must be sincere in all we say or do. Flattery and adulation can include saying or doing something just to be agreeable. Flattery and adulation is a venial sin when these attitudes and actions are limited to the desire to be agreeable and do not bring harm to others. Flattery and adulation can be a grave sin when they cause serious harm to someone.

WHAT ABOUT YOU PERSONALLY?

- Think about your desire to belong to a group of friends.
- How much does that desire impact what you say or do?
- What might be the cost of speaking up when what is being said or done is downright wrong?

FROM THE CATECHISM
The virtue of truth gives another his just due. Truthfulness keeps to the just mean between what ought to be expressed and what ought to be kept secret; it entails honesty and discretion.

—CCC, no. 2469

RESPECT FOR THE REPUTATION AND HONOR OF "NEIGHBORS"

When we are requested to provide information about another person or group, we must judge our responsibility in the light of the gospel command to love others and whether it is appropriate for us to share such information. Sometimes, we may have the responsibility to not share information because "the good and safety of others, respect for privacy, and the common good are sufficient reasons for being silent about what ought not be known or for making use of a discreet language" (CCC, no. 2489).

Sometimes there is an obligation to share what someone has told us; but sometimes there is no obligation to do so. Sometimes silence and discretion are the more appropriate responses. Keeping secrets and confidences is not the same as lying. Some confidences, such as professional secrets, must be kept; for example, doctor/patient, lawyer/client and confessor/penitent confidentiality. The words spoken by a penitent to a bishop or priest confessor may never be revealed by the confessor to another

person. "The sacramental seal is inviolable" (CIC, can. 983 §1; quoted in CCC, no. 2511). Betraying such confidences is a serious offence against the Eighth Commandment and the love of neighbor.

Sometimes, however, a person who has a professional relationship with someone is *required* by both moral law and civil law to share information relating to such confidences. For example, if a teacher hears about or even suspects child abuse, she or he is obligated to report that knowledge or suspicion to the proper authority. The spirit of these laws is to protect those in our society who are most vulnerable and who cannot protect themselves. This duty also applies to all of us if we know that someone is planning to do harm to others or to himself or herself. Meeting this responsibility can be very difficult, but it is necessary. Such behavior is truly life-giving. God's grace will strengthen us to meet this *responsibility and obligation.*

People sometimes speak the truth just to be mean, spiteful or hurtful. While everything we say must be true, we need not and should not say everything that is true—especially when doing so would harm people. If we give in to this temptation and harm another person with our lying or spiteful speaking of what is true, we must make **reparation**, or repair the harm, we have caused. We must do everything we can to be reconciled with the people who have suffered because of our speech.

FROM THE CATECHISM
Honor is the social witness given to human dignity, and everyone enjoys a natural right to the honor of his name and reputation and to respect.
—CCC, no. 2479

DISHONORING THE REPUTATION OF PEOPLE
We have previously explored the unbreakable connection between a person and his or her name. The Eighth Commandment warns against every attitude and action that dishonors the reputation or good name of others. In the Book of Proverbs we read: "For lack of wood the fire goes out, / and where there is no whisperer, quarreling ceases" (Proverbs 26:20). We will now take a brief look at some very common ways of dishonoring the name of another person, namely, by gossip, calumny, detraction, rash judgment, and irony or sarcasm.

Gossip: Gossip is an act of violence that brings harm to a person. **Gossip** can be defined as the *unnecessary* sharing of personal information about someone in a way that can harm them— no matter the reason. Today gossip via the internet or text messaging can spread like a raging wildfire; hosts of news shows engage in gossip to improve ratings; tabloids gossip about entertainers. We cannot control who has seen or heard gossip or how far it has spread even in a short space of time. On the surface, gossip may seem to be *harmless fun*, but its consequences are far from fun. For example, you are well aware of the many cases where young people have taken their own lives because of the pain they suffered as a result of gossip. We are obligated to resist the temptation to *have fun* by taking part in gossip. A good rule of thumb to follow is: "If you cannot say something good about another person or group, say nothing!"

Calumny and detraction: Calumny and detraction are often connected with gossip. While gossip may be based on half-truths, calumny is the spreading of lies about a person or a group of people. Detraction is the disclosing of another person's faults and failings, even if true, with the sole purpose of harming or even destroying their reputation and good name.

Rash judgment: Rash judgment is judging others before we know all the pertinent facts. We give in to the temptation of judging others rashly when we assume "as true, without sufficient foundation, the moral fault of a neighbor" (CCC, no. 2477). St. Ignatius of Loyola offers this advice when we are faced with such a temptation: "Every good Christian ought to be ready to give a favorable interpretation to another's statement rather than to condemn it" (*Spiritual Exercises*, 22).

Irony and sarcasm: When irony or sarcasm are used to maliciously ridicule and belittle someone, they are enemies of the truth and contrary to the Eighth Commandment. A good rule to follow is to T-H-I-N-K before you speak.

T-H-I-N-K

Five questions to ask and answer in order to avoid giving in to the temptation to dishonor someone's good name and reputation:

Is what I am about to say or do:

T rue?
H elpful?
I nspiring?
N ecessary?
K ind?

THINK, PAIR AND SHARE
⊙ Share with a partner specific examples of people bringing harm to the good name of a person or group of people.
⊙ Identify which acts contrary to the Eighth Commandment these examples represent.
⊙ Talk about the harm such actions bring to an individual or group of people.

WHAT ABOUT YOU PERSONALLY?
⊙ What can you do to follow the advice given in James 3:1–12?

in quenching our daily thirst for information by feeding us not only with truth but also with half-truths and unsubstantiated facts. Social communication media have the obligation to help in the formation of sound truthful public opinion, and users of such media have the duty to use them in a disciplined and responsible way. The Catholic Church teaches:

> The proper exercise of this right demands, however, that the news itself that is communicated should always be true and complete, within the bounds of justice and charity. In addition, the manner in which the news is communicated should be proper and decent. This means that in both the search for news and in reporting it, there must be full respect for the laws of morality and for the legitimate rights and dignity of the individual. For not all knowledge is helpful, but "it is charity that edifies" (1 Corinthians 8:1).
>
> —Vatican II, *Decree on Social Communications*, no. 5

SCANDAL

Check out Matthew 18:6–7. In this passage Jesus speaks of giving **scandal**. Jesus demands that all of our attitudes and actions are to be life-giving. Scandal is *not* life-giving. "Scandal is an attitude or behavior which leads another to do evil" (CCC, no. 2284). Both individuals and society can give scandal, which can lead to harm of themselves or of others. Jesus had extremely harsh words for those who give scandal.

THINK, PAIR AND SHARE

- Work with a partner. Check out Matthew 7:15–20, 18:6–7; Luke 17:1–2.
- What does Jesus tell us about the gravity of giving scandal?

FROM THE CATECHISM

"The information provided by the media is at the service of the common good. Society has a right to information based on truth, freedom, justice, and solidarity" (CCC, no. 2494). "One should practice moderation and discipline in the use of the social communications media" (CCC, no. 2512).

THE RESPONSIBILITIES OF THE MEDIA AND ART

We are a media-driven society. The communications media play a major role

People who work in the entertainment media should always be aware of the fact that their communications can have deep and lasting effects on viewers, especially the young. **Pornography** and portrayals of excessive violence and of other lifestyles contrary to the moral order are degrading of the dignity of human life. We can say the same about art. Good art reflects the truth and beauty in life. Art that is true and beautiful can uplift people, move them toward contemplation and, ultimately, lead them to worship and thankfulness to God, who is the source of all beauty and goodness.

OVER TO YOU

- There are many images of beautiful art in this textbook and in the other texts of the *Credo* series. Select one image that can be a special path to God for you.
- Spend some time in silence reflecting on this image.
- What does this image say to you?

Choose life so that you may live

⊙ What does it mean to choose life, to be pro-life?

⊙ Give reasons for your responses.

FROM THE CATECHISM

"*Human life is sacred* because from its beginning it involves the creative action of God and it remains for ever in a special relationship with the Creator, who is its sole end. God alone is the Lord of life from its beginning until its end: no one can under any circumstance claim for himself the right directly to destroy an innocent human being" (Congregation on the Doctrine of the Faith, *Instruction on Respect for Human Life*, February 22, 1987).

—CCC, no. 2258

A CULTURE OF LIFE VERSUS A CULTURE OF DEATH

Natural law and revealed law demand that we embrace a "culture of life." The right to life is the fundamental right of every person. The Fifth Commandment, "You shall not kill," teaches this foundational moral principle. This Commandment prohibits directly destroying the life of any "innocent human being" (CCC, no. 2258). Our very nature and God's Revelation call us to be life-givers, not life-takers. Violation of that principle leads, as St. John Paul II taught, to a "culture of death."

Human history gives clear testimony to the reality that "murderous violence" (CCC, no 2260) is part of the human story. The background to the covenant between God and humankind reminds us of God's gift of human life and of the capacity of human beings to engage in death-bearing violence. In the very first chapters of the Book of Genesis, God addresses this violence. In the covenant he made with Noah and, through Noah, with humankind, God says to Noah and his sons:

CAIN AFTER KILLING HIS BROTHER ABEL | HENRI VIDAL

For your own lifeblood I will surely require a reckoning: from every animal I will require it and from human beings, each one for the blood of another, I will require a reckoning for human life.
> Whoever sheds the blood of a human,
>> by a human shall that person's
>>> blood be shed;
> for in his own image,
>> God made humankind.

—Genesis 9:5–6

Beyond condemning murder, the Fifth Commandment mandates choosing life over all forms of death-bearing attitudes and actions. Moses, in his exhortation on the life-giving power of obeying the Commandments, reminded the Israelites:

"See, I have set before you today life and prosperity, death and adversity. . . . I call heaven and earth to witness against you today that I have set before you life and death, blessings and curses. Choose life so that you and your descendants may live, loving the LORD your God, obeying him, and holding fast to him; for that means life to you and length of days, so that you may live in the land that the LORD swore to give to your ancestors, to Abraham, to Isaac, and to Jacob."

—Deuteronomy 30:15, 19–20

In the Sermon on the Mount Jesus teaches:

"You have heard that it was said to those of ancient times, 'You shall not murder'; and 'whoever murders shall be liable to judgment.' But I say to you that if you are angry with a brother or sister, you will be liable to judgment."

—Matthew 5:21–22

Reverence for the sacredness of every human life from the moment of its conception is the best antidote to a culture of death; it is the only way to the fullness of life that God promised for individuals and for families, for the People of God and for nations.

PAUSE AND REFLECT

- ⊙ If you were to make "Choose Life" your personal motto, what actions would you be motivated to make part of your daily living?
- ⊙ What sort of actions would you be motivated to avoid?

ACTS OF VIOLENCE AGAINST HUMAN LIFE

The Fifth Commandment forbids *direct and intentional killing* of an innocent person as gravely sinful. This prohibition teaches us to examine as individuals and as a society how we are contributing to building a culture of life—and not taking part in the building of a culture of death. Acts contrary to the Fifth Commandment include direct abortion, embryonic research, intentional euthanasia, suicide and the intentional neglect of one's bodily and mental health.

Direct abortion: Abortion is the taking of the life of an unborn child from the first moment of her or his conception. Recalling the teaching of the prophet Jeremiah, "Before I formed you in the womb I knew you, / and before you were born I consecrated you" (Jeremiah 1:5), the Catholic Church teaches that the *life of a human person* begins at the moment of conception. Formal

Reverence for the sacredness of every human life is the best antidote to a culture of death

cooperation in a direct abortion is gravely contrary to the moral law. This teaching of the Church has not changed and is unchangeable:

> From its conception, the child has the right to life. Direct abortion, that is, abortion willed as an end or a means, is a "criminal" practice (*Pastoral Constitution on the Church in the Modern World*, no. 27), gravely contrary to the moral law. The Church imposes the canonical penalty of excommunication for this crime against human life.
>
> —CCC, no. 2322

God's mercy and love commands us to show love and understanding to those who have had an abortion. Abortion can cause crippling guilt and regret. God does not want to increase those feelings but wants to heal and have mercy on every wrong. Revelation teaches that there is no such thing as an "unforgivable" sin when we reach out to God for forgiveness. Log on to the United States Conference of Catholic Bishops at *www.usccb.org* for their recommendations on post-abortion healing.

We must distinguish between direct abortion and indirect abortion. For example, a pregnant woman may be diagnosed with a cancerous tumor in or on or in close proximity to her uterus. In such a case a woman might choose to have the tumor removed. In directly removing the tumor, the life of the unborn child may indirectly be aborted. Such a choice is not contrary to the teaching of the Catholic Church.

Catholics must strive to understand why our faith opposes direct abortion so that they are able to articulate the Church's teachings in a clear and compassionate way. We can work against laws that allow "legal" abortion by offering care, support and financial aid to women who need help to nurture the life of their unborn child. The Church does so by providing comprehensive social services that give parents with an unplanned or unwanted pregnancy the resources to bring their baby to birth. Likewise, we can encourage adoption as an alternative to abortion. Some one third of American couples of child-bearing age are now deemed medically infertile; many of these couples long to offer a home to an adopted son or daughter. All these efforts can and do drastically reduce the number of direct abortions.

The right of every human being to life is an inalienable right. Civil laws that deny or take away this right from any person, born or unborn, such as the United States of America has done under "Roe versus Wade," are illegitimate laws. They are contrary to the moral law, both natural and revealed. Even in a society that continues to allow direct abortions, Christians must practice a consistent ethic of choosing for life. This means that we are to both actively oppose abortion and work to end these acts of "murderous violence." One way Christians foster and work to build a consistent ethic for contributing to a culture of life is in how they cast their votes in elections.

THINK, PAIR AND SHARE

- ◉ Imagine you are to make a persuasive presentation to a group of young people who do not know the Catholic position on abortion.
- ◉ Work with a partner to identify the points you would be sure to make.

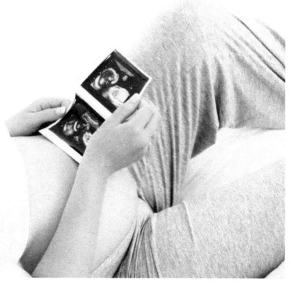

Embryonic stem cell and other scientific research: Human life begins with the fusion of a sperm cell and an egg. An embryo is a human being in his or her earliest stage of development. Because of this biological fact "the embryo must be defended in its integrity, cared for and healed like every other human being" (CCC, no. 2323). Producing and using stem cells from embryos (ESCs) for research contradicts this fact. What is true of the use of embryos for scientific research is not true of the use of adult stem cells (cells obtained from adult tissue samples). Research conducted on adult stem cells does not infringe the dignity of the human person. Such research is therefore in harmony with the moral law.

All expectant parents wonder, "Is our child a boy or a girl?" "Does our child suffer from any genetic or developmental abnormalities that we need to know about before his or her birth, so we can take proper care of our child?" Some parents seek to get answers to those questions prior to the birth of their child. Such prenatal diagnosis is acceptable "if it respects the life and integrity of the embryo and the human fetus. . . . It is gravely opposed to the moral law when this is done with the thought of possibly inducing an abortion, depending upon the results" (Congregation for the Doctrine of the Faith, *Instruction on Respect for Human Life*, I, 2; quoted in CCC, no. 2274).

Scientific, medical or psychological experiments on human beings that *can contribute* to healing the sick and to the advancement of public health must be at the service of the human person and in conformity with the law of God. "Research or experimentation on the human being cannot legitimate acts that are in themselves contrary to the dignity of persons and to the moral law" (CCC, no. 2295).

LET'S PROBE DEEPER: RESEACH ACTIVITY
- ⊙ Work with a partner or group of three or four students.
- ⊙ Research the position of both civil law in the United States and the Catholic Church on embryonic stem cell research. Compare the two.
- ⊙ Present your findings to the class at the completion of the study of this chapter.

Intentional euthanasia: People whose lives are weakened or threatened by sickness or disability deserve special care and respect. Euthanasia denies a person this respect and care. Euthanasia is the ending of a human life in order to end the suffering of a person. Intentional euthanasia, or acts committed with the purpose of directly ending a suffering person's life, is murder and is gravely contrary to the Fifth Commandment. Intentional euthanasia "is gravely contrary to the dignity of the human person and to the respect due to the living God, his Creator" (CCC, no. 2324).

When a terminally ill person is facing imminent death or suffering greatly, we have the responsibility to provide the normal and ordinary care due to the person. Any act or the omission of treatment to directly end a person's life, even if it is done with the intention of eliminating suffering, is murder. Voluntary euthanasia, also known as "assisted suicide," is a form of intentional suicide. In such cases, the terminally ill or suffering individual no longer wants to live, and enlists the help of a medical professional, or another person, to either directly end their life or allow them to die by directly ceasing treatment. The Catholic Church's teaching is that we are always required to take the best "ordinary means" to preserve life. Of course, ordinary means can vary according to advances in medical science.

In summary: "The dying should be given attention and care to help them live their last moments in dignity and peace. They will be helped by the prayer of their relatives, who must see to it that the sick receive at the proper time the sacraments that prepare them to meet the living God" (CCC, no. 2299). The medical and pastoral practice of hospice care can assist us in treating terminally ill persons, family and non-family, in a caring and compassionate manner that is in harmony with the moral law.

LET'S PROBE DEEPER: RESEARCH ACTIVITY

- ◉ With a partner, find out more about the vision and ministry of hospice care.
- ◉ You might begin by contacting your parish ministry to the sick or your diocesan office to find out who offers hospice care in your community.
- ◉ Interview a hospice worker. With the permission of the school principal and your teacher, make your findings available to the school community.

Suicide: Suicide is tragic not only for the individual who commits suicide but also for the family, friends and all those who share life with him or her. Suicide is the intentional taking of one's own life. Sometimes, a person feels that life is so painful or so meaningless they cannot face another day and they decide to end their physical life. When a person both knowingly and freely chooses to end their own physical life, they are acting in a way that is contrary to the Fifth Commandment. Suicide is a tragedy which often results from giving in to the temptation to despair. You will recall that despair is the loss of hope. It is the loss of belief and trust in the saving presence of God who is with us every moment of our life.

"Suicide is seriously contrary to justice, hope and charity" (CCC, no. 2325). It is a profound failure of one's love for God, for one's self and for one's neighbor. Taking one's own life is contrary to love of neighbor because it unjustly breaks the ties of solidarity with family and others. Voluntary cooperation in the suicide of another person is also contrary to the Fifth Commandment. When we become aware of a person's intention to commit suicide it is a life-giving act of love to make that situation known to someone who can help; for example, to a parent, parish priest or youth minister, principal, school nurse, teacher or coach, or some other trusted adult who has legitimate authority over that person.

Christ calls us not to judge others. We cannot know the depth of pain another person is suffering and how that pain has impacted their decision to take their own life. The Catholic Church recognizes this and teaches: "Grave psychological disturbances, anguish, or grave fear of hardship, suffering, or torture can diminish the responsibility of the one committing suicide" (CCC, no. 2282). The Church prays for and invites us to pray for God's mercy for those who have taken their own lives.

TALK IT OVER

- Young people have taken their own lives as a response to the bullying or gossiping or rumor-spreading of their classmates and friends. What responsibility might someone have who helps create the circumstances that contribute to a friend or classmate taking their own life?
- What should you do if you have even the slightest suspicion that a sibling, friend or classmate is contemplating suicide?

Intentional disregard of our bodily and mental health: The Fifth Commandment also demands that we respect both our own bodily well-being and that of others. A consistent ethic of choosing life demands that we care for the health of our own minds and bodies. This includes doing our best to make choices to eat healthy foods, to exercise and to get sufficient sleep. Developing and practicing the virtue of temperance helps us meet that obligation. Temperance is the cardinal virtue that strengthens us to avoid every kind of excess, such as the abuse of food, alcohol or tobacco, the use of or selling of illegal drugs and the misuse of legal drugs that can harm our bodily and mental health.

Other concerns: The human person, in both body and soul, must be respected from womb to tomb. Catholics show respect for the dead body of a person in a number of significant ways that attest to our faith and hope that our beloved dead are "gone home to God" and will rise to eternal life in the final resurrection. It is a traditional pastoral practice for Catholics to bury the remains of a dead person in the earth. Burying the dead is one of the seven corporal works of mercy. For many reasons, including the lack of sufficient burial space, the Catholic Church also permits cremation, provided that cremating a body is not an act of denial of faith and hope in the final resurrection of the body.

According to Catholic teaching, autopsies, organ donation and cremation do not dishonor or disrespect the human body. These choices are morally permitted for legal inquests or scientific research. Organ donation by a living donor and by a donor after death is a genuine service to one's neighbor. Such donation can also be made by a legal proxy of a dying person. Organ donation can help lengthen or improve the quality of life of the recipient of the donated organs and contribute to the peace of the recipient's family.

WHAT ABOUT YOU PERSONALLY?
- How do the demands of the Fifth Commandment help you to choose life?
- How can you take better care of your mental and physical health?

Love and respect for ALL human life—even those who call themselves your enemy

SEAN PENN AND SUSAN SARANDON IN *DEAD MAN WALKING*

Dead Man Walking

In the highly acclaimed film *Dead Man Walking* Sister Helen Prejean describes her insights and experiences of ministering to men facing execution, and, later, to the families of murder victims. The film allows audiences to see the reality of murder and punishment from the viewpoints of death row inmates, their families, the families of the victims, and prison officials. Here is an extract:

PRISON GUARD:
   Tell me something sister, what's a nun doing in a place like this? Shouldn't you be teaching children? Didn't you know what this man has done? How he killed them kids?

SISTER HELEN PREJEAN:
   What he was involved with was evil. I don't condone it. I just don't see the sense of killing people to say that killing people's wrong.

PRISON GUARD:
   You know what the Bible say, "An eye for an eye."

SISTER HELEN PREJEAN:
   You know what else the Bible asks for death as a punishment? For adultery, prostitution, homosexuality, trespass upon sacred grounds, profaning a Sabbath and contempt to parents.

PRISON GUARD:
   I ain't gonna get into no Bible quoting with no nun cause I'm gonna lose.

The prison guard is right. One can find quotes from the Scriptures both to support the death penalty and to oppose it. Meanwhile, as Christians, our challenge is always to try to follow the radical demands of the preaching of Jesus. Everything we find in the Scriptures must be interpreted through Jesus' teaching. Later in the film, the father of one of the victims becomes angry when he sees Sister Helen with the man who murdered his child:

CLYDE PERCY:
   How can you stand next to him?

SISTER HELEN PREJEAN:
   Mr. Percy, I'm just trying to follow the example of Jesus, who said that a person is not as bad as his worst deed.

- Reflect on the excerpt from *Dead Man Walking*. Then share your views on: "Is killing always wrong?"
- Stand at the top of the room if you agree, stand at the bottom of the room if you disagree, and stand in the middle of the room if you are undecided.
- Share the reasons for your position with someone in another group. Working one on one, try to convince others to join your group.

LEGITIMATE SELF-DEFENSE

The Fifth Commandment does not deny the right of a person or a society to defend itself and protect itself legitimately from an unjust aggressor. Legitimate defense against aggression is not only a right; for someone who bears responsibility for the lives of others it can even be a duty. St. Thomas Aquinas explained: "The act of self-defense can have a double effect: the preservation of one's own life; and the killing of the aggressor. . . . The one is intended, the other is not" (*Summa Theologiae* II–II, 64, 7; quoted in CCC, no. 2263). In other words, every person has the right to defend one's own life and other people's lives (the intended outcome) even when the exercise of that right includes the justifiable killing of another person. Engaging in a just war and capital punishment are two of the means by which a society exercises its right and duty of legitimate self-defense.

FROM THE CATECHISM

Because of the evils and injustices that all war brings with it, we must do everything reasonably possible to avoid it. The Church prays: "From famine, pestilence and war, O Lord, deliver us."

—CCC, no. 2327

THE CHURCH FAVORS NON-VIOLENCE, NOT WAR

While the Church favors the non-violent resolution of differences, the teachings of the Church also affirm that a nation may engage in a war under very strict conditions. The key condition for going to war is that it must be the last resort a society has to defend itself. When war is the *last resort*, "the Church and human reason assert the permanent validity of the moral law during armed conflicts. Practices deliberately contrary to the law of nations and to its universal principles are crimes" (CCC, no. 2328).

The development and storing of arms is a common strategy used by nations to assure their ability to defend themselves. On this practice the Church teaches: "The arms race is one of the greatest curses on the human race" (*Pastoral Constitution on the Church in the Modern World*, no. 81; quoted in CCC, no. 2329). Our bishops remind us of the criteria for entering and fighting a just war:

First, whether lethal force may be used is governed by the following criteria:

- *Just Cause*: force may be used only to correct a grave, public evil, that is, aggression or massive violation of the basic rights of whole populations;
- *Comparative Justice*: while there may be rights and wrongs on all sides of a conflict, to override the presumption against the use of force the injustice suffered by one party must significantly outweigh that suffered by the other;
- *Legitimate Authority*: only duly constituted public authorities may use deadly force or wage war;
- *Right Intention*: force may be used only in a truly just cause and solely for that purpose;
- *Probability of Success*: arms may not be used in a futile cause or in a case where disproportionate measures are required to achieve success;
- *Proportionality*: the overall destruction expected from the use of force must be outweighed by the good to be achieved;
- *Last Resort*: force may be used only after all peaceful alternatives have been seriously tried and exhausted.

These criteria (*jus ad bellum*), taken as a whole, must be satisfied in order to override the strong presumption against the use of lethal force. Second, the just-war tradition seeks also to curb the violence of war through restraint on armed combat between the contending parties by imposing the following moral standards (*jus in bello*) for the conduct of armed conflict:

- *Noncombatant Immunity*: civilians may not be the object of direct attack, and military personnel must take due care to avoid and minimize indirect harm to civilians;
- *Proportionality*: in the conduct of hostilities, efforts must be made to attain military objectives with no more force than is militarily necessary and to avoid disproportionate collateral damage to civilian life and property;
- *Right Intention*: even in the midst of conflict, the aim of political and military leaders must be peace with justice, so that acts of vengeance and indiscriminate violence, whether by individuals, military units or governments, are forbidden.

—From *The Harvest of Justice Is Sown in Peace*, United States Conference of Catholic Bishops, November 1993

'THIS IS OUR CRY. THIS IS OUR PRAYER. PEACE ON EARTH.' MEMORIAL TO 12-YEAR-OLD SADAKO SASAKI, HIROSHIMA PEACE PARK, JAPAN

THINK, PAIR AND SHARE

- Read and think about these teachings of Jesus from the Sermon on the Mount:
  - "Blessed are the peacemakers, for they will be called children of God" (Matthew 5:9).
  - "Do not resist an evildoer. But if anyone strikes you on the right cheek, turn the other also" (Matthew 5:39).
- Share with a partner what these teachings of Jesus contribute to your understanding of a nation engaging in a just war.

JOURNAL EXERCISE

- How has your study of the Catholic Church's teaching on entering a just war affected your understanding of the use of violence?
- How do you show that you hunger and thirst for justice?

TORTURE AND GUN VIOLENCE: CONTRIBUTORS TO A CULTURE OF DEATH

Torture: The use of torture has long been a wartime practice, justified as a necessary element of self-defense. Torture shows complete and grave disregard for the dignity of human life; it contributes to building a culture of death. The Catholic bishops of the Church in the United States have issued a four-chapter guide, *Torture is a Moral Issue*, which is available online at *www.usccb.org*.

Gun violence: Death by guns has reached epidemic proportions in the United States of America. Agreeing on a treatment plan to deal with this epidemic has been conflicted by the diversity of understandings of the Second Amendment of the Constitution of the United States. Our bishops have had much to say on the need of both society and the Church to address this issue. You may also find these teachings and suggestions for working to reduce gun violence at *www.usccb.org*.

CAPITAL PUNISHMENT

In addition to Jesus' words during his trial, there is only one incident in the four Gospels where Jesus addressed the death penalty. With a partner, read John 8:1–11.

- How were Jesus' actions on this occasion consistent with the declaration that he would later make in this Gospel, "I am the way, and the truth, and the life" (John 14:6)?
- What do Jesus' words and actions here reveal about God's treatment of those who, according to human law, deserve capital punishment?

Following the example of Jesus, the Catholic Church teaches and advocates for mercy and forgiveness for sinners and criminals. Yet, the Church for a long time has taught that capital punishment is a form of legitimate defense for capital crimes. The Church has, in her past, even pursued and promoted the death penalty for people considered to be heretics. The Inquisition is a horrendous witness to this practice. The teaching of the Catholic Church, however, has evolved to her current teaching, which essentially opposes the death penalty in all but the rarest of circumstances.

The Catholic Church teaches and upholds the right of a government to protect its citizens by punishing those who commit heinous crimes and who will remain a threat to the safety and lives of her citizens. But, this purpose can be achieved by sentencing a criminal to life in prison without parole. The exercise of the right of self-defense is a practice of the virtue of justice. We are to exercise that right to self-defense in relationship to every person's right to life and to support the human person and society to work with God's grace in building a world of justice rooted in love.

Retributive justice: Some people and the laws of a few nations limit the practice of justice to retributive justice. They focus on retribution, applying their understanding of the "eye for eye, tooth for tooth" teaching in Exodus 21:24. Such a view is based on a false understanding of that Old Testament directive, which is part of the Torah's law concerning violence. In context, this law reads:

When people who are fighting injure a pregnant woman so that there is a miscarriage, and yet no further harm follows, the one responsible shall be fined what the woman's husband demands, paying as much as the judges determine. If any harm follows, then you shall give life for life, eye for eye, tooth for tooth, hand for hand, foot for foot, burn for burn, wound for wound, stripe for stripe.

—Exodus 21:22–25

Demanding "an eye for an eye" can lead a person and a community to seek revenge. Both the attitude and the practice of expressing revenge are contrary to the Gospel and are death-bearing rather than life-giving.

Restorative justice: The Catholic Church strongly teaches that governments should always exercise restorative justice, even in their treatment of those who commit capital crimes. Restorative justice seeks to rehabilitate the offender. Clearly, the death penalty does not meet that criterion.

TALK IT OVER

⊙ How is the teaching of our Church reflected in our federal and state laws? For example: Who is working for the treatment versus the punishment of people who commit crimes?

OVER TO YOU

⊙ Learn more about the teachings of our bishops on this issue.
⊙ Visit the website of the United States Conference of Catholic Bishops. Search for their document *Responsibility, Rehabilitation, and Restoration: A Catholic Perspective on Crime and Criminal Justice*.

— What are the federal laws and policy on addressing acts of terrorism?
— Do federal and state laws favor retributive or restorative justice?
— How many inmates are currently on death row? What are the profiles of inmates (race, economic background, education and so on)? What do these profiles say about the equal application of justice?
— What is the cost of the death penalty compared to keeping inmates in prison and working to restore them?
— How can you get involved in campaigns to end the death penalty?

Revenge is contrary to the Gospel and is death-bearing rather than life-giving

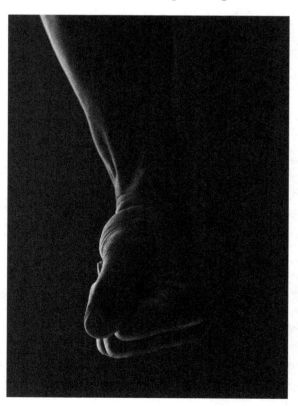

REVIEW AND SHARE WHAT YOU HAVE LEARNED IN THIS CHAPTER

Look back over this chapter and reflect on the teachings of Scripture and Tradition on the Fifth and Eighth Commandments. Share the teachings of the Catholic Church on these statements:

- ⦿ Jesus, the Incarnate Son of God, came that we may "have life, and have it abundantly" (John 10:10).
- ⦿ Human persons are to strive to live as images of God, who is love, truth and the giver of life.
- ⦿ As God is "truth," individuals and society are to be truthful in deeds and in words.
- ⦿ The Gospel calls us to work to develop a "culture of life" and to work against attitudes and behaviors that contribute to a "culture of death."
- ⦿ Every person from their conception has an inalienable "right to life."
- ⦿ Human life must be protected from the first moment of conception until natural death.
- ⦿ Individuals and societies have the right to legitimately defend themselves.
- ⦿ War is justifiable only under strict conditions.
- ⦿ Capital punishment should be used in the rarest of situations.

REFLECT AND DECIDE

- ⦿ What commitments are you willing to make now to choose life and let the commands of the Fifth Commandment and the Eighth Commandment transform your life?

BLESSED ARE THOSE WHO HUNGER AND THIRST FOR JUSTICE

The seemingly endless conflicts in the world point to the imperfection of human beings and our need to work for justice. Jesus names those who work for this justice; they are "blessed." In the Beatitudes Jesus teaches: "Blessed are those who hunger and thirst for righteousness, for they will be filled" (Matthew 5:6). You will recall that in Sacred Scripture the word "righteousness" is a synonym for "justice." People who hunger and thirst for righteousness, or justice, hunger and thirst for the restoration of God's will for human beings and all creation. But there is a cost for living that Beatitude. Four Beatitudes later, Jesus teaches: "Blessed are those who are persecuted for righteousness' sake, for theirs is the kingdom of heaven" (Matthew 5:10).

BLESSED ARE THOSE WHO HUNGER AND THIRST AFTER RIGHTEOUSNESS | CHURCH OF SAINTS DIONYSIUS & SEBASTIAN, KRUFT, GERMANY

Yes, we are to live and work for the justice that Jesus lived and died for. We are to work as Jesus commanded us to bring about the Kingdom of God. As Matthew says in his Gospel, this can lead to people reviling us and persecuting us and uttering all kinds of evil against us falsely. (See Matthew 5:11.)

Sister Helen Prejean, C.S.J

Helen Prejean was born on April 21, 1939, in Baton Rouge, Louisiana. She joined the Sisters of St. Joseph of Medaille (now known as the Congregation of St. Joseph) in 1957. Sr. Helen began her ministry with the imprisoned in 1981. While living with the poor in the St. Thomas housing project in New Orleans, Sr. Helen became a pen pal of Patrick Sonnier. Sonnier, a convicted killer of two teenagers, was incarcerated in Louisiana's Angola State Prison, where he awaited death in the electric chair. Upon Sonnier's request, Sr. Helen visited him on a regular basis as his spiritual advisor. This firsthand experience opened her eyes to the inhumane nature of capital punishment.

Sr. Helen is an outspoken advocate for the elimination of the death penalty. Her renowned book, *Dead Man Walking: An Eyewitness Account of the Death Penalty in the United States*, is an account of her experiences. It has drawn attention to the inhumane cruelty of the death penalty and its contribution to a culture of death. *Dead Man Walking* was nominated for a 1993 Pulitzer Prize, was Number One for thirty-one weeks on the *New York Times'* Best Seller List, and has been translated into ten different languages. In January 1996 the book was developed into a major motion picture starring Susan Sarandon as Sr. Helen; she won an Oscar for Best Actress.

Sr. Helen's second book, *The Death of Innocents: An Eyewitness Account of Wrongful Executions*, was published in December 2004. In it she tells the story of two men, Dobie Gillis Williams and Joseph O'Dell, whom she accompanied to their executions. She believes both men were innocent. In *The Death of Innocents* Sr. Helen takes the reader through all the evidence, including some the juries never heard due to the incompetence of the defense lawyers or the rigid formalities of court procedure. She examines how flaws inextricably entwined in the death-penalty system inevitably lead to innocent people being executed and render the system unworkable.

Sr. Helen has witnessed five executions in Louisiana and today educates the public about the death penalty by lecturing, organizing and writing. As the founder of *Survive*, a victim's advocacy group in New Orleans, she continues to counsel not only inmates on death row but the families of murder victims as well.

TALK IT OVER

- How does Sr. Helen's ministry with the imprisoned on death row and her advocacy for the elimination of the death penalty promote a culture of life?
- What can Christians do each day to help people imprisoned in other ways to "have life, and have it abundantly" (John 10:10)?

WHAT ABOUT YOU PERSONALLY?

- How does Sr. Helen's life and work inspire you to work to build a culture of life?
- How does it inspire you to work against those attitudes and actions that contribute to a culture of death?

SHARE FAITH WITH FAMILY AND FRIENDS

- Think of movies, television shows or music whose message promotes a culture of life. Choose one that you can watch or listen to with your family and friends.
- What does what you have chosen portray about loving and respecting life and speaking and living the truth?
- Share insights that you have learned from your life experience and connect those insights to what you have studied in this chapter.

DECIDE FOR YOURSELF

- Jesus declared himself to be "the way, and the truth, and the life" (John 14:6).
- What are some ways you can live the way of truth and life in imitation of Jesus, and thereby contribute to building a more just society—a society built on truth and the respect for all life?
- List five things you will do. What can you do today?

LEARN BY HEART

"I am the way, and the truth, and the life. No one comes to the Father except through me."

JOHN 14:6

Pray the Sign of the Cross together.

LEADER
Loving God,
help us always to choose the way of truth and life that you revealed in Jesus Christ, your Incarnate Word and Son.
May we show all people the way to abundance of life by being true to your word and our word.
Come, Holy Spirit, Spirit of truth and the giver of life, strengthen us and guide us.
We ask this in the name of Christ Jesus, your truth made flesh.

ALL
Amen.

LEADER
Let us listen to our Lord's words to his disciples.

READER 1
Proclaim John 13:31–35.

READER 2
Proclaim John 16:25–33.

GROUP 1
Tension mounts as terrorists threaten to strike again.

GROUP 2
Jesus said, "Just as I have loved you, you also should love one another." (John 13:34)

ALL
Jesus said, "Peace I leave with you; my peace I give you."

GROUP 1
Gang feud claims three more lives.

GROUP 2
Jesus said, "You have heard that it was said to those of ancient times, 'You shall not murder'; and 'whoever murders shall be liable to judgment.' But I say to you that if you are angry with a brother or sister, you will be liable to judgment." (Matthew 5:21–22)

ALL
Jesus said, "Peace I leave with you; my peace I give you."

GROUP 1
Communities in terror as mindless attacks continue.

GROUP 2
Jesus said, "You have heard that it was said, 'You shall love your neighbor and hate your enemy.'

But I say to you, Love your enemies and pray for those who persecute you, so that you may be children of your Father in heaven." (Matthew 5:43–45)

ALL

Jesus said, "Peace I leave with you; my peace I give you."

GROUP 1

Bloody battle claims four more soldiers' lives.

GROUP 2

Jesus said, "You have heard that it was said, 'An eye for an eye and a tooth for a tooth.' But I say to you, Do not resist an evildoer. But if anyone strikes you on the right cheek; turn the other also." (Matthew 5:38–39)

ALL

Jesus said, "Peace I leave with you; my peace I give you."

LEADER

Let's reflect for a moment on our own lives and ask ourselves: Where is there conflict or untruth in my own life? (*Pause*) In the silence of our hearts let us acknowledge that conflict or falsehood now. (*Pause*) Think about and name one thing that each of us could do alone or with others today to resolve that conflict and restore peace and truth in our own life. (*Pause*)
Let us pray together:

ALL

Loving God, we pray for clear vision to see our lives and the world as it really is.
Remove all hatred and fear and help us accept our differences with a sincere heart.
We pray for politicians and leaders who can do so much to work for peace and truth, and promote a culture of life.
We pray for those who have lost faith and given up hope.
God of perfect love, grant us your peace; send us your Spirit to help us live our life founded on the truth embodied in your Son,
Christ Jesus, our Lord.
Amen.

> Jesus said, "You have heard that it was said, 'An eye for an eye and a tooth for a tooth.' But I say to you, Do not resist an evildoer. But if anyone strikes you on the right cheek; turn the other also."
>
> MATTHEW 5:38–39

CHAPTER 9

The Gift of Human Sexuality

—The Sixth and Ninth Commandments

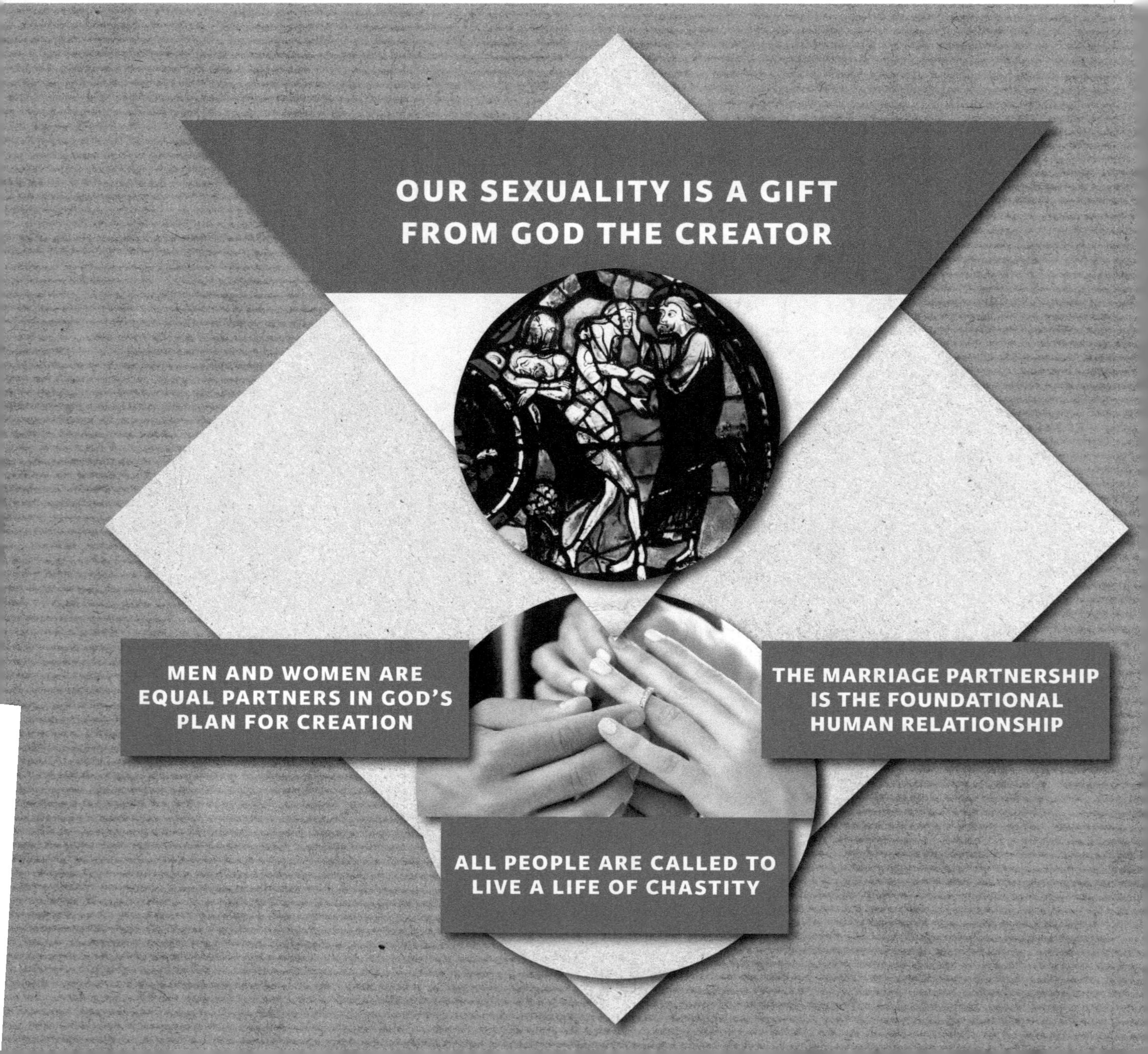

OUR SEXUALITY IS A GIFT FROM GOD THE CREATOR

MEN AND WOMEN ARE EQUAL PARTNERS IN GOD'S PLAN FOR CREATION

THE MARRIAGE PARTNERSHIP IS THE FOUNDATIONAL HUMAN RELATIONSHIP

ALL PEOPLE ARE CALLED TO LIVE A LIFE OF CHASTITY

GOD CREATED HUMAN BEINGS MALE AND FEMALE. Both natural law and revealed law set forth the foundational moral principles that speak to human sexuality and its appropriate expression. In this chapter we explore the Sixth Commandment, "You shall not commit adultery," and the Ninth Commandment, "You shall not covet your neighbor's wife." Both of these Commandments speak directly to the moral attitudes and actions that are to guide us in integrating our sexuality into living a chaste life.

ACTIONS CONTRARY TO LIVING A CHASTE LIFE INCLUDE:

MASTURBATION

PORNOGRAPHY

FORNICATION

PROSTITUTION

RAPE

HOMOSEXUAL ACTS

ATTITUDES AND ACTIONS CONTRARY TO THE MARRIAGE PARTNERSHIP INCLUDE:

ADULTERY

DIVORCE

POLYGAMY

INCEST

FREE UNIONS

Faith Focus: These teachings are the primary focus of the doctrinal content presented in this chapter:

- ⊙ God creates human beings as sexual beings, as men a[nd] women.
- ⊙ Every person should acknowledge, value, respect and [ ] their own sexuality and the sexuality of others.
- ⊙ God creates men and women to be equal partners an[d] complement each other.
- ⊙ Living a chaste life is central to our living a moral life i[n] with the life of holiness that God wills and desires for [ ]
- ⊙ The seeking of sexual pleasures and intimacy needs [ ] and respect the wholeness and oneness of the huma[n]
- ⊙ The development and practice of the virtues of temp[erance] purity of heart and modesty are vital to living a chas[te]
- ⊙ The marriage covenant, which a man and a woman [ ] enter, is a lifelong covenant rooted in faithful love u[ntil] death of one of the spouses.
- ⊙ Grave offenses against the dignity of marriage inclu[de] common social practices of adultery, divorce, polyg[amy] free unions.

Discipleship Formation: As a result of studying this ch[apter] should be better able to:

- ⊙ respect all people, male and female, as images of [God]
- ⊙ grow in attitudes and actions that value, respect a[nd] your sexuality;
- ⊙ build your friendships on the virtues of modesty a[nd] of heart;
- ⊙ avoid viewing and promoting all forms of entertain[ment] promote and foster inappropriate and sinful attitud[es] that offend the dignity of human sexuality and of [ ]
- ⊙ recognize and resist all forms of pornography;
- ⊙ strive to live a chaste life, following the example [ ]

Scripture References: These Scripture references a[re] referred to in this chapter:
OLD TESTAMENT: **Genesis** 1:24 and 27–28, 2:7, 18 an[d] Genesis 4; **Exodus** 20:2; **2 Samuel** 3:2–7, 5:13; **1 King[s]** **Proverbs** 5:15, 12:4, 18:22; **Jeremiah** 31:3
NEW TESTAMENT: **Matthew** 5:8 and 27–28, 19:3–6, [ ] 8:3–11, 13:31–35; **Romans** 1:24–32, 6:13–20, 7:21–25, [ ] 12–23; **1 Corinthians** 3:16, 5:1 and 3–4, 6:19 and 20; [ ] 3:17; **Ephesians** 3:13, 5:25–26 and 31–32; **1 John** 4:8 [ ]

Faith Glossary: Familiarize yourself with the mean[ing] key terms in the Glossary: **abstinence, adultery, a[ ]** **apologist, Capital Sins, celibacy, chastity, concu[piscence]** **divorce, free unions, holiness, homosexuality, in[ ]** **marriage, modesty, passions, polygamy, sexuali[ty]** **temperance, Theology of the Body**

Faith Words: chastity; concupiscence
Learn by Heart: Matthew 5:8
Learn by Example: Blessed Zelie and Louis Marti[n] Thérèse of Lisieux

What responsibilities come with our sexuality?

C.S. Lewis is a widely read Christian writer of fiction classics, such as *The Chronicles of Narnia* (1950–56). Lewis was also an apologist. An **apologist** is someone who speaks or writes to defend and explain a belief, doctrine or idea. Lewis's apologetic writings, such as *Mere Christianity* (1952), are also widely read classics. The following excerpt from *Mere Christianity* is one of his best known defenses and explanations of the Christian teaching on **marriage** and sexual relationships.

The Christian idea of marriage

The Christian idea of marriage is based on Christ's words that a man and wife are to be regarded as a single organism. . . . The male and female were made to be combined together in pairs, not simply on a sexual level, but totally combined. The monstrosity of sexual intercourse outside of marriage is that those who indulge in it are trying to isolate one kind of union (the sexual) from all the other kinds of union which were intended to go along with it and make up the total union. The Christian attitude does not mean that there is anything wrong about sexual pleasure, any more than about the pleasure of eating. It means that you must not isolate that pleasure and try to get it by itself, any more than you ought to try to get the pleasures of taste without swallowing and digesting, by chewing things and spitting them out again.

OPENING CONVERSATION
- In what ways do Lewis's comments reflect contemporary views on human sexuality?
- In what ways do they reflect the teachings of Scripture and the Catholic Church as you have come to know those teachings? Give specific reasons for your responses.

FROM THE CATECHISM
By creating the human being man and woman, God gives personal dignity equally to the one and the other. Each of them, man and woman, should acknowledge and accept his sexual identity.

—*Catechism of the Catholic Church* (CCC), no. 2393

THE WOMAN—MAN/MAN—WOMAN RELATIONSHIP AND PARTNERSHIP

God created human beings as sexual beings. In the Book of Genesis we read: "So God created [man] in his image, / in the image of God he created them; / male and female he created them" (Genesis 1:27). Human **sexuality** is the God-given gift of being a man or a woman. Our sexuality is integral to our human nature and to the divine plan for creation. Each person should accept and acknowledge their sexual identity. Let us briefly review three biblical passages relating to the creation of human beings.

[The LORD God] formed man from the dust of the ground, and breathed into his nostrils the breath of life; and the man became a living being. . . . Then the LORD God said, "It is not good that the man should be alone; I will make him a helper as his partner."

—Genesis 2:7, 18

God blessed them, and God said to them, "Be fruitful and multiply, and fill the earth and subdue it; . . ."

—Genesis 1:28

Therefore a man leaves his father and his mother and clings to his wife, and they become one flesh.

—Genesis 2:24

The marriage partnership revealed in the Book of Genesis is the foundational human relationship that God has willed for human beings. It is central to the divine plan for the creation of new human life. All other human relationships flow from and exist to support and nurture the relationship of a man and a woman united in marriage.

TALK IT OVER

- ⊙ Compare the passage from C.S. Lewis's *Mere Christianity* with the passages from the Book of Genesis. How are the passages similar or different?
- ⊙ What do you think is the connection between the above teachings in Genesis and the Sixth Commandment and the Ninth Commandment?

LIVING AS SEXUAL BEINGS

In *Mere Christianity* Lewis gives his insights into the meaning of the Christian teaching on our living as sexual beings. Desiring and seeking sexual pleasure and intimacy is in itself a created good. But these natural desires cannot be separated from the totality of who God creates the human person to be—an integrated unity of body and **soul** (spirit). Sexual intimacy and intercourse and the seeking of other sexual pleasures need to honor and respect the wholeness and oneness of the human person.

St. John Paul II taught, in what has become known as his **Theology of the Body**, about the goodness and sacredness of the human body and its role in our expressing and sharing our truest and most intimate self. Our sexuality exceeds our physical attributes and it includes the totality of our sexual emotions, feelings and desires. God is the giver of both spiritual and bodily life. God creates us body and soul. Our spiritual and immortal soul is the source of our unity as a person. All our desires for what is good, including our sexual desires, are rooted in and

connected inseparably with our desire for life with and in God.

God creates women and men to be equal sharers of his creative power. The relationship of conjugal love between a man and a woman is ordered to be both *nuptial* (matrimonial) and *generative* (procreative). It is to be love-giving and life-giving. For this reason a man and a woman "become one flesh" (Genesis 2:24).

These truths, revealed in Scripture and taught by the Catholic Church, are the guiding moral principles in our striving to grow into mature sexual persons:

- We are alive by the breath of God. (See Genesis 2:7.)
- God creates us as embodied persons, male and female (see Genesis 1:27), with a body and a soul (see Genesis 2:7).
- Our sexuality (our being a woman or a man) is a gift from God the Creator.
- Our body is a temple of the Holy Spirit, through which we glorify God. (See 1 Corinthians 6:19, 20.)

TALK IT OVER

- What wisdom from Christian faith might you share about responsible human sexuality?
- What is the best advice you can give to someone who is in an unhealthy relationship?

JOURNAL EXERCISE

- In every human relationship that we have entered or are about to enter, we must ask:
  - What attitudes and actions are and will continue to be life-giving and love-giving?
  - What attitudes and actions are and will continue to be destructive and death-bearing to myself and to my partner.
- Look at your friendships and other current significant relationships. Use the two questions above and evaluate those relationships.
- How might you work to ensure that your friendships and other relationships with members of the opposite gender are healthy, life-giving and love-giving?

The universal vocation to live a chaste life

Team Hoyt

Rick Hoyt suffered from oxygen deprivation at the time of his birth, and as a result was diagnosed as a spastic quadriplegic with cerebral palsy. His parents, Dick and Judy, were advised to institutionalize him because there was little hope for Rick to live a "normal" life. Instead, Dick and Judy began the quest for Rick's inclusion in their family life, in sports and education, and one day in the workplace. When Rick was fifteen he told his father that he wanted to participate in a five-mile benefit run for a lacrosse player who had been paralyzed in an accident. Dick agreed to push Rick in his wheelchair and, while they finished next to last, they completed all five miles.

That night, Rick told his father, "Dad, when I'm running, it feels like I'm not handicapped." With that, Team Hoyt went on to complete 1,000 races, including marathons, duathlons and triathlons. Also adding to their list of

achievements, Dick and Rick biked and ran across the United States, completing a full 3,735 miles in forty-five days. Rick was once asked, if he could give his father one thing, what would it be? Rick responded, "The thing I'd most like is for my dad to sit in the chair and I would push him for once."

OPENING REFLECTION

- ⊙ What does the story of the Hoyt family tell you about the power of seeing beyond the body of a person?
- ⊙ What does Team Hoyt tell you about the life-giving power of true love?

CHASTITY

The Great Commandment and Christ's new commandment of love (see John 13:31–35) calls us to honor and respect the whole person. **Chastity** is one of the virtues that empowers us to meet this command. Christ himself is the model of living a chaste life.

Developing and practicing the virtue of chastity fosters our growth in the moral attitudes and behavior that enable us to honor and respect our own dignity and the dignity of other people as sexual persons. Chastity fosters "the integration of sexuality within the person" (CCC, no. 2395). It nurtures the unity and wholeness of the human person, both body and soul. Living a chaste life is being true to one's sexual identity.

Chastity differs from celibacy. **Celibacy** is integral to the way of life of those who have chosen to remain unmarried. Some members of the Church choose to embrace a life of celibacy in order to give themselves entirely to God and to the service of his people. They give witness to our call to live for the sake of the Kingdom of Heaven.

All the faithful are required to live chaste lives. Living a chaste life is central to our living the life of **holiness** that God wills and desires for all people. God invites all people—single or married, those engaged to be married, ordained, lay or religious, young or old—to live a life of chastity. This includes the practice of abstinence by unmarried persons. **Abstinence** is refraining from sexual intercourse and other inappropriate expressions of intimacy until one marries. For married persons, living a chaste life requires exclusivity and faithfulness between spouses. "As a couple grows in virtue, they grow in holiness. In other words, the couple acquires, by prayer and discipline, those interior qualities that open them to God's love and allow them to share in his love more deeply" (*Marriage: Love and Life in the Divine Plan. A Pastoral Letter of the United States Conference of Catholic Bishops*, 46).

FAITH WORD

Chastity

Connected to purity of heart, this is a virtue that moves us to love others with generous regards for them. It excludes lust and any wish to exploit them sexually. It helps us see and put into practice God's plan for the body, person, and sexuality. All people are called to pursue and live the virtue of chastity according to one's state in life.

—USCCA, Glossary, 506

We are social beings. There is "an interdependence between personal betterment and the improvement of society" (CCC, no. 2344). That is why practicing the virtue of chastity involves a cultural effort that supports and does not undermine this moral command.

WHAT ABOUT YOU PERSONALLY?

- ◉ How would you describe your commitment to live a chaste life?
- ◉ What obstacles do you face? What support do you have?
- ◉ What can you do now to deepen your commitment to live a chaste life?

CHASTITY AND TEMPERANCE

Chastity also calls for self-mastery, or self-control. The fire in our soul requires discipline to deal with the fires ignited by our **passions**. The cardinal virtue of temperance strengthens us to develop this self-control. "The virtue of chastity comes under the virtue of temperance" (CCC, no. 2341). **Temperance** is the virtue by which one moderates the desire and attraction of pleasure and provides balance in the use of created goods. Among those created goods is the pleasure associated with the appropriate expression of our sexuality. "Temperance ensures the mastery of the will over instinct, and keeps natural desires within proper limits" (CCC, Glossary, "Temperance").

You will recall that self-control is one of the fruits of the Holy Spirit. The discipline of self-mastery leads to a life of freedom. Self-mastery, or self-control, can be a difficult thing to accomplish, particularly during adolescence as changing bodies and hormones ignite powerful feelings. The practice of chastity and temperance and the other moral virtues of prudence, justice and fortitude lead to a self-mastery right here and now. This discipline prepares people both for marriage and for developing and living in healthy human relationships in whatever state of life one has a vocation—lay single life, consecrated life or the ordained life.

JOURNAL EXERCISE

- ⊙ Describe your own understanding of what it means to live a chaste life.
- ⊙ Why does striving to live a chaste life help to set a person free to truly love God and other people?

TEMPERANCE, PURITY OF HEART AND MODESTY

In the Sermon on the Mount Jesus teaches us, "Blessed are the pure in heart, for they will see God" (Matthew 5:8). This Beatitude urges us to make our every attitude and behavior stem from our love for God, our love for our neighbors and for our self.

Purity of heart is central to living a chaste life. Purity of heart enables us to *see* as God sees. It "lets us perceive the human body—ours and our neighbor's—as a temple of the Holy Spirit, a manifestation of divine beauty" (CCC, no. 2519). Purity of heart is not the denial of physical, sexual pleasures. These are created goods that flow from our God-given sexuality and that are to be valued. The pure of heart, with the help of the grace of God, respect the mystery and dignity of all human persons and respond to the desire for physical and sexual pleasures in a disciplined and temperate manner.

The pure of heart, strengthened by the virtue of temperance, live a life of **modesty**. "A modest person dresses, speaks, and acts in a manner that supports and encourages purity and chastity and not in a manner that would tempt or encourage sinful sexual behavior" (USCCA, Glossary, "Modesty," 520). Modesty is a virtue and also one

of the fruits of the Holy Spirit; it is a sign that we are cooperating to live our life in Christ with the grace of the Holy Spirit.

The virtue of modesty awakens respect for the human person—for oneself and for other people. Modesty "protects the mystery of persons and their love. It encourages patience and moderation in loving relationships" (CCC, no, 2522). Modesty protects both men and women from being used as objects of pleasure, as if they were only some *thing*—a mere object used by another to fulfill their desire for sexual pleasure.

THINK, PAIR AND SHARE

- ⊙ Share stories of people who witness to the values of modesty and purity.
- ⊙ What practical advice do these stories have for you?

"MALE AND FEMALE GOD CREATED THEM"

These three fundamental revealed truths speak to our human sexuality: (1) God creates every person in the divine image and likeness; (2) God creates every person male or female; and (3) everyone is to be treated with dignity and respect as an image and child of God. These truths guide the respect and understanding and love that people must show to one another, regardless of their sexual orientation, including people who are sexually attracted to others of the same gender.

The treatment of homosexuals and lesbians is a widely discussed global social issue that was one of the key deliberations at the 2014 Extraordinary Synod on the Family. The issue is even more complicated in the face of growing acceptance of and legalization for same-sex marriages in the United States of America. These teachings of the Catholic Church serve as our guide in the respect we are to show people who are sexually attracted to others of the same gender:

- ⊙ Those who experience same-sex attraction and come to accept themselves as homosexual or lesbian are children of God.
- ⊙ It is not a sin to be attracted to persons of the same gender.
- ⊙ Homosexual and lesbian persons are called to live a chaste life, as are all persons. (See CCC, no. 2359.)
- ⊙ Homosexual and lesbian persons are not to be treated with disrespect or be subject to discrimination.
- ⊙ Christians must always condemn and avoid prejudicial attitudes and behavior toward homosexuals and lesbians.
- ⊙ Homosexual and lesbian persons are fully welcome and included in the Body of Christ.

These teachings of the Catholic Church are to be understood within a holistic sexuality. God creates men and women as partners to complement each other physically, emotionally and spiritually. This equal and complementary partnership is fulfilled in the marriage of a man and a woman. For these reasons, the Catholic Church teaches that "homosexual acts are intrinsically disordered" (CCC, no. 2357).

OVER TO YOU

- ⊙ Compile a list of all the ways you show love and affection for another person. Which of these support your living a chaste life? Which do not?
- ⊙ What special grace do you need from God at this time? Ask for it.
- ⊙ Pray, "Come, Holy Spirit, fill me with the fire of your love! May your love guide and strengthen me as I try to obey your command to love."

Living a Chaste Life

With the help of God's grace, every day and every moment is an opportunity to respect yourself and others as sexual beings—to live a chaste life. Here are some tips to consider:

- ⊙ Build healthy friendships with all persons— support one another as good friends.
- ⊙ Set boundaries if you have a boyfriend or a girlfriend.
- ⊙ Practice respect for yourself and others; remember that "you are God's temple and that God's Spirit dwells in you" (1 Corinthians 3:16).
- ⊙ Avoid situations that lead you into temptation.
- ⊙ Guard your mind—get rid of the stuff that makes you fall.
- ⊙ Pray often and talk over your relationships with God.
- ⊙ Take part in the celebration of the Eucharist regularly.
- ⊙ Celebrate the Sacrament of Penance and Reconciliation regularly.
- ⊙ Take your time with relationships.

Self-control fosters the freedom to love

OPENING REFLECTION -CONVERSATION

Before he gave them the Ten Commandments, God reminded the Israelites, "I am the LORD your God, who brought you out of the land of Egypt, out of the house of slavery" (Exodus 20:2).

◉ What is the connection and paradox between the Israelites being free and their keeping the Commandments?

◉ What forms of freedom do you see or hear about that result from living the Commandments?

◉ What forms of slavery do you see or hear about that result from not living the Commandments?

CHASTITY AND LOVE

All human life finds its deepest meaning and fulfillment in relationships rooted and centered in love of God, others and one's self. The theological virtue of charity—the God-given ability to love God, neighbor (all people) and oneself because of our love for God—is the central force behind our living a moral life. The practice of the virtue of chastity is driven by charity, and empowers people to live the Great Commandment and the law of love taught by Jesus.

You have seen that a chaste person strives to live free from the slavery of a self-centered life driven by his or her unbridled passions. The chaste person desires, above all, not to enter relationships for self-serving reasons that enslave themselves and other people. The chaste person strives to enter and live in loving relationships that are free, faithful and life-giving. True love (*agape*) is the generous self-giving of one person to another. When we love in such a way, as Jesus did, we are most like our God, for "God is love" (1 John 4:8).

JOURNAL EXERCISE

◉ Take a moment and reflect on your experiences of dating.

◉ How is what you have learned so far about chastity reflected in your "dating" relationships?

◉ What might you do to ensure your dating relationships are chaste?

FROM THE CATECHISM

The ninth commandment warns against lust or carnal concupiscence.

—CCC, no. 2529

TRUE LOVE VERSUS LUST

Lust is the enemy of freedom, true love and living a chaste life. Even after Baptism the inclination toward sin remains, as a result of Original Sin. This inclination is called **concupiscence**. We enslave ourselves when we give in to carnal concupiscence and misuse our passions. St. Paul addressed this conflict and inclination within himself. (Check out Romans 7:21–25, 8:1–8, 12–23.)

beings and gives us the gift of life to love and to be loved, not to be used and then disposed of. We need to distinguish between love and lust. True love is free, total, faithful and fruitful. True love is chaste! Acts contrary to living a chaste life include masturbation, fornication, pornography, prostitution, rape and homosexual acts.

THINK, PAIR AND SHARE
- Reread the opening reflection.
- With a partner, compare its teaching with the teaching of St. Paul in Romans.
- Share how St. Paul's teaching helps you understand Exodus 20:2.

Masturbation: Masturbation is the deliberate stimulation of the genital organs of oneself or another person in order to derive sexual pleasure without having sexual intercourse. It is an offense against love because it makes the excitement of sexual pleasure an end in itself. Oral sex and petting have a similar purpose to masturbation and are also sins against chastity.

The sexual act of masturbation leads to a "dead end." It circumvents the true purpose of our sexuality and replaces it with self-centered erotic pleasure. Sexual erotic love differs from self-giving and self-sacrificing love, or *agape*.

Pornography: Pornography is sexually explicit material that offends against chastity. It perverts and abuses the sexual act and sexual intimacy by exhibiting it to others for base erotic pleasure or profit. St. John Paul II taught that the problem with pornography is not that it shows too much of a person, but too little.

OVER TO YOU
Take a moment and reflect on St. John Paul II's description of pornography.
- What do you think St. John Paul II meant?
- What do you think are the dangers of pornography for young people today?
- What are the best reasons and ways to avoid it?

Pornography is contrary to the moral order because it objectifies and strips men and women, youth and children, of their dignity. This sin reduces a person to his or her body parts. This

Concupiscence

The disorder in our human appetites and desires as the result of Original Sin. These effects remain even after Baptism and produce an inclination to sin.
—USCCA, Glossary, 507

We commit the sin of lust when we knowingly and freely give in to the temptation and desire to seek sexual pleasures *inordinately*, or in ways that are contrary to the moral order that God created. Lust is one of the seven Capital Sins, or sins that lead to other sins and vices.

Lust has its origins in an inordinate and false love of self. It is the setting of one's mind on the flesh and living according to the flesh. (See Romans 8:5, 12.) It is about abusing the freedom to love by misusing other people's or one's own body for sexual pleasure in ways that are contrary to the "law of the Spirit of life in Christ Jesus" (Romans 8:2). It is setting one's mind "on the flesh [that] is hostile to God" (Romans 8:7).

Lust involves treating people, including oneself, as an object and not a person. It is about abusing people. But the human person is not a thing—not simply an object. God creates human

abuse of human sexuality is destructive of both the dignity of persons and the common good of society. Anyone who produces, buys or consumes pornographic materials violates human dignity and seduces others to sin. Pornography is gravely offensive to God, to the person or persons abused, and to the person who commits this sin.

Pornography is addictive; like any addiction, it is a trap, or snare, that is easy to fall into but very difficult to get out of. It "immerses all who are involved in the illusion of a fantasy world" (CCC, no. 2354). It is self-indulgence in action; it is not self-control, or self-mastery, which leads to living in "the freedom of the glory of the children of God" (Romans 8:21). (Check out Romans 8:21–23.)

The pornography industry earns over 97 billion dollars every year worldwide and some 13 billion dollars in the United States of America. Disturbingly, child pornography generates some 3 billion dollars every year. Pornography is a business and a social sin that is protected legally, but erroneously, in the United States by the right to freedom of speech guaranteed by the First Amendment to the United States Constitution. The Catholic Church constantly calls on civil authorities to prevent the production and distribution of pornographic materials. (Check out *Renewing the Mind of the Media* and other statements on pornography on the USCCB website.)

TALK IT OVER

- Why is there an explosion of pornography in contemporary society?
- What are its dangers? For individuals? For society?

WHAT ABOUT YOU PERSONALLY?

- Have you or a friend started to watch pornography? Or to text pornographic images? Why?
- Why is it important to resist the temptation to continue? How can you do that?

Fornication and prostitution: Fornication is the carnal union between an unmarried man and an unmarried woman. Prostitution, which often includes fornication, is the selling of sexual intercourse. It reduces the person to an instrument of erotic pleasure and an object for monetary profit. Prostitution usually involves women, but also men, children and adolescents. Often, prostitutes are victims of serious crimes and have been sexually and physically abused.

Those who profit from prostitution—human traffickers, pimps, the client and prostitutes themselves—burden themselves with greater guilt than those who are forced to sell their bodies. The blameworthiness of a prostitute can be lessened when they are under duress or in situations of poverty and other conditions that diminish their freedom. "Prostitution is a social scourge" (CCC, no. 2355). Society needs to reach out to protect and prevent people from being forced into the sexual slavery of prostitution.

OVER TO YOU

Take a few moments to read what St. Paul had to say about fornication and prostitution in his letter to the Church in Rome. Read Romans 1:24–32 and 6:13–20.

- What is the heart of Paul's teaching on fornication and prostitution?
- Why are these acts contrary to living a chaste life?

Rape: Rape is an act of *violence*. It is "the forcible violation of the sexual intimacy of another person. . . . Rape deeply wounds the respect,

freedom, and physical and moral integrity to which every person has a right. It causes grave damage that can mark the victim for life. It is always an intrinsically evil act" (CCC, no. 2356). Rape is a dreadful sin as well as a serious crime. Rape within social, hierarchical, professional or familial relationships, particularly the sexual assault of children, is most despicable (see CCC, no. 2389). It is possible for rape to occur within a marriage. An essential part of sexual union is that the gift of self must be given freely within the context of love.

THINK, PAIR AND SHARE
- Identify with a partner the factors that contribute to the prevalence of these sins in contemporary culture.
- Discuss why they are a denial of the very identity of a Christian.

WHAT ABOUT YOU PERSONALLY?
- What do you know about "date rape"?
- What attitudes and behavior could lead to date rape?
- Check out your own attitudes and behavior. Make a commitment to enter and remain only in healthy and chaste relationships.

FROM THE CATECHISM
"The Good News of Christ continually renews the life and culture of fallen man" (*Pastoral Constitution on the Church in the Modern World*, no. 58).

—CCC, no. 2527

GOD OF MERCY, FORGIVENESS AND HEALING
Stories of people sinning against chastity are a recurring theme in the human story. Resisting concupiscence is a reality that every person, believer and nonbeliever, must master, as St. Paul so eloquently and passionately taught. Jesus showed and shared the compassion and mercy of God with those who sinned against the Sixth and Ninth Commandments. In John 8:3–11 we read the account of Jesus saving a woman who was caught in the act of adultery from a mob intent on killing her. Notice what Jesus said to the woman after she was safe. When we give in to

carnal concupiscence and sin, we need to repent, seek forgiveness and strengthen our efforts to live a chaste life.

In the Sacrament of Penance and Reconciliation we encounter the risen and glorified Christ, the Incarnate Son of God. Through this ministry that he has given his Church, God treats us with compassion, assures us of forgiveness and offers us the grace to renew our efforts to live a holy and chaste life. We respond by reaffirming our commitment to live a holy and chaste life.

THINK, PAIR AND SHARE
- With a partner, identify ways in which the media create an environment that fosters and promotes fornication, prostitution and even rape.
- Why are these sins offenses against God? Against individuals? Against society?
- What attitudes and behavior must a person develop so as to avoid these sins and live a chaste life?

JOURNAL EXERCISE
- How might you be cooperating with and supporting the media in the creation of a society that offends the dignity of human sexuality?
- What are you doing or can you do to avoid this?

JESUS AND THE SINFUL WOMAN | AFTER ALEXANDRE BIDA

The sacramental covenant of marriage—the Sacrament of Matrimony

OPENING CONVERSATION

Recall for a moment what you have learned about human sexuality in this chapter.

- ⊙ What do the first two chapters of Genesis teach about human sexuality and its connection with marriage?
- ⊙ What are the predominant social attitudes and behavior that are shaping our culture's view of marriage?
- ⊙ Compare these with the teachings of Genesis and the Catholic Church.

FROM THE CATECHISM

"The matrimonial covenant, by which a man and a woman establish between themselves a partnership of the whole of life, is by its nature ordered toward the good of the spouses and the procreation and education of offspring; this covenant between baptized persons has been raised by Christ the Lord to the dignity of a sacrament" (*Code of Canon Law*, canon 1051; see also Vatican II, *Pastoral Constitution on the Church in the Modern World*, no. 48).

—CCC, no. 1601

THE SACRAMENT OF MARRIAGE

Marriage in the divine plan for humanity is a covenant; it is much more than a civil and legally binding contract. It is an "intimate communion of life and love" (CCC, no. 1660). Marriage is a holy union between a man and a woman—an image and a living sign of the covenant love that God and his people have freely and irrevocably entered. God did not name conditions and write loopholes in the covenant that would free him to abandon his people when and if they would not live up to their part of the covenant. God would

always love them; he would *always be faithful* to them; and, even if they turned their back on him, he would *always be their God*.

Jesus Christ, the Incarnate Son of God, is the new and everlasting covenant. He is the fullest, clearest and the final Revelation of the communion of life and love uniting God, his people and all human beings. Christ the Lord raised the marriage between a baptized woman and a baptized man to the dignity of a sacrament that signifies the love uniting Christ and his Church. (Check out Ephesians 5:25–26, 31–32.) The married life of the baptized is always in the service of building up the Body of Christ, the Church, and the kingdom that Jesus inaugurated.

The proper celebration and faithful living of the Sacrament of Marriage is a source of grace and holiness for the spouses, for their families and for the whole Church. The Sixth and Ninth Commandments teach that not only the man and

woman who enter the marriage covenant but everyone, individuals and society, must respect and support the sanctity of the marriage vows that spouses freely and fully commit to live. In the next section we look more closely at the elements of a true and valid marriage. These provide parameters for our respecting and supporting the sanctity of a marriage.

THINK, PAIR AND SHARE

- What other contracts do people enter? What happens when one party breaks the terms of a contract?
- Why is marriage more than a contract?
- Why must everyone respect the sanctity of the marriage vows?

ENTERING THE SACRAMENTAL MARRIAGE COVENANT

A Catholic woman and a Catholic man, or a Catholic and a baptized member of another ecclesial communion, or denomination, who wish to celebrate the Sacrament of Marriage are required to marry according to the laws of the Catholic Church. These laws are based on the indispensable elements for a true and valid sacramental marriage, and reflect both the *nuptial* and *generative* purposes of marriage revealed in Scripture and beautifully explained by St. John Paul II.

For a marriage to be an authentic image of the love of God and a true and valid sacramental marriage, the following elements must be present at the time the spouses enter the marriage.

- **Free and freely entered**: Freedom is an essential dimension of all true relationships.
- **Unity**: Marriage is a covenant that by its very nature brings about a bodily, an intellectual and a spiritual communion of life and love between a man and a woman. It is the total giving of the partners to each other so that they become as one.
- **Indissolubility**: Marriage lasts until the death of one of the spouses.
- **Fidelity**: Marriage is a partnership that excludes other sexual partners.
- **Fecundity**: The marital act by its very purpose is an intimate sharing of love that both deepens the love uniting the spouses *and* is open to offspring.

TOTAL UNITY FREELY ENTERED

St. John Paul II, in his teaching on married love, wrote: "Conjugal love involves a totality, in which all the elements of a person enter—appeal of the body and instinct, power of feeling and affectivity, aspiration of the spirit and of will. It aims at a deeply personal unity, the unity that, beyond union in one flesh, leads to forming one heart and soul" (*The Christian Family in the Modern World*, no. 13.)

At the beginning of the celebration of the rite for the Sacrament of Marriage, the celebrant asks the bridegroom and bride three questions. The first question is: "Have you come here freely and without reservation to give yourselves in marriage?" The giving of oneself in marriage *must be freely given*, that is, "the exchange of consent between the spouses [is] the indispensable element that 'makes the marriage' [*Code of Canon Law*, Canon 1057]" (CCC, no. 1626). Being free to marry and being able to give free consent include that neither the woman nor the man (1) is hindered, or impeded, from marrying by any natural law or Church law, or (2) is coerced or constrained by a physical, emotional and/or mental condition preventing her or him from giving their consent freely.

Conjugal love, the love proper to marriage, is the sign and expression of the marriage covenant. "Conjugal love establishes a unique communion of persons through the relationship of mutual self-giving and receiving between husband and wife, a relationship by which 'a man leaves his father and mother and clings to his wife, and the two of them become one body [flesh]' [Genesis 2:24]" (USCCB, *Marriage: Love and Life in the Divine Plan*).

THINK, PAIR AND SHARE

⊙ Reflect on this teaching of St. Paul: "Now the Lord is the Spirit, and where the Spirit of the Lord is, there is freedom" (2 Corinthians 3:17).
⊙ Share how these words of St. Paul apply to the vocation of marriage.

FAITHFUL AND INDISSOLUBLE

The second question the celebrant asks the man and woman about to marry is: "Will you love and honor each other as man and wife for the rest of your lives?" Take a moment and read Matthew 19:3–6. What does Jesus' teaching say about the answer to this question?

In his teaching in this passage Jesus asserts that marriage by *its very nature* requires inviolable fidelity until the death of one of the spouses. "Love seeks to be definitive; it cannot be an arrangement 'until further notice'" (CCC, no. 1646). Nuptial fidelity shares in and gives witness to God, who reminded his people in exile, "I have loved you with an everlasting love; / therefore I have continued my faithfulness to you" (Jeremiah 31:3).

LET'S PROBE DEEPER

The Old Testament Books of Ruth and Tobit give witness to the ideals of marriage.
⊙ Recall or look up the stories of Ruth and Tobit.
⊙ How does each help you understand marriage?
⊙ Write your thoughts in your journal.

OPENNESS TO THE GIFT OF CHILDREN

Marriage and the conjugal act are intended in the divine plan to be life-giving in two ways:

RUTH AND BOAZ | 18TH-CENTURY ENGRAVING

life-giving for the good of the spouses and life-giving in the procreation of a new human person. "Called to give life, spouses share in the creative power and fatherhood of God" (CCC, no. 2367; see also Ephesians 3:13; Matthew 23:9). This is why the Catholic Church teaches that making love in a marriage must always be open to the possibility of offspring, the gift of children.

FROM THE CATECHISM
The regulation of births represents one of the aspects of responsible fatherhood and motherhood. Legitimate intentions on the part of the spouses do not justify recourse to morally unacceptable means (for example, direct sterilization or contraception).

—CCC, no. 2399

FAMILY PLANNING
By responding to God's command, "Be fruitful and multiply," that is, by being open to the gift of children, spouses fulfill one of the two inseparable and fundamental purposes of

One third of American couples who desire to have children find that they are infertile

marriage, namely, to be at the service of life. Being open to the procreation of a new life does not command the married couple to "generate" a new life in an irresponsible way. All children are a grace and a great blessing. A married couple should carefully discern how many children they can raise responsibly. They need to consider the health of each spouse and the family's economic and social situation. Family life requires a secure and loving environment for nurturing and educating children, spiritually and physically.

For just reasons, a couple may choose to space the births of their children through morally acceptable means. The Catholic Church recommends the refined methods of self-observation, such as Natural Family Planning (NFP), as responsible methods of deliberately regulating conception. These methods make use of the natural alternation of fertile and infertile days in the woman's cycle to achieve or avoid pregnancy. Natural Family Planning is ecological, holistic, healthy and an exercise in partnership between the couple.

On the other hand, the Catholic Church rejects all artificial means of contraception that separate the conjugal act from its procreative potential and block the total self-giving of husband and wife. These include chemical methods (the pill), mechanical methods (condoms) and surgical methods (direct sterilization). No government has the authority to promote the regulation of births by means that are contrary to the moral law, such as the direct sterilization of a person.

TALK IT OVER
⊙ What issues are spouses to consider in planning the size of their family?
⊙ What moral principle should guide spouses in planning the size of their family?

THOSE WHO CANNOT HAVE CHILDREN
Some one third of married couples in the United States of America who desire to have children find that they are infertile. Infertility is a cause of much suffering for spouses. The Catholic Church supports research into reducing infertility that is "at the service of the human person, of his inalienable rights, and his true and integral

good according to the design and will of God" (Congregation for the Doctrine of the Faith, *The Gift of Life: Instruction on Respect for Human Life In Its Origins and the Dignity of Procreation* (1987), Introduction, 2).

Medical science has developed methods and procedures to help infertile couples. All methods that *substitute or suppress* the need for marital intercourse in the procreation of new life are immoral. Some of these methods are gravely immoral and, therefore, unacceptable because they "dissociate the sexual act from the procreative act" (CCC, 2377). There are also "legitimate medical procedures" (CCC, no. 2379) that assist marital intercourse in the procreation of new life that couples can seek to treat infertility. The Catholic Church is sensitive to the desire of infertile couples to give birth to and nurture children. The Church and others reach out to these couples and provide them with the opportunity for adoptive parenting and foster-care parenting.

Artificial insemination and fertilization: Artificial insemination and fertilization are procedures during which conception becomes a medical act outside of sexual union in marriage. These occur in one of two ways. *Heterologous* artificial insemination and fertilization involves a person other than the couple (a sperm or egg donation or a surrogate uterus). *Homologous* artificial insemination and fertilization involves only the married spouses. Out of respect for human dignity and God's design, the Catholic Church teaches that both of these medical methods are contrary to the generative purpose of marriage and are morally unacceptable.

Adoptive parenting and foster parenting: In every society there are numerous children who need the blessing of a caring home and loving parents. Adoption is an act of love on the part of birth parents who recognize their inability to provide a good home, and by the adoptive parents who receive the child as their own. To provide a caring home to an adopted child is an act of love as great as that of birth parents who care for their own children. Adoptive parents and children can bond as readily as any family.

Widespread practice of adoption has also been found very effective in reducing the number of abortions in a society.

Parenting in God's kingdom goes far beyond physical childbirth or parenting through adoption and foster care. Parenting is about nurturing, both spiritually and physically. Many spouses who have neither conceived and given birth to a child, nor welcomed a child into their family through adoption or foster care, overflow with the ability and passion to nurture others. Godparents and mentors and many others can also play a significant role in the care of children and youth.

THINK, PAIR AND SHARE
- Discuss with a partner the attitudes in our society toward adoption and foster care.
- Share ideas on how we could act to place greater value on adoption and foster care as ways to parent a child.

ATTITUDES AND ACTIONS CONTRARY TO THE DIGNITY OF MARRIAGE
The Sixth and Ninth Commandments name attitudes and actions that are contrary to

We follow the example of Christ and do not judge those whose marriages fail

the good of the marriage partnership. These attitudes and actions are offenses against God, the dignity and vocation of spouses and the dignity of the offender. Adultery, divorce, polygamy, incest and free unions are among those attitudes and actions.

Adultery: Adultery is "marital infidelity, or sexual relations between two partners, at least one of whom is married to another party. The sixth commandment and the New Testament forbid adultery absolutely" (CCC, Glossary, "Adultery"). Both the desire for and the act of adultery are a fundamental betrayal of married love. This sin is an injustice and a violation of the lifelong fidelity promised in the marriage covenant that spouses freely entered into in God's presence.

Jesus taught, "You have heard that it was said, 'You shall not commit adultery.' But I say to you that everyone who looks at a woman with lust has already committed adultery with her in his heart" (Matthew 5:27–28).

⊙ How seriously does our contemporary society take this teaching of Jesus? Give specific examples.

⊙ What impact does adultery have on spouses, families and the common good of society?

Divorce: Over fifty percent of spouses who enter marriage in the United States of America seek and obtain a civil divorce. The Catholic Church does not recognize that a civil divorce ends a marriage because no government can dissolve what divine law reveals to be indissoluble. However, if "civil divorce remains the only possible way of ensuring certain legal rights, the care of the children, or the protection of inheritance, it can be tolerated and does not constitute a moral offense" (CCC, no. 2383).

Spousal abuse and child abuse within a family is an outrage and a scandal. A spouse or children may suffer severe physical, mental and spiritual harm as a result of abuse; and the home can become a place where a spouse and children are at risk. In such situations, spouses may separate and discontinue living with each other. If and when this happens, the marriage still exists, and the separated spouses are still bound to fidelity to their marriage promises even if they receive a civil divorce. "The remarriage of persons divorced from a living, lawful spouse contravenes the plan and law of God as taught by Christ. They are not separated from the Church, but they cannot receive Eucharistic communion. They will lead Christian lives especially by educating their children in the faith" (CCC, no. 1665).

In some cases it becomes evident, after careful review of a marriage by Church authority, that one or more of the indispensable conditions for a true and valid marriage were not present at the time the spouses married. The Church has the authority to make a decision about the nullity of the marriage, that is, whether a true and valid marriage never existed. This decision and declaration is known as an annulment. Once the Church declares that a true and valid marriage never existed, the man and the woman are free to marry provided there are no other impediments to their marrying.

Whatever the reason behind a marriage failing severely, we follow the example of Christ and do not judge those whose marriages fail. It is often difficult and a tragedy for those who experience divorce or a separation. Anger and a sense of betrayal are often experienced by spouses and children alike when a divorce or separation impacts their home.

Polygamy: Polygamy is the "practice of having more than one wife at the same time, which is contrary to the unity of marriage between one man and one woman, and which offends against the dignity of the woman" (CCC, Glossary, "Polygamy"). While it is an historical fact that in the Old Law polygamy was practiced among God's people (see Genesis 4, 2 Samuel 3:2–7, 5:13, 1 Kings 11:3), the evidence shows that there was little polygamy after the Exile. Monogamy, or being married to only one person at a time, was taught and valued as the ideal state (see Proverbs 5:15, 12:4,

18:22). The practice of polygamy, while it is illegal, exists in the United States; for example, it is the current practice of the Fundamentalist branch of the Church of the Latter-Day Saints (FLDS). The Church of the Latter-day Saints (LDS) has renounced polygamy and declared monogamy the law of the Mormons.

Incest: Incest is "intimate relations between relatives or in-laws within a degree that prohibits marriage between them (see Leviticus 18:7–20)" (CCC, no. 2388). Incest corrupts family life and debases those who commit this sin. St. Paul addressed the practice of incest in the early Church. He scolded Christians in Corinth: "It is actually reported that there is sexual immorality among you, and of a kind that is not found even among pagans; for a man is living with his father's wife. . . . For though absent in body, I am present in spirit; and as if present I have already pronounced judgment in the name of the Lord Jesus on the man who has done such a thing" (1 Corinthians 5:1, 3–4).

Our society has become plagued by an outrageous and scandalous form of incest; it is the rape of children committed by their parents or the rape of children and adolescents committed by adults responsible for their education or entrusted with their care in any other way. This sin cries to heaven for vengeance.

Think about ways that society proposes and supports attitudes that are contrary to marriage

Free unions: The term "free unions" refers to several relationships between a man and a woman. These include trial marriages, cohabitation and concubinage, as well as the "rejection of marriage as such, or inability to make long-term commitments" (CCC, no. 2390). All these relationships have one thing in common: the partners choose to live together without entering a full marriage commitment and union. Such partnerships are contrary to the dignity of marriage and the moral law. The partners do not commit themselves to all or some of the indispensable elements that make a marriage a marriage. They seek sexual intimacy outside of marriage and destroy the very idea of the family. "Carnal union is morally legitimate only when a definitive community of life between a man and a woman has been established" (CCC, no. 2391). "Outside of marriage it always constitutes a grave sin and excludes one from sacramental communion" (CCC, no. 2390).

Similar to free unions is the current phenomenon of "hooking up." Father Robert Barron, a priest and theologian of the Archdiocese of Chicago and Rector and President of Mundelein Seminary, has described hooking up as "sex as mere recreation, as contact sport, as a source only of superficial pleasure [that] has produced armies of the desperately sad and anxious, many who have no idea that it is precisely their errant sexuality that has produced such deleterious effects in them."

THINK, PAIR AND SHARE

⊙ Think about ways that society proposes and supports the attitudes and actions that are contrary to marriage.
⊙ What impact does entering those relationships have on the life of the partners? On family life? On society?

JOURNAL EXERCISE

⊙ What kind of self-control and self-sacrifice do you practice now in your relationships with members of the opposite gender? Might you be more disciplined in your efforts? Why is doing so important? Write your thoughts on this in your journal.

JUDGE AND ACT

REVIEW AND SHARE WHAT YOU HAVE LEARNED IN THIS CHAPTER

Look back over this chapter and reflect on the teachings of Scripture and Tradition on the Sixth and Ninth Commandments. Share the teachings of the Catholic Church on these statements:

- ⊙ We are to honor and respect human sexuality as a gift of God.
- ⊙ We are to accept our sexuality and live a chaste life whatever our state of life, or vocation.
- ⊙ The virtues of modesty, purity of heart and temperance strengthen us to live a chaste life.
- ⊙ Jesus Christ is the model for living a chaste life.
- ⊙ The human person is not some "thing" but some "one".
- ⊙ Resisting concupiscence is a reality that every person must master.
- ⊙ Masturbation, fornication, rape, pornography and homosexual practices are contrary to chastity.
- ⊙ Marriage is a covenant between a man and a woman.
- ⊙ Christ raised marriage to a sacrament.
- ⊙ We are to respect the sanctity of the marriage vows.
- ⊙ Freedom, unity, indissolubility, fidelity and openness to children are the essential elements of a true marriage.
- ⊙ Adultery, divorce, polygamy and free unions show disrespect for the sanctity of marriage vows and are offenses against the dignity of marriage.

REFLECT AND DISCERN

- ⊙ What is the best wisdom you have learned about the gift of sexuality in this chapter?
- ⊙ How can you imagine living out such wisdom?

LEARN BY EXAMPLE

Blessed Louis and Zelie Martin, the parents of St. Thérèse of Lisieux

On October 19, 2008, World Mission Sunday, Louis and Zelie Martin were declared blessed in Lisieux, France. It was only the second time in history that a married couple had been beatified. Here are adapted excerpts from their biography.

When Louis and Zelie met they quickly came to appreciate and love each other. Their spiritual harmony established itself so rapidly that a religious engagement sealed their mutual commitment without delay. From the beginning, they placed their love under God's protection. They celebrated their marriage on July 13, 1858.

Shortly afterward they welcomed into their home a five-year-old boy whose widowed father was crushed by the burden of raising eleven children. In their marriage, Louis and Zelie would always serve God as their first priority. They were blessed by the birth of nine children, of which five girls survived, all of whom became nuns. Zelie taught them the morning offering of their hearts to God, the simple acceptance of daily difficulties to please Jesus. This became the basis of "The Little Way" taught by the most celebrated of their children, Thérèse, whom the Catholic Church would name a saint and Doctor of the Church. The spiritual life of Zelie and Louis Martin, which was at the heart of their vocation to family life, was the basis of the growth in holiness of St. Thérèse and the religious vocations of her sisters.

On August 28, 1877, Zelie died, leaving Louis with five children to care for: Marie, Pauline, Leonie, Celine, and Thérèse who was four and a half years old. Louis moved the family to Lisieux, where he could take better care of the children. In the last years of his life Louis, who was affectionately named "the patriarch" by those close to him, experienced several health problems and he died peacefully on July 29, 1894.

When the Church named Zelie and Louis blessed of the Church, Cardinal Saraiva Martins, the retired Prefect of the Congregation for the Cause of Saints, said that in a time of crisis for families, the family has in the Martin couple a true model. Here is an excerpt from his homily:

Among the vocations to which individuals are called by providence, marriage is one of the highest and most noble. Louis and Zelie understood that they could become holy not in spite of marriage, but through, in, and by marriage, and that their becoming a couple was the beginning of an ascent together. The conjugal love of Louis and Zelie is a pure reflection of Christ's love for his Church.

In a letter Thérèse wrote:

While reading the Apostolic Letter of the Holy Father, I thought of my father and mother, and now I invite you to think of your parents that together we may thank God for having created and made us Christians through the conjugal love of our parents. The gift of life is a marvelous thing, but even more wonderful for us is that our parents led us to the Church which alone is capable of making us Christians. For no one becomes a Christian by oneself.

HOUSE OF LOUIS AND ZÉLIE MARTIN, BIRTHPLACE OF ST. THÉRÈSE, ALENÇON, FRANCE

TALK IT OVER

- What does the married life of Zelie and Louis teach about the connection between one's sexuality and one's spirituality?
- What did you find most inspirational in their story?

WHAT ABOUT YOU PERSONALLY?

- What can you learn about your current friendships from the example of Louis and Zelie? About preparing for future relationships, including marriage should that be your vocation?

SHARE FAITH WITH FAMILY AND FRIENDS

- Reflect: Modesty, chastity and purity of heart require the loving support of family and friends.
- Discuss with family and friends how well you integrate these virtues into your family and friendships.
- Share ideas on some practical ways you can better support one another in making these virtues part of your daily life.

JUDGE AND DECIDE

- How do the ways in which the media and the entertainment industry exploit the human inclination toward carnal concupiscence contribute to injustice and violence?
- What might you do to work against sexually based injustice and violence?

JOURNAL EXERCISE

- Reflect on your understanding of chastity. Be honest with yourself about what aspects you find most challenging.
- Write an action plan to help you succeed in living the virtue of temperance.
- Talk your plan over with the Holy Spirit.

LEARN BY HEART

"Blessed are the pure in heart, for they will see God."

MATTHEW 5:8

NOTRE-DAME, PARIS, FRANCE

Pray the Sign of the Cross together.

READER
A reading from the holy Gospel according to John.
Proclaim John 8:3–11.
The Gospel of the Lord.
ALL
Praise to you, Lord Jesus Christ.
Prayerfully reflect on the Word of God and apply it to your life.

LEADER
Let us give thanks to God for the beautiful gift of our sexuality and ask for the grace and strength necessary to live out chastity in thought, word and deed. Let us pray:

READER
God, giver of life and love, you created us male and female to complement each other and to be co-creators with you.
Help us open our minds and hearts to the gift of our sexuality.
Help us live in accordance with our responsibility to honor the gift and sacredness of our body and our power to create new life.
ALL
Lord, hear our prayer.

READER
God, giver of life and love, you call us to resist and reject the limited view of sex that is prevalent in our society.
You call us to respect and celebrate the wonderful gift of our sexuality and to integrate it with our spirituality— our relationship with you.
ALL
Lord, hear our prayer.

READER
God, giver of life and love, you have warned us against the dangers of lust.
Protect our minds and hearts so that all our thoughts, desires and actions will be pleasing to you and will help us establish loving relationships in our lives.
ALL
Lord, hear our prayer.

READER
God, giver of life and love, Jesus showed mercy to the woman who committed adultery and he then asked her to go and sin no more.
Help us to show the same compassion to those who struggle to live out chastity in their lives, including ourselves.
We ask this through Jesus Christ, your Incarnate Son, who lives and reigns with you and the Holy Spirit, one God, for ever and ever.
ALL
Amen.

Pray the Sign of the Cross together.

Help us to show compassion to those who struggle to live out chastity in their lives

CHAPTER 10

Building a Just and Compassionate Society
—The Seventh and Tenth Commandments

GOD HAS ENTRUSTED HUMANITY WITH THE STEWARDSHIP OF HIS CREATION

WE ARE TO LIVE A LIFE OF JUSTICE AND CHARITY

THE RIGHT TO PRIVATE PROPERTY IS LIMITED BY CONCERN FOR THE QUALITY OF LIFE OF OTHERS

GOD CREATED THE WORLD FOR THE BENEFIT OF EVERYONE

IN THIS CHAPTER WE CALL OUR ATTENTION TO GOD the Creator's command to our first parents: "Have dominion over the fish of the sea, and over the birds of the air . . . and over every living thing that moves upon the earth" (Genesis 1:28). We explore both the Seventh Commandment, "You shall not steal," and the Tenth Commandment, "You shall not covet . . . anything that belongs to your neighbor." These two Commandments reveal that we are to treat all material things as gifts from God and use them with justice and charity for the good of all people.

TYPES OF JUSTICE:

- ORIGINAL JUSTICE
- COMMUTATIVE JUSTICE
- DISTRIBUTIVE JUSTICE
- LEGAL JUSTICE
- SOCIAL JUSTICE
- RETRIBUTIVE JUSTICE
- RESTORATIVE JUSTICE

Faith Focus: These teachings are the primary focus of the doctrinal content presented in this chapter:

- ⊙ God gave humanity the responsibility to be good stewards of creation.
- ⊙ We are to treat all created goods as gifts from God.
- ⊙ We are to use all creation justly, showing concern and compassion for others, especially the poor.
- ⊙ God the Creator is always at work caring for his creation and bringing it to its fulfillment.
- ⊙ We must respect the possessions of others.
- ⊙ The right to private property includes acquiring and using it for personal needs *and* the good of others.
- ⊙ All people have a right to the basic necessities required to live a decent and dignified life.
- ⊙ Society must work for the common good.
- ⊙ Working for justice requires showing special concern for those who are most in need.
- ⊙ God desires justice and solidarity among all people and all nations.

Discipleship Formation: As a result of studying this chapter you should be better able to:

- ⊙ value your possessions as gifts to be generously shared, especially with people in need;
- ⊙ become more aware of your solidarity with others as children of the one God, Father and Creator of all;
- ⊙ treat others justly and with love out of love for God;
- ⊙ speak out against social structures that are unjust and that dishonor the dignity of people.

Scripture References: These Scripture references are quoted or referred to in this chapter:

OLD TESTAMENT: **Genesis** 1:26–29, 2:15, 3:6; **Exodus** 20:15, 17, 21:24; **Deuteronomy** 5:21; **Psalm** 119:12, 14–15 164–165; **Proverbs** 6:34, 15:27; **Isaiah** 1:17
NEW TESTAMENT: **Matthew** 5:40, 42, 6:19–21, 25–34, 20:1–16; **Mark** 2:15, 12:30, 31, 38–44; **Luke** 4:16–19, 11: 54, 12:13–23, 27–31, 41–48, 14:1–24, 16:1–13, 19–31, 18: 25, 19:1–10, 24:30; **John** 2:1–11, 13:34; **Romans** 8:18–25 **2 Corinthians** 8:9; **Galatians** 5:24; **James** 3:13–14, 16

Faith Glossary: Familiarize yourself with the meaning of these key terms in the Glossary: **almsgiving, consumerism, covetousness, divine providence, jus Kingdom of God, social sin, social teachings (doctri the Church, solidarity, stewardship, theft, Works o**

Faith Word: covetousness
Learn by Heart: Matthew 6:19–21
Learn by Example: St. Martin de Porres, Dominic brother

What responsibilities come with God's gifts?

- How does the Blackfoot chief's response reflect the teachings of Genesis?
- Compare the Blackfoot chief's response with what you have learned from your study of the social doctrine of the Catholic Church in your theology courses.

FROM THE CATECHISM

In the beginning God entrusted the earth and its resources to the common stewardship of mankind to take care of them, master them by labor, and enjoy their fruits (see Genesis 1:26–29). The goods of creation are destined for the whole human race.

—*Catechism of the Catholic Church* (CCC), no. 2402

A GIFT FOR ALL

Divine Revelation, both Sacred Scripture and Sacred Tradition, is clear: it is the plan and will of God that we use the goods of creation for both the glory of God and the benefit of all human beings.

You will recall that in the first creation account in Genesis, after God has created the first human beings, he blesses them and says:

"Be fruitful and multiply, and fill the earth and subdue it; and have dominion over the fish of the sea and over the birds of the air and over every living thing that moves upon the earth. . . . See, I have given you every plant yielding seed that is upon the face of all the earth, and every tree with seed in its fruit; you shall have them for food."

—Genesis 1:28–29

And in the second account of creation, we read: "The LORD God took the man and put him in the garden of Eden to till it and keep it" (Genesis 2:15).

When European settlers arrived on the North American continent, they found a vast expanse of largely unexplored land rich in an abundance of natural resources. With such a wealth of resources available to them, these settlers saw that the possibilities for their future were endless. Many families and business enterprises came to the New World with the intention of buying land and beginning new lives. You can imagine the surprise of the settlers who offered to purchase land from the Blackfoot people in the 1800s when they received this response from a Blackfoot chief: "We cannot sell the lives of men and animals; therefore we cannot sell this land."

OPENING CONVERSATION

- What would your response have been to the Blackfoot chief?

PRIVILEGE AND RESPONSIBILITY GO HAND IN HAND

God the Creator has been exceedingly generous to humanity from the start; however, God's generosity also involves a responsibility on our part. God entrusts the gift of his creation to the entire human race with the requirement that we "till and keep it" for the good of all. This responsibility includes our being good stewards of creation. **Stewardship** means caring for goods and possessions that have been entrusted to a person by their rightful owner. (Check out Luke 12:41–48, 16:1–13.)

As creatures, we receive the gift of life and all creation solely through God's gratuitous generosity. We have no gift of our own making to offer God in return; what we can offer is our gratitude, and we do this best when we take good care of the gifts God has given us.

The "Christian life strives to order this world's goods to God and to fraternal charity" (CCC, no. 2401). We do this by coming to know and work toward implementing God's original plan of justice for his creation. God wills that all creation live in justice, in "right order" and "harmony." The Church reminds us:

The seventh commandment enjoins respect for the integrity of creation. Animals, like plants and inanimate beings, are by nature destined for the common good of past, present, and future humanity (see Genesis 1:28–31). Use of the mineral, vegetable, and animal resources of the universe cannot be divorced from respect for moral imperatives. Man's dominion over inanimate and other living beings granted by the Creator is not absolute; it is limited by concern for the quality of life of his neighbor, including generations to come; it requires a religious respect for the integrity of creation (see St. John Paul II, Encyclical Letter, *On the Hundredth Year* (May 1, 1991), nos. 37–38).
—CCC, no. 2415

In the Seventh Commandment God directs us to acknowledge and live by his divine plan for all creation, namely, the goods of creation are "destined for the common good of past, present and future humanity." The Catholic Church names this revealed truth "the universal destination of goods." This moral principle is fundamental to the **social doctrine, or teaching, of the Catholic Church.** It is God's will that everyone benefit from God's creation. For anyone to possess an excess of goods

and to hold on to them irresponsibly while others go without a just share in the basic necessities of life is an offense against the generosity of God and against one's neighbor. God gave humanity dominion over creation so that all people can live a decent and dignified life. No personal right is more basic than the right to life and to what is needed to sustain it.

LET'S PROBE DEEPER: SCRIPTURE ACTIVITY

- Read Luke 12:13–21, the first part of the parable of the rich fool.
- How would you describe the rich man's attitude toward his wealth?
- What does Jesus teach about material possessions?
- How does the rich man's attitude square with the Catholic Church's social teaching on the universal destination of goods?

WHAT ABOUT YOU PERSONALLY?

- Reflect: Everything you have is ultimately a gift from God and a reflection of God's generosity.
- What kinds of responsibilities might this imply in your life now?

GENEROSITY STARTS WITH SMALL ACTS

A little research will show that the world is desperately in need of a greater commitment to justice and generosity. Homelessness, world hunger, lack of drinking water and of medical care are all offenses that work against divine providence. **Divine providence** is "God's loving care and concern for all he has made; he continues to watch over creation, sustaining its existence and presiding over its development and destiny" (*United States Catholic Catechism for Adults* [USCCA], Glossary, "Divine Providence," 510).

Conditions that prevent some people from possessing their rightful share of the earth's goods are a scandal to and offense against the solidarity that binds the human family. Such conditions begin with and continue through personal acts of turning our back on individuals in need, as the rich man did on Lazarus. (Check out the parable of the rich man and Lazarus in Luke 16:19–31.) In the parable of the widow's mite Jesus teaches that the degree of generosity with which we give, and the amount we give, is the measure of our charity, or love, for others. (Check out Mark 12:38–44 or Luke 20:45—21:4.)

We live in a time when the material wealth and the necessary technologies exist to provide the means to address world hunger and other tragedies. The seemingly small acts of individuals and the social policies of nations that withstand the sharing of goods as generously as the widow in the gospel parable continue to contribute to these great **social sins**. You will recall from your study of social sin in chapter 4 that social sins are the result of personal sins. They "produce unjust social laws and oppressive institutions" (USCCA, Glossary, "Social Sin," 528).

Great moral evils start as small ones. For this reason, we must be diligent to develop and live the moral virtues of justice and generosity, even in the smallest details of our daily life. This enables us to follow the example and teachings of Christ to express both in our words and actions our concern for others.

TALK IT OVER

⊙ Explain in your own words the meaning of the Catholic social teaching on the universal destination of goods.

⊙ What are the implications of this moral teaching for your school community?

⊙ In what concrete ways can your school community put that teaching into practice?

JOURNAL EXERCISE

⊙ Read Mark 12:41–44, the account of the widow's offering in the Temple.

⊙ Discuss whether your generosity resembles that of the widow or of the rich people in the parable.

⊙ Describe how you can show your gratitude for God's gifts to you.

"This poor widow . . . has put in everything she had, all she had to live on."

MARK 12:43–44

THE WIDOW'S OFFERING | OTTOBEUREN ABBEY, GERMANY

The Seventh Commandment: much more than not stealing

A Gut-Wrenching Violation

A study into the psychological effects of home burglary revealed these findings:

Half described the experience as feeling "like a violation or rape." . . . The feelings of violation led several women to wash all of their clothes after a burglar had rummaged through them. One laundered everything three times. In a third of adults, sleeplessness and anxiety lingered for months after the break-in, but kids were especially shaken by the experience. One first-grader began hiding favorite toys before leaving for school each day.

OPENING CONVERSATION
⊙ Have you or anyone whom you know ever been the victim of theft? What impact did it have?
⊙ What do we lose in addition to our material possessions when someone steals from us? Give reasons for your responses.

A BASIC TRUST AND RESPECT
The Israelites were living in a state of great vulnerability when they received the Ten Commandments. They were wandering nomads living in the desert somewhere between Egypt and Canaan, the land God had promised them. As wandering nomads, they were subject to other nomadic tribes that were often hostile to them. They lived in constant fear of thieves moving stealthily among them and of enemies raiding their encampments and seizing the goods they depended upon for their survival. Theft and its devastating consequences were realities in their lives. **Theft** is "usurping another's property

against the reasonable will of the owner" (CCC, no. 2408).

The Seventh Commandment spoke to this insecurity and warned God's people of the importance of trust and respect for the property of others, including within their own communities. If members of a community cannot trust that others will respect what belongs to them, everyone's life becomes filled with anxiety. In an environment in which stealing, or theft, is a constant threat, the safety and well-being that God desires and wills for all people can be reduced to a mere wish.

TALK IT OVER
⊙ How does a climate of theft contribute to the vulnerability of people?
⊙ What virtues or moral qualities do you think the commandment "You shall not steal" is asking us to develop as individuals and as a society?
⊙ How do these virtues contribute to the peace of mind and well-being of people?

THE RIGHT TO PRIVATE PROPERTY

God created the world for the benefit of everyone. Among those benefits is the right to private, or personal, property that is acquired justly and as a result of one's work. Acquiring personal property justly contributes to the stewardship of creation. It guarantees the freedom and dignity of persons and helps individuals, families and members of society to meet their basic needs. The moral law, however, forbids the acquisition of private property unjustly. For example, it "forbids acts which, for commercial or totalitarian purposes, lead to the enslavement of human beings, or to their being bought, sold or exchanged like merchandise" (CCC, no. 2455).

As we acquire and care for our personal possessions, we must keep our neighbors in mind and follow the mandate of the Great Commandment. We must maintain a balance between our personal needs and the needs of other people, especially the poor. We are to be just and prudent stewards of creation, whose origin is God the Creator and whose end, ultimately, is to give glory to God and to serve the common good. Concern for others is always a responsibility and characteristic of the disciples of Christ.

THINK, PAIR AND SHARE

- ⊙ Think about some of your favorite possessions. Talk with a partner about how you can use them for your own good in a way that gives glory to God.
- ⊙ Then share how you can use them for the bodily and spiritual good of others.

FROM THE CATECHISM

Man is himself the author, center and goal of all economic and social life. The decisive point of the social question is that goods created by God for everyone should in fact reach everyone in accordance with justice and with the help of charity.

—CCC, no. 2459

A BIG RESPONSIBILITY

The wisdom of God at the heart of the Seventh Commandment directs us to acquire and use the goods of creation *in accordance with justice and with the help of charity.* "The dominion granted by the Creator over the mineral, vegetable, and animal resources of the universe cannot be separated from respect for moral obligations, including those toward generations to come" (CCC, no. 2456).

When we work, or "till and keep [the earth]" (Genesis 2:15), we participate in the divine work of creation and in the redemptive work of Christ's new creation. This wisdom is reflected in the practice of **almsgiving**, which has always been a hallmark of God's people. The Church reminds us: "Giving alms to the poor is a witness to fraternal charity: it is also a work of justice pleasing to God" (CCC, no. 2462).

This responsibility to share God's gifts extends not only to personal possessions but also to our larger economic and political dealings. The moral law requires that individuals and boards of directors who oversee corporations and owners of smaller businesses use the means at their disposal for the common good of all, even as they pursue a reasonable profit. Greater privilege and power brings greater responsibility. In the words of Pope Benedict XVI: "[I]investment always has moral, as well as economic significance" (*Charity in Truth*, no. 40).

Fundamental to the social doctrine of the Catholic Church is the Church's right and ministry to make "a judgment about economic and social matters when the fundamental rights of the person or the salvation of souls requires it. She is concerned with the temporal common good of men because they are ordered to the sovereign Good, their ultimate end" (CCC, no. 2458). One way the Church does this is by reading and addressing the signs of the times in light of the Gospel. For example, in his first major speech on the global financial system on May 18, 2013, Pope Francis decried the "cult of money" that is tyrannizing the poor and turning humans into expendable consumer goods. He said:

"If investment in banks fall, it is a tragedy, and people say, 'What are we going to do?' But if people die of hunger, have nothing to eat or suffer from poor health, that's nothing. This is our crisis today. A Church that is poor and for the poor has to fight this mentality."

"Money has to serve, not rule," Pope Francis stated as he encouraged world leaders to accept their responsibility to transform the financial system and make it more ethical and concerned for the common good. Pope Francis' teaching clearly reflects the constant teaching of the

Catholic Church that "political authority has the right and duty to regulate the legitimate exercise of the right to ownership for the sake of the common good" (CCC, no. 2406).

TALK IT OVER
- What are the effects when the decisions of business and political leaders disregard their responsibility to the common good?
- How can youth participate in the responsibility of the Church to speak out on economic and social issues?

ACTIONS CONTRARY TO THE SEVENTH COMMANDMENT
The Seventh Commandment reveals that the respect that is due every person *includes* respecting their goods as you want other people to respect you and your possessions. The violation of this moral principle is not always as cut-and-dry as someone stealing your lunch money from your backpack. Some acts contrary to justice demanded by the Seventh Commandment are not so obvious and clear cut and acknowledged, for example, the widespread and common business practices of making exorbitant profits to satisfy investors and shareholders at the expense of employees and customers.

Other acts contrary to the Seventh Commandment include business fraud, paying unjust wages, doing poor work for which one is paid, not keeping promises made in a legal contract that has been freely entered, the unjust destruction of another person's property, and avoiding or not paying social obligations such as social security contributions and taxes. Whatever its form, theft is an act of injustice that requires reparation and restitution.

TALK IT OVER
- Give examples of laws or social policies that support the Seventh Commandment. How do these contribute to promoting peace and the well-being of people?
- Give examples of laws or social policies that work against living the Seventh Commandment. What impact do these laws have upon individuals and society?

THE FULFILLMENT OF THE LAW
Jesus, the Incarnate Son of God, fulfilled the Law and the Prophets. He did not abolish the Seventh Commandment; he revealed its spirit and inner meaning. Where Moses taught the Israelites God's law "You shall not steal," Jesus challenges us to go deeper and live out its spirit of generosity. He taught, "If anyone wants to sue you and take your coat, give your cloak as well. . . . Give to everyone who begs from you, and do not refuse anyone who wants to borrow from you" (Matthew 5:40, 42).

LET'S PROBE DEEPER
- Review the corporal **works of mercy** in the "Catholic Prayers, Devotions and Practices" section of this text.
- How do the works of mercy guide us in living the Seventh Commandment to its fullest?

THINK, PAIR AND SHARE
- Share with a partner why living the Seventh Commandment is essential for promoting peace and creating a just and compassionate society.

JOURNAL EXERCISE
- Reflect upon and describe the changes you need to make in your own life in order to live more fully the life of justice and charity at the heart of the Seventh Commandment.

The social teaching of the Catholic Church

feed upon the powerless. As a consequence, masses of people find themselves excluded and marginalized: without work, without possibilities, without any means of escape. . . . The excluded are not the 'exploited' but the outcast, the 'leftovers'" (*The Joy of the Gospel*, no. 53).

OPENING CONVERSATION

⊙ Brainstorm specific examples of ways the economy may be contrary to the Seventh Commandment.

⊙ What would be morally appropriate responses for a disciple of Jesus to make to an unjust economic situation?

FROM THE CATECHISM

In economic matters, respect for human dignity requires the practice of the virtue of *temperance*, so as to moderate attachment to this world's goods; the practice of the virtue of *justice*, to preserve our neighbor's rights and render him what is his due; and the practice of *solidarity*, in accordance with the golden rule and in keeping with the generosity of the Lord, who "though he was rich, yet for your sake . . . became poor so that by his poverty, you might become rich" (2 Corinthians 8:9).

—CCC, no. 2407

AN ECONOMY OF EXCLUSION: THE SURVIVAL OF THE FITTEST

Human history is, in part, the story of "the few" profiting from their use of the goods of the earth primarily for themselves to the detriment of "the majority." Pope Francis has addressed this situation directly: "Just as the commandment 'Thou shalt not kill' sets a clear limit in order to safeguard the value of human life, today we also have to say 'thou shalt not' to an economy of exclusion and inequality. Such an economy kills. How can it be that it is not a news item when an elderly homeless person dies of exposure, but it is news when the stock market loses two points? This is a case of exclusion. Can we continue to stand by when food is thrown away while people are starving? This is a case of inequality. Today everything comes under the laws of competition and the survival of the fittest, where the powerful

CONNECTING THE DOTS: FOUNDATIONS OF CATHOLIC SOCIAL TEACHING

The great body of Catholic social doctrine rests upon the foundational principle that every human being is created in the "image of God" (Genesis 1:27). Every person has fundamental rights and responsibilities that flow from that dignity. Created by God in the divine image and likeness, every person and every social entity created by human beings has the responsibility and obligation to live in just and loving relationships. Put another way: every person has the vocation to work for the **Kingdom of God** that Jesus announced and inaugurated. (Check out Luke 4:16–19.)

Working for the Kingdom of God aims to bring about the common good of a society in a just and compassionate way. This work is not optional for disciples of Jesus. Joined to Christ in Baptism, our work makes us participants in the divine works of creation and redemption. Working in cooperation with the grace of the Spirit of Christ for a just and compassionate society is an essential part of building up the Kingdom of God. Certain implications follow from this understanding of the social nature and calling of human beings and human societies.

"'Work is for man, not man for work (see St. John Paul II, *On Human Work*, no. 6).' Everyone should be able to draw from work the means of providing for his life and that of his family, and of serving the human community" (CCC, no. 2428). The true and full development of the whole person includes the value their work brings to their ability to respond to God's call.

All social structures and political and economic systems must work for the good of all human beings. All systems that lead to the enslavement of human beings and exploit human beings or their labor are sinful social structures. Christians are to resist and work for the reformation of such sinful structures; for example, strikes that workers conduct in a moral way are legitimate and just ways to work for a more just society. But a good end (better working conditions) does not justify the use of an evil means (use of unjust force that brings harm to people or property). A strike is morally unacceptable when it uses unjust violence or is undertaken for reasons other than improving the working conditions of workers or when it works against the common good.

THINK, PAIR AND SHARE

⊙ Work with a partner and review the key teachings of the social doctrine of the Catholic Church, which are summarized at the end of the "Catholic Prayers, Devotions and Practices" section of this text.

⊙ Discuss how each of these teachings contributes to the building of a just society, the Kingdom of God.

THE VIRTUE OF JUSTICE

The four cardinal moral virtues empower us to live the Seventh Commandment. These virtues are, as you have learned, justice, temperance, fortitude and prudence. The more we make these virtues part of our daily living, the more we truly live out both the letter *and* the spirit of the Seventh Commandment.

Work is for man, not man for work.

ST. JOHN PAUL II

Justice is the "cardinal moral virtue which consists in the constant and firm will to give their due to God and to neighbor" (CCC, Glossary, "Justice"). A justice founded in charity is not that of the blind Lady Justice, weighing out evenly on the scale of justice what people deserve. Giving everyone their "due" is only the most basic notion of justice.

By contrast, the justice God desires and wills is revealed in his original plan of justice for creation. This justice, as we have already learned, is achieved only "with the help of charity" (CCC, no. 2459). It demands showing special concern for those who are most in need. This is the justice that the prophets preached. In the Book of Prophet Isaiah we read: "Seek justice, rescue the oppressed, defend the orphan, plead for the widow" (Isaiah 1:17). Given the biblical understanding of justice, we can better

appreciate how the Seventh Commandment challenges us to see that all people receive their "full due."

LET'S PROBE DEEPER: SCRIPTURE ACTIVITY

- ☉ Work in groups. Read Matthew 20:1–16, the parable of the laborers in the vineyard.
- ☉ Discuss what this parable says about justice.
- ☉ Describe the society in which everyone lives according to this gospel understanding of justice.

TYPES OF JUSTICE

People have different understandings of the nature of justice and the ways of seeking justice. These differences can result in a diversity of opinions on how to build a just society.

Original justice: Original justice is God's plan and will for all creation. It is "the state of holiness in which God created our first parents" (CCC, Glossary, "Justice"). This justice will be restored fully in the Kingdom of God when Christ comes again in glory at the end of time and the new creation that he inaugurated is completed. (Check out Romans 8:18–25.)

Commutative justice: Commutative justice ensures that we deal fairly and honestly with one another in our daily interactions. We are to respect for the rights of others, pay our debts, make good on our promises and fulfill any obligations for which we have freely contracted with another person or institution.

> "Friend, I am doing you no wrong. . . . I choose to give to this last the same as I give to you."
>
> MATTHEW 20:13–14

Distributive justice: Distributive justice "regulates what the community owes its citizens in proportion to their contributions and needs" (CCC, Glossary, "Justice"). It is the just and fair distribution of a society's resources so that everyone has enough to meet their basic needs. Distributive justice guards against a few people appropriating more than their fair share of resources for themselves.

Legal justice: Legal justice "concerns what the citizen owes to the community" (CCC, Glossary, "Justice"). This includes paying taxes, using resources, such as water, wisely and responsibly, obeying fire, traffic and other safety laws.

Social justice: Social justice refers to the ordering of society that promotes "respect for the fundamental rights that flow from the intrinsic dignity of the person" (CCC, no. 1944). We achieve social justice when everyone's dignity and rights are respected in Church and society. Distributive, commutative and legal justice set the parameters for fair dealings among people within a society, and they contribute to social justice.

But what is the proper response when social justice is thwarted? Retributive justice and restorative justice are the two fundamental approaches to repairing the damage and harm done by acts of injustice. We explored the difference between retributive justice and restorative justice in the treatment of capital punishment in chapter 8. In summary:

Retributive justice: Retributive justice focuses on the punishment of offenders and is aimed at balancing the scales held by Lady Justice. This approach claims that it is implementing the Old Testament Law of an eye for an eye, a tooth for a tooth (see Exodus 21:24).

Restorative justice: Restorative justice focuses on the dignity of the human person, both the victim and the offender, as an image of God. While this form of justice does not ignore the evil of acts of injustice and other crimes, restorative justice also aims at the rehabilitation of the offender and reparation to victims. Restorative justice demands that offenders work to repair the harm caused by their acts and that the victim's suffering be acknowledged and addressed.

- Choose a crime that is making the headlines.
- Evaluate and discuss the crime according to the forms of justice. How is that crime an offense against God, against individuals and against society, as expressed in the Seventh Commandment?
- How can justice best be served?

THE PRINCIPLE OF SOLIDARITY

The Son of God took on flesh and entered into solidarity with human beings. Jesus' solidarity with all humanity is the root and foundation of solidarity among all people. Let us look, once again, at the principle of solidarity, which you explored earlier in this course. A commitment to building a just society is rooted in the principle of solidarity. The moral principle of solidarity enjoins us to unite ourselves with others, to look upon each other as another self, and to share compassionately in each other's joys and sufferings. It guides us in developing the habit of practicing the central command of the law of God, "You shall love the Lord your God with all your heart, . . . You shall love your neighbor as yourself" (Mark 12:30, 31). Jesus revealed how we are to live that Great Commandment in solidarity with others; he taught, "Just as I have loved you, you also should love one another" (John 13:34). Jesus Christ, the Incarnate Son of God, is the source of our salvation and our solidarity with one another. He is the source of justice in society.

LET'S PROBE DEEPER

Recall that solidarity "is an eminently Christian virtue. It practices the sharing of spiritual goods even more than material ones" (CCC, no. 1948). In our age of rapid advances in technology, communications and transportation, the world is more interconnected than ever. We have more means of assisting one another when injustice becomes wound up in international systems, as Pope Francis so clearly reminded us. Because of the complexity of the age we live in, the Catholic Church constantly calls upon countries and organizations to form international collaborations in order to ensure that all people receive their just share of earthly goods.
- Put in your own words what it means to practice the principle of solidarity. Give examples of people living in solidarity.
- Share experiences of times when you have acted in solidarity with others.
- Why is the principle of solidarity absolutely essential to building a just society and the new creation, the Kingdom of God announced and inaugurated by Jesus?

WHAT ABOUT YOU PERSONALLY?
- What wisdom can you take away from Catholic social teaching for how to live the Seventh Commandment more fully?
- What can you do, alone or with others, in your own community to promote social justice?

HABITAT FOR HUMANITY BUILDS HOMES IN OAKLAND, CALIFORNIA

Attitudes and actions count in living the Christian moral life

NEVER ENOUGH

A 2011 survey of 1,000 millionaires possessing an average of $3.5 million found that 42 percent did not feel wealthy. And how much would they need to feel rich? $7.5 million—more than double what they already have! Money has not made them feel secure and satisfied! So what is their solution? More money!

OPENING REFLECTION

⊙ What do you have to say about the attitude of the millionaires described in this survey?

⊙ What material things do you and your family count on for your security or well-being?

⊙ What does the Gospel teach about the true source of human security and well-being? Need help? Check out Matthew 6:25–34.

FROM THE CATECHISM

Desire for true happiness frees man from his immoderate attachment to the goods of this world so that he can find his fulfillment in the vision and beatitude of God. "The promise [of seeing God] surpasses all beatitude.... In Scripture, to see is to possess.... Whoever sees God has obtained all the goods of which he can conceive" (St. Gregory of Nyssa, *On Happiness*, 6).
—CCC, no. 2548

DO NOT COVET; LIVE IN TRUE FREEDOM

The wisdom of the Tenth Commandment instructs us to examine our innermost desires and attitudes—the desires of our mind, heart and inner self. It enjoins us both as individuals and as the community of God's people, "You shall not covet . . . anything that belongs to your neighbor" (Exodus 20:17; see also Deuteronomy 5:21).

What does it mean to covet? The verb "to covet" means "to desire [what belongs to another] inordinately or culpably" (*Merriam Webster Online Dictionary*). Covetousness is one of the seven Capital Sins by which we seek happiness everywhere but in God. Human beings, who are at once bodily and spiritual beings, are, as a consequence of Original Sin, conflicted by covetousness. The Tenth Commandment, as the Ninth Commandment does, responds to this reality.

God has warned human beings of the seduction of things that appear as "a delight to the eyes" (Genesis 3:6). We can crave inordinately for earthly goods. St. Paul addressed the Church in Galatia about our power to resist these seductions; he wrote: "[T]hose who belong to Christ Jesus have crucified the flesh with its passions and desires" (Galatians 5:24).

Jesus embraced and experienced the joy of using earthly goods. At the wedding feast in Cana he transformed water into wine . . . and

THE WEDDING FEAST AT CANA | DUCCIO DI BUONINSEGNA

very good wine at that. (Check out John 2:1–11.) He often shared meals with friends, and invited all, saints and sinners and sundry others, to join him at table. (Check out Mark 2:15; Luke 11:37–54, 14:1–24, 19:1–10, 24:30). Still, Jesus knew that people sometimes get caught up in desiring, seeking and enjoying worldly pleasures and possessions. They lose sight of the true treasure that God has given them—life in communion and friendship with him—and they often replace it by giving in to the desire for material goods. In the Sermon on the Mount Jesus warned us of the seduction of this temptation. He taught:

"Do not store up for yourselves treasures on earth, where moth and rust consume and where thieves break in and steal; but store up for yourselves treasures in heaven, where neither moth nor rust consumes and where thieves do not break in and steal. For where your treasure is, there your heart will be also."

—Matthew 6:19–21

The inordinate longing for and enjoyment of earthly goods is similar to an addiction—a state of slavery. The wisdom of the Tenth Commandment sets us free from addictive attitudes toward possessions, which never fully satisfy us. This final Commandment of the Decalogue enjoins us to value earthly goods appropriately. Only by putting the one true God at the center of our lives—the deepest desire of our heart—can we live as the truly free persons God creates and desires us to be.

FAITH WORD

Covetousness

A disordered inclination or desire for pleasure or possessions. One of the capital sins.

—CCC, Glossary

THINK, PAIR AND SHARE

In *The Lion, the Witch and the Wardrobe* by C.S. Lewis, the character Edmund becomes so obsessed with enchanted sweets that he betrays his own siblings in order to get more. In one memorable line, Lewis writes: "There is nothing that spoils the taste of ordinary good food half so much as the memory of bad magic food."

- Share with a partner the insights Edmund's behavior gives you into the meaning of the Tenth Commandment.
- What do you think Lewis's statement means? Share examples of "ordinary good food" spoiled by "bad magic food."

READ AND REFLECT
- Reread Matthew 6:19–21. Where is your heart's treasure?
- How might your desire for worldly treasures be an addiction?
- How might seeking those treasures be getting between you and your relationship with God, with family and with friends? What will you do about it?

ATTITUDES AND BEHAVIOR CONTRARY TO THE TENTH COMMANDMENT

Our inordinate desires for material goods may not be as obvious as an addiction to drugs. Offenses against the Tenth Commandment include the Capital Sins of greed (avarice), envy and gluttony and the sinful choices that flow from these Capital Sins. Pause and review the definitions of the Capital Sins in chapter 4, "Think It Through," of this text.

Greed (avarice): The wisdom of Proverbs warns us: "Those who are greedy for unjust gain make trouble for their households" (Proverbs 15:27). The culture around us and the media, through advertising, can lure us into believing that giving in to the temptation of greed is in our best interests. Such is the case with the consumerism that is an addiction for many in our society.

Envy: The Letter to James, which counsels us that we must put our faith into action, teaches: "Who is wise and understanding among you? Show by your good life that your works are done with gentleness born of wisdom. But if you have bitter envy and selfish ambition in your hearts, do not be boastful and false to the truth. . . . For where there is envy and selfish ambition, there will also be disorder and wickedness of every kind" (James 3:13–14, 16). We combat the seduction of envy "through good-will, humility, and abandonment to the providence of God" (CCC, no. 2554).

Jealousy: Jealousy is an "attitude related to envy as well as greed; a jealous person is possessive of what one has or thinks one should have, as well as resentful toward others for what they have" (USCCA, Glossary, "Jealousy," 516). The wisdom of Proverbs warns us of the power of jealousy to destroy both the jealous person and their relationships with others. We read: "For jealousy arouses a husband's fury, / and he shows no restraint when he takes revenge" (Proverbs 6:34).

Gluttony: Gluttony, you will recall, is "eating and drinking more than is necessary" (USCCA, Glossary, "Gluttony," 513). This sin is an offense against God and the dignity of the person committing this sin.

OVER TO YOU
- At home tonight, pay attention to the programs and to the commercials advertising those programs.
- Compare the messages they are sending with what you have learned about the Tenth Commandment.

A LIFE OF SIMPLICITY, A LIFE OF FREEDOM

Jesus told his disciples, "And do not keep striving for what you are to eat and what you are to drink, and do not keep worrying. . . . Instead,

strive for his kingdom, and these things will be given to you as well" (Luke 12:29, 31). The Tenth Commandment encourages taking Jesus' command to heart and living the gospel precept of detachment with a poverty of heart and simplicity.

Joined to Christ in Baptism, we receive from the Spirit of Christ the wisdom and courage to transform our attitudes and behavior into those of Christ. We receive the grace to resist the seduction of the world's prevailing attitudes toward earthly goods, which are contrary to both natural and revealed law. It is this grace that enables us to strive to grow into the likeness and image of God.

Jesus showed that he understood truly and compassionately the inner conflict within every heart. He taught: "How hard is it for those who have wealth to enter the kingdom of God! Indeed, it is easier for a camel to go through the eye of a needle than for someone who is rich to enter the kingdom of God" (Luke 18:24–25). Imagine a camel loaded with goods trying to enter the city of Jerusalem through a small opening in a gate to the city!

In this teaching Jesus reminds his disciples of the need to detach ourselves from over-indulging in material goods and, instead, to abandon ourselves to the caring presence of God who "frees us from anxiety about tomorrow" (CCC, no. 2547; see also Matthew 6:25–34).

JOURNAL EXERCISE

- ◉ Describe in your own words the destructive power that greed, envy and jealously has had in your life.
- ◉ Identify concrete actions you can take right now to cultivate a lifestyle of detachment and simplicity, in accordance with the Gospel.

JUDGE AND ACT

REVIEW AND SHARE WHAT YOU HAVE LEARNED IN THIS CHAPTER

Look back over this chapter and reflect on the teachings of Scripture and Tradition on the meaning of the Seventh and Tenth Commandments. Share the teachings of the Catholic Church on these statements:

- ⊙ God has given the human race responsibility to care for and develop his creation.
- ⊙ God has given his entire creation for the good of all people.
- ⊙ We are to be just and generous in our use of earthly goods.
- ⊙ Theft and the taking and using unjustly of another person's property is contrary to the Seventh Commandment.
- ⊙ We are to balance our personal desires and acquiring of wealth and other material goods with the rights and needs of others.
- ⊙ Greed (avarice), envy, jealously and gluttony are acts contrary to the Tenth Commandment and lead to an abuse of the goods of creation.
- ⊙ There is a fundamental solidarity among all people.
- ⊙ Disciples of Christ, as are all people, are to strive to live a life of simplicity and detachment.

TALK IT OVER

- ⊙ Describe how living the Seventh and the Tenth Commandments might make a difference to the way you and other young people live today. Give specific examples.

REFLECT AND DISCERN

- ⊙ Where might you personally struggle with living the Seventh and the Tenth Commandments?
- ⊙ What can help you deal successfully with that struggle?

THE BLESSED LIFE OF LIVING THE COMMANDMENTS

The Jewish people have always valued the Ten Commandments as a blessing more than

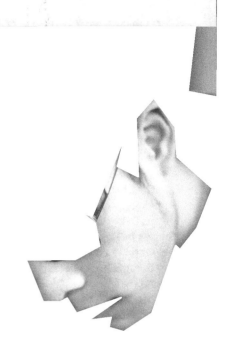

a burden. The Israelites realized that the law of God both takes into account our human condition and also guides us in a way of life that will lead us to happiness and true freedom. The psalmist passes on this wisdom to us:

> Blessed are you, O LORD;
>   teach me your statutes. . . .
> I delight in the way of your decrees
>   as much as in all riches.
> I will meditate on your precepts,
>   and fix my eyes on your ways. . . .
> Open my eyes, so that I may behold
>   wondrous things out of your law. . . .
> Seven times a day I praise you
>   for your righteous ordinances.
> Great peace have those who love your law;
>   nothing can make them stumble.
>   —Psalm 119:12, 14–15, 18, 164–165

St. Martin de Porres (1579–1639), the transforming power of living a life of gospel simplicity

Juan Martin de Porres was born in Lima, Peru, on December 9, 1579. Born the son of a Spanish nobleman and of a Black free-woman, Martin described himself as a "mulatto," or a person born of a black and a white parent. At the age of fifteen Martin entered the Dominican Friary in Lima and he became a Dominican lay brother at the age of twenty-four. Brother Martin lived a life of gospel simplicity and service. He embodied what it means to be detached from earthly goods and to use one's resources for the good of others. He put on the mind of Christ, emptied himself and became poor in order to serve the poor.

Brother Martin worked in the kitchen, did the laundry and cleaned the Friary. He served the friars as farmer, barber (surgeon), nurse and steward of the Friary community's resources. On one occasion when the Friary was in debt, Martin actually suggested that his superiors sell him as a slave to raise their needed funds, saying, "I am only a poor mulatto, sell me."

Brother Martin also reached out to the sick and hungry and homeless. He founded a home in Lima to care for orphans and children abandoned by their families. On an average day he would feed over a hundred people. His superiors often became annoyed with him for bringing sick people to the Friary and caring for

METROPOLITAN CATHEDRAL, BUENOS AIRES, ARGENTINA

them in his own bed. Martin did not limit his service to people. His compassion for animals moved him to set up a clinic for abandoned dogs and cats in his sister's home.

Martin de Porres died on November 3, 1639 and was named a blessed of the Church in 1837. St. John XXIII named Brother Martin a saint on May 6, 1962. The Church celebrates his memory and life each year on November 3 and honors him as the patron saint of barbers, people of mixed race and public health workers.

TALK IT OVER

- In what ways is St. Martin de Porres a model for living the gospel mandate to renounce worldly goods in the service of God and others?
- Do you know a similar model today? Describe that person.
- What wisdom can young people today learn for their lives from St. Martin de Porres?

SHARE FAITH WITH FAMILY AND FRIENDS

- Reflect with family and friends on this fact: In addition to consuming more material goods than most of the world, in our country we literally waste tons of the world's resources every year. For example, the average American generates fifty-two tons of garbage by age seventy-five.
- Share ideas on what you can do to promote a gospel-focused view of the use of material goods.
- Choose one of your ideas and work together to implement it.

WHAT ABOUT YOU PERSONALLY?

⊙ St. Martin held nothing back when it came to serving others. What inspiration does his example offer you for your life right now?

JUDGE AND DECIDE

⊙ Read and reflect: Becoming self-sufficient and independent is highly valued in our society. However, not all cultures value these things as highly. Many Central and South American as well as African cultures believe that it is more important to be loyal to one's family and community and to work well with others, than to become self-sufficient and independent.

⊙ What wisdom do you think we can learn from these different cultures? Make that wisdom part of the way you live the Ten Commandments, as Jesus taught us to do.

PREPARATION FOR THE PRAYER REFLECTION

In preparation for the Prayer Reflection, bring to class something that you enjoy having or using, or an image of that thing; for example, a favorite food, cell phone, basketball or tennis racket, musical instrument and so on.

"Do not store up for yourselves treasures on earth, where moth and rust consume and where thieves break in and steal; but store up for yourselves treasures in heaven, . . . For where your treasure is, there your heart will be also."

MATTHEW 6:19–21

PRAYER REFLECTION

Note: Students will need the "favorite things" referred to in the "Preparation for the Prayer Reflection" note at the end of the previous section.

All gather, form a circle and sit on the floor. Pray the Sign of the Cross together.

LEADER
Loving God,
give us hearts that long for you.
Purify our desires so that we may use the gifts
you have given us for our good, for the good of
our neighbors, and for your greater glory.
Move in our midst as we pray and try to grow
closer to you and one another.
ALL
Amen.

READER
A reading from the holy Gospel according to Luke.
ALL
Glory to you, O Lord.

READER
Proclaim Luke 12:22–23, 27–31.
The Gospel of the Lord.
ALL
Praise to you, Lord Jesus Christ.

LEADER
Gracious God,
we thank you for the care that you show us.
Help us to display our gratitude to you
by taking care of and sharing the gifts you give us
in your service and in the service of the people
you put in our lives.
ALL
Amen.

LEADER
Aware of this responsibility and blessing,
we will now lay some of these gifts before God.
As you lay your gift in the center of the circle,
speak aloud how you can give glory to God
by using it for the good of neighbor and self.

Students take turns offering gifts.

LEADER
I now invite everyone to bring their prayers
before God the Creator, who is Father, Son and
Holy Spirit.
Feel free to offer either prayers of thanksgiving
and praise for the gifts God has given us
or prayers of intercession for the needs of the
world.
Our response after each prayer will be, "Lord,
hear our prayer."

Students offer their intentions aloud.

LEADER
Great and generous God,
you are the source and goal of our happiness,
you are the cause of our joy.
Send your Spirit to enrich us with the gift of
wisdom to help us see you in all good things
and to use the resources we have to bring others
closer to you.
We pray in the name of Jesus Christ, your
Incarnate Son, who is the Revelation of your
justice and love.
ALL
Amen.

Pray the Sign of the Cross together.

CHAPTER 11

Living New Life in Christ Jesus
—The Universal Call to Holiness of Life

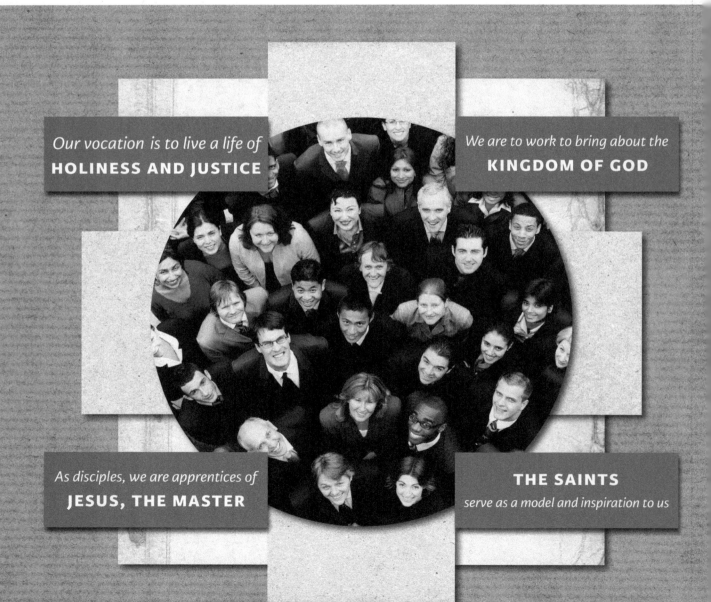

Our vocation is to live a life of
HOLINESS AND JUSTICE

We are to work to bring about the
KINGDOM OF GOD

As disciples, we are apprentices of
JESUS, THE MASTER

THE SAINTS
serve as a model and inspiration to us

GOD THE CREATOR IS THE GIVER OF LIFE. GOD calls every person to the holiness of life that was lost as a consequence of Original Sin. In this chapter we explore the call to every Christian to live as a disciple of Jesus Christ, the Incarnate Son of God, by following the "way" that he preached and taught and modeled for us. We reflect on the many ways that individuals and groups choose to follow the way of Christ and how we might do likewise.

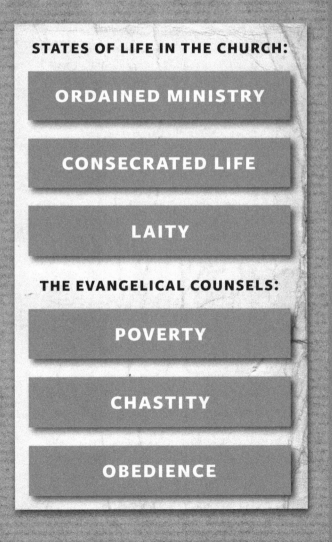

STATES OF LIFE IN THE CHURCH:

ORDAINED MINISTRY

CONSECRATED LIFE

LAITY

THE EVANGELICAL COUNSELS:

POVERTY

CHASTITY

OBEDIENCE

Faith Focus: These teachings are the primary focus of the doctrinal content presented in this chapter:

⊙ God calls every person to a life of holiness and justice.
⊙ The faithful can live out their vocation to a life of holiness and justice according to three states of life; namely, Holy Orders, consecrated life, and marriage.
⊙ The laity in their daily activities contribute to the bringing about of the Reign of God.
⊙ The faithful who accept the vocation to the consecrated life vow to live the evangelical, or gospel, counsels poverty, chastity and obedience.
⊙ Christ calls every disciple of Christ to live the evangelical counsels according to their vocation in life.
⊙ The Church is the sacrament of Christ and the the Kingdom of God.
⊙ The Church's primary mission in the world is announce the Gospel to all people.

Discipleship Formation: As a result of studying this you should be better able to:

⊙ discern the vocation God has given you to live as a disciple of Jesus Christ;
⊙ understand and value your discipleship as an apprenticeship to Christ, our Lord and Master;
⊙ live the spirit of the evangelical counsels right now;
⊙ work in whatever way you can to improve the situation of those oppressed by poverty in any form;
⊙ identify ways in which the lives and influence of the saints of the Church can support you in living your vocation;
⊙ commit yourself to announcing the Gospel in all you say and do.

Scripture References: These Scripture references are quoted or referred to in this chapter:

OLD TESTAMENT: **Exodus** 3:1–12; **1 Samuel** 3:1–18; **Isaiah** 11:1–9; **Jeremiah** 1:4–19

NEW TESTAMENT: **Matthew** 4:18–22, 5:13–16, 48, 6:9–11, 9:35–38, 13:1–53, 16:15–18, 19:16–30, 26:69–75, 28:20; **Luke** 1:26–38, 4:18–19, 5:10, 6:20, 10:2; **John** 1:1–18, 14:6, 17:9, 21:15–17; **Acts of the Apostles** 1:15–26, 2:14, 9:1–19; **1 Corinthians** 2:16, 12:8–10, 27; **Colossians** 1:15; **1 Timothy** 5:3, 5; **Revelation** 14:4

Faith Glossary: Familiarize yourself with the meaning of these key terms in the Glossary: **apostolate, charism, consecrated life, contemplation, disciple, evangelical councils, evangelization, hierarchy, holiness, Kingdom of God, laity, lay ecclesial ministers, ministerial priesthood, parable, perpetual virginity, vocation**

Faith Words: vocation; evangelical counsels
Learn by Heart: Matthew 19:21
Learn by Example: Simon Peter, apostle and evangelize

What is your vocation?

REAL LIFE CHOICES

In *The Game of Life* players travel around the game board landing on spaces that simulate various life events, from graduating high school to retirement. Along the way players encounter jobs, lawsuits, children, property and life tiles. The tiles represent major life events which are revealed at the end of the game; each tile adds different amounts of money to a player's retirement total. The player who ends their life with the most money *wins* the game—at least on this playing board.

What to do with one's life is the ultimate question every person must answer. Each one of us makes myriad choices—great and small—as we navigate our path through life and attempt to answer that question. How we decide what we do with our time, money, work and relationships reflects the values we treasure and contributes significantly to how we grow as a person.

For a Christian, the response to this ultimate life question must also answer the questions "What enables us best to follow Jesus?" and "What enables us best to live our Baptism?" Following "the Way," who is Jesus, must give heart and substance to our life. It must lie behind every other decision we make. In other words, for Christians, all of life is about responding to our **vocation** from God that began with our Baptism.

The word "vocation" comes from the Latin verb *vocare*, which means "to call." A vocation implies a call-receiver and a call-giver. Many voices may call us to follow a particular path through life. But God is our primary call-giver; he invites us to **holiness** of life, to use our gifts and talents to bring about his desire and will

IS LIFE A GAME?

In 2009 the classic edition of *The Game of Life* appeared as an iPhone App. The promotional blurb ran as follows: "Stay single or say, 'I do.' Retire rich or lose it all. ANYTHING can happen in EA MOBILE'S *THE GAME OF LIFE!* Play it safe with sensible choices like college, marriage and kids. Play it risky with high-stake investments and lavish luxuries. Navigate your car through a 3D environment of winding roads and lush landscapes. Pass 'N Play with up to three friends to see who can get richest the quickest!"

OPENING CONVERSATION

- ⊙ The aim of *The Game of Life* is to make as much money as possible. In your opinion, is this a worthy life aim? Will it bring true and lasting happiness? Why or why not?
- ⊙ What other worthy aims might a person aspire to in his or her life?

OVER TO YOU

- ⊙ Look deep inside yourself. What do you treasure? What might make your life a real success?

Vocation

The term given to the call to each person from God; everyone has been called to holiness and eternal life, especially in Baptism. Each person can also be called more specifically to the priesthood or to religious life, to married life, and to single life, as well as to a particular profession or service.

—*United States Catholic Catechism for Adults* (USCCA), Glossary, 531

for creation, the Kingdom, or Reign, of God. The fundamental vocation for every Christian, regardless of what particular path we take in life, is to cooperate with the grace of the Holy Spirit and live as a disciple of Jesus Christ, the Incarnate Son of God, who is one God with the Father and the Holy Spirit.

TALK IT OVER
⊙ Draw up a list of particular ways in which you see Christians living out their call to live as disciples of Jesus Christ.
⊙ How might they be making a difference in the world?
⊙ Which of these vocations interests you right now? Why is that?

LET'S PROBE DEEPER
⊙ God calls every Christian to the vocation to live as a disciple of Jesus. God also calls each of us to our own particular way of living out that vocation.
⊙ Read and think about these three descriptions of a vocation:
  – A vocation is about searching for the deepest inclination of your heart and following it.

  – A vocation is a purpose for being in the world that is related to the purposes of God.
  – A vocation is the place where your deep gladness meets the world's deep need.
⊙ Which description of vocation do you like most, and why? Share your answer.

Notice that all three descriptions of a vocation have something in common. Each suggests that a vocation has to do with listening to your own deepest desires and aligning them with what you discern is God's will for you. These three simple but great questions can help us listen to our hearts: (1) What am I good at? (2) What would I enjoy doing? (3) Does this need to be done? As you reflect on these or similar questions, be sure to ask the Holy Spirit for guidance. The deeper we search our own hearts, the more likely we are to hear, listen and discern our particular vocation to live as a disciple of Jesus Christ.

READ, REFLECT AND SHARE
⊙ Read and reflect on one or more of these Bible stories about "calls" from God: the call of Moses in Exodus 3:1–12; the call of Samuel in 1 Samuel 3:1–18; the call of Jeremiah in Jeremiah 1:4–19; the call of Mary in Luke 1:26–38; the

The saints serve as a model and inspiration to us

faithful]" (USCCA, Glossary, "Saint," 527); for example, St. Peter and the other Apostles, St. Francis of Assisi, St. Thérèse of Lisieux, St. Martin de Porres, St. Katharine Drexel, and others such as St. John XXIII, St. John Paul II, as well as others whose canonization is in process. These include Blessed Mother Teresa of Calcutta and Servant of God Dorothy Day. The Blessed Virgin Mary is, of course, the greatest among the saints of the Church. All the saints of the Church can inspire and help us discern and live our own particular vocation.

TALK IT OVER
An ancient story from Hasidic Jewish wisdom tells that when Rabbi Zusya was an old man, he said, "In the coming world, they will not ask me: 'Why were you not more like Moses?' They will ask me: 'Why were you not Zusya?'" The vocation we choose must truly be our own, not just a replica of someone else's.
- ⊙ How might thinking about their vocation in life help young people grow to be the people whom God created and calls them to be—to be truly more like themselves?
- ⊙ How can young people think, right here and now, about what their vocation might be in the future? What might they do? Who can help them?

WHAT ABOUT YOU PERSONALLY?
- ⊙ What do you think is at the heart and soul of your vocation in life? What might God be calling you to do—even now?
- ⊙ Is your name the name of a saint? How might coming to know more about the life of that saint and of other saints of the Church help you come to know and live your vocation?

call of the first disciples in Matthew 4:18–22; and the call of Saul (St. Paul) in Acts of the Apostles 9:1–19.
- ⊙ Share with a partner the wisdom each passage gives you for discerning and responding to your call from God.

LIFE MODELS FOR CHRISTIANS
In discerning how best to live one's life, it certainly helps to have models. Jesus Christ, the Incarnate Son of God, is the first and foremost model for Christians—and for all human beings. He is the firstborn of all creatures. "He is the image of the invisible God, the firstborn of all creation" (Colossians 1:15).

It can also help us to have more immediate models of those who have faithfully lived out their vocation for following the way of Jesus. The Catholic Church canonizes, or names as saints, certain deceased members of the faithful to "serve as [models] and inspiration to [the Christian

A Christian's vocation is good news

JESUS' VOCATION IS GOOD NEWS

The Gospel according to Luke gives this account of Jesus' announcement of his vocation, which Jesus read from the scroll of the prophet Isaiah in the synagogue in his hometown of Nazareth:

> "The Spirit of the Lord is upon me,
>   because he has anointed me
>   to bring good news to the poor.
> He has sent me to proclaim release to the
>   captives
>   and recovery of sight to the blind,
>   to let the oppressed go free,
> to proclaim the year of the Lord's favor."
>   —Luke 4:18–19

OPENING CONVERSATION

◉ What does Jesus' announcement reveal about his understanding of his vocation?

◉ Compare the passage in Luke with John 1:1–18. What does the passage from John add to your understanding of the passage in Luke?

WHY DID THE FATHER SEND THE SON?

Central to Jesus' preaching and teaching was his proclamation and inauguration of the **Kingdom of God**. The Kingdom of God is the "actualization of God's will for human beings proclaimed by Jesus Christ as a community of justice, peace, mercy, and love, the seed of which is the Church on earth, and the fulfillment of which is in eternity" (USCCA, Glossary, "Kingdom of God," 517). For this reason the essence of our Christian vocation is to "seek the kingdom of God" (CCC, no. 898) by keeping "God's commandments as Christ taught us, by loving God and our neighbor" (*Rite of Baptism for Children*, no. 39).

Jesus taught us to pray, "Our Father in heaven, / hallowed be your name. / Your kingdom come. / Your will be done, on earth as it is in heaven"

(Matthew 6:9–10). He then enjoined us to ask for God's grace to put the words of our prayer into action, "Give us this day our daily bread. . . ." (Matthew 6:11). In other words, it is not enough for Christians just to pray for the coming of the Kingdom of God; we must ask for and cooperate with God's grace to do on earth what God wills. We are to partner with God to bring about God's reign, which will come about fully when Jesus Christ comes again in glory at the end of time.

The Kingdom of God is not a particular place or territory; it is a *way of living* in communion and peace with God and all his creation. Imagine what a wonderful world we would have if everyone worked toward bringing about God's will of fullness of life for all people, of love and freedom, of peace and justice. This is the good news the Church brings to the world through the lives of its members. Life on earth is to foreshadow eternal life with God.

This is the kingdom that the prophet Isaiah envisioned in Isaiah 11:1–9. This is the kingdom that Jesus preached and lived and died and rose from the dead to bring about. By his life and the events of his Paschal Mystery Jesus released what St. Paul calls "an abundance of God's grace." This grace is the catalyst that will bring about the restoration of God's desire and will for his creation, to be restored to a "home" of justice and love.

The Spirit of Christ offers every Christian the grace to accept and live this vocation. We are to work to bring this life-giving good news that foreshadows the life to come in the heavenly kingdom to every dimension of society. We are to use our gifts to contribute in some way to the transformation of the world toward the Kingdom of God. We are to strive to do our best to see to it that all family, societal and world affairs are in harmony with God's will and plan for creation as we cooperate with the grace of the Spirit of "righteousness and peace and joy" and journey toward eternal life in the eternal kingdom.

OVER TO YOU

⊙ Pause for a moment and add to the list from your deepest desires.

LET'S PROBE DEEPER

In the **parables** of the Kingdom of God, or Kingdom of Heaven, Jesus, the Incarnate Son of God, used very ordinary examples from the daily life of his listeners to reveal the mystery of the Kingdom of God. For example, Jesus taught that the Kingdom of Heaven is *like* a farmer sowing seed, *like* a mustard seed, *like* yeast mixed with flour, *like* a treasure hidden in a field, *like* a merchant buying fine pearls, *like* catching and sorting fish. (Check out Matthew 13:1–53.)

By comparing the Kingdom of Heaven with experiences from their daily lives, Jesus also revealed that what people do with their everyday lives is integral to bringing about God's reign. All the events of our everyday lives—learning and teaching, driving a car or riding on a school bus, playing in the school band or orchestra, texting and blogging, singing in a choir or playing a minor role in a play—can and should be directed toward God's kingdom.

TALK IT OVER

⊙ What do you think: Is God's will for the world a possibility? Give reasons for your opinion.
⊙ What might be some concrete signs of that kingdom?

ENVISAGING THE REIGN OF GOD

One way to get a sense of God's desire and will for humanity is to imagine all the deepest and best desires of the human heart being fulfilled in abundance—a life in communion with God, "righteousness and peace and joy in the Holy Spirit" (CCC, no. 2819; see also Romans 14:7). Such is the desire and destiny of every person, as St. Augustine of Hippo so eloquently reminded us in his *Confessions*.

Our vocation on earth is to join with the Spirit of Christ and work toward bringing about that "righteousness and peace and joy." This task would surely include working for a decent life for everyone, an end to hunger and injustice, and worldwide peace. It would mean working to bring about a world in which the God-given dignity and rights of all people are fully respected and realized, a world filled with compassion and mercy for all. It would mean working to bring about a world in which all people and societies would live as good stewards of creation and would use the world's resources wisely and fairly, a world in which everyone protected the environment and all of nature; the list could go on and on.

CREATIVE ACTIVITY

⊙ Create a kingdom parable around an everyday life experience.
⊙ Share your parable.

"BLESSED ARE YOU WHO ARE POOR"

God's love for the poor is a major theme in Sacred Scripture. Among the four accounts of the Gospel, Luke makes it one of his central themes. The first of his Beatitudes is: "Blessed are you who are poor, / for yours is the kingdom of God" (Luke 6:20). This proclamation by Jesus was, indeed, good news for the poor of his time, as it is for the poor today. Jesus' teaching turned the attitudes and behavior of the religious and political leaders of his time toward the poor inside out. His teaching does the same today.

Whatever our vocation, we are to have a preferential love for the poor, as Jesus revealed God has. The Christian life of holiness and justice demands that we reach out to those oppressed by poverty of any kind—the hungry, the homeless, the imprisoned and those living on the margins because of poverty. This is the gospel message, the good news, that we are to preach by our words *and* by our deeds.

When we love others as Jesus did, we take part in the Church's work of evangelization. **Evangelization** is "the ministry and mission of proclaiming and witnessing Christ and his Gospel with the intention of deepening the faith of believers and inviting others to be baptized and initiated into the Church" (USCCA, Glossary, "Evangelization," 512). The 1971 World Synod of Bishops reaffirmed this truth, teaching: "Action on behalf of justice and participation in the transformation of the world fully appear to us as a constitutive dimension of the preaching of the Gospel" (*Justice in the World*, no. 6). Every Christian has a responsibility to take part in this mission of the Church. It is an essential responsibility of Christian discipleship.

THINK, PAIR AND SHARE

⊙ Work with a partner. Think of an unjust social or cultural issue that cries out for healing.
⊙ Discuss what Christians can do to help bring compassion and justice to the situation.

OVER TO YOU

⊙ A friend says: "Isn't it true that charity begins at home? So why all this stuff about helping someone else before I have enough to care for myself?"
⊙ Use Jesus' teaching about the Kingdom of God to respond to your friend. Give examples from your own life of how your living the Gospel is making a difference both to you and to others.

DISCIPLES: APPRENTICES OF THE MASTER

Our new life of being a **disciple** of Christ begins with our response to his invitation, "Follow me" (Matthew 4:19). The root word of "disciple" is the Greek *mathetes*, which can have the meaning "apprentice." Christ calls us to follow him as apprentices learning from a master. He calls us to learn his way, his truth, and come to new life in him. What is that new life? It is the life of being one with him and the Father through the power of the Spirit. The *Catechism* puts it this way: "He who believes in Christ has new life in the Holy Spirit. The moral life, increased and brought to maturity in grace, is to reach its fulfillment in the glory of heaven" (CCC, no. 1715).

St. Paul came to understand what that call means. He taught that we are to "have the mind of Christ" (1 Corinthians 2:16). We are to respond to the grace of the Spirit and work to transform our minds and hearts—our whole being from the inside out—into the mind and heart of Christ. We are to be apprentices of Jesus. We are to fashion our lives after the life of our master.

We enter this new life in Christ at Baptism. Through the graces of the other sacraments and through prayer and the development of the virtues, we become strengthened to live this new life in Christ. We are to love God with all our heart, soul, strength and mind and to love our neighbor as we love our own self. We are to obey this part of the Great Commandment as Jesus commanded us to do—to love one another and all people as he loves us. By living this gospel command in our daily life and work, whether we are married or unmarried, we bring good news to one another and to the world.

READ, REFLECT AND SHARE

- Work with a partner. Choose and page through one of the four accounts of the Gospel. Identify ways in which Jesus our master models how he calls his disciples, his apprentices, to live.
- What difference does making those ways part of how we live bring to one's own life and the life of other people?

WHAT ABOUT YOU PERSONALLY?

- You no doubt have heard the saying, "What would Jesus do?" What new insights has your study of the vocation to Christian discipleship given to your understanding of that saying?
- How will you integrate those insights into your daily living of the Gospel?

ST. PAUL | LUCAS CRANACH THE YOUNGER

Seeking the Kingdom of God in the world

OPENING ACTIVITY

⊙ Work alone. Create a mind map under the heading "The People and Things That Most Influence What I Want to Do with My Life."
⊙ List the people and things that have influenced or are now influencing your life significantly. Then rank those influences in order of priority, with the most important being number 1.
⊙ Pair up with a partner. Compare lists and share the reasons for your ranking.

OVER TO YOU

⊙ Where was Jesus on your list? Why?
⊙ Where was the Church on your list? Why?

DISCIPLES OF JESUS DO NOT GO IT ALONE!

At the time of Paul, there were many issues dividing the Church in Corinth that he addressed head on. Using the image of the human body, he wrote: "Now you are the body of Christ and individually members of it" (1 Corinthians 12:27). Pause for a moment and reflect on what Paul's words mean to you.

The Church is the Body of Christ. Christ is the Head of the Church and the baptized are its members. Jesus, the Head of his Church, is always with us—as he promised! Recall his final words just before he ascended to his Father: "And remember, I am with you always, to the end of the age" (Matthew 28:20). Fifty days later he and the Father fulfilled another promise that Jesus had previously made at the Last Supper. The Holy Spirit came upon the disciples. God did not abandon them and leave them alone to live out their call to discipleship.

The Church, the Body of Christ, is the community of Jesus' disciples. United in solidarity with the Father and the Son and the

Holy Spirit, and with one another, we learn, celebrate, pray and live the new life in Christ that we first received in Baptism. We serve the Church and announce the Good News. We are called to make our own particular contribution to building up God's reign in the world. God calls the faithful to meet this responsibility as bishops, priests or deacons; or as members of the consecrated life; or as married or single lay members of the Church.

TALK IT OVER

⊙ Where do you see young people cooperating with the Holy Trinity in order to take part in the Church's mission of building up God's reign in the world?

The Gospel is the leaven that God is kneading into the world

⊙ Can you identify something more that young people could do? How can you take part in that work?

WHAT ABOUT YOU PERSONALLY?

⊙ Think back over the last twenty-four to forty-eight hours. Where do you recognize a "God moment"—a time when God's grace might have been at work in your life?

⊙ How was God offering his grace to you? (Remember, God offers his grace in *ordinary* ways.) How well did you respond?

REBORN INTO NEW LIFE IN CHRIST

As members of the Church, "we live our discipleship together." In the Sacrament of Baptism the newly baptized are anointed with the consecrated oil of sacred Chrism. This anointing is a sign that the Holy Spirit has made the newly baptized sharers in the threefold mission of Christ the Priest, Prophet and King. The Church outlines three essential responsibilities that flow from Baptism:

⊙ The baptized have the responsibility to be active and faithful members of the Church as members of the hierarchy (ordained ministry), of the lay faithful, or of the consecrated life.

⊙ The baptized, guided by the Spirit of truth, have the responsibility to proclaim the Gospel.

⊙ Baptism calls all Christians to serve their neighbors—*all people*. This includes those who are not members of the Church and non-believers.

THE PRIMARY VOCATIONS OF THE BAPTIZED

The Gospel is the leaven that God is kneading into the world. Reread Jesus' parable of the yeast, or leaven, in Matthew 13:33. God sends all the baptized forth to live the Gospel in the midst of the world. This is our common vocation as disciples of Jesus. We are to bring the leaven of the Gospel to our whole life—into our private lives, into our personal relationships and into our life as faithful citizens in society.

The Catholic Church names three primary vocations through which God invites the baptized to live out their discipleship. These vocations are (1) a vocation to the ordained ministry of bishop, priest (the ministerial priesthood) or deacon; (2) the vocation of the laity, as a single or a married person, or (3) a vocation to the consecrated life by the "profession of the evangelical counsels within a permanent state of life recognized by the Church, that characterizes the life consecrated to God" (CCC, no. 915)

In the next section of this chapter we will explore the consecrated life. Now, let's take a look at the vocation to ordained ministry and the vocation of the lay faithful.

THE ORDAINED MINISTRY

The pope and the other bishops in communion with him are members of the **hierarchy** of the Church. The term "hierarchy" refers to the "Apostles and their successors, the college of bishops, to whom Christ gave the authority to teach, sanctify, and rule the Church in his name" (CCC, Glossary, "Hierarchy"). In the Sacrament of Holy Orders a baptized man is ordained to serve the People of God as a bishop, priest or deacon. Recalling the teachings of St. Ignatius of Antioch (c. 50 – c. 117), the *Catechism* teaches: "The ministries conferred by ordination are irreplaceable for the organic structure of the Church: without the bishop, presbyters, and deacons, one cannot speak of the Church" (CCC, no. 1593).

Through the Sacrament of Holy Orders, the mission Christ entrusted to his Apostles continues to be exercised in the Church. The ordained ministers of the Church exercise their service for the People of God by teaching, divine worship and pastoral governance. This authority includes "the right always and everywhere to announce moral principles, including those pertaining to the social order, and to make judgments on any human affairs to the extent that they are required by the fundamental rights of the human person or the salvation of souls" (*Code of Canon Law*, canon 747; quoted in CCC, no. 2032).

FROM THE CATECHISM

[The Sacrament of Holy Orders] configures the recipient to Christ by a special grace of the Holy Spirit, so that he may serve as Christ's instrument for his Church. By ordination one is enabled to act as a representative of Christ, Head of the Church, in his triple office of priest, prophet and king.

—CCC, no. 1581

THINK, PAIR AND SHARE

- What do you recall from chapter 3 on the role of the Magisterium, or teaching office of the Church, in the formation of conscience? Relate what you learned to the above.
- What moral issues are you aware of that the Church has recently addressed?
- Share with a partner how those teachings are guiding you in living as a disciple of Christ.

LAYPEOPLE—A WIDE VARIETY OF CALLINGS AND RESPONSIBILITIES

Laypeople, married and single, fulfill their vocation in many ways. For example, Christian parents share in the mission of Christ through their intimate love of each other and through educating and forming their children in the faith of the Church. Laypeople serve as catechists and teachers in schools and parishes and as teachers of theology

FROM THE CATECHISM

"By reason of their special vocation it belongs to the laity to seek the kingdom of God by engaging in temporal affairs and directing them according to God's will. . . . It pertains to them in a special way so to illuminate and order all temporal things with which they are closely associated that these may always be effected and grow according to Christ and may be to the glory of the Creator and Redeemer" (*Dogmatic Constitution on the Church*, no. 31).

—CCC, no. 898

Lay ecclesial ministers: Some laypeople have the vocation to serve the Church full time. The Catholic Church uses the term lay ecclesial ministers to describe this particular vocation. Lay ecclesial ministers are appointed by the Church to serve in parishes, schools, diocesan agencies and Church institutions. These laypeople work in close mutual collaboration with the pastoral ministry of bishops, priests and deacons. They fulfill certain leadership responsibilities entrusted to them in particular areas of ministry.

LET'S PROBE DEEPER

⊙ Read more about some of these associations of the laity; for example, check out the International Associations of the Faithful at the Vatican website, *www.vatican.va*.

Third Orders and Oblates: Laypeople sometimes commit to supporting one another by associating themselves with a religious order or institute; for example, the Third Order of St. Francis, the Third Order of St. Dominic, the Third Order of the Blessed Virgin Mary of Mount Carmel or the Lay Oblates of St. Benedict. Members of a third order are also known as tertiaries. Tertiaries often make promises and some take simple vows to study, adapt and adopt the vision and rule of the order's founder as their way of striving to grow in holiness of life. Diocesan priests can also belong to third orders.

Confraternities and other lay groups and movements: Laypeople have always recognized their need to come together to support one another in living the Gospel. Such groups and movements formed by laypeople and approved

in colleges and universities. In whatever way of life they choose, by living just and truthful lives with care and compassion for all those around them, laypeople share in the mission of Christ.

The lay faithful take part in the celebration of the sacramental life of the Church in many diverse ways. First and foremost, united with Christ and his sacrifice and with the other members of the Body of Christ, they offer themselves to the Father in thanksgiving as a "holy and living sacrifice" (Eucharistic Prayer III, *The Roman Missal*). The lay faithful may serve as greeters, readers and altar servers, musicians and choir members during the celebration of Mass. As extraordinary ministers of the Eucharist they may also distribute Holy Communion and bring the Real Presence of the Body and Blood of Christ to the sick and the homebound. Laypeople may also lead prayer services and, in an emergency, baptize.

Laypeople also take part in the governance of the Church. They participate in the work of parish councils, diocesan synods, pastoral councils, finance committees and ecclesiastical tribunals. They have a right and sometimes a duty to dialogue with their pastors and with other members of the Church and to share their views concerning the good of the Church.

by the Church can be described as associations. The members pool resources to put flesh and blood on their discipleship in a particular way; for example, to live the works of mercy, to work for justice and peace, and so on. Examples of longstanding lay groups and movements include the Legion of Mary, the Knights of Columbus, the Daughters of Isabella, the Altar/Rosary Society and the Society of St. Vincent de Paul.

There are also new movements in the Church, among them Focolare, Communion and Liberation, Sant'Egidio, and other religious movements, such as charismatic renewal, which exists in over two hundred countries throughout the world. The charismatic renewal movement emphasizes the mission and work of the Holy Spirit in the Church and the charisms the Spirit gives to the Church to fulfill the mission Christ gave her. (Check out 1 Corinthians 12:8–10.) All seek to contribute to the transformation of the world into the Reign of God.

The Community of Sant'Egidio

The Sant'Egidio movement began in Rome in 1968 with a group of high school students. Today its members include over 50,000 Christian laypeople in more than seventy countries. Sant'Egidio communities work to tear down the walls of prejudice, fear and loneliness that separate people from one another within society.

Solidarity, friendship, peace, ecumenism and interreligious dialogue are central to the life of the Sant'Egidio community. The members' special vocation is to foster friendships with the poor, the elderly, immigrants and children who are their neighbors in the cities in which they live. Sant'Egidio communities also serve the imprisoned and build friendships and strong foundations for peace; for example, they create Schools of Peace wherever children need a safe place to learn. They have also realized dreams of friendship across

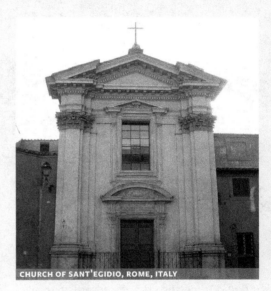

CHURCH OF SANT'EGIDIO, ROME, ITALY

international borders; for example, with a HIV/AIDS treatment program in sub-Saharan Africa.

RESEARCH AND SHARE
⊙ Work alone or with a partner. Research one of the many lay associations and movements in the Catholic Church.
⊙ Discuss: What appeals to you about belonging to such a group of laypeople? What is not so appealing?
⊙ Share your research with the class.

TALK IT OVER
⊙ Right now, as a member of the laity, you have a vocation. Describe the vocation of a young Christian of high school age.

⊙ How are your parish and high school communities supporting young people to live their vocation? How do you see youth responding to that support?

OVER TO YOU
⊙ Read Matthew 9:35–38 and Luke 10:2.
⊙ What is Jesus saying to you about the importance of your vocation right here, right now?

Leaven in the world

CAMEL AND THE EYE OF A NEEDLE | ST. BONIFACE CHURCH, DORTMUND, GERMANY

OVER TO YOU

- Think about the rich young man's question and Jesus' response.
- What might you learn for your own life right now from the encounter of the rich young man with Jesus? How willing are you to do more to follow Jesus?

FROM THE CATECHISM

Christ proposes the evangelical counsels, in their great variety, to every disciple.

—CCC, no. 915

THE EVANGELICAL COUNSELS

The Benedictines, Carmelites, Franciscans, Dominicans, Jesuits, Salesians and Ursulines are just a few of the many religious communities who enrich the life of the Church. These and other religious communities dedicate themselves to living the radical demands of the Gospel. Traditionally, the Church describes the decision to live in this way as "entering the religious life."

Professing publicly to live a life of holiness rooted in the evangelical, or gospel, counsels of poverty, chastity and obedience is a core aspect of *religious life*. The evangelical counsels, in general, are "the teachings of the New Law proposed by Jesus to his disciples which lead to the perfection of Christian life. . . . The public profession of the evangelical counsels of poverty, chastity, and obedience is a constitutive element of state of consecrated life in the Church" (CCC, Glossary, "Evangelical Counsels").

Poverty: Pope Emeritus Benedict XVI distinguished "chosen poverty" (being "poor in spirit") from "poverty to be fought" (unjust

Recall the account of the encounter of the rich young man with Jesus in Matthew 19:16–30. The rich young man seemingly takes great pride in having lived his life according to *all* the Commandments. He approaches Jesus and asks, "Teacher, what good deed must I do to have eternal life?" (Matthew 19:16) The young man is somewhat taken back and disappointed with Jesus' response, "If you wish to be perfect, go, sell your possessions, and give the money to the poor, and you will have treasure in heaven; then come, follow me" (Matthew 19:21). In other words, "You can do more!"

OPENING CONVERSATION

- What do the names Benedictine, Carmelite, Franciscan, Dominican, Jesuit, Salesian and Ursuline mean to you?
- Do you know someone who has responded to Jesus and is "doing more"? Share their story.

Evangelical counsels

Those vows taken by men or women who enter religious life; there are three vows: poverty, chastity, and obedience.

—USCCA, Glossary, 511

16TH-CENTURY STONE PLAQUE GIVING DIRECTIONS TO A MONASTERY

and imposed poverty). By professing and living the evangelical counsel of poverty, members of the consecrated life choose to commit themselves freely to be "poor in spirit" *and* "poor in possessions." They become living reminders that the "poor in spirit" alone truly find the blessedness and happiness that the human heart craves. They become living reminders of God's preferential option for the poor. True poverty—that is, attachment to God above all else and detachment from possessions—brings true freedom and abundance of life.

Chastity: We explored the virtue of chastity in detail in chapter 9. Recall the many ways this virtue strengthens the faithful to grow in true love of God, neighbor and self. By professing and living the evangelical counsel of chastity, a member of a religious community *consecrates* himself or herself totally to God, and serves the Church as a living reminder that God desires and calls everyone to live in intimate communion and friendship with him.

Obedience: The Latin verb *oboedire*, which means "to listen well," is the root of the English word "obedience." The baptized who live the consecrated life vow or promise to "listen well" and freely respond to the Lord. This includes obedience to the Church and to the authority of their religious community. By living the evangelical counsel of obedience, members of the consecrated life remind all the baptized to listen to the Spirit of Christ, who dwells within our heart, as the young Blessed Virgin Mary did when she responded, "Here am I, the servant of the Lord; let it be with me according to your word" (Luke 1:38).

FROM THE CATECHISM

In the consecrated life, Christ's faithful, moved by the Holy Spirit, propose to follow Christ more nearly, to give themselves to God who is loved above all and, pursuing the perfection of charity in the service of the Kingdom, to signify and proclaim in the Church the glory of the world to come (see *Code of Canon Law*, canon 573).

—CCC, no. 916

THE CONSECRATED LIFE

The Latin verb *consecrare*, which means "to dedicate or set apart for a holy purpose," is the root of the word "consecrate." Jesus spoke to that holy purpose in the Sermon on the Mount. He instructed his disciples, "Be perfect, therefore, as your heavenly Father is perfect" (Matthew 5:48). All Christians are to strive for that perfection, to live a life of holiness and justice.

God also calls some of the faithful, lay and ordained, to *profess* the evangelical counsels within a permanent state of life. The Church names this state of life the consecrated life. In his teaching on the consecrated life, St. John Paul II wrote:

ST. ANTHONY AND ST. PAUL IN THE DESERT | DIEGO VELÁZQUEZ

The eremitic life, or the life of a hermit: The term "eremitic" means "one who lives in the desert." Eremites, also called hermits or anchorites, live apart from the world. They "manifest to everyone the interior aspect of the mystery of the Church, that is, personal intimacy with Christ" (CCC, no. 921). While they may or may not profess the three evangelical counsels, hermits devote their lives to the praise of God by living in silence, by the practice of prayer and the discipline of penance. The Old Testament prophet Elias and St. John the Baptist lived the eremitic life. St. Anthony of the Desert (c. 251–356) and Julian of Norwich (c. 1342–1416) are well-known Christian hermits whose lives and writings continue to be a blessing for the Church.

The contemplative life: The sixteenth-century mystic St. Teresa of Jesus (St. Teresa of Ávila) described contemplative prayer as "nothing else than a close sharing between friends; it means taking time frequently to be alone with him who we know loves us" (*The Book of Her Life*, 8, 5; quoted in CCC, no. 2709). The contemplative way of life imitates Christ praying on the mountain in solitude and silence, directing his whole life to the Father and to the fulfillment of his Father's will.

The Son, who is the way which leads to the Father (see John 14:6), calls all those whom the Father has given to him (see John 17:9) to make the following of himself the whole purpose of their lives. But of some, those called to the consecrated life, he asks a total commitment, one which involves leaving everything behind (see Matthew 19:27) in order to live at his side and to follow him wherever he goes (see Revelation 14:4).

—Apostolic Exhortation, *On the Consecrated Life and Its Mission in the Church and in the World*, no. 18

Let us look now at some of the more formal ways of living the consecrated life that are part of the spiritual tradition of the Church.

The Poor Clares and Trappists are examples of the faithful who center their life in the prayer of contemplation. As members of the Body of Christ, contemplatives are a unique source of grace and blessing for the apostolic life of the Church and for the growth of the People of God. The Church has affirmed this belief by naming the contemplative St. Thérèse of Lisieux as the patron saint of missionaries.

TALK IT OVER

⊙ In what ways do you see the contemplative life supporting and complementing putting the Gospel into action?

⊙ Why is it important for all Christians to set aside time to pray the prayer of contemplation?

Consecrated virgins: God the Father blessed Mary, the Mother of his Incarnate Son, with the singular grace of perpetual virginity. Consecrated virgins vow or promise to live a life of perpetual virginity. Through this commitment they live totally for the sake of the Kingdom of God. Consecrated virgins may live alone or in community. They live out their commitment through prayer, penance and service of others.

JOURNAL EXERCISE

In her liturgy the Church remembers a long list of virgins whose lives have blessed the Church from her earliest days; for example, St. Agnes (January 21), St. Katharine Drexel (March 3), St. Kateri Tekakwitha (July 14) and St. Teresa of Jesus (October 15).

- ⊙ Research the lives of virgins whom the Church remembers and celebrates in her liturgy.
- ⊙ Write down the wisdom you learn and describe specific ways in which you can integrate that wisdom into your living the Gospel.

Consecrated widows and widowers: In his first letter to his companion St. Timothy, St. Paul wrote, "Honor widows who are really widows. . . . The real widow, left alone, has set her hope on God and continues in supplications and prayers night and day" (1 Timothy 5:3, 5). St. John Paul II encouraged the renewal of this apostolic way of life. He wrote: "These women and men, through a vow of perpetual chastity as a sign of the Kingdom of God, consecrate their state of life in order to devote themselves to prayer and the service of the Church" (*On the Consecrated Life and Its Mission in the Church and in the World*, no. 7).

Secular institutes: Members of secular institutes have the vocation and charism to live out their consecration in the marketplace of the world. A charism is a "specific gift or grace of the Holy Spirit which directly or indirectly benefits the Church, given in order to help a person live out the Christian life, or to serve the common good in building up the Church" (CCC, Glossary, "Charism").

Both laity and ordained members of the Church profess to live the Gospel as members of secular institutes. They are "a leaven of wisdom and a witness of grace within cultural, economic and political life. Through their own specific blending of presence in the world and consecration, they seek *to make present in society the newness and power of Christ's Kingdom*" (*On the Consecrated Life and Its Mission in the Church and in the World*, no. 10).

Societies of apostolic life: Societies of apostolic life are associations of the faithful who take simple promises, not religious vows. These societies support their members to pursue a specific apostolate, such as education, or care of the sick or elderly. The Church uses the term "apostolate" to name the "activity of the Christian which fulfills the apostolic nature of the whole Church by working to extend the reign of Christ to the entire world" (CCC, Glossary, "Apostolate").

ST. TERESA OF JESUS | SALAMANCA, SPAIN

For example, the Daughters of Charity of St. Vincent de Paul live in community and serve Christ through their full-time work for and with the poor. St. Louise de Marillac (1591–1660) and St. Vincent de Paul (1581–1660) founded this society. Today, there are over 18,000 Daughters of Charity who serve people in over 2,000 communities in ninety-one countries throughout the world.

OVER TO YOU

⊙ What power do you see in the evangelical counsels of poverty, chastity and obedience to transform your life?

⊙ How might you be called to live these in your own life now?

THE CHURCH: THE SACRAMENT OF CHRIST AND SEED OF THE KINGDOM

The Church is the sacrament of Christ. She is "catholic" and the seed of the Kingdom of God. She has the mission to knead the leaven of the Gospel into every part of society. In other words, the Church makes Christ and his way of life *visibly present* in the home, in the local community and in all parts of the world. We might say that the Church puts flesh and blood on the mystery of the risen and glorified Christ until he comes again in glory.

Those who live the consecrated life, including hermits and members of contemplative religious communities, take part in this evangelizing and missionary work in a real way. Let us turn once again to the words of St. John Paul II:

The evangelical basis of consecrated life is to be sought in the special relationship which Jesus, in his earthly life, established with some of his disciples. He called them not only to welcome the Kingdom of God into their own lives, but also to put their lives at its service, leaving everything behind and closely imitating his own *way of life.*

—*On the Consecrated Life and Its Mission in the Church and in the World,* no. 14

Religious communities have a long history of taking part in the missionary and evangelizing work of the Church. Many religious live the Gospel in lands other than their own; others travel within their own countries to minister with the poor; others, such as contemplatives, as we have seen, are missionaries and evangelizers through their life of prayer.

JOURNAL EXERCISE

⊙ What wisdom does the life of Christians living the consecrated life offer to you and other young Christians?

⊙ Identify several ways you can make that wisdom part of your life as a disciple of Jesus Christ.

THE FIRST MISSIONARIES | ENGRAVING OF A 15TH-CENTURY TAPESTRY

REVIEW AND SHARE WHAT YOU HAVE LEARNED IN THIS CHAPTER

Look back over this chapter and reflect on the teachings of Scripture and Tradition on the many ways the faithful are called to live the Gospel. Share the teachings of the Catholic Church on these statements:

- ⊙ God calls every person to a life of holiness and justice.
- ⊙ God's love for the poor is a major theme in Sacred Scripture.
- ⊙ The Gospel calls all believers to work to bring about the Kingdom of God.
- ⊙ The faithful live out their vocation to live a holy and just life as members of the hierarchy, the lay faithful or the consecrated life.
- ⊙ By living the evangelical counsels of poverty, chastity and obedience according to one's state of life, every disciple strives to live the Christian life to its fullness.
- ⊙ Laypeople seek holiness of life and work to bring about the Kingdom of God by living the Gospel in a variety of ways.
- ⊙ The Church, the Body of Christ, is the community of Jesus' disciples, living in communion with the Father and the Son and the Holy Spirit, and with one another.
- ⊙ The Church is the sacrament of Christ and the seed of the Kingdom of God.

TALK IT OVER

- ⊙ Describe how the many ways of living the Gospel reveal God's desire and will that all people live a life of holiness and justice.

REFLECT AND DISCERN

- ⊙ How do you understand the call to Christian discipleship—what is involved, its major demands, its best hopes?
- ⊙ What will you do about choosing your own particular vocation in life?
- ⊙ What practical decisions will you make in response to what you have learned in this chapter?

LEARN BY EXAMPLE

Simon Peter, meeting the challenges of being a disciple of Jesus Christ

Simon (Peter) was a native of Bethsaida, near Lake Tiberias. He worked, like his brother Andrew, as a fisherman. Andrew introduced Simon to Jesus, who called him to become a disciple: "Do not be afraid; from now on you will be catching people" (Luke 5:10).

During a trip that Jesus took with his disciples to Caesarea Philippi to Jews living outside of Palestine, they encountered many people who had a variety of opinions as to who Jesus was. Turning to his disciples, Jesus asked, "But who do you say that I am?" Peter responded for the rest, declaring, "You are the Messiah, the son of the living God."

DETAIL OF ST. PETER (BRANCACCI CHAPEL) | MASACCIO

Whereupon Jesus responded, "Blessed are you Simon son of Jonah! For flesh and blood has not revealed this to you, but my Father in heaven. But I tell you, you are Peter, and on this rock I will build my church" (Matthew 16:15–18). The name Peter, or Cephas, means "rock."

From then on it was clear that Jesus named Peter to be the first among, or leader of, his closest disciples, the Apostles. The leadership ministry of Peter continues today through the pope, the successor of Peter and Bishop of Rome. Peter was always listed as the first of the disciples in the New Testament. He is recorded as speaking more than any other disciple, and he was at Jesus' side throughout his ministry.

Peter also had his human failings. After Jesus was arrested, a woman asked Peter three times whether he was a disciple of Jesus. Three times Peter denied even knowing "the man." Peter, Matthew tells us, then "went out and began to weep bitterly." (Read this whole account of Peter's betrayal and repentance in Matthew 26:69–75.)

After his Death and Resurrection, the risen Christ appeared to Peter and the other disciples on the shores of the Sea of Tiberias where they were fishing. Jesus asked Peter three times, "Do you love me?" Three times Simon Peter professed his commitment to and faith in Jesus. Jesus responded each time by entrusting the care of the Church to Peter, saying, "Feed my lambs" (John 21:15), "Tend my sheep" (John 21:16), and "Feed my sheep" (John 21:17).

St. Luke tells us that, upon Jesus' Ascension, Peter was the unquestionable leader among the Apostles. It was Peter who called for an election of an apostle to replace Judas (check out Acts of the Apostles 1:15–26). After the descent of the Holy Spirit upon the Apostles and others in an upper room in Jerusalem at Pentecost, it was Peter, "standing with the eleven" (Acts of the Apostles 2:14), who addressed the Jewish pilgrims and began the work the risen Jesus had commissioned them to do. Under the leadership of Peter, the work of the Church had begun. The remainder of the Acts of the Apostles details the work of St. Peter (along with that of St. Paul) in such cities as Antioch, Corinth and, eventually, Rome, where he was martyred, probably in AD 64. According to an ancient tradition, Peter requested to be crucified upside down because he declared himself unworthy to die in the same manner as Jesus.

TALK IT OVER
- What can we learn about discipleship from Peter's life?
- What might Peter's discipleship have to say to young Christians today?

SHARE FAITH WITH FAMILY AND FRIENDS
- Read Matthew 5:13–16.
- Then share with family and friends how you can support one another to live your vocation as disciples of Jesus Christ to bring about the Kingdom of God.

JUDGE AND DECIDE
- Research ways your parish is taking part in the Church's mission to build a just and compassionate society. For example, read the parish bulletin board, visit its website and talk to several of the leaders of your parish.
- Which of these projects most appeals to you?
- How might you participate in this work of your parish?

LEARN BY HEART

"Go, sell your possessions and give the money to the poor, and you will have treasure in heaven; then come, follow me."

MATTHEW 19:21

PRAYER REFLECTION

All reflect quietly and acknowledge the presence of Christ. (Pause)

Pray the Sign of the Cross together.

LEADER
Today I invite you to transport yourself in spirit to a courtyard. It's chilly. A warm charcoal fire is ablaze. Let us go to the fire and warm our hands. (*Pause*)
All reflect and apply what you are hearing to your lives as disciples of Jesus.

LEADER
A man joins us. He is bearded, strong, commanding. He too warms himself by the fire. A woman appears. She is composed, firm in her conviction, and says to him, "You too were with Jesus." The man denies it, saying, "I do not even know the man." (*Pause*)
All reflect and apply what you are hearing to your lives as disciples of Jesus.

LEADER
The man, whom we know is Peter, had sworn to Jesus, "I will never forsake you." He now denies that he ever knew Jesus. Why? Fear. Fear overcame Peter. For Peter, the woman represents the religious and political leaders who have just arrested Jesus. Peter's fear is so great that he denies Jesus. Jesus is now in the hands of the ruling power. Experience has taught Peter that crucifixion is imminent. So he slips away . . . in fear for his own life. (*Pause*)
All reflect and apply what you are hearing to your lives as disciples of Jesus.

LEADER
Jesus was always on the side of the oppressed. In reaching out in love, he spoke against the evils of the barriers of his day. He treated all people with respect. He was a just man. He spoke to the Samaritan woman; Jews and Samaritans did not mix. He healed the leper; lepers were despised. He healed on the Sabbath; in so doing he was a threat to the religious ruling bodies of his day. And so they feared him and plotted his death. Jesus' faithfulness to his mission through "his loving obedience to his Father" (CCC, no. 623) led to his death. (*Pause*)
All reflect and apply what you are hearing to your lives as disciples of Jesus.

LEADER
Not much has changed. Conflict between oppressor and the oppressed is still very much with us. The times and circumstances may have changed. The conflict between the powers of this world and the Reign of God continues. Christ's disciples do not flee from that conflict; they face it head on. Blessed Mother Teresa of Calcutta (1910–97) spoke out and cared for the dying and destitute in India. Blessed Archbishop Oscar Romero (1917–80) worked tirelessly for the poor and oppressed to bring about a just and compassionate society in El Salvador. Martin Luther King Jr. (1929–68) spoke out and gave his life for the cause of African Americans and the equality of all people in the United States. The list of faithful disciples goes on . . . a list that is filled with the names of unknown disciples dedicated to the work of establishing the Reign of God. Who else can you add to this litany? (*Pause*)
All reflect and apply what you are hearing to your lives as disciples of Jesus.

LEADER
Christ asks you by name, "_____, do you love me?" You reply, "Lord, you know I love you." In reply he says, "Care for one another. Love one another." (*Pause and reflect*)

LEADER
Come, Holy Spirit, fill us with your fire. Strengthen us to glorify you, and the Father and the Son, with our lives.
ALL
We will care for one another as you care for us. We will love one another as you love us. Thanks be to God.

Pray the Sign of the Cross together.

CHAPTER 12

Sustaining the Moral Life as Disciples of Jesus

—The Life of Grace, the Virtues and Prayer

THE HUMAN VIRTUES
help us to live the New Law of love

We acquire these virtues by
OUR EFFORTS, AIDED BY GOD'S GRACE

God's grace comes to us through
THE HOLY SPIRIT

The Christian life is guided by the threefold law of
BELIEVING, PRAYING AND LIVING

THE CHURCH
is our guide for living a moral life

PRAYER AND THE CHRISTIAN LIFE
are inseparable

LIVING THE MORAL LIFE AS A DISCIPLE OF JESUS Christ is an invitation to live the New Law revealed by Jesus Christ. In this chapter we explore the role of the theological virtues of faith, hope and charity (love) and the four cardinal virtues of prudence, justice, fortitude and temperance in the Christian life. We discover that participating in the celebration of the sacraments, especially the Eucharist, and living a life of prayer are a source of grace and strength to live a virtuous life.

THEOLOGICAL VIRTUES:

- FAITH
- HOPE
- LOVE

CARDINAL VIRTUES:

- PRUDENCE
- JUSTICE
- FORTITUDE
- TEMPERANCE

GRACE:

- SANCTIFYING GRACE
- SACRAMENTAL GRACES
- ACTUAL GRACES

Faith Focus: These teachings are the primary focus doctrinal content presented in this chapter:
- ⊙ The theological virtues and the human moral virtues empower us to live as children of God.
- ⊙ The human virtues are positive attitudes and habits that help us live the New Law revealed by Jesus Christ.
- ⊙ The heart and soul of the New Law is the New Commandment, which Jesus gave to his disciples and to the whole Church at the Last Supper.
- ⊙ The Holy Spirit always offers us the grace to live a virtuous life.
- ⊙ The cardinal virtues are the central moral virtues.
- ⊙ The Church, guided by the Holy Spirit, is our teacher for living a moral life.
- ⊙ Prayer is an essential and vital part of the Christian life.
- ⊙ The Lord's Prayer is a summary of the Gospel

Discipleship Formation: As chapter you should be b
- ⊙ understand the central role your life as a disciple of Jesus;
- ⊙ live as a disciple of Christ with courage;
- ⊙ reach out to Mary as the model for your discipl
- ⊙ come to understand the Church to be your surest gu to living a moral life;
- ⊙ grow as a person of prayer,
- ⊙ discover the Lord's Prayer to be a guide in your s to bring about the Kingdom of God.

Scripture References: These Scripture references a quoted or referred to in this chapter:
OLD TESTAMENT: **Genesis** 1:26–27, 31; **Psalms** 5:1–3, 19:7–9, 31:23–24; **Wisdom** 8:7; **Isaiah** 58:6
NEW TESTAMENT: **Matthew** 6:5–8, 9–13, 7:7–11, 21– 13:45–46, 28:19–20; **Mark** 8:31—9:1, 13:45–46; **Luke** 2:25–35, 3:21, 5:16, 31–32, 6:12, 9:18–20, 28, 11:1–4, 2 41–44; **John** 8:32, 10:10, 13:31–35, 15:1–17, 19:26–27; the Apostles 2:2–4; **Romans** 5:5; **1 Corinthians** 13:1 **2 Corinthians** 6:16, 9:8; **Galatians** 5:6, 22–25; **Ephe** 1:9; **Philippians** 2:5–11; **Colossians** 3:14; **1 Thessalo** 5:17; **1 John** 3:1

Faith Glossary: Familiarize yourself with the mean these key terms in the Glossary: **actual graces, ca law, charity (love), faith, fortitude, fruits of the H Spirit, gifts of the Holy Spirit, grace, hope, huma virtues, indefectibility, infallibility, justice, Magi merit, New Commandment, New Law, Paschal M prayer, prudence, sacramental graces, sanctifyi temperance, theological virtues**

Faith Word: human virtues
Learn by Heart: 1 Corinthians 13:13
Learn by Example: Nuestra Señora de la Caridad a symbol of faith, hope and love for the Cuban p

What sustains your moral life?

People who are healthy don't rush into emergency rooms, healthcare clinics and doctors' offices. You certainly would wonder why if they did. We go to the doctor when we are sick or injured. Jesus used this fact of life to reveal to his disciples, the Pharisees, scribes and others, the nature of his work among them. He stated unequivocally, "Those who are well have no need of a physician, but those who are sick; I have come to call not the righteous but sinners to repentance" (Luke 5:32).

OPENING CONVERSATION

⊙ In addition to illness of our body or mind, what other kinds of sickness might a person suffer?

⊙ Who might give them a treatment plan?

⊙ How does our experience of being sick help us understand the teaching of Jesus in Luke 5:32?

OVER TO YOU

⊙ Think of a time when you have been spiritually sick. Describe what that was like. How did you find healing?

FROM THE CATECHISM

The theological virtues dispose Christians to live in a relationship with the Holy Trinity. They have God for their origin, their motive, and their object—God known by faith, God hoped in and loved for his own sake.

—*Catechism of the Catholic Church* (CCC), no. 1840

NEW LIFE: THE FRUIT OF THE THEOLOGICAL VIRTUES

Jesus came to heal the relationship, or covenant, between God and humanity that human beings first broke by Original Sin and continued to break after that by personal sin. Jesus fulfilled the Old Law, which centered on the Ten Commandments, and established the New Law. The **New Law** is the "title given to the manner of living and acting taught by Jesus. When we follow the New Law, we are maintaining our part of the covenant with God" (*United States Catholic Catechism for Adults* [USCCA], Glossary, "New Law," 521).

The heart and soul of the New Law is the **New Commandment** that Jesus gave to his disciples and to the whole Church at the Last Supper. (Reread the episode in John 13:31–35.) St. Paul describes the heart and soul of living the New Commandment in his great hymn on love in 1 Corinthians 13:1–13. Paul concludes his hymn, "And now faith, hope, and love abide, these three; and the greatest of these is love" (1 Corinthians 13:13).

Faith, hope and love are three **theological virtues**. These virtues are three great pillars and foundations of our relationship with God. You will recall from chapter 5 that they are called "theological" because God is their origin, and life with God is their end. They are free gifts, or graces, God gives us that enable us to live and act as his children and to attain eternal life and happiness. Accepting and living these three great virtues is the source and power of our receiving the abundant life that Jesus promised to his disciples (see John 10:10).

READ, OBSERVE AND SHARE

⊙ Read and reflect on 1 Corinthians 13:13 and John 10:10. Then look carefully at the images and the colors the artist used in these stained-glass images of the theological virtues.

⊙ Work with a partner and share responses to these questions:
  - What do the images and colors say to you about Faith (*Fides*), Hope (*Spes*) and Love (*Caritas*)?
  - Do you think that the artist deliberately placed "Caritas" in the center? Why or why not?

WHAT ABOUT YOU PERSONALLY?

⊙ How would you depict Paul's teaching in 1 Corinthians 13:13? Share your ideas.

FAITH, HOPE AND LOVE

Throughout this course of study you have been learning that the theological virtues and the human moral virtues are central to living the New Law. Faith, hope and charity inform all the human virtues. The threefold dimension of believing, praying *and* living has traditionally been used to describe the Christian life. We join with the whole Church in *professing* her teachings in the creeds; in *celebrating* our new life in Christ in the sacraments; and in *living* that new life with the grace and guidance of the Spirit of Christ and his Church. Let us briefly recall what you have learned about the theological virtues. (We will explore the human virtues in the next section of this chapter.)

Faith: Faith is "submission" to God; it includes assent to all that God has revealed to us about himself and to what the Church proposes for our belief. For Christians, faith is the giving of our whole person to the Incarnate Son of God, Jesus Christ, and following his way. We profess our faith in words and deeds. (Check out Matthew 7:21–23.) St. Paul put it this way, "the only thing that counts is faith working through love" (Galatians 5:6).

Hope: St. Paul writes that "hope does not disappoint us, because God's love has been poured into our hearts through the Holy Spirit that has been given to us" (Romans 5: 5). **Hope** is the gift by which "we desire, and with steadfast trust await from God, eternal life and the graces to merit it" (CCC, no. 1843). The term **"merit"** does not mean "earn" or "have a right to" as a result of our own unassisted efforts. "We can have merit in God's sight only because of God's free plan to associate man with the work of his grace" (CCC, no. 2025). The Catholic Church uses the term "merit" to identify the "reward which God promises and gives to those who love him and by his grace perform good works" (CCC, Glossary, "Merit").

No one can earn the initial grace of sharing in the life of God or the gift of eternal life on their own. The **Paschal Mystery** of the Passion, Death, Resurrection and Ascension of the Incarnate Son of God is the source of our merit—of our sharing in the life and love of God, both now and in eternal life. "Uniting us by faith and Baptism to the Passion and Resurrection of Christ, the Spirit makes us sharers in his life" (CCC, no. 2017). The Paschal Mystery assures humanity that life will triumph over death, good over evil, love over hatred, and the Reign, or Kingdom, of God over the powers of the kingdom of the world.

JOURNAL EXERCISE

- Quietly pray the Lord's Prayer. As you pray, listen for words of hope from the Holy Spirit.
- What do those words mean for your life right now? Write your reflections in your journal.

Charity (love): Charity (love) is the theological virtue "by which we give love to God for his own sake and love to our neighbor on account of God" (USCCA, Glossary, "Charity (Love)," 506). Jesus places love above all laws and at the center of the life of each of his disciples and of the community of his disciples, the Church. St. John the Evangelist has much to say about love. Open your Bible and read John 15:1–17. Jesus entreats his disciples: "As the Father has loved me, so I have loved you; abide in my love" (John 15:9). And again: "This is my commandment, that you love one another as I have loved you" (John 15:12). We are to love as Jesus, the Incarnate Son of God, loves. The model of our love is God's love for us.

"Charity, the form of all the virtues, 'binds everything together in perfect harmony' (Colossians 3:14)" (CCC, no. 1844). When we truly love God, self and neighbor we experience joy, peace and mercy. We stand before God not as slaves fearful of punishment but as children responding to the love of God, who loves us beyond our wildest dreams. A life that begins and ends in love brings about friendship and communion at every level. Love is the energy that inspires all the other virtues.

THINK, PAIR AND SHARE

- Look back at the stained-glass images of the theological virtues and notice, once again, the artist's placement of *Caritas* (Love).
- Why might the artist have placed the works in that particular order? Share your views with a partner.

LET'S PROBE DEEPER

- Father Pedro Arrupe, S.J. (1907–91) was the Superior General of the Society of Jesus (the Jesuits) from 1965 to 1983. He wrote: "Nothing is more practical than finding God, than falling in Love in a quite absolute, final way. What you are in love with, what seizes your imagination, will affect everything. It will decide what will get you out of bed in the mornings, what you do with your evenings, how you spend your weekends, what you read, who you know, what breaks your heart, and what amazes you with joy and gratitude. Fall in Love, stay in love, and it will decide everything."
- What are young people today "in love with"? Does that love reflect Father Arrupe's description of love? Why or why not? Give examples.
- What about your search for love? Do Father Arrupe's words "What you are in love with, what seizes your imagination, will affect everything" have meaning for you? How do they apply to your life?

JOURNAL EXERCISE

Violent conflicts, injustice, excessive economic or social inequalities, envy, pride and distrust among people and nations constantly threaten peace and cause wars.

- How do the virtues of faith, hope and love empower Christians to partner with the Spirit of Christ to work to transform such situations and bring about the Reign of God?
- Write a short prayer asking the Holy Spirit for the courage to take your part in that work.

Striving to live a virtuous life

Both believers and non-believers have taught and continue to teach the value of living a virtuous life. The Greek word *arete*, which is translated "virtue," means "moral excellence." Socrates (469–399 BC) equated virtue with the knowledge of good and evil. Aristotle (384–322 BC) taught that virtue is excellence of character achieved by training and repeatedly choosing to do good and avoid evil. All the major religious traditions, Christian and non-Christian, call their members to lead a moral life rooted in the virtues.

OPENING CONVERSATION

⊙ Who do you know personally or have you learned about that you would describe as a person of excellence of character?

⊙ What traits in a person would lead you to acknowledge them to be of excellence of character?

⊙ How are the saints of the Church persons of excellence of Christian character? Give examples.

OVER TO YOU

⊙ What about yourself? Would your friends and teachers and neighbors describe you as a person of excellence of character? What would move them to describe you that way?

FROM THE CATECHISM

A virtue is an habitual and firm disposition to do the good. It allows the person not only to perform good acts, but to give the best of himself. The virtuous person tends toward the good with all his sensory and spiritual powers; he pursues the good and chooses it in concrete actions. "The goal of a virtuous life is to become like God" (St Gregory of Nyssa, *Homilies on the Beatitudes*, 1).

—CCC, no. 1803

THE HUMAN VIRTUES

The **human virtues** strengthen us to build our life on the true, the good and the beautiful. They are positive attitudes and habits that help us to live the New Law. We acquire these virtues by our efforts, aided by God's grace. While God's grace prompts and sustains our efforts, we must work at developing and living a virtuous life. A virtue only becomes part of who we are if we practice it.

We all know that it takes hours of practice to become really skilled at anything. So it is with any virtue. We need to cultivate the practice of virtue in order to grow to be the persons whom God creates us to be. (See Genesis 1:26–27, 31;

PRUDENCE | PIERRE COURTEYS

Human virtues

The human virtues are stable dispositions of the intellect and the will that govern our acts, order our passions and guide our conduct in accordance with reason and faith. They can be grouped around the four cardinal virtues: prudence, justice, fortitude, and temperance.

—CCC, no. 1834

THE CARDINAL, OR "HINGE," VIRTUES

In the Book of Wisdom we read: "And if anyone loves righteousness, / her labors are virtues; / for she teaches self-control and prudence, / justice and courage; / nothing in life is more profitable for mortals than these" (Wisdom 8:7). The four human moral virtues of **prudence**, **justice**, **fortitude** and **temperance** (self-control) are the foundation for leading a virtuous life, and for this reason they are called the cardinal virtues. The Latin word *cardo*, which means "hinge," is the root of the word "cardinal." All the other human virtues hinge upon and flow from the four cardinal virtues. Let's take a look at each of them.

Prudence: This virtue provides guidance for our conscience in making moral choices. We can gain insight into the importance of the virtue of prudence from the story of the merchant who finds a pearl of great value, in Mark 13:45–46. Pause and read that parable.

Prudence helps us know and choose the true treasures in life. It "disposes a person to discern the good and choose the correct means to accomplish it" (CCC, Glossary, "Prudence"). Prudence is *cardinal* because in order to lead a truly virtuous life one must grow in the habit of knowing and choosing the "good" and the "true." Clearly, then, all the other virtues hinge on prudence. Only a prudent person can apply the virtues of justice, fortitude and temperance to do good in daily life. A person becomes prudent by developing the habit and ability to:

⊙ discern what is good and right in real-life situations,

⊙ distinguish what is essential from what is non-essential,

Psalm 8:5; 1 John 3:1.) The human virtues lay the foundation for meaningful and right relationships with others and with oneself. Virtues grow through education, through the deliberate choices we make to act in particular ways, and through perseverance, especially in times of struggle.

JOURNAL EXERCISE

⊙ Create a virtue self-portrait. List all the virtues that contribute to your good character.

⊙ Think about and describe what you need to do to continue to grow as a person of good character. Make your decision and act upon it.

- set the correct and wisest goals, and
- choose the best means of attaining them.

Justice: Justice is the constant and firm recognition of what is rightfully due to God and to others. You have explored this cardinal virtue throughout this course of study. Take a moment and recall what you have learned.

The Scriptures describe justice as living in right relationship with God, others, ourselves and all creation. For example, the prophet Isaiah teaches that true worship of God includes "to loose the bonds of injustice, / to undo the thongs of the yoke, // to let the oppressed go free, . . ." (Isaiah 58:6). The practice of this virtue promotes fairness in all situations and at every level of existence—personal, communal and social.

TALK IT OVER
- Name people whom you consider to be both just and prudent?
- Why do you recognize them as living these virtues? Give concrete examples.

Fortitude: "Fortitude (sometimes called strength, courage and might) is also one of the seven gifts of the Holy Spirit" (CCC, Glossary, "Fortitude"). The psalmist encourages all God's people: "Love the LORD, all you his saints. / The LORD preserves the faithful, / but abundantly repays the one who acts haughtily. // Be strong, and let your heart take courage, / all you who wait for the LORD" (Psalm 31:23–24).

Fortitude (courage) is firmness of spirit, especially in times of difficulty. It includes the courage to confront our personal weaknesses and sinfulness honestly and to make the changes needed. Someone who practices fortitude perseveres in their commitment to do or say the good they recognize, regardless of the cost or danger to themselves. It is a willingness to go beyond the call of duty, to make sacrifices, to act on one's convictions, even if doing so costs you something that you value, such as a friendship, membership in a group, and so on.

Temperance: You have explored the virtue of temperance in your study of the Fifth, Sixth, Eighth, Ninth and Tenth Commandments.

Which cardinal virtue do you consider to be important for young people today?

Temperance is also known as moderation and self-control. Coupled with prudence, it enables us to see, respect and value the true beauty and goodness of creation. Temperance does not ask us to denounce all earthly goods and pleasures as evil. Rather, temperance guides us in enjoying these created gifts as signs of God's love. "It ensures the mastery of our will over instinct, and keeps natural desires within proper limits" (CCC, Glossary, "Temperance"). Living such a life, St. Paul tells us, is a sign that we are cooperating with the grace of the Holy Spirit. (Check out Galatians 5:22–25.)

THINK, PAIR AND SHARE
- Take a moment to look up the definition of temperance in the Faith Glossary of this text.
- Share what you recall about the importance of the virtue of temperance in the life of a disciple of Jesus.

OVER TO YOU
- Which of the four cardinal virtues do you consider to be important for young people today? Why?
- Which might be most difficult to develop in one's life? Explain.
- Which cardinal virtue would you like to cultivate more earnestly in your own life right now? Why? How will you go about that?

We live by the Spirit; we walk by the Spirit

Images can give us insight into the deeper meaning of realities in a way that words alone cannot. For example, Sacred Scripture uses many images for God. "Fire" and "wind" are key images used for the Holy Spirit. You will recall that in the account of Pentecost the disciples are engulfed by the "sound of the rush of a violent wind" and "tongues, as of fire, appeared among them, and a tongue rested on each of them." Luke explains: "All of them were filled with the Holy Spirit and began to speak in other languages, as the Spirit gave them ability" (Acts of the Apostles 2:2–4).

OPENING CONVERSATION

⊙ What is Scripture teaching us about the Holy Spirit by using images of wind and fire?

WHAT ABOUT YOU PERSONALLY?

⊙ When have you been "on fire" to do something good? Did you recognize that fire as the presence and power of the Holy Spirit? Explain.

THE WORLD OF GRACE

Christians live by the Spirit and walk by the Spirit. Through God's abundant grace in Jesus Christ, we are always assured of the presence and help of the Holy Trinity to sustain our efforts at living virtuously. The word "grace" comes from the Latin word *gratia*, which means "free." Grace is the free and undeserved gift of God's love to us. God shares his divine life with us and invites us to live a life of intimate communion with him.

An old Gaelic proverb runs, "There is an ebb to every tide, except the tide of God's grace." God's grace—his effective love—is always at high tide in our lives. God's grace is ever at work in our lives, inviting and helping us to live as children of God and disciples of Jesus. The Catholic Church passes on this truth of faith when she teaches: "The divine initiative in the work of grace precedes, prepares, and elicits the free response of man. Grace responds to the deepest yearnings of human freedom, calls freedom to cooperate with it, and perfects freedom" (CCC, no. 2022).

At Baptism every Christian receives the gift of sanctifying grace. Baptism makes us sharers once again in the very life of God and heals us of all sin, Original Sin and personal sins, and restores us to holiness of life, a life of intimate communion with God. We become adopted children of God, temples of the Holy Spirit, and brothers and sisters of Christ, and are joined to him and initiated into his Body, the Church. In the Sacrament of Confirmation we receive the fullness of the gift of the Holy Spirit. In the Eucharist we join with the risen Christ in offering himself to the Father and we receive the Body and Blood of Christ. Receiving Holy Communion unites us more closely with Christ and with his Church and strengthens us to live as his disciples.

In the Sacraments of Healing (Penance and Reconciliation, and Anointing of the Sick) God offers us many graces so that we may be healed in body and spirit when we are weakened by sin or illness. We are strengthened in our relationship with him and with the whole Church. In the Sacraments of Holy Orders and Marriage God offers special graces to the faithful whom he calls to serve his Church. **Sacramental graces** strengthen the faithful to grow in their love for God and for one another.

God also offers us **actual graces** and charisms. He walks with us through life as our companion, guiding and supporting us to know and respond to his will and live as his adopted children.

OVER TO YOU

- ☉ Look up and review the definition of "grace" in the Faith Glossary of this text. What does it mean to you to live in a grace-filled world?
- ☉ How might you grow in the awareness that God is your constant companion and respond to the many graces he offers you?

FROM THE CATECHISM

The gifts of the Holy Spirit "complete and perfect the virtues of those who receive them" (CCC, no. 1831). "The *fruits* of the Spirit are perfections that the Holy Spirit forms in us as the first fruits of eternal glory" (CCC, no. 1832).

THE GIFTS AND THE FRUITS OF THE HOLY SPIRIT

In the Nicene Creed we profess our faith in "the Holy Spirit, the Lord, the giver of life, / who proceeds from the Father and the Son, / who with the Father and the Son is adored and glorified." At Baptism the Holy Spirit comes to abide in and with us and offers us the grace to abide in and with God. Through the graces of Baptism we are made sharers in the life of God so intimately that we become temples of the Holy Spirit.

At Baptism we first receive the seven **gifts of the Holy Spirit**. These gifts, namely, wisdom, understanding, counsel, fortitude, knowledge, piety, and fear of the Lord, are strengthened in Confirmation. These seven gifts strengthen us to respond knowingly and freely to God's holy will in the very circumstances of daily life. The Holy Spirit sustains us to become God's special agents to bear fruit in the world. Building on the list in Galatians 5:22–23, the Catholic Church names twelve **fruits of the Holy Spirit**, which are signs that we are cooperating with the Holy Spirit. They are: charity, joy, peace, patience, kindness, goodness, generosity, gentleness, faithfulness, modesty, self-control, chastity. Through God's abundant love in Jesus Christ, we are always assured of the grace of the Holy Spirit to sustain our efforts at living a virtuous life.

OVER TO YOU
- Imagine a world in which the fruits of the Holy Spirit overshadowed all other traits. How are you contributing to building such a world?
- What could you do today? How will you go about doing it?

FROM THE CATECHISM

In the liturgy and the celebration of the sacraments, prayer and teaching are conjoined with the grace of Christ to enlighten and nourish Christian activity. As does the whole of the Christian life, the moral life finds its source and summit in the Eucharistic sacrifice.

—CCC, no. 2031

THE CHURCH: THE TEMPLE OF THE HOLY SPIRIT

We do not and cannot strive to live a life of virtue alone. We profess, celebrate and live our faith as members of the Church. The Church is the temple of the Holy Spirit (see 2 Corinthians 6:16). Guided by the Spirit of Christ the Church is our Mother and Teacher; she is our most reliable guide for living a moral life. St. Irenaeus reminded us of this mystery of faith when he taught: "For where the Church is, there is also God's Spirit; where God's Spirit is, there is the Church and every grace" (*Against Heresies*, 3, 24, 1).

Jesus told his disciples that when they live according to his teachings "you will know the truth, and the truth will make you free" (John 8:32). And he gave the Church the mission and authority to "make disciples of all nations . . . teaching them to obey everything that I have commanded you" (Matthew 28:19–20). The Church continues to fulfill that commission, as she has done from her earliest days. She scrutinizes the *signs of the times* and interprets them in light of the Gospel. She addresses new questions that arise in medicine and healthcare, politics, economics and all issues that affect the well-being and dignity of people. She guides us in making moral decisions in the everyday of our lives.

The Magisterium has the authority and responsibility, handed on to her by Christ, to teach authentically and authoritatively not only on matters of faith (doctrine) but also on morality. This is true in respect of matters of personal morality and social morality. All people have the ability to understand the Church's basic moral teaching because God has written the natural law on the heart of every person. When the Church fulfills this responsibility, she is not imposing her views on others; she is making known the truth of God's word to all.

The Magisterium, reflecting on the faith of the people (*sensus fidelium*), seeks to "preserve God's people from deviations and defections . . . seeing to it that the People of God abides in the truth that liberates" (CCC, no. 890). The Church exercises this authority in many ways, for example, through the Councils of the Church, through encyclicals and other official teaching documents, as well as through church law, or canon law. Canon law is the "rules (canons or laws) which provide the norms for good order in the visible society of the Church. Those canon laws that apply universally are contained in the Codes of Canon Law" (CCC, Glossary, "Canon Law").

The Holy Spirit blesses the Church with many graces to guide her in this office. These include the gifts of indefectibility and infallibility. These graces of the Holy Spirit assure us that the Church will always teach the Gospel of Christ without error in spite of the defects of her members. All other members of the Church are to teach in harmony with the Magisterium.

⊙ Work with a partner. Brainstorm a list of moral issues the Catholic Church has recently addressed. (Hint: You might visit the website of the United States Conference of Catholic Bishops (*www.usccb.org*).

⊙ Choose one issue and research and write a summary of the Church's teaching on that issue. Include in your summary how the Church guides you in addressing the issue.

⊙ Present your findings at the completion of your study of this chapter.

MARY FULL OF GRACE

The Blessed Virgin is the greatest saint of the Church and the model disciple of the Lord. She is our clearest and primary guide for living as disciples of her Son. Mary's consent when told that she was to be mother of the Messiah was, "Here am I, the servant of the Lord; let it be with me according to your word" (Luke 1:38). From Mary we learn to keep the word of God in our heart, treasure it and live it as she did. The total giving of oneself to God and to others is to be the life's work of every disciple, as it was the work of Mary—and as it was the work of her Son. (Check out Luke 2:25–35, Mark 8:31—9:1 and Philippians 2:5–11.)

Mary is not only the model disciple, she is also our Mother. She is the Mother of the Church and the Mother of all Christians. St. John's Gospel tells the amazing story of Jesus' final words to his Mother: "When Jesus saw his mother and the disciple whom he loved standing beside her, he said to his mother, 'Woman, here is your son.' Then he said to the disciple, 'Here is your mother'" (John 19:26–27).

In the countless hymns and antiphons to Mary, the Mother of God, two movements usually alternate with each other. This twofold movement of prayer to Mary is found in a privileged way in the *Ave Maria* (Hail Mary)—the great prayer to Mary in Catholic tradition. The first part of the Hail Mary praises and gives thanks to God for the great things done for this lowly servant and, through her, for all human beings. The second entrusts Mary to bring our supplications and praises to God. We trust Mary to care for us as she did for Jesus, and we bring our needs to her as Jesus

himself did. We believe that she is ever ready to pray for us that we may say our own radical and total self-giving "Yes" to God as she did and as Jesus did to the Father.

THINK, PAIR AND SHARE

⊙ Reflect on the mysteries of the Rosary, which you will find in the "Catholic Prayers, Devotions and Practices" section of this text.

⊙ Share with a partner what each mystery tells you about the virtues in Mary's life.

OVER TO YOU

⊙ Check out some classical versions of the *Ave Maria*, such as those by Bach, Gounod or Schubert. Then research some contemporary songs inspired by the *Ave Maria*.

⊙ Choose a version of the *Ave Maria*, classical or contemporary, that appeals to you. Why does that version appeal to you?

⊙ How does praying the *Ave Maria* deepen your own devotion to Mary and your commitment to live as a disciple of her Son?

"WOMAN, HERE IS YOUR SON" | ST. JAMES' CHURCH, GLENBEIGH, IRELAND

The "way" of Christian prayer

FROM THE CATECHISM
In the New Covenant, prayer is the living relationship of the children of God with their Father who is good beyond measure, with his Son Jesus Christ and with the Holy Spirit. . . . Thus, the life of prayer is the habit of being in the presence of the thrice-holy God and in communion with him.

—CCC, no. 2565

THE LIFE OF PRAYER

Prayer and the Christian life are inseparable. In prayer we bless and adore God; we praise and give thanks to him; we pray for others; we pray for ourselves and ask for forgiveness. The Christian family is the first place where we learn to lead a life of prayer. This life of prayer is nourished and deepened by participation in the prayer life of the Church. The Church has a regular rhythm of prayer, in which she invites the faithful to participate. This includes daily prayers, the Liturgy of the Hours, Sunday Eucharist and the feasts of the liturgical year.

The Christian life is a way of prayer that imitates the life of Jesus. (Check out Luke 3:21; 5:16; 6:12; 9:18–20, 28; 22:32, 41–44.) Christians address their prayer primarily to the Father, as Jesus did. "The whole prayer of Jesus is contained in [his] loving adherence of his human heart to the mystery of the will of the Father (see Ephesians 1:9)" (CCC, no, 2603).

The wonderful thing about prayer is that we can pray anywhere and at any time. In the words of St. Paul, we can "pray without ceasing" (1 Thessalonians 5:17). Why is that? Prayer is really about living in the presence of God and responding to God's invitation to open our minds and hearts to him. God is always with us wherever we are. God's loving presence is the one great constant in our lives.

OPENING CONVERSATION

- ⊙ When you hear the word "prayer," what do you think of?
- ⊙ If someone asked you, in a more formal way, "What is prayer," what would you say?
- ⊙ A time-honored definition of prayer is "raising the mind and heart to God." Why the "mind," do you think? Why the "heart"?
- ⊙ How do you imagine prayer might help a person to live a virtuous life as a disciple of Jesus?

Prayer takes work. It "is both a gift of grace and a determined response on our part. It always presupposes effort" (CCC, no. 2725). Prayer has been described as a spiritual battle in which we must confront many temptations and obstacles. These include a false notion of prayer, distraction, dryness, discouragement, and lack of faith and trust. The Holy Spirit offers us the grace to help us strive to overcome these obstacles to prayer.

PAUSE AND REFLECT
- What helps you to pray? What are some of the things that get in the way of your prayer?
- Talk things over with God. Ask for his help in your efforts to grow as a person of prayer.

THE MANY WAYS TO PRAY
Christian tradition speaks of three expressions of prayer, or ways of praying. These are vocal prayer, meditation and contemplation. We will now explore each and its role in the life of a disciple of Jesus Christ.

Vocal prayer: Jesus taught his disciples about prayer, through both his words and his actions.

For example, check out his words to his disciples in Matthew 6:5–8. Vocal prayer is a prayer of words, either spoken or unspoken. We can meet God in prayer with others or in the quiet of our heart. Jesus reminds us that the length of our prayer, the number of words we use, is not the key to prayer.

We can speak with God in our own words or using a prayer formula, such as the Our Father and the Hail Mary. As we talk with God using a traditional prayer formula, it is important to mean what we say. The words of a formal prayer should not be so routine that they lose their meaning. Isn't it amazing to realize that God invites each person to speak heart-to-heart with him? Jesus assures us that God listens to the prayers of every person, and, through the deep listening of our hearts, we can discern his response.

OVER TO YOU
- Check out Matthew 7:7–11. What advice do you hear Jesus giving you?

The prayer of meditation: Meditation is a deeper kind of talking with God that is more focused on figuring out how to respond to his word. Meditation helps us understand and apply

ST. TERESA OF JESUS | GUIDO CAGNACCI

St. Teresa of Jesus described contemplative prayer as "nothing else than a close sharing between friends; it means taking time frequently to be alone with him who we know loves us"

Jesus' teachings to our life. Meditation usually begins with reading and reflecting on a text that communicates God's word to us. The text we choose may be a written Scripture passage, a visual text such as a sacred image, or a life text from "the great book of creation, and that of history—the page on which the 'today' of God is written" (CCC, no. 2705). Indeed, whatever helps us to go deeper into thoughtful reflection and conversation with God is a source of meditation.

Meditation not only engages thought; it also engages our heart and soul, our imagination, emotions and desires. We sit with the text, hold its word in our minds and hearts, and lift our deepest sentiments to God. We ask God for the grace to be open to hear and put into practice what he is saying to us through what we are reading or seeing or hearing.

THINK, PAIR AND SHARE

⊙ Talk with a partner about both vocal and meditative prayer. How do you understand them now?

⊙ How might these ways of praying inform your own prayer life?

The prayer of contemplation: In the prayer of contemplation the Father strengthens our inner being with power through the Spirit so that Christ may dwell in our hearts. Contemplation is a gift, or grace, and an intense time of prayer that reaches beyond words. St. Teresa of Jesus described contemplative prayer to be "nothing else than a close sharing between friends; it means taking time frequently to be alone with him who we know loves us" (*The Book of Her Life*, 8, 5; quoted in CCC, no. 2709). In this deep inner prayer we keep our attention off of our self and on God. We listen to God speaking to our hearts. We let our masks fall and turn our hearts to God, who loves us unconditionally.

The Church describes contemplation to be "*a gift*," "intense," a "*gaze* of faith," "*hearing*" and "*silence*" that has the power to transform us. "Words in this kind of prayer are not speeches; they are like kindling that feeds the fire of love" (CCC, no. 2717). In this silence the Father speaks to us and the Spirit enables us to be in communion with Jesus so that the way we act reflects the life of a true disciple.

TALK IT OVER

⊙ Create your own personal prayer profile. Draw a circle or another shape and divide it into three parts. The sections are to be proportionate in size to the role that vocal prayer, meditation and contemplation have in your prayer life.

- Share and discuss your profile with a partner.
- Which way of praying is represented by the smallest section of your profile? What suggestions can you make to each other to grow that section?

FROM THE CATECHISM

The Sermon on the Mount is teaching for life, the Our Father is a prayer; but in both the one and the other the Spirit of the Lord gives new form to our desires, those inner movements that animate our lives. Jesus teaches us this new life by his words; he teaches us to ask for it by our prayer.

—CCC, no. 2764

THE LORD'S PRAYER: A GUIDE FOR DISCIPLESHIP

The Evangelists Luke and Matthew tell us that when the disciples asked Jesus to teach them to pray, Jesus taught them the Our Father. (Check out Luke 11:1–4; see also Matthew 6:9–13.) The Our Father, or Lord's Prayer, is, in capsule form, a plan for living the heart and essence of the Gospel and imitating the master of prayer, Jesus Christ. It is the exemplary prayer of the Church, a summary of the Gospel. In his teachings on the Our Father St. Thomas Aquinas writes:

Jesus teaches us this new life by his words; he teaches us to ask for it by our prayer

"The Lord's Prayer is the most perfect of prayers. . . . In it we ask, not only for all the things we can rightly desire, but also in the sequence that they should be desired. This prayer teaches us not only to ask for things, but also in what order we should desire them" (*Summa Theologiae* II–II, 83, 9).

—CCC, no. 2763

In the Lord's Prayer we respond to the divine invitation to deepen our communion with God. We acknowledge God to be our origin and end, the source of our life and the means of living as his children. We petition God for the graces to face all the challenges that come our way as we strive, with his grace, to bring about the Kingdom of God.

JOURNAL EXERCISE

- Quietly pray the Lord's Prayer as a prayer of meditation.
- Pause frequently to reflect on what the words mean for your life as a disciple of Jesus. Write your reflections in your journal.
- Repeat this activity often.

THE SERMON ON THE MOUNT | 19TH-CENTURY ENGRAVING

JUDGE AND ACT

REVIEW AND SHARE WHAT YOU HAVE LEARNED IN THIS CHAPTER

Look back over this chapter and recall its teachings on the importance of developing virtue and on how life in the Church sustains you in a life of Christian virtue. Share the teachings of the Church on these statements:

- ⊙ God always offers us the grace to live as his children.
- ⊙ Jesus Christ has revealed the law of grace.
- ⊙ The Christian life is a life of virtue.
- ⊙ The theological virtues make it possible for us to live the law of grace.
- ⊙ All the human moral virtues hinge on the four cardinal virtues.

- ⊙ The Church is our Teacher and Mother who guides us and nurtures us for living a moral life.
- ⊙ We cannot live our new life in Christ without prayer.
- ⊙ The Lord's Prayer teaches us how to live and how to pray.

REFLECT AND DISCERN

- ⊙ What insights and wisdom have you learned about virtue and prayer and the links between the two?
- ⊙ What difference will those insights make to your life—to your efforts to live your faith?

LEARN BY EXAMPLE

Nuestra Señora de la Caridad del Cobre: a symbol of faith, hope and love for Cuban people

CATHEDRAL SANTUARIO DE GUADALUPE, DALLAS, TEXAS

About the year 1600 Juan and Rodrigo de Hoyos, twin brothers, and Juan Moreno, a ten-year-old African slave, set out to collect sea salt for the Spanish colony's settlement of El Cobre, Cuba. Crossing the Bay of Nipe, on the island's northeast coast, in a small craft, the three came upon "a white thing floating on the foam." As it drew closer, the brothers saw that it was a statue of Mary holding the Christ child in her left arm and with a gold cross in her right hand. The statue was fastened to a board with the inscription, "Yo soy la Virgen de la Caridad (I am the Virgin of Charity)." And despite the recent storm and the motion of the waves, neither the figure of the Virgin, nor her clothing, was wet.

The three carried the statue to El Cobre. The statue soon became an object of veneration. Ever since, this Marian devotion has been part of the history of the island and an integral aspect of the prayer life of its people. The image is often shown rising above a stormy sea before the gaze of three awestruck voyagers in a tiny boat.

Devotion to our Lady of Charity is a vital part of the prayer life of the Cuban community in the United States of America. During the celebration in Miami, Florida, of the 400th anniversary of the finding of the statue, Father Juan Rumin Dominquez, rector of the Shrine of Our Lady of Charity, summed up the devotion of the Cuban people to *Cachita*: "Our Lady of Charity covers us all with her mantle and, in her, we are one people of faith."

In 1916 Pope Benedict XV declared Our Lady of Charity the patroness of Cuba. In 1997 Blessed Pope Paul VI raised the sanctuary holding *Cachita* to a basilica. In 1988 St. John Paul II named Our Lady of Charity, once again, the queen and patron of Cuba. The Cuban people celebrate her feast day on September 8.

THE BASILICA HOLDING OUR LADY OF CHARITY, CUBA

THINK, PAIR AND SHARE

⊙ With a partner, brainstorm a list of devotions to Mary that are part of the prayer life of a Catholic.

⊙ Which of these devotions are rooted in your heritage? Talk about how you celebrate those devotions.

⊙ Share how devotion to Mary strengthens your faith in her Son and your commitment to live as his disciple.

SHARE FAITH WITH FAMILY AND FRIENDS

⊙ Justice is one of the cardinal virtues. Identify with family and friends the other virtues and blessings that hinge on justice, or that cannot be realized without justice.

⊙ Discuss how your relationships are built on these virtues. In other words, how do they guide you in living in right relationship with one another as God desires and wills you to live?

WHAT ABOUT YOU PERSONALLY?

⊙ Earlier in this chapter you learned: "The goal of a virtuous life is to become like God" (St. Gregory of Nyssa, *Homilies on the Beatitudes*, 1).

⊙ Do St. Gregory's words describe your efforts to live a moral life? Explain.

All reflect on the mystery of God's presence—with each one of us individually and with the group.

LEADER
Our thrice-holy God, the Father, the Son and the Holy Spirit, always invites us to encounter him in prayer. Today, we use the threefold expression of prayer to respond to that invitation.

Vocal Prayer

ALL
In the name of the Father, and of the Son, and of the Holy Spirit. Amen.
Glory to you, O Lord, to you we lift up our prayer.
SIDE 1
Give ear to [our] words, O LORD;
    give heed to [our] sighing.
Listen to the sound of [our] cry,
    [our] King and [our] God,
        for to you [we] pray.
SIDE 2
O LORD, in the morning you hear [our] voice;
    in the morning [we] plead [our] case to you,
        and watch.

—Psalm 5:1–3

ALL
Glory to you, O Lord, to you we lift up our prayer.

SIDE 1
The law of the LORD is perfect,
    reviving the soul;
the decrees of the LORD are sure,
    making wise the simple;
the precepts of the LORD are right,
    rejoicing the heart;

SIDE 2
the commandment of the LORD is clear,
    enlightening the eyes;
the fear of the LORD is pure,
    enduring forever;
the ordinances of the LORD are true
    and righteous altogether.

—Psalm 19:7–9

ALL
Glory to you, O Lord, to you we lift up our prayer.

Prayer of Meditation

*All silently read the verses from Psalms 5 and 19.
Pause often throughout the reading and ask, "What are these words saying to me?"*
All silently reread verses again and ask, "What is God asking me to do?"
Each person responds by making a decision to put into practice God's word to them.

Prayer of Contemplation

All sit in silence in the presence of God, who abides in you and with you. Open your heart and mind to God, friend to friend.

LEADER
Let us lift our minds and hearts together and give glory to our thrice-holy God, who is always inviting us to live in friendship with him.
ALL
Glory be to the Father,
and to the Son,
and to the Holy Spirit;
as it was in the beginning,
is now, and ever shall be,
world without end. Amen.

CATHOLIC PRAYERS, DEVOTIONS AND PRACTICES

SIGN OF THE CROSS
In the name of the Father,
and of the Son,
and of the Holy Spirit. Amen.

OUR FATHER (LORD'S PRAYER)
Our Father who art in heaven,
hallowed be thy name;
thy kingdom come,
thy will be done
on earth as it is in heaven.
Give us this day our daily bread,
and forgive us our trespasses,
as we forgive those who trespass against us;
and lead us not into temptation,
but deliver us from evil. Amen.

GLORY PRAYER (DOXOLOGY)
Glory be to the Father,
and to the Son,
and to the Holy Spirit;
as it was in the beginning
is now, and ever shall be,
world without end. Amen.

PRAYER TO THE HOLY SPIRIT
Come, Holy Spirit, fill the hearts of your faithful.
Enkindle in them the fire of your love.
Send forth your Spirit and they shall be created.
And you shall renew the face of the earth.

O God, by the light of the Holy Spirit you have
    taught the hearts of your faithful.
In the same Spirit, help us to know what is truly
    right and always to rejoice in your consolation.
We ask this through Christ, our Lord. Amen.

HAIL MARY
Hail Mary, full of grace,
the Lord is with thee.
Blessed art thou among women
and blessed is the fruit of thy womb, Jesus.
Holy Mary, Mother of God,
pray for us sinners,
now and at the hour of our death. Amen.

APOSTLES' CREED
I believe in God,
the Father almighty,
Creator of heaven and earth,
and in Jesus Christ, his only Son, our Lord,
who was conceived by the Holy Spirit,
born of the Virgin Mary,
suffered under Pontius Pilate,
was crucified, died, and was buried;
he descended into hell;
on the third day he rose again from the dead;
he ascended into heaven,
and is seated at the right hand of God the Father
    almighty,
from there he will come to judge the living and
    the dead.

I believe in the Holy Spirit,
the holy catholic Church,
the communion of saints,
the forgiveness of sins,
the resurrection of the body,
and life everlasting. Amen.

NICENE CREED
I believe in one God,
the Father almighty,
maker of heaven and earth,
of all things visible and invisible.

I believe in one Lord Jesus Christ,
the Only Begotten Son of God,
born of the Father before all ages.
God from God, Light from Light,
true God from true God,
begotten, not made, consubstantial with the
    Father;
through him all things were made.
For us men and for our salvation
he came down from heaven,

and by the Holy Spirit was incarnate of the Virgin
    Mary,
and became man.

For our sake he was crucified under Pontius Pilate,
he suffered death and was buried,
and rose again on the third day
in accordance with the Scriptures.
He ascended into heaven
and is seated at the right hand of the Father.
He will come again in glory
to judge the living and the dead,
and his kingdom will have no end.

I believe in the Holy Spirit, the Lord, the giver of life,
who proceeds from the Father and the Son,
who with the Father and the Son is adored and
    glorified,
who has spoken through the prophets.

I believe in one, holy, catholic and apostolic
    Church.
I confess one Baptism for the forgiveness of sins
and I look forward to the resurrection of the dead
and the life of the world to come. Amen.

JESUS PRAYER

Lord Jesus Christ, Son of God, have mercy on me,
    a sinner. Amen.

ACT OF FAITH

O my God, I firmly believe that you are one God
in three divine Persons, Father, Son, and Holy
Spirit. I believe that your divine Son became man
and died for our sins and that he will come to
judge the living and the dead. I believe these and
all the truths which the Holy Catholic Church
teaches because you have revealed them, who
are eternal truth and wisdom, who can neither
deceive nor be deceived. In this faith I intend to
live and die. Amen.

ACT OF HOPE

O Lord God, I hope by your grace for the pardon
of all my sins and after life here to gain eternal
happiness because you have promised it, who are
infinitely powerful, faithful, kind, and merciful. In
this hope I intend to live and die. Amen.

ACT OF LOVE

O Lord God, I love you above all things and I love
my neighbor for your sake because you are the
highest, infinite and perfect good, worthy of all
my love. In this love I intend to live and die. Amen.

PRAYER FOR VOCATIONS

Loving Mother, Our Lady of Guadalupe,
you asked Juan Diego to help build a Church that
    would serve a new people in a new land.
You left your image upon his cloak as a visible
    sign of your love for us,
so that we may come to believe in your Son, Jesus
    the Christ.
Our Lady of Guadalupe and St. Juan Diego,
help us respond to God's call to build your Son's
    Church today.
Help us recognize our personal vocation to serve
    God as married or single persons or priests,
    brothers or sisters as our way to help extend
    the Reign of God here on earth.
Help us pay attention to the promptings of the
    Holy Spirit.
May all of us have the courage of Juan Diego to
    say "Yes" to our personal call!
May we encourage one another to follow Jesus,
    no matter where that path takes us. Amen.

Daily Prayers

Morning Prayer
CANTICLE OF ZECHARIAH (THE BENEDICTUS)
(based on Luke 1:67–79)
Blessed be the Lord, the God of Israel;
for he has come to his people and set them free.
He has raised up for us a mighty Savior,
born of the House of his servant David.
Through his prophets he promised of old
    that he would save us from our enemies,
    from the hands of all who hate us.
He promised to show mercy to our fathers
and to remember his holy covenant.
This was the oath he swore to our father Abraham:
to set us free from the hand of our enemies,
free to worship him without fear,
holy and righteous in his sight
    all the days of our life.

You, my child, shall be called the prophet of the
 Most High,
for you will go before the Lord to prepare his way,
to give his people knowledge of salvation
by the forgiveness of their sins.
In the tender compassion of our God
the dawn from on high shall break upon us,
to shine on those who dwell in darkness and the
 shadow of death,
and to guide our feet into the way of peace.
Amen.

MORNING OFFERING
O Jesus, through the Immaculate Heart of Mary,
I offer you my prayers, works, joys and sufferings
 of this day
for all the intentions of your Sacred Heart,
in union with the Holy Sacrifice of the Mass
 throughout the world,
for the salvation of souls, the reparation for sins,
 the reunion of all Christians,
and in particular for the intentions of the Holy
 Father this month. Amen.

Evening Prayer
CANTICLE OF MARY (THE *MAGNIFICAT*)
My soul proclaims the greatness of the Lord;
my spirit rejoices in God my savior
for he has looked with favor on his lowly servant.
From this day all generations will call me blessed:
the Almighty has done great things for me
and holy is his name.
He has mercy on those who fear him
in every generation.
He has shown the strength of his arm,
and has scattered the proud in their conceit.
He has cast down the mighty from their thrones,
and has lifted up the lowly.
He has filled the hungry with good things,
and the rich he has sent away empty.
He has come to the help of his servant Israel
for he has remembered his promise of mercy,
the promise he made to our fathers,
to Abraham and his children forever. Amen.

GRACE BEFORE MEALS
Bless us, O Lord, and these your gifts,
which we are about to receive from your bounty,
through Christ our Lord. Amen.

GRACE AFTER MEALS
We give you thanks for all your benefits, almighty
 God, who lives and reigns forever.
And may the souls of the faithful departed,
 through the mercy of God, rest in peace.
 Amen.

PRAYER OF ST. FRANCIS (PEACE PRAYER)
Lord, make me an instrument of your peace:
where there is hatred, let me sow love;
where there is injury, pardon;
where there is doubt, faith;
where there is despair, hope;
where there is darkness, light;
where there is sadness, joy.

O divine Master, grant that I may not so much seek
to be consoled as to console,
to be understood, as to understand,
to be loved as to love.

For it is in giving that we receive,
it is in pardoning that we are pardoned,
it is in dying that we are born to eternal life.
Amen.

Contrition and Sorrow
CONFITEOR
I confess to almighty God
and to you, my brothers and sisters,
that I have greatly sinned,
in my thoughts and in my words,
in what I have done and in what I have failed to
 do,
through my fault, through my fault,
through my most grievous fault;
therefore I ask blessed Mary ever-Virgin,
all the Angels and Saints,
and you, my brothers and sisters,
to pray for me to the Lord our God. Amen.

ACT OF CONTRITION
O my God, I am heartily sorry for having offended
you, and I detest all my sins because of your
just punishments, but most of all because
they offend you, my God, who are all good and
deserving of all my love. I firmly resolve with the
help of your grace to sin no more and to avoid
the near occasion of sin. Amen.

Prayers before the Holy Eucharist

THE DIVINE PRAISES

Blessed be God.
Blessed be his holy name.
Blessed be Jesus Christ, true God and true man.
Blessed be the name of Jesus.
Blessed be his most Sacred Heart.
Blessed be his most precious Blood.
Blessed be Jesus in the most holy Sacrament of the altar.
Blessed be the Holy Spirit, the Paraclete.
Blessed be the great Mother of God, Mary most holy.
Blessed be her holy and Immaculate Conception.
Blessed be her glorious Assumption.
Blessed be the name of Mary, Virgin and Mother.
Blessed be St. Joseph, her most chaste spouse.
Blessed be God in his angels and in his saints.

ANIMA CHRISTI (SOUL OF CHRIST)

Soul of Christ, sanctify me.
Body of Christ, save me.
Blood of Christ, inebriate me.
Water from the side of Christ, wash me.
Passion of Christ, strengthen me.
O good Jesus, hear me.
Within your wounds hide me.
Permit me not to be separated from you.
From the malicious enemy defend me.
In the hour of my death call me.
And bid me come to you,
that with your saints I may praise you
forever and ever. Amen.

AN ACT OF SPIRITUAL COMMUNION

My Jesus, I believe that you are present in the Most Blessed Sacrament.
I love you above all things, and I desire to receive you into my soul.
Since I cannot at this moment receive you sacramentally, come at least spiritually into my heart.
I embrace you as if you were already there and unite myself wholly to you.
Never permit me to be separated from you. Amen.

Prayers to Mary, Mother of God

ANGELUS

Verse: The Angel of the Lord declared unto Mary.
Response: And she conceived of the Holy Spirit.
Hail Mary, full of grace,
the Lord is with thee.
Blessed art thou among women
and blessed is the fruit of thy womb, Jesus.
Holy Mary, Mother of God,
pray for us sinners,
now and at the hour of our death. Amen.
Verse: Behold the handmaid of the Lord.
Response: Be it done unto me according to your Word.
Hail Mary. . . .
Verse: And the Word was made flesh,
Response: And dwelt among us.
Hail Mary. . . .
Verse: Pray for us, O holy Mother of God,
Response: That we may be made worthy of the promises of Christ.

Let us pray. Pour forth, we beseech you, O Lord, your grace into our hearts: that we, to whom the Incarnation of Christ your Son was made known by the message of an Angel, may by his Passion and Cross be brought to the glory of his Resurrection. Through the same Christ our Lord. Amen.

MEMORARE

Remember, O most gracious Virgin Mary, that never was it known that anyone who fled to your protection, implored your help, or sought your intercession, was left unaided. Inspired by this confidence, I fly unto you, O Virgin of virgins, my mother; to you do I come, before you I stand, sinful and sorrowful. O Mother of the Word Incarnate, despise not my petitions, but in your mercy hear and answer me. Amen.

REGINA CAELI (QUEEN OF HEAVEN)

Queen of Heaven, rejoice, alleluia:
for the Son you were privileged to bear, alleluia,
is risen as he said, alleluia.
Pray for us to God, alleluia.

Verse: Rejoice and be glad, O Virgin Mary, Alleluia!

Response: For the Lord is truly risen, Alleluia.

Let us pray. O God, who gave joy to the world through the resurrection of your Son, our Lord Jesus Christ, grant, we beseech you, that through the intercession of the Virgin Mary, his Mother, we may obtain the joys of everlasting life. Through the same Christ our Lord. Amen.

SALVE, REGINA (HAIL, HOLY QUEEN)

Hail, holy Queen, Mother of Mercy: Hail, our life, our sweetness and our hope. To you do we cry, poor banished children of Eve. To you do we send up our sighs, mourning and weeping in this valley of tears. Turn then, most gracious advocate, your eyes of mercy toward us; and after this our exile show unto us the blessed fruit of your womb, Jesus. O clement, O loving, O sweet Virgin Mary. Amen.

PRAYER TO OUR LADY OF GUADALUPE

God of power and mercy,
you blessed the Americas at Tepeyac
with the presence of the Virgin Mary of
    Guadalupe.
May her prayers help all men and women
to accept each other as brothers and sisters.
Through your justice present in our hearts
may your peace reign in the world. Amen.

THE ROSARY

THE JOYFUL MYSTERIES: Traditionally prayed on Mondays and Saturdays and on Sundays of the Christmas Season.

1. The Annunciation (Luke 1:26–38)
2. The Visitation (Luke 2:39–56)
3. The Nativity (Luke 2:1–20)
4. The Presentation in the Temple (Luke 2:22–38)
5. The Finding of Jesus after Three Days in the Temple (Luke 2:41–50)

THE LUMINOUS MYSTERIES: Traditionally prayed on Thursdays.

1. The Baptism at the Jordan (Matthew 3:13–17)
2. The Miracle at Cana (John 2:1–11)
3. The Proclamation of the Kingdom and the Call to Conversion (Mark 1:14–15)

4. The Transfiguration (Matthew 17:1–13)
5. The Institution of the Eucharist (Matthew 26:26–28)

THE SORROWFUL MYSTERIES: Traditionally prayed on Tuesdays and Fridays and on the Sundays of Lent.

1. The Agony in the Garden (Matthew 26:36–56)
2. The Scourging at the Pillar (John 18:28—19:1)
3. The Crowning with Thorns (John 19:2–3)
4. The Carrying of the Cross (John 19:17)
5. The Crucifixion and Death (John 19:18–30)

THE GLORIOUS MYSTERIES: Traditionally prayed on Wednesdays and Sundays, except on the Sundays of Christmas and Lent.

1. The Resurrection (Matthew 28:1–8)
2. The Ascension (Matthew 28:16–20/Acts 1:1–11)
3. The Descent of the Holy Spirit at Pentecost (Acts 2:1–13)
4. The Assumption of Mary (See CCC, no. 966)
5. The Crowning of the Blessed Virgin as Queen of Heaven and Earth (See CCC, no. 966)

How to pray the Rosary

1. Pray the *Sign of the Cross* and pray the *Apostles' Creed* while holding the crucifix.
2. Touch the first bead after the crucifix and pray the *Our Father*, pray the *Hail Mary* on each of the next three beads, and pray the *Glory Prayer* on the next bead.
3. Go to the main part of your rosary. Say the name of the Mystery and quietly reflect on the meaning of the events of that Mystery. Pray the *Our Father*, and then, fingering each of the ten beads, pray ten *Hail Marys*. Then touch the next bead and pray the *Glory Prayer*. (Repeat the process for the next four decades.)
4. Pray the *Salve Regina (Hail, Holy Queen)* and conclude by praying:

    Verse: Pray for us, O holy Mother of God.

    Response: That we may be made worthy of the promises of Christ.

    Let us pray. O God, whose only-begotten

Son, by his life, death and Resurrection, has purchased for us the rewards of eternal life, grant, we beseech you, that meditating on these mysteries of the most holy rosary of the Blessed Virgin Mary, we may imitate what they contain and obtain what they promise, through the same Christ our Lord. Amen.

5. Conclude by praying the *Sign of the Cross*.

STATIONS, OR WAY, OF THE CROSS

The tradition of praying the Stations, or Way, of the Cross dates from the fourteenth century. The tradition, which is attributed to the Franciscans, came about to satisfy the desire of Christians who were unable to make a pilgrimage to Jerusalem.The traditional Stations of the Cross are:

FIRST STATION: Jesus is condemned to death
SECOND STATION: Jesus is made to carry his Cross
THIRD STATION: Jesus falls the first time
FOURTH STATION: Jesus meets his mother
FIFTH STATION: Simon helps Jesus to carry his Cross
SIXTH STATION: Veronica wipes the face of Jesus
SEVENTH STATION: Jesus falls the second time
EIGHTH STATION: Jesus meets the women of Jerusalem
NINTH STATION: Jesus falls the third time
TENTH STATION: Jesus is stripped of his garments
ELEVENTH STATION: Jesus is nailed to the Cross
TWELFTH STATION: Jesus dies on the Cross
THIRTEENTH STATION: Jesus is taken down from the Cross
FOURTEENTH STATION: Jesus is laid in the tomb.

In 1991 St. John Paul II gave the Church a scriptural version of the Stations. The individual names given to these stations are:

FIRST STATION: Jesus in the Garden of Gethsemane—Matthew 25:36–41
SECOND STATION: Jesus, Betrayed by Judas, Is Arrested—Mark 14:43–46
THIRD STATION: Jesus Is Condemned by the Sanhedrin—Luke 22:66–71
FOURTH STATION: Jesus Is Denied by Peter—Matthew 26:69–75

FIFTH STATION: Jesus Is Judged by Pilate—Mark 15:1–5, 15
SIXTH STATION: Jesus Is Scourged and Crowned with Thorns—John 19:1–3
SEVENTH STATION: Jesus Bears the Cross—John 19:6, 15–17
EIGHTH STATION: Jesus Is Helped by Simon the Cyrenian to Carry the Cross—Mark 15:21
NINTH STATION: Jesus Meets the Women of Jerusalem—Luke 23:27–31
TENTH STATION: Jesus Is Crucified—Luke 23:33–34
ELEVENTH STATION: Jesus Promises His Kingdom to the Good Thief—Luke 23:39–43
TWELFTH STATION: Jesus Speaks to His Mother and the Disciple—John 19:25–27
THIRTEENTH STATION: Jesus Dies on the Cross—Luke 23:44–46
FOURTEENTH STATION: Jesus Is Placed in the Tomb—Matthew 27:57–60

Some parishes conclude the Stations with a prayerful meditation on the Resurrection.

The Way of Jesus: Catholic Practices

THE SEVEN SACRAMENTS
Sacraments of Christian Initiation
BAPTISM: The sacrament by which we are freed from all sin and are endowed with the gift of divine life, are made members of the Church, and are called to holiness and mission.
CONFIRMATION: The sacrament that completes the grace of Baptism by a special outpouring of the gifts of the Holy Spirit, which seals and confirms the baptized in union with Christ and calls them to a greater participation in the worship and apostolic life of the Church.
EUCHARIST: The ritual, sacramental action of thanksgiving to God which constitutes the principal Christian liturgical celebration of and communion in the Paschal Mystery of Christ. This liturgical action is also traditionally known as the Holy Sacrifice of the Mass.

Sacraments of Healing
PENANCE AND RECONCILIATION: The sacrament in which sins committed after Baptism are forgiven,

which results in reconciliation with God and the Church. This sacrament is also called the Sacrament of Confession.

ANOINTING OF THE SICK: This sacrament is given to a person who is seriously ill or in danger of death or old age which strengthens the person with the special graces of healing and comfort and courage.

Sacraments at the Service of Communion

MARRIAGE (MATRIMONY): The sacrament in which a baptized man and a baptized woman enter the covenant partnership of the whole of life that by its nature is ordered toward the good of the spouses and the procreation and education of offspring.

HOLY ORDERS: The sacrament in which a bishop ordains a baptized man to be conformed to Jesus Christ by grace, to service and leadership in the Church as a bishop, priest, or deacon.

GIFTS OF THE HOLY SPIRIT

The seven gifts of the Holy Spirit are permanent dispositions which move us to respond to the guidance of the Spirit. The traditional list of these gifts is derived from Isaiah 11:1–3.

WISDOM: A spiritual gift which enables one to know the purpose and plan of God.

UNDERSTANDING: This gift stimulates us to work on knowing ourselves as part of our growth in knowing God.

COUNSEL (RIGHT JUDGMENT): This gift guides us to follow the teaching the Holy Spirit gives us about our moral life and the training of our conscience.

FORTITUDE (COURAGE): This gift strengthens us to choose courageously and firmly the good, despite difficulty, and also to persevere in doing what is right, despite temptation, fear or persecution.

KNOWLEDGE: This gift directs us to a contemplation, or thoughtful reflection, on the mystery of God and the mysteries of the Catholic faith.

PIETY (REVERENCE): This gift strengthens us to grow in respect for the Holy Trinity, for the Father who created us, for Jesus who saved us, and for the Holy Spirit who is sanctifying us.

FEAR OF THE LORD (WONDER AND AWE): This gift infuses honesty into our relationship with God.

FRUITS OF THE HOLY SPIRIT

The fruits of the Holy Spirit are the perfections that the Holy Spirit forms in us as the "first fruits" of eternal glory. The Tradition of the Church lists twelve fruits of the Holy Spirit. They are: love, joy, peace, patience, kindness, goodness, generosity, gentleness, faithfulness, modesty, self-control and chastity.

VIRTUES

The Theological Virtues

Gifts from God that enable us to choose to and to live in right relationship with the Holy Trinity.

FAITH: The virtue by which the believer gives personal adherence to God (who invites his or her response) and freely assents to the whole truth that God revealed.

HOPE: The virtue through which a person both desires and expects the fulfillment of God's promises of things to come.

CHARITY (LOVE): The virtue by which we give love to God for his own sake and love to our neighbor on account of God.

The Cardinal Moral Virtues

The four moral virtues on which all other human virtues hinge.

FORTITUDE: The virtue by which one courageously and firmly chooses the good despite difficulty and also perseveres in doing what is right despite temptation.

JUSTICE: The virtue by which one is able to give God and neighbor what is due to them.

PRUDENCE: The virtue by which one knows the true good in every circumstance and chooses the right means to reach that end.

TEMPERANCE: The virtue by which one moderates the desire for the attainment of and pleasure in earthly goods.

THE NEW LAW

The Great, or Greatest, Commandment

"You shall love the Lord your God with all your heart, and with all your soul, and with all your mind. . . . You shall love your neighbor as yourself."

—Matthew 22:37, 39, based on Deuteronomy 6:5 and Leviticus 19:18

THE NEW COMMANDMENT OF JESUS

"Love one another. Just as I have loved you, you also should love one another." John 13:34

THE BEATITUDES

Blessed are the poor in spirit, for theirs is the kingdom of heaven.

Blessed are those who mourn, for they will be comforted.

Blessed are the meek, for they will inherit the earth.

Blessed are those who hunger and thirst for righteousness, for they will be filled.

Blessed are the merciful, for they will receive mercy.

Blessed are the pure in heart, for they will see God.

Blessed are the peacemakers, for they shall be called children of God.

Blessed are those who are persecuted for righteousness' sake, for theirs is the kingdom of heaven.

Blessed are you when people revile you and persecute you and utter all kinds of evil against you falsely on my account. Rejoice and be glad, for your reward is great in heaven, for in the same way they persecuted the prophets who were before you.

—Matthew 5:3–11

SPIRITUAL WORKS OF MERCY

Admonish and help those who sin.
Teach those who are ignorant.
Advise those who have doubts.
Comfort those who suffer.
Be patient with all people.
Forgive those who trespass against you.
Pray for the living and the dead.

CORPORAL WORKS OF MERCY

Feed the hungry.
Give drink to the thirsty.
Shelter the homeless.
Clothe the naked.
Visit the sick and those in prison.
Bury the dead.
Give alms to the poor.

THE TEN COMMANDMENTS, OR THE DECALOGUE

Traditional Catechetical Formula

FIRST: I am the LORD your God: you shall not have strange gods before me.

SECOND: You shall not take the name of the LORD your God in vain.

THIRD: Remember to keep holy the LORD's Day.

FOURTH: Honor your father and mother.

FIFTH: You shall not kill.

SIXTH: You shall not commit adultery.

SEVENTH: You shall not steal.

EIGHTH: You shall not bear false witness against your neighbor.

NINTH: You shall not covet your neighbor's wife.

TENTH: You shall not covet your neighbor's goods.

Scriptural Formula

FIRST: I am the LORD your God, who brought you out of the land of Egypt, out of the house of slavery; you shall have no other gods before me.

SECOND: You shall not make wrongful use of the name of the LORD your God, for the LORD will not acquit anyone who misuses his name.

THIRD: Observe the sabbath day to keep it holy. . . .

FOURTH: Honor your father and your mother. . . .

FIFTH: You shall not murder.

SIXTH: Neither shall you commit adultery.

SEVENTH: Neither shall you steal.

EIGHTH: Neither shall you bear false witness against your neighbour.

NINTH: Neither shall you covet your neighbor's wife.

TENTH: Neither shall you desire . . . anything that belongs to your neighbor.

—From Deuteronomy 5:6–21

PRECEPTS OF THE CHURCH

The precepts of the Church are positive laws made by the Church that name the minimum in prayer and moral effort for the growth of the faithful in their love of God and neighbor.

FIRST PRECEPT: Participate in Mass on Sundays and on holy days of obligation and rest from work that impedes keeping these days holy.

SECOND PRECEPT: Confess serious sins at least once a year.

THIRD PRECEPT: Receive the Sacrament of the Eucharist at least during the Easter Season.

FOURTH PRECEPT: Fast and abstain on the days established by the Church.

FIFTH PRECEPT: Provide for the materials of the Church according to one's ability.

SOCIAL DOCTRINE OF THE CHURCH

These seven key principles are at the foundation of the social doctrine, or social teaching, of the Catholic Church:

1. *Life and dignity of the human person.* Human life is sacred and the dignity of the human person is the foundation of the moral life of individuals and of society.
2. *Call to family, community and participation.* The human person is social by nature and has the right to participate in family life and in the life of society.
3. *Rights and responsibilities.* The human person has the fundamental right to life and to the basic necessities that support life and human decency.
4. *Option for the poor and the vulnerable.* The Gospel commands us "to put the needs of the poor and the vulnerable first."
5. *Dignity of work and workers.* Work is a form of participating in God's work of creation. "The economy must serve people and not the other way around."
6. *Solidarity.* God is the Creator of all people. "We are one human family whatever our national, racial, ethnic, economic and ideological differences."
7. *Care for God's creation.* Care of the environment is a divine command and a requirement of our faith.

APOLOGETICS: RESPONDING TO FREQUENTLY ASKED FAITH QUESTIONS

Your friends and other people might sometimes ask you questions about your Catholic faith. Some of those questions might deal with morality. The teachings of Scripture and the Church that you have been studying in this theology course will guide you in responding to those questions. Here are five questions and summaries of key points you might include in your response to such questions. When you dialog with others about the faith of the Catholic Church, you are taking part in the Church's work of proclaiming Jesus Christ and the Gospel. This is the work of evangelization; it is the primary work of the Church.

Question 1: If God created me free, doesn't that mean that I alone can decide what is right and wrong?

The simple response is "No; not really?" Think about it? But first let's agree on a definition of freedom. "Freedom is the power, rooted in reason and will, to act or not to act, to do this or that, and so perform deliberate actions on one's own responsibility. By free will one shapes one's own life. Human freedom is a force for growth and maturity in truth and goodness; it attains perfection when directed toward God, our beatitude" (*Catechism of the Catholic Church* [CCC], no. 1731).

You can just imagine what it would be like if everyone, without exception, could decide what is right or wrong for themselves, on their own and without regard to how their decisions affect other people. What a mess! The reality is: the way we use or abuse our freedom affects both ourselves and others. A simple example: Choosing to stop at a red light results in our own safety and the safety of other drivers and pedestrians. If, on the other hand, I decide, perhaps because I am running late, that it is good for me to run a red light, such a misuse of freedom could not only bring about bodily harm or even death, but it actually lessens our own and others' freedom.

Yes, it is true God has created every person with a free will. God has also created us with an intellect that gives us the natural ability to reason and come to know what is good (right) and what is evil (wrong), that is, to know the natural moral law that God has planted in our heart. The common universal experience of humanity is that there are certain truths that are universally known about what is "right" or "good" and what is "wrong" or "evil." The example and writings of philosophers and the teachings of the world's religions give witness to this reality.

One of the great mysteries of life is that we do have a free will. Why do people deliberately harm others? Why apartheid? Why genocide? Why direct abortion? The list goes on. Our intellect and free will work together. We can choose not to use our intellect and remain ignorant of what is true and good. We can also act according to what we learn to be true and good, or we can choose not to do so. Jews and Christians believe that these fundamental human moral behaviors have also been revealed in the Scriptures (for example, the moral behaviors revealed in the Commandments) and that their meaning is understood by the wisdom of their faith communities. Many other truths about human acts and choices that are "right" and "wrong" flow from those truths and have been applied to human personal and social life throughout the ages. Catholics and other Christians believe Jesus Christ is the fullest and clearest Revelation of the principles underlying moral behavior. We can come to know what is truly right from what is wrong from the teachings and the life, Death and Resurrection of Jesus Christ. Catholics state this truth by saying that our reason aided by the Spirit of Christ is guided in coming to know right from wrong by listening to Sacred Scripture, especially the Gospel, and Sacred Tradition.

All people, both believers and non-believers, have the responsibility to make an honest effort to educate themselves to know the truth about good and evil and to act morally. All people also face the challenge to resist the temptation to knowingly and freely choose what is evil, or to sin. Sin is an offense against the Creator, who made all things good; against the human person, and against creation. We are tempted to abuse our freedom and choose what only appears to be good. (Recall the story of the serpent's temptation of Eve, who was taken in by the serpent's deceit, and Adam and Eve's consequent choice and its results.)

As the story of the fall teaches: "Sin is an offense against reason, truth, and right conscience; it is failure in genuine love for God and neighbor caused by a perverse attachment to certain goods. It wounds the nature of man and injures human solidarity" (CCC, no. 1849). As such, sin is the deliberate choice of evil over good; it is "a deliberate thought, word, deed, or omission contrary to the eternal [natural and revealed] law of God" (CCC, Glossary, "Sin").

In short, it is an abuse of our intellect to name what is right or what is wrong solely on our own; it is truly an arrogant and "perverse attachment." Sinful acts diminish freedom; moral, or good, acts increase our freedom so we can live in the freedom of the children of God. The kingdom announced and inaugurated by Jesus—human life rooted in justice and love—is true freedom.

Question 2: Isn't it wrong to judge other people by telling them something they are doing is wrong?

In the Gospel Jesus teaches his disciples many truths about human relationships. One of those truths is: "Do not judge, so that you may not be judged. For with the judgment you make you will be judged, and the measure you give will be the measure you get. Why do you see the speck in your neighbor's eye, but do not notice the log in your own eye?" (Matthew 7:1–3).

We need to be careful not to interpret Matthew 7:1–3 in isolation from other teachings of Jesus. In this passage Jesus is not teaching us to turn a blind eye to sin or to approve of sinful words and deeds. Why do we say that? Jesus also taught that we are to name sinful acts for what they are. In Matthew 18:15 Jesus instructs us to point out to others their sins. But we are to

do so in a loving and forgiving way that reflects the mercy of God and that calls for a change of heart. We have the responsibility to encourage one another to live a life free of sin, free of deliberate acts that bring physical and spiritual harm to others—and to one's self. We are to encourage and support others to love others and themselves as the Great Commandment teaches. To do that, we must remember and acknowledge that sin is real and be willing to call what is sinful a "sin."

Who would not warn a friend or even a passerby of a physical evil in order to help them avoid harm? You would agree that doing so is an act of love—even if our expression of love is rejected. Spiritual evil, or sin, also harms a person. It is an act of love to address the spiritual evil a friend or relative is facing in the same way we would address a physical evil and harm. Recall the example of Jesus and the expression of compassionate love he offered the woman caught in adultery. Jesus' words and actions teach that we are to love the sinner, hate the sin.

To challenge someone or a group of people to stop sinning and hurting themselves or others and to seek forgiveness and reconciliation is an expression of love. This is not so easy to do. We are often told, "Mind our own business!" There is widespread pressure in society to be politically correct and to practice "tolerance" toward all, even when what they (or we) say or do is harmful. There is a cost for us to face that pressure. These pressures are an expression of a moral relativism that has been woven into the fabric of our society. Moral relativism presents a false understanding of tolerance. Moral relativism teaches that moral rules and standards are irrelevant. It teaches that no act is good or evil in and of itself. In other words, moral relativism erroneously claims that the morality of any act is "relative" to what a person thinks, the circumstances of a person's life, the time and culture in which a person lives. In other words, there is no objective good or truth.

"To tolerate," however, is not synonymous with "to ignore." "Honesty is the best policy" is still a wise and proven adage. Open and honest correction is an act of charity, of love revealed by God and lived fully by Jesus Christ. Objective, truthful and honest moral judgment prevents personal and social chaos and contributes to healthy personal relationships and social life. Moral actions, our own, those of others, and those of society, must always be measured by truth.

So the loving truth is, "No; it is not wrong to judge other people by telling them something they are doing is wrong."

Question 3: Isn't it wrong for the Church to impose her views of morality on others?

The Church does not *impose*, or force anyone to accept, her views on morality. The Church, as Pope Francis is doing, proclaims and shares with all people, both members of the Church and non-members, what she has received. She takes to heart the responsibility the risen Jesus gave to his Church. She strives with the guidance of the Spirit of Christ, the Spirit of truth, to openly and honestly fulfill the responsibility Christ has given to her to invite all people to come to know and freely "obey everything that I have commanded you" (Matthew 28:20) so that individuals and society may come to know and enjoy the fullness of life.

In fulfilling this responsibility the Church makes known and promotes the universal moral law. All people have the "natural" ability to come to understand the "natural" moral law and to choose to live by it. Fundamental and universal moral truths, such as the fundamental dignity of every person from which flows every person's right to life, are part of the very fiber of the human heart. They are truths that God has written in every human heart and has revealed to us.

In promoting and defending these truths the Church is sharing and promoting what she has come to know and understand that God has revealed about the divine plan for creation and salvation. In so doing, the Church is fulfilling her Christ-given mission to pass on to everyone, as persuasively as possible, the truths God has revealed about how he created people to live, act and treat one another.

Many disagree with what the Church teaches about the moral law. There are those who reject that there are universal objective moral truths. We see this pattern of disagreement and objection in the many responses to Pope Francis' teaching on evil and the sinful structures of society that contribute to the violation of the dignity of persons, especially the poor, and the widespread addiction to a consumerist view of the world. The Church meets this rejection head-on, declaring that living by such a relative moral code, as history attests, leads to both personal and social chaos and to a dead end in the search for happiness.

Question 4: Why can't we make up our own minds and be in control over everything?

Actually, the Catholic Church does teach that we are free to make up our own mind and, therefore, are in control of our moral decision-making. But the Church also teaches that we have a serious responsibility to make sure that we have the necessary and correct information to make those decisions—decisions that not only affect us personally but also impact the well-being of others and the common good of all people. So the first question is, What does it mean to "make up our own minds" and "be in control over everything"?

The Catholic Church's response to that question is: We are to strive honestly to form our conscience correctly, and then we must follow a well-formed conscience. The Church defines our conscience as "the interior voice of a human being, within whose heart the inner law of God is inscribed. Moral conscience is a judgment of practical reason about the moral quality of a human action. It moves a person at the appropriate moment to do good and to avoid evil" (*Catechism of the Catholic Church* [CCC], Glossary, "Conscience").

This freedom is so sacred that the Church teaches that "a human being must always obey the certain judgment of his conscience. If he were deliberately to act against it, he would condemn himself" (CCC, no. 1790). The key to understanding this teaching is that a person must honestly and responsibly strive to ensure that their conscience is well formed, that it is upright and truthful. Our experience tells us that human intelligence is finite. We cannot know everything and there are forces at work in the world that obscure and even hide what is good and true. The Catholic Church puts it this way: "The education of conscience is indispensable for human beings who are subjected to negative influences and tempted by sin to prefer their own judgment and to reject authoritative teachings" (CCC, no. 1783). This reality points out that the education of our conscience is a lifelong task.

Catholics believe that there is more to educating our conscience than the gift of reason. We believe that a "good and pure conscience is enlightened by true faith, for charity proceeds at the same time from 'a pure heart and a good conscience and a sincere faith' (1 Timothy, 5)" (CCC, no. 1794). We believe and trust that the Spirit of Christ dwells within the Church, teaching her to know and teach in the name of Christ what is true and good.

Catholics trust in Jesus' promise, "If you love me, you will keep my commandments. And I will ask the Father, and he will give you another Advocate, to be with you forever. This is the Spirit of truth, whom the world cannot receive, because it neither sees him nor knows him. You know him, because he abides with you, and he will be in you" (John 14:15–17). We believe that the baptized are temples of the Holy Spirit, "the Spirit of truth," who knows, sees and understands more than any of us can. We believe that the Holy Spirit enlightens our minds and hearts to assist us in forming a conscience that is "upright and truthful" (CCC, no. 1783).

The many tragic conflicts resulting from the choosing of evil out of ignorance or under the pretense of doing good that still exist in the world point to a moral blindness that can only be overcome by the grace of God merited for us by God's saving work made present among us in Christ. Striving to form and follow a well-formed conscience with the assistance of the grace of the Spirit of truth and the guidance of the Church is our surest way to use our gift of freedom to make choices that "guarantee freedom and engender peace of heart" (CCC, no. 1784).

Question 5: There's an old saying about charity beginning at home. Doesn't this mean that I don't have to worry about helping anyone else until I have enough to take care of me and my family?

Let's begin by coming to a shared understanding of "home." By "home," are we speaking about "the social unit formed by a family living together" (*Merriam-Webster* Online Dictionary); "the people living under the same roof"; "our biological or adoptive family, including grandparents, aunts, uncles and cousins"? Or do we have a broader view of our home?

Yes, it is true that the Fourth Commandment teaches we have a primary responsibility to show our love and care for our immediate family. But today, more than ever, we have come to realize that Earth is our home and all people are family. The impact of world events, past and current, such as the international response to the human suffering from Hurricane Katrina in 2005, the tsunami devastation in 2011 in Japan and in the Philippines in 2013, the displacement of peoples in Syria and Iraq in 2013–2015, and the Ebola outbreak in 2014, gives witness that "home" and "family" extend beyond the place where we reside and the people with whom we live.

The Acts of the Apostles attests that the Church has given witness to this truth from her earliest days. Individual Christians, religious congregations and organizations have arisen to reach out and care for people in need. Today, Church organizations, such as Catholic Relief Services and Catholic Charities, combine the efforts of the baptized to give witness to the truth that the charity we practice at home is to be extended beyond our immediate home. The reality, as so many believers and non-believers have experienced, is that it is in giving that we receive.

Before we conclude, let us open our minds to the meaning of "charity." Charity is a God-given virtue that enables us to "love God above all things for his own sake, and our neighbor as ourselves for the love of God" (*Catechism of the Catholic Church*, Glossary, "Charity"). Acts of charity are expressions of this love. In the parable of the widow's mite, which we find in Mark 12:38–44 and Luke 20:45—21:4, Jesus teaches that the value of an act of charity is not to be determined by the size of our bank account. Our generosity is not measured by the "amount" we give; our giving, even of pennies, from our hearts out of love is the measure of true and authentic charity.

How central is living such a life of charity? Jesus answered that question in the parable of the judgment of nations in Matthew 25:31–46.

FAITH GLOSSARY

Abbreviations: CCC = *Catechism of the Catholic Church;* Compendium = *Compendium of the Catechism of the Catholic Church*; USCCA = *United States Catholic Catechism for Adults*

A–B

abortion: The intentional destruction of an unborn child; such an act is gravely contrary to the moral law and [to] the will of the Creator. (USCCA, 503)

abstinence: The term "abstinence" is used in two ways. (1) "*Abstinence* is refraining from eating meat. The Church identifies specific days and times of fasting and abstinence to prepare the faithful for certain special feasts; such actions of sacrifice can also help us to grow in self-discipline and in holiness" (USCCA, 335).
(2) Abstinence is also related to the virtue of chastity. In this instance, it is refraining from sexual intercourse and other inappropriate expressions of intimacy until one marries.

actual graces: God's interventions in our lives, whether at the beginning of [our] conversion or in the course of the work of [our] sanctification. (USCCA, "Grace," 514) *See also* **grace**.

adoration: The acknowledgment of God as God, Creator and Savior, the Lord and Master of everything that exists. (CCC, Glossary).

adultery: Marital infidelity, or sexual relations between two partners, at least one of whom is married to another partner. The sixth commandment and the New Testament forbid adultery absolutely. (CCC, Glossary)

agape: In 1 John 4:8, 16 we read: "God is love." The Greek word used here for "love" is *agapē*. The word *agape* describes God's total "self-gift" of unconditional and infinite love, both among the Persons of the Blessed Trinity and for each and every one of us.

almsgiving: Money or goods given to the poor as an act of penance or fraternal charity. Almsgiving, together with prayer and fasting, are traditionally recommended to foster the state of interior penance. (CCC, Glossary)

annulment: The consent of the spouses entering into marriage must be a free act of the will, devoid of external or internal invalidating factors. If this freedom is absent, the marriage is invalid. For this reason, the Church, after an examination of the situation by a competent Church court, can declare the nullity of a marriage, i.e., that the sacramental marriage never existed. In this case, the contracting parties are free to marry, provided the natural obligations of the previous union are discharged. (USCCA, 503–504).

apologist: Someone who speaks or writes to defend and explain a belief, doctrine or idea.

apostasy: The total repudiation of the Christian faith. (CCC, Glossary)

apostolate: The activity of the Christian which fulfills the apostolic nature of the whole Church by working to extend the reign of Christ to the entire world. (CCC, Glossary)

ark of the covenant: This revered chest was a symbol of God's presence with and among his people. The two tablets on which Moses wrote the Ten Commandments were deposited in the ark of the covenant.

authority: "The quality by virtue of which persons or institutions make laws and give orders to men, and expect obedience from them" (CCC, no. 1897). "The duty of obedience requires all to give due honor to authority and to treat those who are charged to exercise it with respect, and, insofar as it is deserved, with gratitude and good-will" (CCC, no. 1900).

Beatific Vision: The seeing of God face to face; being and living in the presence of God in heavenly glory. "The contemplation of God in heavenly glory, a gift of God which is a constitutive element of the happiness (or beatitude) of heaven" (CCC, Glossary).

beatitude: Happiness or blessedness, especially the eternal happiness of heaven, which is described as the vision of God, or entering into God's rest by those whom He makes "partakers of the divine nature." (CCC, Glossary)

Beatitudes: The eight Beatitudes form part of the teaching given by Jesus during the Sermon on the Mount, which set forth fundamental attitudes and virtues for living as a faithful disciple. (USCCA, 505) *See also* **Sermon on the Mount.**

blasphemy: Speech, thought, or action involving contempt for God or the Church, or persons or things dedicated to God. Blasphemy is directly opposed to the second commandment. (CCC, Glossary)

C

canon law: The rules (canons or laws) which provide the norms for good order in the visible society of the Church. Those canon laws that apply universally are contained in the Codes of Canon Law. (CCC, Glossary)

Capital Sins: Those seven sins, sometimes called "deadly," that can lead us into more serious sin. The Capital Sins are lust, avarice (greed), envy, pride, sloth, gluttony and anger. (USCCA, 506) *See also* **mortal sin; sin; venial sin.**

cardinal virtues: Four pivotal human virtues (from the Latin *cardo*, "pivot"): prudence, justice, fortitude, and temperance. (CCC, Glossary). *See also* **fortitude; human virtues; justice; prudence; temperance.**

celibacy: "The state or condition of those who have chosen to remain unmarried for the sake of the kingdom of heaven in order to give themselves entirely to God and to the service of his people" (CCC, Glossary). Celibacy should not be confused with the virtue of chastity.

charism(s): Special graces of the Holy Spirit given to the Church and the baptized for the building up of the Church.

charity (love): The Theological Virtue by which we give love to God for his own sake and love to our neighbor on account of God. (USCCA, 506) *See also* **faith; hope.**

chastity: Connected to purity of heart, this is a virtue that moves us to love others with generous regards for them. It excludes lust and any wish to exploit them sexually. It helps us see and put into practice God's plan for the body, person, and sexuality. All people are called to pursue and live the virtue of chastity according to one's state in life. (USCCA, Glossary, 506).

civil disobedience: The refusal to obey an unjust law, or the choice to display one's judgment that a law is unjust. If authority enacts unjust laws, such laws would not be binding in conscience. (Based on CCC, no. 1903)

cohabitation: An unmarried couple living together. *See also* **free unions.**

common good: By common good is to be understood "the sum total of social conditions which allow people, either as groups or as individuals, to reach their fulfillment more fully and more easily" (CCC, no. 1906, quoting *Pastoral Constitution on the Church in the Modern World*, no. 26). "The common good consists of three essential elements: respect for and promotion of the fundamental rights of the person; prosperity, or the development of the spiritual and temporal goods of society; the peace and security of the group and its members" (CCC, no. 1925).

compassion: In the Bible, the English word "compassion" is a translation of a Greek word meaning "womb" and of a Hebrew word that is also translated as "mercy." Compassion is the quality of a person who so closely identifies with the suffering and condition of another person that the suffering of the other becomes their own, or "enters their womb." The Latin roots of the English word "compassion" are *cum* and *patior*, which mean "suffering with."

concupiscence: The disorder in our human appetites and desires as the result of Original Sin. These effects remain even after Baptism and produce an inclination to sin. (USCCA, 507)

conscience: The interior voice of a human being, within whose heart the inner law of God is inscribed. Moral conscience is a judgment of practical reason about the moral quality of a human action. It moves a person at the appropriate moment to do good and to avoid evil. (CCC, Glossary)

consecrated life: A permanent state of life recognized by the Church, entered freely in response to the call of Christ to perfection, and characterized by the profession of the evangelical counsels of poverty, chastity, and obedience. (CCC, Glossary)

consumerism: Consumerism is the inordinate desire for and consumption of goods. It encourages the purchase of goods and services in ever-greater amounts and is deeply rooted in secularism and materialism. *See also* **materialism; secularism**.

contemplation: "Wordless prayer in which a person focuses the whole person in loving adoration on God and his very presence" (USCCA, 508). Contemplation is one of the three forms of Christian prayer.

conversion: Conversion means turning around one's life toward God and trying "to live holier lives according to the Gospel" (Vatican II, *Decree on Ecumenism*; quoted in CCC, no. 821).

covenant: A covenant is a solemn agreement made between human beings or between God and a human being involving mutual commitments or guarantees. The Bible speaks of covenants that God made with Noah and, through him, "with every living creature" (Genesis 9:10). Then God made the special covenant with Abraham and renewed it with Moses. The prophets constantly pointed to a new covenant that God would establish with all humankind through the promised Messiah—Jesus Christ.

covetousness: A disordered inclination or desire for pleasure or possessions. One of the capital sins. (CCC, Glossary)

creation: The act by which the eternal God gave a beginning to all that exists outside of himself. Creation also refers to the created universe or totality of what exists, as often expressed by the formula "the heavens and the earth." (CCC, Glossary)

Creator: Title for God; God alone is the Creator. God—Father, Son and Holy Spirit—out of love for us created the world out of nothing, wanting to share divine life and love with us.

D–E

Daily Examen: A form of daily prayer rooted in principles of the spiritual practices that were practiced and taught by St. Ignatius of Loyola, during which a person looks back over the day and evaluates her or his response to the presence of the Spirit in his or her life.

Decalogue: Another name for the Ten Commandments. "The Ten Commandments (literally, "ten words") given by God to Moses on Sinai. In order to be faithful to the teaching of Jesus, the Decalogue must be interpreted in the light of the great commandment of love of God and neighbor" (CCC, Glossary).

despair: The abandonment of hope in salvation and the forgiveness of sins. (CCC, Glossary)

disciple: Name given in the New Testament to all those men and women who followed Jesus and were taught by him while he was alive, and who, following Jesus' death, Resurrection, and Ascension, formed the Church with the Apostles and helped spread the Good News, or Gospel message. Contemporary members of the Church, as followers of Jesus, can also be referred to as disciples. (USCCA, 509–510)

divine filiation: An effect of Baptism and Confirmation: becoming adopted sons and daughters of God, participating in God's life and love. (USCCA, 510)

divine providence: God's loving care and concern for all he has made; he continues to watch over creation, sustaining its existence and presiding over its development and destiny. (USCCA, 510)

divorce: The claim that the indissoluble marriage bond validly entered into between a man and a woman is broken. A civil dissolution of the marriage contract (divorce) does not free persons from a valid marriage before God; remarriage would not be morally licit. (CCC, Glossary)

doubt, voluntary: "*Voluntary doubt* about the faith disregards or refuses to hold as true what God has revealed and the Church proposes for belief" (CCC, no. 2088).

doubt, involuntary: "*Involuntary doubt* refers to hesitation in believing, difficulty in overcoming objections connected with the faith, or also anxiety aroused by its obscurity" (CCC, no. 2088).

euthanasia: An action or an omission which, of itself or by intention, causes the death of handicapped, sick, or dying persons— sometimes with an attempt to justify the act as a means of eliminating suffering. Euthanasia violates the fifth commandment of the law of God. (CCC, Glossary)

evangelical counsels: Those vows taken by men or women who enter the religious life; there are three vows: poverty, chastity, and obedience. (USCCA, 511)

evangelization: The "ministry and mission of proclaiming and witnessing Christ and his Gospel with the intention of deepening the faith of believers and inviting others to be baptized and initiated into the Church" (USCCA, 512). Evangelization is the primary work of the Church.

Examen: *see* Daily Examen.

F–G

faith: Faith is one of the three theological virtues. Faith "is both a gift of God and a human act by which the believer gives personal adherence to God (who invites his or her response) and freely assents to the whole truth that God has revealed" (USCCA, 512).

family: "A man and a woman united in marriage, together with their children, form a family. This institution is prior to any recognition by public authority, which has an obligation to recognize it. It should be considered the normal reference point by which the different [authentic] forms of family relationship are to be [recognized]." (CCC, no. 2202).

fortitude: "The Cardinal Virtue by which one courageously and firmly chooses the good despite difficulty and also perseveres in doing what is right despite temptation, fear or persecution" (USCCA, 513). One of the seven gifts of the Holy Spirit, also named "courage." *See also* cardinal virtues.

freedom: "Freedom characterizes properly human acts. It makes the human being responsible for acts of which he is the voluntary agent. His deliberate acts properly belong to him" (CCC, no. 1745). "The more one does what is good, the freer one becomes. Freedom attains its proper perfection when it is directed toward God, the highest good and our beatitude. Freedom implies also the possibility of choosing between good and evil. The choice of evil is an abuse of freedom and leads to the slavery of sin" (*Compendium*, no. 363).

free unions: The term "free unions" refers to several types of intimate relationships between a man and a woman. These include trial marriages, cohabitation and concubinage. All these relationships have one thing in common: the partners have chosen to live together without being married and they remain "free" from entering a full marriage commitment. The partners do not commit themselves to all or some of the indispensable elements that make a marriage a marriage.

free will: Our God-given power and ability to choose what we have come to know and understand to be good and true, and to love God, others and ourselves because of our love for God. Our free will and our intellect are the bases of our responsibility and accountability for our moral choices. *See also* **freedom; intellect/reason.**

fruits of the Holy Spirit: The Tradition of the Church lists twelve fruits of the Holy Spirit: love, joy, peace, patience, kindness, goodness, generosity, gentleness, faithfulness, modesty, self-control and chastity. (USCCA, 513)

genocide: "The deliberate and systematic destruction of a racial, political, or cultural group" (*Merriam-Webster* Online Dictionary).

gifts of the Holy Spirit: These gifts are permanent dispositions that move us to respond to the guidance of the Spirit. The traditional list of these gifts is derived from Isaiah 11:1–3: wisdom, understanding, knowledge, counsel [right judgment], fortitude [courage], reverence (piety), and wonder and awe in God's presence (fear of the Lord). (USCCA, 513)

gossip: Gossip is contrary to the Eighth Commandment. It is the unnecessary sharing of personal information about someone in a way that can harm them.

grace: The word "grace" comes from the Latin *gratia*, which means "free." Grace is the "free and undeserved gift that God gives us to respond to our vocation to become his adopted children" (CCC, Glossary). *See also* **actual graces; charism(s); sacramental grace(s); sanctifying grace.**

H–I–J

heresy: "The obstinate denial after Baptism of a truth which must be believed with divine and Catholic faith" (CCC, Glossary). "A religious teaching that denies or contradicts truths revealed by God" (USCCA, 514).

hierarchy: The Apostles and their successors, the college of bishops, to whom Christ gave the authority to teach, sanctify, and rule the Church in his name. (CCC, Glossary)

holiness: "A state of goodness in which a person—with the help of God's grace, the action of the Holy Spirit, and a life of prayer—is freed from sin and evil" (USCCA, 514). A person in the state of holiness lives in communion with God, who is Father, Son and Holy Spirit.

holy days of obligation: "Principal feast days on which, in addition to Sundays, Catholics are obliged by Church law to participate in the Eucharist; a precept of the Church" (CCC, Glossary). In the United States of America there are six holy days of obligation for Latin (Roman) Catholics. They are (1) Mary, the Holy Mother of God [January 1]; (2) The Ascension of the Lord [forty days after Easter or the following Sunday]; (3) The Assumption of the Blessed Virgin Mary [August 15]; (4) All Saints' Day [November 1]; (5) The Immaculate Conception of the Blessed Virgin Mary [December 8]; and (6) The Nativity of the Lord—Christmas [December 25].

homosexuality: Sexual attraction or orientation toward persons of the same sex and/or sexual acts between persons of the same sex. Homosexual acts are morally wrong because they violate God's purpose for human sexual activity. (CCC, Glossary)

hope: One of the three theological virtues "through which a person both desires and expects the fulfillment of God's promises of things to come" (USCCA, 515). Hope is the desire and expectation of the salvation God promised. It is based on God's unwavering fidelity to keeping and fulfilling his promises. *See also* **charity; faith.**

human person: The human individual, made in the image of God; not some thing but some one, a unity of spirit and matter, soul and body, capable of knowledge, self-possession, and freedom, who can enter into communion with other persons—and with God. The human person needs to live in society, which is a group of persons bound together organically by a principle of unity that goes beyond each one of them. (CCC, Glossary, "Person, human")

human virtues: The human virtues are "stable dispositions of the intellect and the will that govern our acts, order our passions, and guide our conduct in accordance with reason and faith. They can be grouped around the four cardinal virtues: prudence, justice, fortitude, and temperance" (CCC, no. 1834) *See also* **theological virtues; virtue.**

humility: The virtue by which a Christian acknowledges that God is the author of all good. Humility avoids inordinate ambition or pride, and provides the foundation for turning to God in prayer. Voluntary humility can be described as "poverty of spirit." (CCC, Glossary)

hypocrisy: Hypocrisy is a form of pretending; it gives false witness to what one truly believes. Hypocrisy is "the practice of claiming to have moral standards or beliefs to which one's own behavior does not conform" (*Oxford Dictionaries* online). Hypocrisy is contrary to the Eighth Commandment.

idolatry: The divinization of a creature in place of God; the substitution of some one (or thing) for God; worshiping a creature (even money, pleasure, or power) instead of the Creator. (CCC, Glossary).

incest: "Intimate relations between relatives or in-laws within a degree that prohibits marriage between them. . . . Incest corrupts family relationships" (CCC, no. 2388) and debases those who commit this sin.

incredulity (unbelief): The "neglect of revealed truth or the willful refusal to assent to it" (CCC, no. 2089).

indefectibility: The Lord Jesus ensures that his Church will remain until the Kingdom of God is fully achieved. Indefectibility means that the Church does not and cannot depart from proclaiming the authentic Gospel without error in spite of the defects of her members. (USCCA, 515)

infallibility: This is the gift of the Holy Spirit to the Church whereby the pastors of the Church—the pope, and bishops in communion with him—can definitively proclaim a doctrine of faith and morals, which is divinely revealed for the belief of the faithful. This gift flows from the grace of the whole body of the faithful not to err in matters of faith and morals. The pope teaches infallibly when he declares that his teaching is *ex cathedra* (literally, "from the throne"); that is, he teaches as supreme pastor of the Church. (USCCA, 516)

intellect/reason: Our God-given power and ability to know what is good and true. Our intellect enables us to come to know God through creation and to know and understand the order that God wills among things. Our intellect and free will are the bases of our responsibility and accountability for our moral choices. *See also* **freedom; free will.**

involuntary doubt: See **doubt, involuntary.**

Jesus [name]: The name given to the Son of God, the Second Person of the Trinity. This name, which means, "God Saves," was revealed both to the Blessed Virgin Mary and to St. Joseph [see Luke 1:31; Matthew 1:21]. (USCCA, 516)

justice: The Cardinal Virtue by which one is able to give God and neighbor what is due to them. (USCCA, 517) *See also* **cardinal virtues.**

K–L–M

kenosis: A Greek word meaning "emptiness"; the term is used by St. Paul in Philippians 2:7 to teach the mystery of God's love revealed in the Incarnation and redemption; Jesus, the Incarnate Son of God, emptied himself for our salvation.

Kingdom [Reign] of God: The actualization of God's will for human beings proclaimed by Jesus Christ as a community of justice, peace, mercy, and love, the seed of which is the Church on earth, and the fulfillment of which is in eternity. (USCCA, 517)

laity: Members of the Church, distinguished from the clergy and those in consecrated life, who have been incorporated into the People of God through the Sacrament of Baptism. (USCCA, 517)

lay ecclesial ministers: The men and women of every race and culture who serve in parishes, schools, diocesan agencies and Church institutions. Lay ecclesial ministers are laypeople who give their lives full time to carrying out the ministries of the Church.

law: A code of conduct established by competent authority. (USCCA, 517) *See also* **moral law; natural law; New Law**

Lord's Day: A name used synonymously for Sunday, the day of the Lord Jesus' Resurrection. (USCCA, 518)

lust: One of the Capital Sins; it is an inordinate desire for earthly pleasures, particularly sexual pleasures. (USCCA, 519)

lying: "Lying consists in saying what is false with the intention of deceiving [one's] neighbor" (CCC, no. 2508). Lying is contrary to the Eighth Commandment.

Magisterium: The living, teaching office of the Church, whose task it is to give authentic interpretation to the word of God, whether in its written form (Sacred Scripture), or in the form of Tradition. The Magisterium ensures the Church's fidelity to the teaching of the Apostles in matters of faith and morals. (CCC, Glossary).

Marriage (Matrimony), Sacrament of: "The marriage covenant, by which a man and a woman form with each other an intimate communion of life and love, has been found and endowed with its own special laws by the Creator. By its very nature it is ordered to the good of the couple, as well as to the generation and education of children. Christ the Lord raised marriage between the baptized to the dignity of a sacrament" (CCC, no. 1660).

martyr: From the Greek word *martyr*, which means "witness." In a Christian context, a martyr is a person "who witnesses to Christ and the truth of faith, even to the point of suffering" (USCCA, 519).

martyrdom: Martyrdom is the ultimate form of commitment to living a truthful life in the Lord. Throughout history, literally millions of Christians have given their lives in witness to the truth, who is Jesus Christ. This witness continues today.

materialism: A philosophy or view of the world "in which the world is understood to have come from pre-existing matter that developed naturally and not as a result of any type of divine action or plan" (USCCA, 54). It is the preoccupation with material rather than spiritual things, which drives one to pursue and turn created goods into idols or "gods."

merit: The reward which God promises and gives to those who love him and by his grace perform good works. One cannot "merit" justification or eternal life, which are the free gift of God; the source of any merit we have before God is due to the grace of Christ in us. (CCC, Glossary)

ministerial priesthood: This priesthood, received in the Sacrament of Holy Orders, differs in essence from the priesthood of the faithful. The ministerial priesthood serves the priesthood of the faithful by building up the Church in the name of Christ, who is head of the Body, by offering prayers and sacrifices to God on behalf of people. A priest is given the power to consecrate the Eucharist, forgive sins, and administer the other Sacraments, except Holy Orders. (USCCA, 519–520)

modesty: A virtue and fruit of the Holy Spirit connected with the virtues of respect and reverence. "A modest person dresses, speaks, and acts in a manner that supports and encourages purity and chastity and [does not act] in a manner that would tempt or encourage sinful sexual behavior" (USCCA, 520).

monogamy: The state of being married to only one spouse.

morality: Morality refers to the goodness or evil of human acts. For a Catholic, morality "refers to the manner of life and action formed according to the teaching laid down by Christ Jesus and authoritatively interpreted by the Church" (USCCA, 520).

moral law: In biblical terms, the *moral* law is the fatherly instruction of God, setting forth the ways which lead to happiness and proscribing those which lead to evil. The *divine* or eternal law can be either *natural* or revealed (*positive*). Natural moral law is inscribed in the heart, and known by human reason. Revealed law is found in the *ancient* law (Old Testament), notably the ten commandments, and in the *new* law (Law of the Gospel), the teaching of Christ, notably the Sermon on the Mount, which perfects the ancient law. (CCC, Glossary, "Law, Moral")

moral virtues: *see* **human virtues; virtue.**

mortal sin: A grave infraction of the law of God that destroys the divine life in the soul of the sinner (sanctifying grace), constituting a turn away from God. For a sin to be mortal, three conditions must be present: grave matter, full knowledge of the evil of the act, and full consent of the will. (CCC, Glossary) *See also* **Capital Sins; sin; venial sin.**

N–O–P

natural law: The natural law is our rational apprehension of the created moral order, an ability we have due to our being made in God's image. It expresses the dignity of the human person and forms the basis of our fundamental rights. (USCCA, 521)

New Commandment: The Commandment Jesus gave to his disciples at the Last Supper: "I give you a new commandment, that you love one another. Just as I have loved you, you also should love one another. By this everyone will know that you are my disciples, if you have love for one another" (John 13:34–35). The New Commandment summarizes the manner of living and acting that Jesus taught. When we live by the New Commandment we are following the New Law that Jesus revealed.

New Law: "The title given to the manner of living and acting taught by Jesus. When we follow the New Law, we are maintaining our part of the covenant with God" (USCCA, 521). It is "the grace of the Holy Spirit received by faith in Christ, operating through charity. It finds its expression above all in the Lord's Sermon on the Mount and uses the sacraments to communicate grace to us" (CCC, no 1983).

obedience (virtue): "The submission to the authority of God which requires everyone to obey the divine law. Obedience to the Church is required in those things which pertain to our salvation; . . . . In imitation of [the] obedience of Jesus, as an evangelical counsel, the faithful may profess a vow of obedience; a public vow of obedience, accepted by Church authority, is one element that characterizes the consecrated life" (CCC, Glossary). Obedience is also due to parents and to legitimate civil authority.

original holiness: The "grace of original holiness was to share in divine life" (CCC, no. 375). The state of living in communion with God and sharing in the gift of divine life enjoyed by our first parents from the moment of their creation until the fall, when they freely chose to disobey God's command (Original Sin).

original innocence: "Original innocence" is the term used for this teaching of the Church: "The first man was not only created good, but was also established in friendship with his Creator and in harmony with himself and with the creation around him, in a state that would be surpassed only by the glory of the new creation in Christ" (CCC, no 374).

original justice: The state of living in harmony or right relationship with God and all creation enjoyed until the fall, or Original Sin. "The inner harmony of the human person, the harmony between man and woman (see Genesis 2:25), and finally the harmony between the first couple and all creation, comprised the state called 'original justice'" (CCC, no. 376).

Original Sin: The personal sin of disobedience committed by the first human beings, resulting in the deprivation of original holiness and justice and the experience of suffering and death. (USCCA, 522)

parables: A characteristic feature of the teaching of Jesus. Parables are simple images or comparisons which confront the hearer or reader with a radical choice about his invitation to enter the Kingdom of God. (CCC, Glossary)

Paschal Mystery: In speaking of the Paschal Mystery we present Christ's death and Resurrection as one, inseparable event. It is *paschal* because it is Christ's passing into death and passing over it into new life. It is a *mystery* because it is a visible sign of an invisible act of God. (USCCA, 522–523)

passions, moral: The emotions or dispositions which incline us to good or evil actions, such as love and hate, hope and fear, joy and sadness, and anger. (CCC, Glossary)

Passover: The name of the Jewish feast that celebrates the deliverance of Israel from Egypt and from the Angel of Death who passed over their doors marked by the blood of sacrificed lamb. Jesus Christ inaugurated the new Passover by delivering all people from death and sin

through his blood shed on the Cross. The celebration of the Eucharist is the Passover feast of the New Covenant. (USCCA, 523)

perjury: Giving one's word under oath falsely, or making a promise under oath without intending to keep it. Perjury violates the second and eighth commandments. (CCC, Glossary)

perpetual virginity: Mary was a virgin in conceiving Jesus, in giving birth to him, and in remaining always a virgin ever after. (USCCA, 523)

piety: One of the seven gifts of the Holy Spirit which leads one to devotion to God. Filial piety connotes an attitude of reverence and respect by children toward their parents. Popular piety refers to the religious sense of a people, and its expression in popular devotions. (CCC, Glossary). *See also* **reverence.**

polygamy: The practice of having more than one wife at the same time, which is contrary to the unity of marriage between one man and one woman, and which offends against the dignity of the woman. (CCC, Glossary)

pornography: "*Pornography* consists in removing real or simulated sexual acts from the intimacy of the partners, in order to display them deliberately to third parties" (CCC, no. 2354).

prayer: "The raising of one's mind and heart to God in thanksgiving and in praise of his glory. It can also include the requesting of good things from God. It is an act by which one enters into an awareness of a loving communion with God" (USCCA, 523–524). "Prayer is the response of faith to the free promise of salvation and also a response of love to the thirst of the only Son of God" (CCC, no. 2561).

precepts of the Church: Positive laws (sometimes called commandments) made by Church authorities to guarantee for the faithful the indispensable minimum in prayer and moral effort, for the sake of their growth in love of God and neighbor. (CCC, Glossary)

presumption: An act or attitude opposed to the theological virtue of hope. Presumption can take the form of trust in self without recognizing that salvation comes from God, or of an over-confidence in divine mercy. (CCC, Glossary)

proverb: "A statement of traditional wisdom, supported by long experience and expressed in memorable form. . . . Proverbs are quoted in many books of the Bible, but the major collection is in Proverbs. There are also proverbs in Wisdom and, in a longer 'essay' form, in Sirach" (*The Catholic Study Bible, Second Edition: New American Bible*, Glossary, 1707).

prudence: The cardinal virtue "by which one knows the true good in every circumstance and chooses the right means to reach that end" (USCCA, 525). *See also* **cardinal virtues**.

R–S

redemption: "The salvation won for us by Jesus. By his Incarnation, ministry, death and Resurrection, Jesus has freed us from original and actual sin and won eternal life for us" (USCCA, 525). By his paying the price of his own sacrificial death on the Cross to ransom us, he has set us free from the slavery of sin.

relativism (moral): Any teaching that denies the existence of absolute values and teaches that all points of view are equal and relative to the individual. Moral relativism makes sin a non-reality. It teaches that no act is good or evil in and of itself, and that moral rules and standards are irrelevant. The morality of any act is relative to what a person thinks, the circumstances of a person's life, and the time and culture in which a person lives.

religion: A set of beliefs and practices followed by those committed to the service and worship of God. The first commandment requires us to believe in God, to worship and serve him, as the first duty of the virtue of religion. (CCC, Glossary)

reparation: Making amends for a wrong done or for an offense, especially for sin, which is an offense against God. By his death on the cross, the Son of God offered his life out of love for the Father to make reparation for our sinful disobedience. We are obliged to make reparation for personal sins against justice and truth, either through restitution of stolen goods or correcting the harm done to the other's good name. (CCC, Glossary)

reverence (piety): The gift of the Holy Spirit and virtue by which we show God the Father (Creator), Son (Savior) and Holy Spirit (Sanctifier) the respect due to him alone, and also show all his creation the respect due them as images and manifestations of the Creator. *See also* **piety**.

Sabbath: In Scripture, the Sabbath was the seventh day of the week that the people of Ancient Israel were to keep holy by praising God for the creation and the covenant and by resting from their ordinary work. For Christians, the observance of the Sabbath has been transferred to Sunday, the day of the Lord's Resurrection. (USCCA, 526)

sacramental grace(s): [G]ifts of the Holy Spirit received in the sacraments to help us live out our Christian vocation. (CCC, Glossary, "Grace") *See also* **grace**.

sacrilege: Profanation of or irreverence toward persons, places, and things which are sacred, that is, dedicated to God; sacrilege against the sacraments, especially the Eucharist, is a particularly grave offense against the first commandment. (CCC, Glossary)

salvation history: The story of God's reaching out to humanity to fulfill the divine plan of salvation, and also of humanity's response to God.

sanctifying grace: The word "sanctifying" means "that which makes holy." Sanctifying grace is "a habitual gift of God's own divine life, a stable and supernatural disposition that enables us to live with God and to act by his love" (USCCA, "Grace," 514). *See also* **grace**.

scandal: An attitude or behavior which leads another to do evil. (CCC, Glossary)

schism: Refusal of submission to the Supreme Pontiff, or of communion with the members of the Church subject to him. (CCC, Glossary)

secularism: Secularism is a vision and philosophy of life that separates religion and society. It is rooted in the material dimension of human existence and denies that God is the source and center of all life.

Sermon on the Mount: The summary of Jesus' teaching on discipleship found in Matthew 5:1—7:29; it is a blueprint on how to live as his Church, the new People of God. *See also* **Beatitudes**.

Sermon on the Plain: The shorter version of the Sermon on the Mount found in Luke 6:17–49.

sexuality, human: Human sexuality is the God-given gift of being a man or a woman. Our sexuality is integral to human nature and the divine plan of goodness and creation. It is fundamental to the woman–man partnership of fulfilling God's command to create new life and to be stewards of the gift of creation. The man–woman partnership is an image of God the Creator, who is love. It is a glimpse into the mystery of the absolute and unfailing love with which God loves the entire human family.

simony: The buying or selling of spiritual things, which have God alone as their owner and master. (CCC, Glossary)

sin: Sin is an offense against God as well as against reason, truth, and right conscience; it is a failure in genuine love for God and neighbor caused by a perverse attachment to certain goods. It wounds the nature of man and injures human solidarity. (USCCA, 528). *See also* **Capital Sins; mortal sin; social sin; venial sin.**

sin of commission: A sin a person knowingly and freely chooses to do or say that is contrary to God's law. Sins of commission may be of thought, of word or of deed.

sin of omission: Something a person knowingly and freely chooses not to do that is good, which he or she has the responsibility to do and can do.

sloth: "One of the Capital Sins; it involves a lack of effort in meeting duties and responsibilities to God, to others, and to oneself" (USCCA, 528). Also called acedia or laziness.

social sin: Sins that produce unjust social laws and oppressive institutions. They are social situations and institutions contrary to divine goodness. Sometimes called "structures of sin," they are the expression and effect of personal sins. They lead the victims to do evil. (USCCA, 528)

social teachings (doctrine) of the Church: The official social doctrine of the Church developed by the Catholic Church "to respond to the social problems that have arisen because of the industrial and technological revolutions" (USCCA, 528). The social doctrine is built on the Church's reaching out and responding to orphans, widows, aliens and others from the days of the early Church.

solidarity: "The principle of solidarity, also articulated in terms of 'friendship' or 'social charity,' is a direct demand of human and Christian brotherhood" (CCC, no. 1939). This involves a love for all peoples that transcends national, racial, ethnic, economic, and ideological differences. It respects the needs of others and the common good in an interdependent world. (USCCA, 529)

soul: "The spiritual principle of human beings. The soul is the subject of human consciousness and freedom; soul and body together form one unique human nature. Each human soul is individual and immortal, immediately created by God" (CCC, Glossary). "The immortal spiritual part of a person; the soul does not die with the body at death, and it is reunited with the body in the final resurrection" (USCCA, 529).

state of grace: A condition in which our sins have been forgiven and we are reconciled with

God, though purification from sin's effects may still be needed. A person is first in a state of grace, sharing in God's life, following Baptism. If a person falls out of that state, he or she can be subsequently reconciled to God, especially through the Sacrament of Penance. (USCCA, 529)

states of life: Term used to designate ways the faithful participate in the mission and ministry of Christ and fulfill their vocation as members of the Church. The term "states of life" specially refers to those in the ordained ministry, in the consecrated life, in married life, and to those in the single life who make a personal consecration or commitment that takes on a permanent, celibate gift of self to God.

stealing/theft: Unjustly taking and keeping the property of another, against the reasonable will of the owner. Stealing is a violation of the seventh commandment of God, "You shall not steal." (CCC, Glossary)

steward/stewardship: A steward is someone who has the responsibility of caring for what belongs to another person or group of people. In the biblical accounts of creation, God gives humanity dominion over creation. The root word for "dominion" is *domus*, which means household. God has entrusted creation, his household, to the care of humanity.

suicide: "The willful taking of one's own life; a grievous sin against the fifth commandment. A human person is neither the author nor the supreme arbiter of his life, of which God is sovereign master" (CCC, Glossary). "One who is psychologically disturbed or is experiencing grave fear may have diminished responsibility" (*Compendium*, no. 470).

T–Z

temperance: The Cardinal Virtue by which one moderates the desire for the attainment of and pleasure in earthly goods. (USCCA, 530) *See also* **cardinal virtues**.

temptation: An attraction, either from outside oneself or from within, to act contrary to right reason and the commandments of God. (CCC, Glossary)

theft: *See* **stealing/theft**.

theological virtues: Gifts "infused by God into the souls of the faithful to make them capable of acting as his children and of meriting eternal life" (CCC, no. 1813). The theological virtues are faith, hope, and charity (love).

Theology of the Body: The teachings of St. John Paul II about the goodness and sacredness of the human body guide us in understanding how we express our truest and most intimate selves through our bodies. God is the giver of spiritual and bodily life. God creates us body and soul. Our spiritual and immortal soul is the source of our unity as a person. All our desires for what is good, including our sexual desires, are rooted in and connected inseparably with our desire for life with and in God.

theophany: From two Greek words meaning "a manifestation of God," or "an appearance of God." "A revelation or visible appearance of God, as in the case of Moses at Mount Sinai" (CCC, Glossary).

Torah: A Hebrew word meaning "instructions," "teachings" and "laws." The term is used to name the first five books of the Bible, which are also known as the Law or the Pentateuch.

trial marriage: *see* **free unions**.

truth: "Truth or truthfulness is the virtue which consists in showing oneself true in deeds and truthful in words, and guarding against duplicity, dissimulation, and hypocrisy" (CCC, no. 2505).

Twelve (the): The Apostles chosen by Jesus before his Death, Resurrection and Ascension. From among the Twelve, Jesus appointed St. Peter to be the leader of the Apostles (see John 21:15–19).

venial sin: Sin which does not destroy divine life in the soul, as does mortal sin, though it diminishes it and wounds it. Venial sin is the failure to observe necessary moderation, in lesser matters of the moral law, or in grave matters acting without full knowledge or complete consent. (CCC, Glossary) *See also* **Capital Sins; mortal sin; sin.**

vice: Vice is the habitual practice of repeated sin. (USCCA, 531)

virtue: "A habitual and firm disposition to do good" (CCC, no. 1833). *See also* **cardinal virtues; human virtues; theological virtues.**

vocation: The term given to the call to each person from God; everyone has been called to holiness and eternal life, especially in Baptism. Each person can also be called more specifically to the priesthood or to religious life, to married life, and to single life, as well as to a particular profession or service. (USCCA, 531) *See also* **states of life.**

voluntary doubt: *see* **doubt, voluntary.**

works of mercy: Charitable actions by which we come to the aid of our neighbors in their bodily and spiritual needs. The spiritual works of mercy include instructing, advising, consoling, comforting, forgiving, and patiently forbearing. Corporal works of mercy include feeding the hungry, clothing the naked, visiting the sick and imprisoned, sheltering the homeless, and burying the dead. (CCC, Glossary)

worship: Adoration and honor given to God, which is the first act of the virtue of religion. Public worship is given to God in the Church by the celebration of the Paschal Mystery of Christ in the liturgy. (CCC, Glossary)

YHWH: The divine name God revealed to Moses in Exodus 3:13–15; the Hebrew letters YHWH are the first letters of the words meaning "I Am Who I Am," or "I Am He Who Is," or "I Am Who Am." The divine name is so sacred that the people of ancient Israel did not speak or write it, nor do Jews today. In its place they use the words Adonai or Lord. Jews today also write G—D.

Acknowledgments

Scripture quotations taken from or adapted from the New Revised Standard Version Bible: Catholic Edition, copyright © 1989, 1993, Division of Christian Education of the National Council of Churches of Christ in the USA; used by permission; all rights reserved.

Excerpts from the English translation of the *Catechism of the Catholic Church* for use in the United States, second edition, copyright © 1997, United States Catholic Conference, Inc., Libreria Editrice Vaticana; all rights reserved.

Excerpts from the *Compendium of the Catechism of the Catholic Church*, copyright © 2005, Libreria Editrice Vaticana; all rights reserved.

Excerpts from documents of Vatican II from A. Flannery (ed.), *Vatican Council II: Constitutions, Decrees, Declarations* (New York/Dublin: Costello Publishing/ Dominican Publications, 1996).

Excerpts from the *United States Catholic Catechism for Adults*, copyright © 2006, United States Conference of Catholic Bishops, Washington D.C.; all rights reserved.

Excerpts from *Catholic Household Blessings & Prayers*, Revised Edition, copyright © 2007, Bishops Committee on the Liturgy, United States Conference of Catholic Bishops, Washington, D.C.

Excerpts from the English translation of *Rite of Baptism for Children* © 1969, International Commission on English in the Liturgy Corporation (ICEL); excerpts from the English translation of the Act of Contrition from *Rite of Penance* © 1974, ICEL; excerpts from the English translation of *The Roman Missal* © 2010, ICEL; all rights reserved. Texts contained in this work derived whole or in part from liturgical texts copyrighted by the International Commission on English in the Liturgy (ICEL) have been published here with the confirmation of the Committee on Divine Worship, United States Conference of Catholic Bishops.

Excerpt on p. 7 from CNNMONEY article taken from: *http://money.cnn.com/*.

"The Summer Day," p. 10, from the volume *House of Light* by Mary Oliver, published by Beacon Press, Boston, copyright © 1990 by Mary Oliver, used herewith by permission of the Charlotte Sheedy Literary Agency, Inc.

Story of university student, p. 12, from *Stories for All Seasons* by Gerard Fuller (Twenty-Third Publications/ The Columba Press).

Story of Patrick Hughes, p. 27, adapted from: *http://patrickhenryhughes.com*, with kind permission of Patrick Hughes.

"Address to Clergy and Laity Concerned," p. 48, from *Strength to Love* by Martin Luther King Jr. (Fortress Press, Minneapolis, 2010).

Excerpt on p. 63 from Victor Frankl, *Man's Search for Meaning*, revised edition (New York, Simon and Schuster, 1962).

Excerpt by David Brooks, p. 75, from the *New York Times*, November 14, 2011.

Excerpt on p. 89 from William Golding, *Lord of the Flies* (London: Faber and Faber, 1954), copyright © William Golding and Faber and Faber Limited.

Quotations on pp. 30, 87 and 131 by John L. Mckenzie, S.J. from *Dictionary of the Bible* (New York: Macmillan Publishing Company, 1965).

Excerpt on p. 149 from Litany of the Holy Name of Jesus, copyright Libreria Editrice Vaticana.

"A Parent's Perspective," p. 155, from Brian Doyle, *Leaping: Revelations and Epiphanies*, NCCL, *CL Weekly*, January 23, 2012, Volume VI, Number 4.

Excerpt on p. 165 from *www.usccb.org*, copyright United States Conference of Catholic Bishops, Washington, D.C.

Excerpts on p. 194 from *Dead Man Walking* © 1995 Orion Pictures Corporation; all rights reserved; courtesy of MGM media licensing.

Excerpts, p. 196, from The Harvest of Justice Is Sown in Peace, a statement by the United States Catholic Conference, November 1993, copyright 1994 United States Conference of Catholic Bishops, Washington, D.C.

Prayer reflection on pp. 202–3 adapted from *We Pray* by Susan Morgan (Dublin, Ireland: Veritas Publications, 2011).

Excerpt on p. 206 from *Mere Christianity* by C.S. Lewis (London: Geoffrey Bless, 1952).

Quotation on p. 246 from *The Lion, the Witch and the Wardrobe* by C.S. Lewis (London: Geoffrey Bless, 1952).

Prayer on p. 280 by Father Pedro Arrupe, S.J. (1907–91) from *Finding God in All Things: A Marquette Prayer Book* (Milwaukee: Marquette University Press, 2005).

Image credits
COVER: *Main image:* Christ Pantokrator; detail from an iconostasis icon from a sanctuary screen (egg tempera on panel). Greek School (16th century). Benaki Museum, Athens, Greece/Gift of the Lilian Boudouris Foundation/The Bridgeman Art Library. *Left center:* © JLP/Jose L. Pelaez/Corbis.

p. 17: Photo: Siren-com
p. 19: Photo: Lauro Mattalucci
p. 27: Photo courtesy of Patrick Hughes
p. 28: Photo: Jim McIntosh
p. 32: Photo: Walters Art Museum (Baltimore, Maryland)
p. 33: Photo: Ralph Hammann
p. 36: Photo: Walters Art Museum (Baltimore, Maryland)
p. 60: Photo: Chihwiedavidliu
p. 62: Canovas Alvaro/Getty Images

p. 68: Photo: Mario Robero Duran Ortiz
p. 77: Photo: Wolfgang Sauber
p. 78: NEW LINE CINEMA/Ronald Grant Archive/Mary Evans Picture Library
P. 83: Phillip Medhurst Collection
P. 86: Photo: Claire and Richard Stracke
P. 87: Photo: Frank Vincentz
P. 92: Photo: Bill Wittman
P 97: Photo: Skier Dude
P. 104: Photo: Johann Jaritz
P. 120: Photo: Malcolm Lidbury
P. 122: Photo: Yair Haklai
P. 140: Phillip Medhurst Collection. Photo by Philip De Vere
P. 144: Photo: Bill Wittman
p. 152: DISNEY/PIXAR/Ronald Grant Archive/Mary Evans
P. 159: Photo: Bill Wittman
P. 171: Photo: Bill Wittman
P. 173: Photo: GFreihalter
p. 187: Photo: Alex E. Proimos
p. 194: Ronald Grant Archive/Mary Evans
p. 199: Photo: Reinhard Hauke
p. 200: Photo: Patrick Riviere/Getty Images
p. 226: Photo: Pierre-Yves Emile
p. 235: Photo: Johannes Böckh & Thomas Mirtsch
p. 250: Photo: Carlos Barcenilla
p. 262: Photo: Wuselig
p. 265: Photo: Bill Wittman
p. 266: Photo: Bill Wittman
p. 267: Photo: LPLT
p. 268: Photo: Mathias Bigge
p. 271: Photo: Basilio
p. 279: Photo: Stan Pritchard Photography, *photographersdirect.com*
p. 282: Photo: P. Poschadel
p. 287: Photo: Andreas Franz Borchert
p. 292: Photo: Andreas Praefcke

Index

Page numbers set in bold italics indicate definitions in Faith Glossary.

commutative justice, 242

compassion, 33, *311*

concupiscence, 213–14, *311*

confession, sacramental seal of, 184

Confessions (St. Augustine), 8, 15, 21, 260

confidences, 183–84

Confiteor, 297

confraternities, 266–67

Congregation of the Religious of Jesus and Mary, 96

Congregation of St. Joseph, 200

Congregation of the Sisters of Our Lady of Mercy, 41

conjugal love, 208, 219

conscience, 59, 60, 306–07, *311*

  and erroneous judgments, 65

  examination of, 61, 65–66, 69–70

  formation of, 60–62

  the freedom of following, 63–65

  and the Holy Spirit, 307

  and moral judgments, 75

  and peer pressure, 64

  and temptation, 63–64

consecrated life, 264, 269–72, *311*

consecrated virgins, 271

consecrated widows and widowers, 271

consumerism, 6, 247, *311*

  see also materialism; secularism

contemplation, 270, 290, *311*

contemplative life, 270

conversion, 20–21, 173, *311*

corporal works of mercy, 302

counsel (right judgment), 301

courage, 283, 301

covenant, 102–03, 107, 109, 110–11, *311*

covetousness, 245–46, *311*

creation, 10–11, 13–15, 138, 232–33, *311*

Creator, *311*

cremation, 193

criminals, 194, 197

Cuba, 292–93

Daughters of Charity of St. Vincent de Paul, 272

Day, Dorothy, Servant of God, 258

de Marillac, Louise, St., 272

Dead Man Walking (Prejean), 94, 200

death

  care for the dying, 191

  culture of death, 187, 197

  see also euthanasia

Death of Innocents (Prejean), 200

death penalty, 197

death row, 194, 200

Decalogue, 102–06, 302, *311*

  see also Ten Commandments

deception, 182–83

Declaration of Independence, 6

despair, 192, *312*

detraction, 185

Deuteronomy, Book of, 108, 123, 138–39, 148

  the Ten Commandments, 103, 109, 110–11, 187–88, 302

Devil (Satan), 16, 17, 75–76, 120, 182

Dickens, Charles, 112

Dictionary of the Bible (McKenzie), 30, 87, 131

dikaiosyne, 34

disciples, 262, *312*

discrimination, 91

dissimulation, 182

distributive justice, 243

divine filiation, *312*

Divine Mercy, 42

Divine Mercy in My Soul (St. Maria Faustina), 41, 42

Divine Praises, The (Felici), 136, 298

divine providence, 29, 234, *312*

divorce, 222–23, *312*

doubt, *312*

Drexel, Katharine, St., 258, 271

duplicity, 182

Egypt, 107–09, 122–23

Elias, 270

embryonic stem cell research, 190

envy, 90, 247

Epictetus, 52

eremitic life, 270

Eucharist, 143–44

Eucharistic Prayer I, 94

euthanasia, 190–91, *312*

evangelical counsels, 268–69, *312*

Evangelii Gaudium, 6

evangelization, 261, 272, *312*

Eve, 16, 75–76, 77

evil, 112

Examen, 65–66, *311*

exclusion, 240

Exodus, Book of, 103, 109, 110, 117, 122, 123

  God's name, 131

  retributive justice, 198

  the Sabbath, 138, 139

  and slavery, 214

Exodus, the, 107

exploitation, 241

faith, 117, 121, 279, 301, *312*

faith questions, 304–08

false gods *see* idols

false witness (lying), 181–82

family, 152–53, 307, *312*

  the domestic church, 163

  and grandparents, 158

  and society, 162–63

  see also children; parents

family planning, 220

family values, 162

fear of the Lord, 301

Felici, Luigi, S.J., 136

filial respect, 156

Finding Nemo (Disney Pixar, 2003), 152

Fisher, John, St., 68

flattery, 183

Forming Consciences for Faithful Citizenship (USCCB), 170, 171

fornication, 215

fortitude, 211, 283, 301, *312*

  see also cardinal virtues

foster parenting, 221

Francis of Assisi, St., 258

Francis, Pope, 37, 42, 81, 115, 118, 121, 306

  and blasphemy, 136

  and the cult of money, 6, 238–39, 240

  and solidarity, 244

Frankl, Victor, 63

fraud, 239

free unions, 222, 224, *313*

free will, 13, 179, 304, *313*

freedom, 59, 114, 304–05, *312–13*

French Revolution, 95

CPSIA information can be obtained
at www.ICGtesting.com
Printed in the USA
LVHW050756300622
722246LV00001B/4

9 781847 306043